Pleasures of Horror

The Pleasures of Horror

MATT HILLS

 **continuum**
LONDON • NEW YORK

Continuum
The Tower Building,
11 York Road,
London SE1 7NX

15 East 26th Street,
Suite 1703,
New York, NY 10010

British Library Cataloguing-in-Publication Data
A catalogue record for this book is available from the British Library.

ISBN: HB: 0-8264-5887-4
        PB: 0-8264-5888-2

Library of Congress Cataloging-in-Publication Data
Hills, Matt, 1971–
   The pleasures of horror / Matt Hills.
   p. cm.
   Includes bibliographical references and index.
   ISBN 0-8264-5887-4—ISBN 0-8264-5888-2 (PB)
   1. Horror tales—History and criticism. 2. Horror
   films—History and criticism. I. Title.
PN3435.H55 2005
809.3'8738—dc 22   2004063444

Typeset by Tradespools, Frome, Somerset
Printed and bound in Great Britain by Antony Rowe, Chippenham, Wiltshire

Dedication

For Emma, who knows the many pleasures of horror.
And in memory of Nelson, never a scaredy cat.

Actually I've no idea why (or if) people like being scared. Furthermore, to put it bluntly, I don't give a shit. I think the assumption that people watch horror films or read horror simply to be scared is insultingly simplistic and reductionist. It strikes me that *a great deal of horror is concerned with a lot more than being scary.* (Kim Newman, writing in *Beyond*, no. 1, April/May 1995, p. 49, my italics)

An active interest in horror fiction strikes many people as being morally offensive ..., or at the very least a sign of immature character development and especially puerile, if not perverse, passions and sensibilities. Since horror fans infrequently regard their own aesthetic tastes in this light, the challenge in this case is to understand why a prevalent aesthetic activity can be celebrated so unabashedly by its participants, while being viewed by others with moral condemnation, aversion, or disdain, and only rarely with indifference. *All in all, then, horror shocks, along many different dimensions, the fan and the philosopher alike.* (Vorobej, 1997, p. 221, my italics)

Contents

Acknowledgements

This book has been written in between, around, and in relation to my teaching at Cardiff University. Thanks must go to my past and present colleagues, especially Gill Branston, Sara Gwenllian Jones, Beccy Harris, John Jewell, Justin Lewis, Jo Marshall, Donald Matheson, Máire Messenger-Davies, Roberta Pearson, James Thomas, Terry Threadgold and Karin Wahl-Jorgensen. Thanks must also go (as ever) to Henry Jenkins and John Tulloch, without whose work in media/cultural studies I probably wouldn't have become an academic in the first place.

In the field of horror and its study, special thanks and much admiration go to Christopher Fowler, Stephen Gallagher, Mark Jancovich, Mark Kermode, Kim Newman and Steven Jay Schneider for their constantly inspiring writings. I would also like to acknowledge and applaud the contributions, discussions and sheer intellectual energy of all the students I've been lucky enough to work with over the past few years, in particular Kirsten Brander, Darrell Chart, Jen Crew, Ben Earl, Emma Follett, Tom Hardcastle, Janine Jones (thanks for the T-shirt), James Lewis, Amy Luther, Jo Menzies, Ross Garner and Rebecca Williams.

Outside the world of academia, hello again to Paul and Helen – I am still alive! – and cheers to Russ, Simon, Mike and all the Nicks. Thanks to Ben for being Ben, and to Tim and Brett for sharing the Whovian excitements of 2003 and 2004.

And thanks, of course, to Mum, Dad and Stu for all their love and support.

Matt Hills, Cardiff, 2004

Preface

Towards a (performative) micro-physics of pleasure

In this study I take a wholly 'performative' approach to the pleasures of horror (partly contra Hills 2002 on fan pleasures; see Sandvoss 2003, p. 178). This means refuting ontological or truth-telling claims as to the experienced realities of such 'pleasures' and instead treating them as performed and constructed (Alasuutari 1999; McKee 2003b, pp. 16–17). Taking such a stance also means ruling out autoethnographic self-accounts (see McKee 2003a, p. 127) as guarantors of the meanings of horror, treating these as one cultural space where horror's pleasures can be discursively fixed by fans and academics alike.

Why is a performative approach particularly useful in this instance? Apart from the fact that theories of performativity have some academic currency at the present moment, especially in fan studies (Hills 2002, pp. 158–60; Thomas 2002, pp. 23–4; Crawford 2004, pp. 122–3), such work allows us to consider horror's pleasures – via the genre's production, reception and wider cultural circulation – as constructions and performances of meaning, rather than as reflections of a brute, positivist reality. That is to say, pleasure is not dealt with here as a mystical, ineffable 'thing' that is somehow outside of culture, thereby 'reducing the problem to non-theorisable dimensions of personal experience' (Mercer 1983, p. 87). Nor is pleasure treated as somehow excessive, as a passional force outrunning social and cultural order in its blissful *jouissance* (Barthes 1976). Neither merely an existent thing, nor magically a disruptive entity, pleasure-as-performative is always a cultural act, an articulation of identity: 'I am the sort of person who takes this sort of pleasure in this sort of media product.' Horror's pleasures – and displeasures – thus work within patterns of cultural reproduction, as fans enact their cultural distinctions from one another, or from non-fans, and as scholars enact their cultural distinctions from one another and from 'untutored' audiences. As Fredric Jameson has put it with regard to the cultural study of pleasure: 'ostensible subjects of individual gratification ... prove to be vehicles for some deeper political and ideological position' (1983, p. 5).

This 'politics of pleasure' has very much been a part of the trajectory and history of Cultural Studies as an (inter-)disciplinary mode of thought (see Harris

1992). However, linking this to a performative approach does introduce a novel element, since it means that pleasure is no longer treated as something empirically present/absent, or as something to be ethnographically captured in its authenticity. Nor is pleasure essentially linked to audience agency via the argument that we enjoy popular culture because it a priori allows us a space for creative action or interpretation (Fiske 1989; Richards 1994, p. 6). Treating pleasure as an essential index of audience 'agency', or assuming its experiential 'reality', would be to adopt a 'constative' approach to the subject. That would mean treating any account of pleasure as a simple *description* of some pre-existent state of affairs.

The performative/constative distinction is J.L. Austin's, and is worth recounting here: '(1) the performative should be doing something as opposed to just saying something; and (2) the performative is happy or unhappy as opposed to true or false' (1976, p. 133). By this, Austin means that performative utterances are not just statements about the world that could be described as 'true' or otherwise – they do not merely reflect existent states of affairs. Instead, they achieve outcomes, or 'do something' to this worldly state of affairs – Austin gives examples such as saying 'I do' in a wedding ceremony, naming a ship, writing a will, and placing a bet (1976, p. 5). All are said to 'not "describe" or "report" or constate anything at all ... [T]he uttering of the sentence is, or is a part of, the doing of an action' (ibid.). 'Happy' performatives are those that achieve their ceremonial and expected outcomes – wedding vows are undertaken, a newly named ship sets sail, and so on. 'Unhappy' performatives, however, are infelicitous in that they are not successful: ritual procedures are not followed or accepted (1976, pp. 26–7).

Austin notes that his examples are all 'explicit' performatives (1976, p. 32). They probably strike us as being quite distinct from a horror fan, say, enthusing about the latest Stephen King or Christopher Fowler novel, or a newly released M. Night Shyamalan film. Surely these 'pleasures' are descriptions of feeling states? Are they not then 'constative', being quite unlike participation in a wedding ceremony or some such? Perhaps, but Austin's distinction cannot be taken as absolute; many statements can be 'implicit' performatives (1976, pp. 32–3), hence blending what seems like description with performative elements (cf. Bourdieu 1991, p. 134). Horror's pleasures, which I will denote and analyse as performative in what follows, should thus be taken as *implicit* performatives. As with expressions of gender identity, or what Judith Butler calls 'gender performatives' (1999a, p. 171), horror's pleasures appear to describe a truth and an interiority – that internal place in the self where our gender is authentically 'felt', or where our pleasures are authentically 'experienced' – but actually work to inscribe 'and create the illusion of an interior and organizing ... core' to the 'pleasure-experiencing self' (Butler 1999a, p. 173). If gender difference has an iterative, imitative structure that drag highlights (Butler 1999a, p. 175), then we might also say that pleasures taken in popular culture have an imitative and iterative structure, especially within the institutions of academic and fan cultures (see Parts I and II). Performativity, whether explicit or implicit, is always a form of iterated 'citationality' (Derrida 1988, p. 18; Butler 1993, p. 12) depending on established cultural codes and ways of doing (or making do). And accounts of the pleasures of horror are just so: they display structural, iterative patterns and repetitions, whether occurring in professional scholars' theories or in fans' practices. For Butler, this citationality necessarily impacts upon theories of socio-cultural agency, since social actors are not just agents who can choose to perform their gender differently. That is, how we perform our gender identity is not a voluntaristic choice (Butler 1993, p. 12).

But isn't being a fan or consumer of horror, by contrast, precisely such a choice? Don't horror's consumers, after all, distinguish themselves by the very virtue of 'paying their money and taking their choice'? Discussing what I have termed 'performative consumption' elsewhere (Hills 2002, p. 159), I note that fans do *not* always represent themselves as voluntaristic agents. Having said that, neither can we fully or theoretically align performed fan identities with performed gender identities. Performativity becomes useful as a way of thinking about the pleasures of popular culture – and here, specifically, the pleasures of horror – precisely because it allows us to treat accounts of pleasure not only as descriptions, and because it also allows us to challenge, from the outset, any notion that consumers of pop culture are simply voluntaristic agents going about their interiorized, individualized business of leisure. As a methodological and heuristic device, it opens the door to addressing 'the question of agency not as a … definite property that fans [and non-fans] do or do not "possess" …, but rather as a claim that can be made at certain points in time but not at others' (Hills 2002, p. 159). The pleasures of horror, on this account, can be analysed as *claims to agency*. They are performative by virtue of arguing for, and constructing, their bearers *as agents who display expertise and authority in relation to horror's texts –* whether this is the authoritative dismissal of horror (as 'perverse', 'weird', 'immoral' and 'unpleasant') enacted by its 'anti-fans' and 'haters' (Gray 2003), or its equally authoritative championing (as 'art') by fans and scholar-fans (Kermode 1997; see Chapter 4 and the Conclusion). The authorization that the 'felicitous' performative requires can be based on a range of socio-cultural institutions, some counter/hegemonic and cultural, some counter/hegemonic and subcultural. So it is that the 'anti-fan' can iterate discourses of moral panic and horror's 'perversion', calling into question its pleasures, while fans can cite discourses of aesthetics and genre history to legitimate 'their' pleasures. And academics can (more literally) cite theoretical discourses, of intertextuality or 'postmodernism', to legitimate horror's pleasures as an ordered object of study, as well as performing their own scholarly expertise (Bordwell 1989; Carroll 1996, p. 26).

Implicit performatives, then, are not restricted to a kind of 'social magic' where only duly authorized speakers can iterate the cultural code of pop culture's pleasures. For as Butler has argued, 'the performative can succeed in producing the effect of authority where there is no recourse to a prior authorization'

(1999b, p. 123). This is what occurs when fans articulate 'pleasure' and 'agency' as expert consumers or connoisseurs, and what has, arguably, led to horror fans being discussed in academic work as displaying 'cultural elitism' (Messenger Davies 2001, p. 162), despite the fact that they lack the authorizing (legal) powers of the State and contest the authorizing (hegemonic) powers of 'common sense' accounts of the genre (Critcher 2003, pp. 64–80).

Tackling the pleasures of horror as performative necessarily requires a focus on the operation of cultural distinctions, thus invoking Pierre Bourdieu's (1986 and 1993) work, as I do most explicitly in Part IV. Types of claimed (aesthetic/moral) and disclaimed (trashy/immoral) pleasures can work to reinforce and re-perform cultural distinctions as bids for horror's cultural valorization or devaluation. And tackling the pleasures of horror as performative requires a focus on discourse, thus involving Michel Foucault's (1977 and 1991) work, which runs like a subterranean labyrinth beneath the explicit intertexts and conclusions of this book. Although I do not repeatedly call up Foucault's symbolic authority and academic authorization in what follows, his work, like that of Bourdieu (1993) and Butler (1999a), underpins the metatheoretical machineries of *The Pleasures of Horror*.

Horror's pleasures, I suggest here, can only be accessed culturally – that is, made sense of, reported, discussed, claimed, disavowed – through grids and templates of meaning or 'discursive practices' that are 'characterized by the delimitation of a field of objects, the definition of a legitimate perspective for the agent of knowledge, and the fixing of norms for the elaboration of concepts and theories' (Foucault 1977, p. 199). As concepts, horror and its pleasures are constituted in a range of cultural sites and within different genres/practices of writing – I focus here on their place within theoretical discourses (Part I); in fans' everyday discourses (Part II); in discourses of the 'authentic' horror genre's boundaries; and in discourses of intertextuality and 'postmodern' citation (Part IV). Like Foucault's infamous 'micro-physics of power', a micro-physics of pleasure cannot 'be localized in a particular type of institution or state apparatus', existing instead between bodies and these 'great functionings' (Foucault 1991, p. 26). But this micro-physics of pleasure is 'ordered' theoretically/academically as well as in industry discourses of genre, and in fan-subcultural institutions (Kendall and Wickham 2001; Mittell 2004).

Analysing theoretical discourses as constructing the 'pleasures' of horror performatively, rather than reflecting constatively on their 'reality', means adopting a metatheoretical stance: 'metatheorizing is a process that occurs *after* theory has been created and takes that theory itself as the object of study' (Ritzer 2001, p. 15). This leaves me open to a charge of logical regression, for as David Bordwell has suggested:

> [A] strong version of constructivism is self-refuting. If all systems of thought are culturally constructed, so is the theory of cultural construction. How, therefore, can it claim that its insights are any more reliable or valid than any

other theory's? More pointedly: How can the intellectual argue that the activities of others are culturally constructed while arrogating to him- or herself a position that purportedly escapes this? (Bordwell 1996:13)

These are good questions. However, their force as critique can be subdued by considering that I am not, in fact, making such a self-contradictory claim: my work here cannot escape its own emphasis on performativity, and must therefore be seen as an instance of that which it seeks to analyse, rather than as a constative reflection on performative consumption and analyses of horror occurring elsewhere. This book – much like the discourses of pleasure circulated in cognitive philosophy, literary theory and psychoanalysis, and in fan practices of connoisseurship – enacts a form of *textual agency*. That is, it constructs my agency (as a scholar-fan) by *doing things with texts*, both other people's theoretical treatises and horror films, TV series, novels and novellas (not to mention 'theory-horror' that monstrously blurs these cultural categories). Rather than reflecting my pre-existent or allegedly essential 'agency' as a fan-consumer, the following pages work together to constitute an implicit performative by constructing, performing and displaying claims to authorial agency. They 'do something with', and 'say something about', the pleasures of horror.

Introduction

The 'Problem' of the Pleasures of Horror

There has been no shortage of academic enquiry surrounding the question of how and why audiences/readers enjoy the horror genre in its many different media incarnations and subgeneric strands. In fact, one could fairly suggest that the cultural popularity and endurance of the horror genre has provoked a monstrous outpouring of academic thought, creating a body of work that seeks to answer the question 'why horror?' Why are audiences drawn to this genre? What is it about horror that its fans especially enjoy and appreciate?

In books such as *Dreadful Pleasures* (Twitchell 1985), *The Delights of Terror* (Heller 1987) and *Horror as Pleasure* (Leffler 2000), as well as in articles such as 'Why horror? The peculiar pleasures of a popular genre' (Tudor 1997) and chapters like 'Conditions of Pleasure in Horror Cinema' (Giles 1984), various critics have suggested answers to the seeming puzzle of horror fictions and their pleasures (see also Modleski 1986; Hoppenstand 1996; Kermode 1997; Hoxter 2000). Some scholars have gone so far as to argue that taking pleasure in horror fictions is a 'paradox' in need of philosophical resolution (Carroll 1990; Markman Ellis 2000, p. 9). It is, I think, possible to identify a boom in such academic writing in the late 1980s – corresponding to, or following, a commercial peak in horror's popularity (see Winter 2000) – with another burst of academic publishing activity following on from the cinematic resurgence of the genre commonly linked to the box-office success of *Scream* (1996, dr: Wes Craven; see Chapter 10).

Unfortunately, a range of academic 'answers' to the supposed 'question' of horror's pleasures have raised further problems: James B. Twitchell (1985) views horror fictions as cautionary tales for adolescent readers, rather essentializing the genre's audiences, if not imputing a certain childishness to horror. Taking a not unrelated tack, Gary Hoppenstand (1996) views much contemporary horror as a critique of pure hedonism, where this quality is equated with evil and monstrous behaviour. In Hoppenstand's argument, as in Twitchell's, horror can apparently be boiled down to the provision of cultural and moral lessons for its attentive viewers.

Aesthetically complicating such views of horror-as-schooling, Noël Carroll (1990) argues that horror fictions provide forms of narrative pleasure alongside emotions of fear and disgust, but his conclusion is, again like Twitchell's work, based on an essentializing notion of what 'counts' as horror in the first place (see Chapter 1). Meanwhile, Terry Heller's (1987) investigation of horror and pleasure turns on an application of a specific theoretical framework (see Chapter 2), as does Dennis Giles's (1984) discussion of horror's invocation and frustration of audience scopophilia (i.e., voyeuristic pleasure taken in seeing). In fact this 'theory-first, pleasure-second' approach has been a repeated problem for work in the field; that is, horror's pleasures have been accounted for in line with (and via) specific, favoured theories. Psychoanalysis has been very often utilized, perhaps as Andrew Tudor has argued because of the 'widespread belief that horror fans are a peculiar bunch who share a perverse predilection. A taste for horror is a taste for something seemingly abnormal and is therefore deemed to require special explanation' (1997, p. 446).

But specific theories, psychoanalysis included, have only proved capable of addressing the pleasures of horror by defining these so as to fit into their grounding assumptions – something that I explore and problematize in Part I of *The Pleasures of Horror*. All such theories (including sociologies and cognitive philosophies of horror) appear to proceed from the basic notion that horror's pleasures stand in need of explanation, whether this is done by relating horror texts to the 'real' cultural anxieties of a time period, or to transhistorical notions of 'the unconscious'. I am suggesting here that theoretical approaches to horror have explained (away) the genre's pleasures by invoking their own disciplinary and theoretical norms. One lives in hope of a sociological study of horror that concludes that real cultural anxieties are not readily replayed or coded into the horror of a period, hence failing to neatly run context and text together; or one hopes vainly for a psychoanalytic study of horror that concludes that the concept of 'the unconscious' is called into question, modified, or problematized by horror texts (due to pressures of space, I do not devote a chapter to sociologies of horror in Part I: see Hills 2003d and 2004e for more on this topic). At worst, theoretical answers seem to be determined in advance of critics' encounters with horror texts, while at best scholarly theories continue to be accorded discursive primacy (that is, academic texts routinely offer pop-cultural examples that somehow mirror, 'prove' or allegorize the writer's chosen/favoured theory).

Explanatory efforts that have taken a multi-theoretical, overview perspective (I am thinking here particularly of Leffler 2000) have avoided such theory-determinist problems, but have nevertheless tended to arrive at vaguely tautological conclusions, for example, fictions of the horror genre are enjoyable because they are fictional and because they are generic (see Leffler 2000, pp. 259–73).

There are thus several pitfalls that this current study must aim to avoid:

- discursively reducing horror's pleasure to the forms and requirements of a favoured theory (see Chapters 1–3);
- proposing 'solutions' to the questions of horror's pleasures that are predominantly tautological (Leffler 2000); and
- proposing 'solutions' to the question of horror's pleasures that essentialize the horror genre and its audiences (as do Twitchell 1985 and Carroll 1990 in different ways).

Indeed, beginning from the very starting point that horror's pleasures *require* explanation may, itself, constitute a further problem to be evaded. I would argue that some horror scholarship (though by no means all) has viewed horror's pleasures as a kind of problem in need of explanation because it has prematurely accepted common-sense, hegemonic accounts of the genre. As represented in the Western news media, horror is frequently depicted as a source of mimetic infection, or of moral pollution – hence it makes sense for one recent overview of the genre to begin (in this case, ironically) with an introduction entitled 'Ban this sick filth!' (Jones 2002, p. 1). The 'video nasties' moral panic of the mid-1980s, one severe outbreak of anti-horror rhetoric in the UK, is by now well documented (for the classic study see Barker (ed.) 1984; the most recent overview at the time of writing is provided in Critcher 2003, pp. 64–80; see also Barlow and Hill 1985 and Barker and Petley (eds) 1997 and 2001). But while critics such as Martin Barker, Julian Petley, David Buckingham (1996) and David Gauntlett (1995 and 2001) have worked to contest mass media narratives of horror's 'effects' on audiences, work on the pleasures of horror seems to have unwittingly adopted media discourses surrounding horror via its willingness to view horror's pleasures as a puzzle, conundrum or a 'problem' in need of further study. Horror's pleasures have been defined, conservatively, as 'aberrant' in sectors of contemporary culture other than academia, with this symbolic equation then being implicitly or explicitly taken up in studies of the genre (Twitchell 1985; Carroll 1990; and according to Tudor (1997), many psychoanalytic readings). Furthermore, studies of horror which conclude that the genre's pleasures stem from its aesthetics can only come as surprising news if the reader, and the theorist, begin with the implicit assumption that horror fictions might somehow be equated with real horror. This assumption occurs, more damagingly, within what I would term a profoundly 'literalist' reading of horror's texts. Such literalist readings treat the genre as a moral problem by collapsing fictional representations into the real, thereby suggesting that watching horror films will either: (a) 'corrupt and deprave' or (b) 'desensitize' viewers. The first type of literalist discourse implies an inevitably mimetic relation between fiction and its viewers (who will imitate screen violence), while the second type relies on a 'folk' or 'lay' theory of media effect, suggesting that watching fictional violence will cause audiences to enjoy, or not be appropriately affected by, real violence.

My point here is that such notions, and their related discourses, do not only occur in UK newspapers participating in moral panics, such as *The Daily Mail* (cf. Critcher 2003, pp. 141–2); they also emerge within academic studies (for an analysis of this see Grixti 1989). For instance, moral philosopher Colin McGinn has argued that sympathetic pain (at another's suffering) can be replaced by pleasure taken in the other's pain if an 'association' is set up between 'the pleasure of entertainment' and the witnessing of suffering (1997, p. 88). McGinn argues that this morally aberrant displacement of sympathy by pleasure can 'be done either by using actual violence or we could just use fictional representations of violence' (1997, p. 88). He goes on to state that 'this is just what happens with the kind of violent entertainment that is so prevalent and popular' in contemporary society (1997, p. 88). McGinn's argument leads to a position where watching violent representations and enjoying them is a problem since this supposedly 'set[s] up hedonic channels in the person … he will find himself reacting to actual violence with confused affect, not knowing whether to laugh or cry' (1997, p. 89). This is a bizarre and pernicious conclusion, and is comparable to Robert Solomon's (2003) conclusion regarding the watching of violence in the news (see Chapter 7). Philosopher Daniel Shaw has responded to such conclusions by noting that 'one would have to be mentally ill to delight in watching a Michael Myers-type serial killer enact his crimes in real life. But most theories of horror-pleasure do not so characterize the fans that revel in such cinematic attractions' (2003, p. 261). And yet the pathologization of horror's pleasures as a 'problem' – and hence also the genre's fans – never seems far from the surface of literalist readings, whether these occur in academics' moral philosophy (McGinn 1997; Solomon 2003) or in mass-mediated moral panics.

McGinn's work offers up one literalist reading of horror since it relies on *collapsing together the real and the fictional*; in McGinn's thought experiment it allegedly does not matter whether real or fictional violence is used to establish links between witnessing suffering and experiencing pleasure (contra Shaw's point that must be false since it assumes psychopathology on the part of audiences). And the alleged result then becomes a further inability to distinguish real and fictional horror; people react inappropriately to real horror because they treat it as if it were fictional. However, note that this logic is twofold; first, *it itself confuses real and fictional violence*, and then it projects this confusion on to the vulnerable Other (in this case, horror's audience) who is allegedly desensitized or depraved. Many rhetorics defining horror's pleasures as a 'problem' tend to rely on this basic two-step structure: as literalist readings, they themselves take fictional representations overly literally, treating fictional violence as if it were real, and then alleging that imagined audiences will be affected such that *they* will not be able to tell the difference (see Schubart 1995, pp. 221–2).

It is through such discourses that horror is constituted as a social, cultural and *moral* problem that requires monitoring and censorship practices (see Chapter 5). Work on the pleasures of horror which begins from the notion that there is a paradox involved in enjoying the horror genre, or which starts from the question 'why horror?', is thus – whether it acknowledges this or not – recapitulating an attenuated literalist reading of the genre. If, instead, we treat horror as an aesthetic, fictional exercise from the outset – rather than arriving at this as a conclusion – then the genre's pleasures do not need to be explained (away). They are no longer a puzzle or a problem (see Oliver and Sanders 2004, p. 257). Instead, we are freed up to investigate the variety of horror's generic pleasures (see Parts I and II), then going on to ask where these aesthetic pleasures exist culturally rather than why they exist (see Part III).

This book could have taken a number of paths. It could have been a study of how horror's audiences take pleasure in horror – which would have involved asking such audiences. Excellent work has been done here by, among others, Shaun Kimber (2002) and Brigid Cherry (1999 and 2002). Or it could have been an experimental study of audiences' preferences (see, e.g., Weaver III and Tamborini (eds) 1996). Or it could have been a study of the details of specific horror texts, discussing the pleasures of horror not through framing theoretical assumptions, but beginning instead with films or books themselves as aesthetic objects (see Freeland 2000, Leffler 2000 and Schneider 2004a for useful movements in this direction).

The Pleasures of Horror is, however, none of these things. Elsewhere, I have offered a critique of asking the (fan) audience to account for its pleasures (Hills 2002). And experimental methods drawing on, for example, uses and gratifications approaches (Lawrence and Palmgreen 1996) are subject to the same theoretical and discursive difficulties of pleasure definition as are seemingly far more speculative psychoanalytic readings of horror (e.g. Creed 1993). Finally, aesthetic approaches, though seeming to negotiate a path through thickets of a priori theoretical assumptions, still tend to fall back on cognitive (Freeland 2001) or psychoanalytic frames (Schneider 2001). Rather unfortunately, academic debates about horror fictions have, all too often, been debates about why one theoretical approach is superior to another, with an openness or free-floating attention to the object of study coming a close second to a priori disciplinary attacks/defences.

This narrowing of options does, however, leave a few possibilities open for exploration. Having clearly stated what I am *not* going to do, here is a brief sense of what the reader can expect from what follows:

- In line with the first epigraph that frames this entire book (Newman 1995, p. 49), I will focus on the multiple pleasures of horror, neither restricting the genre to a singular definition nor linking any 'one' generic definition to an account of its associated, definitional 'pleasure' (e.g. 'scariness').
- I will therefore treat horror's pleasures as discursively constructed both in theory and in fan practices (Parts I and II). This means considering how the pleasures of horror, as recounted by academics and fans, may be similarly restricted by – or defined via – cultural processes such as the

valorization of horror and the construction of fan/academic cultural identities (on such questions, see Jancovich (2000) and Hills (2004e)). Thus, I will not address 'pleasure' as an ineffable 'thing' beyond discourse, but will instead consider horror's pleasures as subject to framing (sub)cultural practices, both inside and outside the academy.

- I will not attempt to foreclose what counts as 'authentic' horror. As already noted, this act is one that often leads theorists astray, since they then focus on their essentializing 'theoretical' definition at the expense of how horror is multiply identified in cultural discourses used by fans, the film industry and so on.

- I will therefore consider horror as significantly intertextual, exploring how its discursively constructed pleasures can also be experienced, via intertextuality, in cultural and media sites beyond those that are usually academically addressed (see Part III). My argument is thus that *the horror genre is not where it is*; it exists, intertextually, rhetorically, and as a 'principle of contamination' (Derrida 1992, p. 227) outside its major and explicitly labelled generic traditions/sites/texts. In Chapters 6, 7 and 8 I will thus focus on horror on TV, in accounts of 'real-life' horror, and in theoretical texts. Due chiefly to lack of space, I will not analyse horror in video games or comics, although others have profitably explored these media/cultural sites, going beyond the critical hegemony of 'horror = films and novels' (e.g. Barker 1992; Ndalianis 1999; Krzywinska 2002a).

- I will also consider popular horror texts themselves as bids for the values and pleasures of the horror genre, rather than such pleasure-constructing and construing discourses being restricted to fan and academic responses (see Part IV). Instead of viewing horror as a pre-reflexive source of 'pleasures', its texts can be analysed as displaying a reflexive knowingness about, even a type of pedagogy over, the pleasures that audiences/readers are expected to experience. By seeking to intertextually cue certain audience reactions, horror texts position themselves in relation to other generic texts as well as in relation to other discourses, such as mass media moral panics and academic theories of horror.

From this series of promissory outlines, it should be immediately apparent that my approach to the pleasures of horror is not a matter of treating pleasure as a 'thing' to be recovered. Although horror's pleasure must be assumed to be felt, materially and affectively by audiences, as soon as this process is theorized by academics (or recounted by fans) then we are necessarily dealing with discourses of pleasure or, more broadly, what I have termed 'discourses of affect' (see Hills 2003a, p. 79). Discourses of affect use the terms of 'pleasure' to mark out powerfully moral coordinates, and to align 'pleasure' with authenticating discourses, thereby defining moral roles or fan identities ('real-life horror' cannot be pleasurable; this is not 'enjoyable' horror, etc.). Where discourses of affect are concerned it is the *result* of any given cultural performance of affect that requires analysis, rather than how or whether a specific pleasure is actually felt by the subject.

One alternative would be to study 'affective discourses' (Hills 2003a, p. 80). These do not directly concern themselves with mediating or discursively constructing 'pleasure', and instead are subjective (but also cultural) moments where extra-discursive affects can be posited as powerfully permeating discourse. Assertions over textual authenticity can act in this way, for example 'this is proper/authentic horror'. Such an approach would have to read 'pleasure' off from the tones, excitements, pacings and rhythms of respondents' discourse: we could interpret 'this isn't authentic horror' as an expression of negative affect, for instance, or the fan statement 'this is real horror' as an expression of pleasure. But any such readings would hinge on extra-discursive cues. Again, this route ultimately and inevitably leads to an analysis of discourses of affect, because interpretations and translations of posited extra-discursive 'pleasures' necessarily require the invocation of an explicatory discursive framework (see Harrington and Bielby 1995, pp. 119–30 for an excellent summary of how audience 'pleasures' have been discursively framed in media studies).

Non-discursive access to the 'pleasures of horror', I am thus suggesting here, is a logical impossibility. Even wiring people up to monitor their heart-rate, 'arousal', etc., will inevitably presuppose discourses of pleasure when it comes to the interpretation of 'experimental' data. And similarly, using psychoanalysis to argue that pleasures are 'outside' discourse is obviously open to the problem of logical-regression; since psychoanalysis is itself a discourse that frames types of pleasure as extra-discursive. Treating horror as part of material culture (see Dant 1999, pp. 20–2; Williamson 2001) and media culture (see Sconce 2000) hence cannot involve adopting a naively realist stance with regard to horror's material pleasures, or its material affects on audiences and critics alike. Yes, it may be important or tempting to consider how horror makes *us* feel (cf. Steinert 2003, p. 58), but even this moment of self-reflexivity will still involve wider cultural systems of value and discourse (cf. Hills 2002).

A rigorously critical and material approach to pleasures taken in cultural artefacts and texts must, seemingly paradoxically, engage with the circulation of *discourses of pleasure* and hence with the cultural values/distinctions of texts and discourses. With this in mind, Part I can be summarized as an investigation of discourses of pleasure in theory, while Part II complements this by considering horror fans' various discourses of pleasure. Part III then analyses how pleasures of horror are discursively policed and ruled out in relation to the genre's intertextual 'para-sites', that is, cultural sites where it is thought not to exist 'properly': on TV, in real-life accounts, and in theoretical texts. Finally, Part IV considers discourses of pleasure (and value) that have been specifically linked to the intertextuality of horror's texts, suggesting that the pleasures of horror can be as much about recognizing generic histories and lineages as about 'being scared'.

To conclude these introductory statements, I want to consider one intriguing example of a discourse of pleasure that may feel all too familiar to some readers:

> During a tutorial on Stephen King's *'Salem's Lot* ... a student offered the following piece of rather stunning resistance to theory: while she was sure that hidden meanings could be found in *Buffy* and *Angel* (no contemporary discussion of vampire narratives could avoid such a digression!) she hoped the lecturer would refrain from doing so because it would *spoil her enjoyment* of those programmes. Her wish in requesting this ... was precisely to preserve the (to her) meaninglessness of *Buffy* and *Angel*. What is stunning, of course, is that thought and enjoyment are characterized as mutually exclusive. (Leane and Buchanan 2002, p. 253)

These authors conclude that the student's statement is an attempt to preserve *Buffy* as her own 'private' text, 'free from the pernicious contaminations of other people's interpretations and associations' (2002, p. 253). Other (academic/theoretical) readings are hence represented as a 'theft of enjoyment' (2002, p. 253). This discursive opposition of 'theory' and 'pleasure' is hardly a new one; although it may be personally felt, and affectively experienced, as a hegemonic discourse of affect it is part of a cultural system of value that marks down 'pleasures' as easy and counter-positions 'theories' as difficult, demanding and requiring labour. Any 'theory' of horror's 'pleasures' might therefore be thought of as distinctly unpleasurable.

However, I want to highlight this theory/pleasure opposition not for its truth value, but rather for its display of cultural conventions. Contra such dominant cultural systems of value – played out differently outside and inside the academy, where difficulty is often revalued as a badge of virtuosity or necessary labour – we might argue that 'theory' offers pleasures of its own, even that these pleasures may be intertextually linked to the horror genre (see Chapter 8). Or we could argue that to discursively construct 'pleasure' as 'easy' is precisely to miss how 'pleasures' are the result of discourses that work, repetitively and insistently, to fix types of pleasures in some cultural sites and not others, always as a question of cultural value/distinction. 'Difficult' pleasures are worth more, culturally, than 'easy' pleasures (see Part IV's comparison of Kim Newman's 'postmodern' fiction with the 'postmodern' *Scream* franchise).

In any case, what this example highlights, for me, is how discourses of pleasure *do things*; the student asking to have her pleasure conserved is seeking to reinforce one interpretation of *Buffy* over another, just as the theorist explaining the pleasures of horror psychoanalytically, sociologically or cognitively is seeking to validate their interpretive framework. Defining and discussing pleasure – what it is, and how it works – is always-already a bid for situated cultural power, involving the (possible) power to interpret and define a situation (e.g. the pleasures of horror are a 'problem'; or 'the pleasures of horror are best understood via psychoanalysis'). And such discussions/definitions also fundamentally involve and invoke morality; in conservative literalist readings the pleasures of horror are a *moral* problem leading to subjective corruption/ desensitization, while in left-wing critical readings the pleasures of horror should be *morally* exposed as ideological (Chapter 3). And yet others may argue that such pleasures should be left in place within a *morality* of 'rights'; here we return to the student plaintively asking for her enjoyment not to be spoilt as well as to a type of fan discourse (Part II). *The pleasures of horror do things*, whether they are discursively defined in theory, in fan practices and anti-censorship arguments, outside the realm of film and fiction, or through the recognition of intertextual references. And these are the stories this book will tell.

I will begin by considering how cognitive philosophies of horror (e.g. Carroll 1990) have discursively restricted horror's pleasures to types of theoretically defined emotion, while also offering restricted definitions of what counts as authentic 'horror'. How have theoretical assumptions caused horror to be analysed as a genre primarily characterized by its monsters rather than its atmospheres and ambiences?

Part I

Theorizing the Pleasures of Horror

A variety of paradigms have explored audience pleasures ... but the two primary paradigms looking to this question are psychoanalysis and cognitive psychology. Though the differences between cognitivism and psychoanalysis are great (as the heated debates between their supporters suggest), the basic approach that each takes in analysing ... genres is similar – *begin with a theoretical model of human psychology and apply it to a series of texts to deduce what audience pleasures drive the given genre.* (Jason Mittell 2004, p. 18, my italics)

Chapter 1

Philosophies of Horror: Cognition ... and Affect

Either explicitly or implicitly, different theories of horror adopt different perspectives on the pleasures of the genre. Audience pleasures are constructed in line with specific theoretical presuppositions, and are then projected on to horror's 'ideal' readers and viewers. In the first section of this chapter I will examine theories of horror that can be broadly grouped together under the category of 'cognitive-based' approaches. None of these theories involve actually interviewing horror audiences about the pleasures that the genre affords them; all are frameworks that make general assertions about how horror will tend to be interpreted by its audiences. Such arguments remain empirically textually derived rather than entirely speculative: that is, on the basis of textual analysis, the critics gathered together here all conclude that horror works in certain ways to engage its audiences in forms of pleasurable cognition.

I will survey the highly influential philosophy of Noël Carroll (1990), then linking this to more recent work done by Cynthia Freeland (2000), Torben Grodal (1999) and Daniel Shaw (2001). For further debate surrounding Carroll's work see Neill (1992), Carroll (1992a), Feagin (1992), Carroll (1992b), Solomon (1992), Gaut (1993), Carroll (1995), Gaut (1995), Vorobej (1997) and Hills (2003b). These academic explorations of horror have, I will argue, constructed the genre's pleasures in limited and restricted ways. Therefore this discussion should not be taken as a somehow 'objective' or 'detached' overview of work in the field: by pointing out how these scholars have theoretically construed and discursively constructed horror's pleasures, my ultimate aim is to suggest an alternative, affective theory of horror. This is sketched out in the chapter's second section, where I draw upon criticisms and developments of cognitive philosophy or 'cognitivism' (Armon-Jones 1991; Greenspan 1993; Matravers 2001). By critiquing cognitive approaches, this chapter will emphasize the need to address audience 'affects' (feelings that are not aimed at, or experienced in response to, a readily identifiable object) *as well as* audience 'emotions' (broadly, feelings that have a cognitive knowledge component and a discriminable object, e.g. I know that I am scared because I am scared of that giant spider scuttling towards me). But I will start by exploring cognitive theories of emotion in relation to horror and its pleasures.

COGNITIVE APPROACHES TO HORROR

Those adopting the precepts of a cognitive philosophy ('cognitivists') stress that what they define as emotions cannot simply be opposed to thought or cognition. To experience an emotion is, by definition for the cognitivist, to be engaged in a process of cognition. In *The Philosophy of Horror or Paradoxes of the Heart*, Noël Carroll explains this as follows:

> I am presupposing that art-horror is an emotion. It is the emotion that horror narratives and images are designed to elicit from audiences. That is, 'art-horror' names the emotion that the creators of the genre have perennially sought to instill in their audiences ... I am also presuming that art-horror is an occurrent emotional state, like a flash of anger, rather than a dispositional state, such as undying envy. An occurrent emotional state has both physiological and cognitive dimensions. (Carroll 1990, p. 24)

We would ordinarily just call art-horror 'horror', but Carroll wants to distinguish the horror we feel in relation to actual, real-life events from that experienced in relation to the horror genre's narratives/images; the former is thus termed 'natural horror' (1990, p. 13), and the latter deemed 'art-horror'. Art-horror has physiological dimensions such as 'tension, cringing, shrinking, shuddering, recoiling, tingling, frozenness, momentary arrests, chilling (hence, 'spine-chilling'), paralysis, nausea, a reflex of apprehension or physically heightened alertness (a danger response), perhaps involuntary screaming, and so on' (Carroll 1990, p. 24). But in Carroll's account these physiological states become linked to the emotion of art-horror thanks only to cognitive elements; he is opposing a *qualia* or 'feeling view of the emotions' (1990, p. 25), which would argue that emotions can be identified purely by the feelings or physical agitations that accompany them. According to the cognitivist position adopted by Carroll:

> Emotions involve not only physical perturbations but beliefs and thoughts, beliefs and thoughts about the properties of objects and situations. Moreover, these beliefs (and thoughts) are not just factual ... but also evaluative. (Carroll 1990, p. 26)

As Robert Solomon has pointed out, '[f]or Carroll, much depends ... on the theory ... of emotion he entertains. Carroll seems particularly attracted and attached to David (sic) Lyons's theory of emotion ... (Lyons, *Emotion*, Cambridge, 1980)' (1992, p. 128). This being the case, Carroll's definition of art-horror – following William Lyons's (1980) theory of emotion – is required to specify what can act as the 'object' of art-horror. What is it in art-horror (as a set of texts) that instils art-horror (the emotion) in audiences?

Carroll's answer, one that has sparked many controversies in academic work on horror, is that horror's monsters provoke the emotion of art-horror (1990, p. 27). Such fictional monsters are further defined by Carroll as referring 'to any being not believed to exist now according to contemporary science' (ibid.) that is regarded as 'threatening and impure' (1990, p. 28). By 'impure' he means noxious and provoking disgust; art-horror is thus a distinctive compound of cognitive/evaluative fear and disgust as far as Carroll is concerned (Miller 1997, pp. 25–8 also argues that disgust and fear are often 'co-experienced' as 'hybrid sentiments' such as horror, while Ahmed 2004, p. 86 notes the significance of disgust within theories of abjection and horror such as Creed 1993 and Stacey 1997).

However, art-horror (and its cognitive component) is not simply cued by the represented, fantastic biologies of the genre's monsters. It is also supported by the diegetic reactions of characters: 'the emotions of the audience are supposed to mirror those of the positive human characters in certain, but not all respects ... This mirroring effect is a key feature of the horror genre' (Carroll 1990, p. 18). This 'mirroring' means that the audience should share characters' assessments of the monster as horrifying. But whereas characters usually believe in the monster's existence, the audience obviously does not, given that they are experiencing *art*-horror.

Carroll's approach has many virtues; it is economical, it accounts for very many examples of art-horror, and it works across media, explaining horror novels as well as it explains horror films. Despite that, later critics have recurrently challenged Carroll's emphasis on the horror monster as a vital characteristic of art-horror. For example, Steven Jay Schneider (2000a), Cynthia Freeland (2000) and David J. Russell (1998) have contested Carroll's definition of 'the monster', arguing that serial killers and 'realistic' monsters must be admitted into Carroll's theory of horror. And Mark Jancovich has usefully observed that '[i]f there is any feature which all horror texts share, it is probably the position of the victim – the figure under threat' (Jancovich 1992, p. 118) rather than the position of a threatening and impure monster that is 'not believed to exist now according to contemporary science'. Of course, Carroll's argument notes the importance of horror's diegetic victims, but he relates their fear and loathing to the 'object' of the monster, making this the central part of his definition rather than the diegetic, narrative suffering of victims.

It would be fair to say that Carroll's definitions of 'the monster' and 'art-horror' have been much challenged – for another example of this, see Hills (2003b) for a discussion of horror films such as *The Blair Witch Project* (1999, dr: Daniel Myrick and Eduardo Sánchez) and *The Haunting* (1963, dr: Robert Wise) that withhold or imply diegetically monstrous agencies rather than clearly representing them. But curiously enough, the Carrollian emphasis on art-horror as an emotion has been far less frequently contested. The close details of Carroll's formulations have been picked apart, but his basic, cognitivist theoretical assumptions have often been left untouched.

Carroll puts forward a specific view of audience pleasure: in his account, audiences enjoy horror for 'universal' and 'general' reasons. The former concerns the curiosity and fascination that horror's monsters engender:

> [T]he objects of horror are fundamentally linked with cognitive interests, most notably with curiosity. The plotting gambits of disclosure/discovery narratives play with ... this initial cognitive appetite ... [T]he objects of art-horror [i.e. monsters] in and of themselves engender curiosity as well. (1990, p. 187)

Hence the 'universal' resolution of horror's apparent paradox – why do we enjoy watching representations of things and events that we would otherwise find repulsive/repellent? – is said to lie in the fascination we hold for monstrous entities, given that these violate standing cultural categories in a variety of ways. Monsters combine cultural meanings in ways that cannot actually exist in our culture; vampires and zombies are both 'alive' and 'dead'; werewolves are 'man' and 'beast', and so on. However, this 'impurity' or 'categorically interstitial' clause is a relatively weak explanation for audience 'fascination' with monsters, for it can be objected that vampires, ghosts, zombies and werewolves are, far from violating cultural categories, exactly what we expect to encounter within the cultural category of the horror genre.

Nevertheless, for Carroll, it is this monstrous fascination that accounts 'universally' for non-narrative and narrative horror. His more 'general' explanation deals only with narrative horror, and emphasizes the way that horror's plots capitalize on audiences' cognitive interest in what the monster is, and what powers it has, by only gradually disclosing the monstrous entity to characters and viewers (1990, p. 190).

Carroll therefore discusses the pleasures of horror as 'co-existentialist' with horror's negative emotions (such as fear and disgust) rather than as 'integrationist'. An integrationist explanation of horror would argue that audiences derive enjoyment directly from the genre's representations of gore and monstrosity; positive and negative emotions would thus be directly integrated, and gore or monstrosity would itself contribute to audience pleasure. By contrast, a co-existentialist account stresses that positive and negative emotions are only contingently connected, with the source and strength of positive emotions outweighing, or compensating for, the source and strength of negative emotions. Following this, Carroll argues that:

> [for] the average consumer of art-horror, the claim is that the art-horror we feel is finally outweighed by the fascination of the monster, as well as, in the

majority of cases, by the fascination engendered by the plot in the process of staging the manifestations and disclosure of the monster. (1990, p. 192)

However, the notion of an 'average consumer' introduces a problem for Carroll's explanation, since it raises the spectre of multiple types of horror audiences. Carroll only considers one 'specialized' consumer group, identifying fans of films such as *Friday the 13th* (1980, dr: Sean S. Cunningham) as an audience that 'seek[s] horror fictions simply to be horrified' (1990, p. 193). This requires an integrationist explanation, as Carroll notes, since audience pleasure in this instance is seemingly directly linked to horrific representations. Carroll explains this as a form of 'metaresponse' whereby consumers treat horror fictions as 'endurance tests' (ibid.), hence reacting primarily to their own responses of disgust or revulsion. Such responses are not captured by Carroll's universal or general theory of art-horror. We might suggest that this logical classification of audience responses, where 'average' consumers act in one way and 'specialized' consumers do something quite different, is open to twin problems of deconstruction and extension.

First, deconstructing this distinction would involve arguing that it is not only 'specialized' audiences – the 'adolescent males' discussed by Carroll (ibid.) – who 'metarespond' to horror; supposedly 'average' audiences may also derive pleasure from feeling that they have 'withstood' horrific representations, even while still being fascinated by monsters and disclosure plots, etc. This possibility would threaten Carroll's neatly logical separation of integrationist and co-existentialist accounts of pleasure, implying that the horror genre may inevitably be experienced by its audiences as a compound of these otherwise conceptually distinguishable approaches.

Secondly, extending the 'average/specialized audiences' argument would involve outlining a range of audience responses that would ultimately tend to disintegrate the notion of stable 'average' and 'specialized' audience groups altogether. For example, horror film audiences may take pleasure in the appearances of certain, well-known genre actors (such as Peter Cushing and Christopher Lee in Hammer films: see Hutchings 1993, p. 59), where cognitive processes would not be entirely narrative based, nor indeed fear or disgust based. Instead, pleasures taken in relation to horror texts could be based on appreciation of a star's performance and/or charisma (and this need not imply that the audience member is necessarily a fan, academic, critic or connoisseur of horror). Because Carroll's theory aims to account for horror across different media, he misses this aspect of horror film. We could extend Carroll's model by adding this type of 'specialized' response, but given the prevalence of star-based readings of popular film, such a consideration may just as well be labelled a part of 'average' consumption. In fact, as this lack of clarity demonstrates, it is really an *empirical* question – a question of how real audiences actually respond to stars in horror films – how to best classify such audience readings. This multiplication or extension of alternative reading positions could be dealt with via a broader range of analytical distinctions (as are contained in Barker and Brooks 1998, for instance), perhaps making star-based reading a further type of 'specialized' response, or a subcategory of 'average' response, but such a scenario begins to strain Carroll's binary opposition, or strict either/or, of 'average' versus 'specialized' horror consumers.

A fellow cognitivist, Murray Smith, has noted the role of film stars in horror narratives, observing that one factor in audience 'allegiances' with 'perverse' characters such as cannibalistic psychopaths can be the casting of a star: 'the "charisma" of stars may ... [work to legitimate] certain imagined desires and their resultant emotions which the spectator herself might frown upon outside of the realm of the fictional' (Smith 1999, p. 227). Thus when 'we watch Hannibal Lecter, we are really watching Anthony Hopkins-playing-Hannibal-Lecter. The presence of a star underlines ... the "playfulness" – unreality, fictionality – of the acts we watch' (ibid.). In such a case we are not merely fascinated by a monster (although recall that Lecter does not readily fit Carroll's definition, despite ad hoc attempts to argue this; see Carroll 2001, p. 240). Instead, we are fascinated by a specific actor's bravura portrayal of such a figure (see also Burn and Parker 2003, pp. 67–74 for a detailed analysis of one audience member's response to the star figure of Anthony Hopkins as Hannibal Lecter).

Whether thought of as part of an 'average' or 'specialized' response to horror, this type of fascination is nevertheless – contra Carroll's (1990) account – not an emotion occurring in relation to narrative or monstrosity *per se*, and nor is it clearly a 'metaresponse' as defined by Carroll. Following Ed Tan's cognitive theory of film as an 'emotion machine' it can be more adequately addressed as an 'A-emotion', this being a category of emotions 'that arise from concerns related to the [film as] artefact [rather than] emotions rooted in the fictional world' (Tan 1996, p. 65). This is a type of response that Carroll downplays or renders absent altogether; it is a response to horror as constructed. A-emotions could also involve the audience taking pleasure in special effects viewed as well crafted (see Chapter 4), or enjoying a plot twist not as a ratiocinative development or clarification of fascinating monstrosity, but simply as evidence of a well-written story (Tan 1995, p. 65 – and see the following chapter). Carroll's account hence pays no attention to audience pleasures of horror that may relate to the genre's stars or *auteurs*, and these are not factored into his distinction between 'average' and 'specialized' audiences. It is perhaps the case that Carroll misses such pleasures because he is concerned to isolate what distinctively characterizes the pleasures of horror, whereas these pleasures of implied creative agency are evidently not specific to the horror genre. Nevertheless, even in his own terms, Carroll seems not to consider cognitive processes that may be linked to treating horror texts as artefacts as well as fictional worlds.

For Carroll, horror is cognitive in terms of the emotion of art-horror, the audience's interest in a fantastic monster, and the genre's typically 'revelatory plotting' (1990, p. 184). Such plotting whets the audience's curiosity with the prospect of 'knowing the putatively unknowable' monster, and then satisfies this appetite 'through a continuous process of revelation, enhanced by imitations of (admittedly simplistic) proofs, hypotheses, counterfeits of causal reasoning, and explanations whose details and movement intrigue the mind in ways analogous to genuine ones' (Carroll 1990, p. 184).

There are many further difficulties with this cognitivist account that go beyond its separation of average/specialized audiences. It appears to hold that horror's physical sensations (fright, etc.) are counterbalanced and compensated for by mindful, cognitive activities that are not strictly speaking emotional. Thus, despite appearing to challenge a cognition/emotion separation by arguing that emotions always have cognitive components, the mind–body or cognition/ emotion distinction is, I would argue, ultimately reinscribed via Carroll's resolution of horror's apparent paradox. Carroll himself is well aware that he could be accused of using 'mindful' cognition to rescue horror as a culturally valuable genre, since he argues proleptically that:

> In claiming that the pleasures derived from horror are cognitive in the broad sense – of engaging curiosity – I am attempting to explain why the genre so often engages us. I am not attempting to justify the genre as worthy of our attention because its appeal is cognitive. Nor by saying that it is cognitive ... am I even implicitly signalling that I think it superior to some other genres whose appeal might be said to be exclusively emotive. (1990, p. 244, n. 46)

While Carroll asserts that he is not valuing or defending horror *because* it is distinctively cognitive, the fact remains that his 'pleasures' of horror are, finally, also the mindful pleasures of analytical philosophy itself, such as proofs, hypotheses, causal reasoning and explanations. Yet the genre's proofs are not quite up to scratch; unlike philosophy (and Carroll's study of horror) they are 'admittedly simplistic' and 'counterfeits' of reasoning. It would appear that the horror genre, in Carroll's account, comes to resemble a type of failed philosophy or metaphysics. Horror seemingly approximates to philosophy, but does not quite imitate it successfully.

In addition, audience 'affects' go significantly astray in this account. Feelings that are cognitively impenetrable (i.e. they do not relate to clear objects framed by cognitive processes of evaluation; they are not 'object directed') are not accounted for, other than the 'startle reflex' where audiences jump when startled by a sudden noise, a fast 'shock edit', or a rapid movement into or within the film frame (Carroll 1990, p. 36; and for more on the 'startle reflex' see Simons 1996). We can thus challenge Carroll's cognitive account of horror's pleasures by attempting to reintroduce the matter of affect. This means challenging cognitivism more generally, as well as Carroll's specific explanation of horror's pleasures. However, before mounting this challenge, I want to examine other broadly cognitive theories of horror, such as those put forward by Torben Grodal (1999), Daniel Shaw (2001) and Cynthia Freeland (2000).

Grodal suggests that horror, like thrillers, deals diegetically with 'problems of cognitive consistency and of paranoia' (1999, p. 245). Such texts generate pleasure by first aligning audiences with characters experiencing arousing cognitive dissonance and then resolving that dissonance, for example there is, after all, a conspiracy to be combated, or there is a supernatural monster to be confronted. As Grodal puts it:

> Key episodes in many horror films are situations in which the protagonists have a powerful experience of causal links which are rejected by 'science' and situations in which protagonists overlook impending danger, because – unlike the viewer – they have 'restricted' concepts of causality. (1999, p. 249)

This is not so far away from Carroll's emphasis on the supposedly philosophy-like pleasures of horror narratives and their ratiocination. Rather than emphasizing the object of these problems with logic, causality and cultural categories (the monster), Grodal focuses instead on the protagonists of horror and their plights. This leads him to conclude that audiences' 'explicit motivation for horror is ... a desire for cognitive and physical control' (ibid.), control that is figured via the protagonists' fight back against the monster or horrifying threat. This account is somewhat problematic insofar as it doesn't seem to account very well for horror fictions where monstrous entities triumph (e.g. David Cronenberg's *Shivers* from 1975) and where autonomy and control are thoroughly dispensed with diegetically in favour of crazed, orgiastic self-absence. This problem has been addressed in a variant on the 'control' explanation of horror's pleasures, put forward by Daniel Shaw (2001). Shaw argues that horror's pleasures are not only related to the power/control of human protagonists:

> [T]he emotion of art-horror is pleasurable in itself ... I propose that we see the horrific force as an embodiment of awesome power, attractive and pleasurable in itself, which repels because of the 'immorality' of the undeserved deaths which inevitably ensue. Such an account is also sufficiently general to cover both impossible beings and human psychopaths. (Shaw 2001, p. 6)

Opposing Carroll's co-existentialist thesis, Shaw argues that horror *is* pleasurable, but not by virtue of curiosity piqued by the 'impossible' and category-violating monster (as this would fail to explain the appeal of human psychopath figures). Rather, it is the psycho-monster's power, their apparent omnipotence or exaggerated agency, that is pleasurable and thrilling for horror's audiences. Both psycho-monsters and protagonists that fight back are usually individuals with the power to 'make a difference' (whether this is to kill or be killed, or to challenge entire cultural systems and ways of life). Their common and extreme diegetic power is what, for Shaw, marks them out as fascinating.

Shaw's account of horror's pleasures is open to the objection that it presents necessary but not sufficient conditions for horror (Carroll 1990, pp. 16–17). That is, forces that are awesomely powerful might also be represented in fairy tales, myths and fantasies, etc., as well as in disaster movies, thrillers and science-fictional texts, so this alone is not sufficient to secure the pleasures of art-horror. Shaw also rather begs the question of how horror is to be defined, stipulating that the forces he is discussing are 'horrific'. In effect, this returns us to Carroll's attempts to delimit the 'monsters' of horror, for we can just as well ask what delimits the 'forces' of horror? Are they necessarily supernatural? Since Shaw includes psychopathic humans this criteria cannot apply. Is the fact that these forces cause characters' deaths a sufficient condition for horror? Arguably not, since such forces will also cause many character deaths in science fiction, fantasy and thriller genres, where a 'momentous struggle for power' and a 'battle for mastery is at the heart of almost every' entry in these genres, just as it may be in horror (Shaw 2001, p. 12). Shaw's main attempt to separate the appeal of horror's powerful forces from 'the bad guys in westerns, Gangster films and Films Noir' is that 'monsters and psychotics are far more powerful than the usual human adversaries ... [by virtue of having] superhuman powers'. But on this account, superhero fantasies such as Superman *et al.* would have to be counted as horror narratives, which seems like a profoundly unhelpful conclusion, and one that Carroll himself has convincingly dispensed with (1990, pp. 40–1). While Shaw's thesis undoubtedly gains over Grodal's at the level of generality, it seems to lack genre specificity. Although attempting a genre-specific explanation of horror's pleasures, Shaw is ultimately driven to uneasily question whether such accounts are even possible (2001, p. 4).

Unlike Carroll (1990) and Shaw (2001), Grodal's (1999) account of horror does not attempt to identify pleasures that are wholly specific to horror, discussing horror and thrillers together. For Grodal, the key 'problem' addressed narratively by thrillers and by horror films is 'choosing the appropriate schemata' (1999, p. 249) within which protagonists must interpret events. This cognitive definition comes very close to Tzvetan Todorov's work that I will consider in the following chapter. Grodal's discussion of horror has the virtue of leaving absent exactly what it is that provokes cognitive dissonance for protagonists (hence his account can link horror and thrillers), but it also carries the same general difficulty as Carroll's work – that is, it focuses on cognitively determined emotions, thereby restricting audience pleasures to theoretically determined versions and discourses of 'pleasure'. Audiences may, entirely contra this style of account which emphasizes cognition and control, desire to be *affected*, that is, to have their mood temporarily altered by the action of an aesthetic artefact such as a horror narrative. Such a desire would not involve any audience fascination with autonomy, control or knowledge; quite the reverse, it would feature a licensed – because aesthetically provoked – self-transformation, one that would not be wholly under the control of the self. In other words, audiences may take pleasure in being affected by horror films or novels via immersion in their textual 'anticipations' and 'moods'.

Such a possibility is also, by definition, discursively and theoretically absent in Cynthia Freeland's otherwise very interesting cognitive account of the horror genre, *The Naked and the Undead: Evil and the Appeal of Horror* (2000). The strength of Freeland's approach lies, in part, in the way that it deals with the problem posed by Carroll's definition of horror monsters. Like Daniel Shaw's (2001) work, Freeland attempts to evade the difficulties implied in Carroll's (1990) *Philosophy of Horror* by broadening what can be thought of as art-horror. Thus, where Shaw includes 'human psycho-killer' fictions as art-horror contra Carroll, Freeland likewise argues for the need to study what she terms 'realist horror' (Freeland 1995). *The Naked and The Undead* tackles 'uncanny horror' (cosmic, possession horror that lacks an obviously embodied 'monster') and 'graphic horror' (distinguished by its emphasis on special effects spectacles akin to the 'numbers' in musicals). Both of these are neglected in Carroll's work. What Freeland terms 'uncanny horror' (2000, pp. 215–40) is not counted as art-horror by Carroll, while Freeland's discussion of 'graphic horror' (2000, pp. 241–71) addresses the absence of 'A-emotions' (Tan 1996, p. 65) in Carroll's discussion of horror, considering effects 'numbers' as offering pleasure on a 'metalevel' where the film-as-artefact is considered by audiences as well as the film-as-fictional-world (Freeland 2000, p. 266).

Freeland's approach displaces Carroll's emphasis on horror's monsters and narratives with a feminist focus on art-horror's representations of evil and its special effects ('SFX') spectacles of confrontation with evil (2000, p. 8). Freeland's discussion of the *Hellraiser* series (beginning with *Hellraiser*, 1987, dr: Clive Barker) is worth considering in this respect:

> On the surface level of the plot or narrative, conventional morality reigns. Wicked people (or monsters) are punished and their evils are defeated ... But on the metalevel, the audience ... is emotionally invested in and desires the survival of the *monster* ... My reading of the monster's maleness is that he represents certain powers ... that are stereotypically coded as male. In particular, the monster is male because he is, like the filmmakers, a magician who makes the visual spectacles possible. The monster is associated with the creativity behind the numbers that constitute the aesthetic pleasures of graphic horror. (Freeland 2000, p. 267)

Freeland's feminist reading contrasts narrative-level genderings of power, where often a 'strong, virtuous, rather pure young woman emerges victorious' (ibid.) with metalevel genderings of power, where the male monster is linked connotatively with male filmmakers. Moral theories and gender ideologies are both said to be 'at tension with one another' (ibid.) across the levels of film-as-fiction and film-as-artefact, that is morality as depicted in the narrative world is contradicted by enjoyment of the film-as-artefact, and similarly, gender ideologies of triumphant femininity in the diegesis are undercut by extra-diegetic forms of masculine (directorial) power. This bivalent cognitive approach complicates the emphasis on 'power/control' taken by Grodal (1999) and Shaw (2001), since these theories only address the level of the fictional world. According to Freeland's account, we might better address the specific pleasures of horror as gendered pleasures of moral ambivalence, if not inversion, where what is condemned at the narrative level is celebrated at the level of manufactured spectacle.

Horror, in this argument, is pleasurable not for inspiring fascination, curiosity, or a desire to possess superhuman powers, but rather because (via monsters as evil forces) it draws attention to its own textuality and its ability to impact upon the audience. On this 'meta' basis, horror's pleasures can be viewed as inherently reflexive. This is not quite the type of 'metaresponse' discussed by Carroll, since Carroll's argument involves an audience member responding to their 'naive' or reflex response to a text, for example steeling themselves to withstand shock and revulsion, and being satisfied at their ability to do so. Freeland's version of metaresponse, by contrast, involves an audience member responding positively to the text's 'creativity' as a source of pleasure.

Thus far I have examined key cognitive accounts of horror, highlighting the candidates for horror's pleasures that have been put forward. Most notably, these have included:

- fascination and curiosity at impossible, monstrous beings;
- disclosure plots that resemble the 'proofs' of philosophy;
- concerns with power/control; and
- evaluations of morality/creativity.

These accounts have shared recurrent problems such as the difficulty of isolating pleasures that are specific to horror, as well as difficulties stemming from their use of cognitive theory itself, in which 'object-directed' audience emotions provoked by the horror genre have been limited to types of fear, disgust, cognitive dissonance, and cognitive reflections on evil. While taking horror very seriously – and promoting it as a serious, mindful genre – such accounts have developed a number of blind spots. One is the way in which much horror veers toward comedy, not only in spoofs or parodies (Miller 2000; Harries 2002), but also in texts that are identified by audiences and critics alike as legitimate or 'authentic' horror (see the belated approach to this in Carroll 2001, and see also Paul 1994; Hoxter 1996; Picart 2003). By focusing on a limited range of emotions such as fear and disgust – by assuming that horror's sole *raison d'être* is to scare or horrify – cognitive theories have undoubtedly downplayed the importance of comedy within horror texts as aesthetic artefacts. However, rather than adding at this point to the range of emotions that cognitivism should deal with, I want to move away from cognitive theories of horror, considering instead an affective theory of the genre.

My central argument here is that cognitive accounts, despite their variations and nuances, have all discursively restricted what counts as 'art-horror' to a theoretically determined version of 'object-directed emotion'. Horror's pleasures have thus been cut to a pre-given theoretical agenda, and this situation of 'theory first, horror second' has rendered invisible a range of alternative perspectives and discourses on the horror genre. In short, by restricting discussion to object-directed emotion, such theories have removed objectless affects (such as mood and anxiety) from scholarly analysis altogether. Thus, although my argument here can be seen as a critical intervention in the field, it most definitely should not be assumed to displace theoretical 'errors' of cognitivism with the 'truth' of an affective analysis. Rather I am seeking to recuperate what appears – on the basis of dominant work in the philosophy of horror – to be a further and very much marginalized discourse of horror's pleasures.

ANXIETY AND ANTICIPATION:
TOWARDS THE AFFECTS OF HORROR

Having suggested that cognitive theories of horror discursively construct specific pleasures for the genre's ideal audience (often 'mindful' pleasures that are akin to those of philosophy itself), what might a non-cognitive approach to horror's pleasures look like? Psychoanalytic theories of horror have usually been taken as the major opponent to cognitive theories (see Chapter 3), since psychoanalysis stresses unconscious processes and affects, striking at the core assumptions of the cognitivist, for whom conscious thought processes and evaluations are crucial. Deleuzian or post-structuralist theories of affect could also be utilized to challenge cognitive theories of emotion, but this is not a direction I will pursue. Deleuzian or post-structuralist accounts of affect (see, for example, Buchanan 2000; Kennedy 2000; Terada 2001; Massumi 2002) tend to view affect as non-personal and desubjectified, as transcending/traversing the subject. I am in agreement with Simon Williams (2001, p. 88) when he writes that this 'radical reconfiguration ... loses too much in the process'. It is unclear how a Deleuzian account of horror's affects could relate to the subjects who choose, and do not choose, to consume horror; arguably, too much of the subject is surrendered by Deleuzians. In this section, then, I want to consider critiques of cognitivism that do not hail from psychoanalytic or Deleuzian quarters, making use instead of amendments to cognitive theory.

The major weaknesses of cognitive theories of horror can be summarized as follows: (i) emotion is theoretically defined as being 'object directed' because it is cognitively evaluative, and (ii) emotion is defined as being 'occurrent', that is, occurring at a given moment rather than lingering like a disposition or mood.

With regard to these assumptions, an affective but non-psychoanalytic theory of horror would make the following counter-assumptions:

- *Horror does not only provoke object-directed emotions*; it also significantly provokes objectless states of anxiety. Although it makes sense to say that fear and disgust are object directed, that is fear of 'X' and disgust at 'Y', anxiety is not definitionally object directed. It is less of an 'emotion', as defined by cognitivists, and more of an affect (affects being feeling states that do not have cognitive, evaluative components).
- *Horror does not only engage audiences in 'occurrent' emotions*, that is emotions which occur at one moment and then pass, like the 'flash of anger' cited by Carroll (1990, p. 24) and distinguished from a disposition such as 'undying envy' (ibid.). This assumption converts horror into a series of cognitive emotions occurring in evaluative succession and in line with narrative events. Contra this notion, horror can immerse its audiences in an 'anticipatory' mood or ambience that endures across the text, and which is not overwritten by specific narrative events or 'occurrent' emotions. That is, horror can generate a saturated affective experience of anticipation, with specific 'emotions' occurring in relation to this affective mood. As Claire Armon-Jones has argued: 'contemporary philosophical theories of affect are cognitive in their theoretical orientation. Moods miss the spotlight of theoretical interest because ... there is a tendency to assume that, if they are objectless then ... they are non-cognitive, and so of no special interest for theories of cognitive states.' (1991, p. 49)

These two leading assumptions of cognitive theory are, of course, inter-connected; it is because emotions are assumed to be object directed that they are also assumed to be occurrent; their object-directedness means that they must arise in response to particular propositions or thoughts, which in this case are themselves occasioned by specific textual cues or moments. However, these assumptions reduce the spectator's experience of horror to a series of computational instances, where as each new textual 'object' is cognitively processed and evaluated new emotions occur somewhat mechanically. Any sense of a horror text as globally constituting a mood or ambience through music, *mise-en-scène*, iconography, etc. is hence neglected.

Some support for the position that cognitive approaches overstate the centrality of object-directed emotion can be drawn from Robert Solomon's commentary on Carroll's *Philosophy of Horror*:

> When we ask, 'What is the object of horror?' is that in fact the proper question, or is that rather shorthand for a more general question about the nature of a kind of experience in which the 'object' is but an abstracted focus? (Solomon 1992, p. 121)

Responding to his own rhetorical question, Solomon then argues that '[m]ere monsters make pretty lousy horror movies ... Horror is not just confrontation with an object. It is an imaginative confrontation with oneself' (1992, p. 128).

Defining the 'object' of art-horror is thus to reduce the complexity of this aesthetic experience. If we extrapolate from Solomon's point, we can argue that horror involves not just an outward-focused 'emotional reaction' to textual content, but that it also, necessarily, involves introspection over one's own emotional and affective states. Confronting an 'object' is compatible with cognitive accounts. Confronting oneself 'imaginatively' is less clearly compatible with such accounts, as it will tend to involve reflecting not only on 'emotions' but also on 'affects'/sensations such as feeling thrilled, tense, edgy or uneasy, which do not carry easily definable objects.

Patricia Greenspan has noted that such affective states can have no object: 'discomfort can sometimes simply "take on" an object. Consider a case of initially objectless sensation – "pure" edginess ... that turns into an emotional state by attaching to an available (external) object' (Greenspan 1993, p. 22). This is referred to as a case of emotion with an 'invented object' (ibid.). But the reverse is also possible; emotions such as fear or disgust could become affects or sensations, if the 'object' of a fear emotion was disregarded introspectively, or if it was textually represented as indeterminate/'cosmic' rather than being clearly object based.

In the first instance, horror audiences would go through the cognitive processes outlined by Carroll, but they might then introspectively reject or 'throw out' their cognitive evaluations. Rather than affect 'taking on' an object and thus becoming an emotion, this process would involve an emotion blocking out or rejecting its object, thus becoming an objectless affect. Horror's audiences may, in line with this account, move between experiencing affects and emotions, refuting or refusing some emotions that would be ideally and textually expected, and rendering these instead as affects – as 'pure' physiological sensations without, or detached from, an object. This dynamic offers one possible solution to the question of whether fear in response to fictional objects is 'really' fear or whether it is fictional fear, etc. (Walton 1990, pp. 195–204). By virtue of the horror audience reflecting on their fear and disgust in response to fictional objects, this 'fear' (or disgust) may in fact then be transformed into objectless affect, for example anxiety.

In the second instance, considered as a purely text-based argument, horror texts that do not clearly identify their horrific 'objects', but which nevertheless imply their existence, leave an objectual indeterminacy in place which sustains objectless affect *and* object-directed emotion. *The Blair Witch Project*, for example, allows for cognitive evaluations that the Witch exists and is a threatening force, but it also withholds confirmation of the Witch as a fully or clearly defined object, hence pushing fear emotions back towards affective saturation (for more on this see Hills 2003b, and see also Higley and Weinstock (eds) 2004). Even at the film's conclusion, clear diegetic delimitation of the Witch as embodied or present is not confirmed, leaving a sense of the Blair Witch as unrestrained in diegetic space and time, and hence as potentially omnipresent. This supports objectless anxiety as well as object-directed emotion (which imagines the Witch propositionally). 'Possession horror' (e.g. *The Exorcist* (1973, dr: William Friedkin); *Fallen* (1998, dr: Gregory Hoblit); *The Shining* (1980, dr: Stanley Kubrick); *The Blair Witch Project*; *Event Horizon* (1997, dr: Paul W.S. Anderson)) offers many instances of the interplay between object-directed emotion (experienced where the possessive force is 'housed' in one specific body) and objectless anxiety, where the possessive force exceeds any one body/object and hence potentially saturates a *mise-en-scène*. Shapeshifting horror monsters can also provoke this shift from object-directed emotion (the gross 'transformation' scene) to objectless anxiety (who is a monster?). And such potential is also sustained by vampire, zombie and werewolf movies, where the question of who is 'infected' by the monstrosity can give rise to object-directed emotion and objectless anxiety. *Demons* (1985, dr: Lamberto Bava) and *Demons 2* (1986, dr: Lamberto Bava) are good examples of this type of 'infection' horror (see Mendik 2001), as is George Romero's (1968) *Night of the Living Dead* (Williams 2003). The ending of John Carpenter's (1982) *The Thing* also offers a clear example of this textual transformation from emotion to affect; where we have perhaps previously been fearful and disgusted in response to the gory, category violations of the Thing, we conclude on a note of uncertainty, not knowing which (if any) of the remaining human characters may actually be an alien (see Billson 1997; Krzywinska 2000; Prince 2004a). The threat hence becomes non-objectual, instead hanging over the text as an indeterminate implication and giving rise to objectless anxiety rather than a cognitive evaluation of fear or disgust.

Although this emotion-transformed-to-affect tendency is more clearly narratively licensed in 'possession horror', it can also emerge through sudden plot twists implying supernatural rather than human agency (see Chapter 2). *Halloween* (1978, dr: John Carpenter), for example, although a slasher movie rather than 'possession horror', concludes by absenting its slasher-killer, Michael Myers, in a way that implies his supernatural omnipresence. A final montage of shots showing the empty house works to reinforce the sense that Michael could be anywhere, but that the gaze of the camera cannot apprehend him. Fearful emotion directed at Michael Myers-as-object is thus textually transformed into objectless anxiety; how can he have disappeared? Where is he? *What* is he? A powerful element of indeterminacy invades the text's final moments.

It may be no accident that horror films sometimes thought of as 'classics' of the genre, like *Halloween* or *The Thing*, shift from object-directed emotion to objectless anxiety (and monstrous indeterminacy) in their closing frames: this movement incites audiences to leave the cinema, or switch the video/DVD off, while still in an anxious, affective mood rather than having just experienced an occurrent 'emotion'. This affect may thus linger – since it is not dependent on cognitive evaluations of an object – spilling outside the experiential time of reading/viewing the horror text, and reinforcing a sense of that text's skilful operation upon its audience.

This line of argument offers a way of thinking about horror's affects as significant rather than trivial or non-essential. Horror, I am arguing here, involves an interplay between 'affect' and 'emotion' as these are defined by cognitivists, with cognitive evaluations transforming affects into emotions, while such evaluations can also be challenged or textually complicated. In this latter case, audience emotion is transformed into objectless affect such as anxiety (this often happening at a horror film's conclusion). Such a perspective stresses that horror may not be an 'emotion machine' *per se* (Tan 1996). Rather, horror's texts may be thought of as a 'machine' for constructing affect and emotion and transforming each into its other; a kind of 'dialectical affect-emotion machine', even if this lacks the rhetorical elegance of Ed Tan's (1996) formulation.

Carroll (1990) and more recent cognitive philosophies of horror appear to view horror's affects – its startle reflexes and shock edits – as inessential to the genre, but I am arguing that we should view such affects very differently: not as opposed and subordinated to object-based emotions, but as potential precursors (and residues) of such emotions. If, as Greenspan argues, 'pure' edginess can resolve itself into an emotion by 'taking on' an object, then we can explain why horror texts may significantly seek to incite such 'pure edginess' in their audiences/readers. Far from being trivial or merely cognitively impenetrable, this affective process would predispose audiences to seek an object to attach their objectless affect to, priming them to experience the emotion of art-horror when a suitable object (whether a 'horrifying' monster or a 'horrific' force) is represented. Indeed, one of the pleasures of horror may in fact lie in the transformation of experienced affect into emotion and vice versa, as objects attach to sensation/ affect, and as emotions that are introspectively refuted or detached from objects 'take off' into affective saturation of a horror text's unsettling mood or 'edgy' ambience.

Continuing this discussion of affect and emotion not as opponents, but as processual partners, Derek Matravers has controversially questioned whether disgust or revulsion can even function as emotions in the way that Carroll suggests:

> Carroll has noted correctly that characters such as Dracula cause feelings of revulsion. Because he thinks such feelings can only be caused by Dracula via the causal intermediary of some cognitive state, he postulates some suitable property of Dracula which can form the content of the requisite beliefs: impurity. It is difficult to see this as anything other than an *ad hoc* move to save the assumption that all the relevant feelings here are caused by cognitive states. (Matravers 2001, p. 93)

Matravers argues that Carroll is, as a matter of theoretical doctrine/dogma, unwilling to concede that 'feelings can be influenced directly' by horror texts, without cognitive intermediaries (2001, p. 92). Since Carroll will not countenance horror as affective or sensational, he fixes his definition of art-horror in purely emotion-based, cognitive terms. By arguing that 'impurity' appears to have no 'single property ... which causes a cognitive state which causes ... reactions' of physical loathing, shuddering, revulsion, etc. (2001, p. 93), Matravers suggests that Carroll has erected a complex thesis to defend his cognitive theory. Following Occam's razor, a far more simple and obvious possibility can be put forward to explain the revulsion felt at horror's monsters:

> To be impure is simply to have the disposition to cause the reactions; there is no role for a cognitive intermediary to play ... whether or not Dracula is horrific depends not only on imagining the relevant propositions, but also on the feelings aroused. (ibid.)

And if these feelings can be aroused directly by a specific filmic representation of Dracula rather than Dracula as a proposition *per se* (Matravers 2001, p. 91), then this is again an affective rather than an 'emotional' relationship between text and audience. However, note that Matravers' challenge to cognitivism does not entirely dispense with cognitive intermediaries. Actually, his account supplements Carroll's: Dracula may both arouse affect *and* act as an object for the cognitive evaluations of emotion. In this argument, affect and emotion are again interconnected rather than affect being discursively and theoretically subordinated to emotion, and hence viewed as trivial. Following Matravers' account, affect may therefore precede the 'emotion' of art-horror felt for Dracula, but it may also persist through this emotion, meaning that rather than felt sensations being entirely transformed into cognitive evaluations aimed at an object, affect may persist as pure physiological feelings (of shuddering, being grossed-out, etc.) even while cognitive evaluations of Dracula-as-object are being made. Hence affects may not even require the full rejection of a cognitive evaluation or object to be reinstated; they may simply persist, colouring the cognitive evaluations made by audiences.

Further supporting the argument that cognitive approaches to horror neglect objectless affect is the work of Chris Meyers and Sara Waller (2001). Like Solomon, Meyers and Waller take issue with Carroll's postulation that the monster is the defining 'object' of art-horror. Instead, they argue that:

> because Carroll focuses on the monster as necessary for horror, he takes this unknown or incomprehensible element to involve *ontological* categories of the nature of the monster ... Instead, we ... see this inconceivability element of horror not as ontological – that is not something wrong with something in the world viz. a monster – but rather as epistemic – maybe there is something wrong with a thing in the world, or may be something wrong with me, or may be I have no idea of what I am up against, (and I know it). (Meyers and Waller 2001, p. 119)

Again, this suggests that it is not the monster and related pleasures of curiosity/fascination that are essential to the horror genre, but rather an 'epistemic deficit': an anxiety-inducing not-knowing in relation to the events and entities of art-horror (see also Dyson 1997, p. xv on the 'sensory incompleteness' of classic supernatural horror films such as Val Lewton's 1940s RKO movies). When art-horror has a clearly defined object then, for Meyers and Waller, this determinacy attenuates the audience's experience of horror, converting it into 'dread' (ibid.). By contrast, objectless horror is intensified:

> by the absence of the *source* of the horror … The epistemic deficit offers us a glimpse of something worse than anything we could describe (in literature) or depict (in painting), because if it could be described or depicted then it would at least be within the limits of what we can grasp. (2001, p. 121)

This argument is also very close to Will H. Rockett's in his (1988) study of horror, *Devouring Whirlwind: Terror and Transcendence in the Cinema of Cruelty*. Rockett defines 'horror' as having an object that inspires fear and loathing: this could be 'repugnant scenes' in the slasher movie, or 'bug-eyed monsters' in the bad science movie (1988, p. 46). By contrast, Rockett discusses 'terror' as 'always [being] of the indeterminate and incomprehensible, of the unseen but sensed or suspected, or of the imperfectly seen' (ibid.). Hence for Dyson, Meyers and Waller, and Rockett, objectless affect is presented as aesthetically superior (or more horrifying) in comparison with object-directed 'dread' (Meyers and Waller) or 'horror' (Rockett).

As well as tackling objectless anxieties of monstrous 'epistemic deficit' or indeterminacy, and transformations of emotion into affect, I have already remarked that an affective theory of horror must also focus on the affects of *anticipatory* anxiety that saturate a horror text's representations prior to object-directed emotion (i.e. affect precedes and can be transformed into art-horror as an emotion). On the question of anticipatory moods, Meyers and Waller have criticized Carroll's 'curiosity' thesis by observing that:

> we could get the curiosity without the unpleasant horror. So why should we still want horror? We seem to be attracted to art … that makes us feel the way we already feel. Many people prefer to listen to sad music when they are sad, angry music when they are angry. (2001, p. 124)

Rather strangely, this implies that horror's audiences may enjoy horror's affective states of edginess, unease and anxiety because they are already anxious prior to viewing a horror movie! Rather like Greenspan's 'invented emotions', horror texts would thus provide objects for audiences to focus their affective states on. However, this proposal seems deeply unhelpful; can we usefully suppose that horror's audiences are all somehow traumatized and seeking to 'escape' from 'real-life horrors'? (Meyers and Waller 2001, pp. 124–5). Such an argument appears, yet again, to pathologize horror's audiences (see Tudor 1997, p. 444). Rather than horror's objectless and edgy ambiences recapping anxious moods felt outside the aesthetic text–audience encounter, then, such textually derived moods may be better thought of as narratively and hermeneutically forward looking. That is, they involve 'anticipatory reading' in which the horror genre is signalled through 'arousing the audience's apprehensions [from the outset through] sinister prophecies, premonitions, omens and dreams' (Leffler 2000, p. 177). The fact that specific devices such as dreams are used should not cause us to suppose that anticipation is strictly object directed. The use of these textual devices is, as Yvonne Leffler goes on to argue, 'vague ... and exists more to create an ominous atmosphere than to give away the story that lies ahead' (ibid.). Since such devices are vague or indeterminate, they involve a type of 'epistemic deficit', but one that is different to the type discussed by Meyers and Waller. The deficit here is not that of a monster implied but undefined; it is rather of a threat yet to materialize, hence raising 'expectations of particular events to come and put[ting] the reader or viewer in a particular mood' (Leffler 2000, p. 178).

Leffler offers many examples of this process. As well as diegetic dreams, instances include the 'mystification of initial events' where remarkable or unexplained events pre-figure the later emergence of monstrous threat (2000, p. 178); setting and the representation of nature (2000, p. 180); 'a specific horror scene [that] raises expectations of further terrors' (2000, p. 181); pre-figuring images, whereby a threat presented in words or as an image within the diegesis is later made diegetically actual (2000, pp. 183–4); filmic 'teasers' of a monster's presence such as the use of musical cues or unusual camera angles (2000, p. 183); and the 'anticipatory function of repetition' (2000, p. 189). For Leffler, all such devices are concerned with the 'mood of horror' (ibid.): they prepare for the audience's experience of art-horror when a monstrous threat or horrific force actually emerges diegetically.

Anticipatory reading and its mood is, according to this argument, a crucial part of establishing the horror genre's identity and its audiences' affective states prior to the appearance of any monstrous threat or horrific force. Although Noël Carroll's *Philosophy of Horror* (1990) focuses on the narratives of horror, and the ways in which they provoke curiosity over the monster's existence and definition, he treats this process as entirely cognitive and as a matter of 'proofs' and 'hypotheses'. By contrast, Leffler's approach usefully highlights the significant presence of 'vague' pre-figurings that build an affective mood of edginess and anxiety.

An affective theory of horror obliges us to consider that art-horror is not solely concerned with cognitively framed emotions (where affects such as the startle reflex are reduced to trivial distractions from cognitive theorizing). I have suggested in the second part of this chapter that art-horror can also provoke and sustain anticipatory moods as well as objectless, anxious affects. Indeed I have argued here that we should not rigorously oppose 'cognitive' and 'affective' approaches to horror. To do so would be to miss the ways in which art-horror potentially works, processually and textually, to transform 'affects' into 'emotions' and vice versa. And it would also mean remaining caught within singular discourses and theoretical definitions of horror's pleasures. I have intervened on the side of 'affects' here, if you like, because the horror genre as an affective process has been considerably neglected by cognitivists, if not defined out of existence. My tentative moves towards composing an affective analysis of horror have thus offered up a type of counter-discourse, shedding light on an otherwise marginalized way of discursively constructing the pleasures of horror. In the next two chapters in this part, as I move on to consider further theories of horror and its pleasures, I will also excavate other counter-discourses, suggesting that theoretical rivals to cognitivism, such as psychoanalysis, have also operated with highly restricted definitions and discourses of horror's pleasures (see Chapter 3).

In the following chapter, though, I want to consider a theoretical approach that has many affinities with cognitive accounts; namely, the work of Tzvetan Todorov (1975) on 'the fantastic'. Like cognitive theories of horror, Todorov emphasizes how the (ideal) audience is called upon to interpret texts. Like cognitive theories, his work places an emphasis on questions of audience knowledge and mastery. But unlike the work I have critically explored in this chapter, Todorov entirely rules audience emotion out of his analysis. What implicit or explicit discourse of audience/reader pleasure might this leave us with?

Chapter 2

'Fantastic' Horror:
Hesitation ... and Shock

In this chapter I want to explore another highly influential theory that has been applied to horror texts: Tzvetan Todorov's literary-critical and partly structuralist account of 'the fantastic' (see Armitt 1996, pp. 30–6). James Donald's excellent (1989) edited collection *Fantasy and the Cinema* includes discussion of Todorov, and the more recent (2000) *Horror Reader* (edited by Ken Gelder) includes an extract from Todorov's (1975) study *The Fantastic: A Structural Approach to a Literary Genre*, confirming the canonical status of Todorovian thought in this academic arena. Todorov's work has also been applied to horror film by Noël Carroll (1990) and Michael Grant (1999), to a range of literary 'horror-thrillers' by Terry Heller (1987), and even to Biblical stories treated as 'sacred horror' (see Donaldson 1997; Lee 1997; Pippin and Aichele 1997). Although what Todorov defines as 'the fantastic' does not fully coincide with the horror genre as this is typically discussed by contemporary critics, audiences and industry alike, Todorov's exploration of other-worldly and potentially supernatural narratives resonates with much that is common-sensically described as 'horror', hence the importance of his literary theory in studies of horror.

Just as cognitive theories frame audience pleasure in line with certain assumptions (e.g. what counts as an emotion; the triviality of affect) so too does the Todorovian approach to horror construct a restricted discourse of audience pleasure. In this instance, audiences are presumed to derive pleasure from the resolution (or, indeed, non-resolution) of very specific narrative puzzles. As such, Todorov's work stresses epistemological questions, that is, questions over what we can know of/about a narrative world. Although not identifiable as a 'cognitive' theory in the sense that it draws on cognitive philosophy, Todorov's work still strongly emphasizes the 'mindful' pleasures of horror. As Will Rockett has remarked, the act of reading literature of the 'fantastic' is a 'process carried out under some stress or tension that for Todorov appears to be primarily intellectual, but that one assumes has emotional ramifications as well' (1988, p. 53). However, Todorov removes audience emotion from his account, in a move that is reminiscent of the cognitivists' typical marginalization of 'affect' (feeling/sensation). Both these theoretical approaches thus discursively limit what can be counted as horror's pleasures, in line with their own definitional and a priori assumptions. And each thereby rules out, or renders definitionally invisible, certain counter-discourses concerning the pleasures of horror. Just as I considered the counter-cognitivist discourse of horror's 'affects' (moods, ambiences, anxieties) in Chapter 1, in the later part of this chapter I will address the counter-Todorovian discourse of 'ontological shock' that is otherwise marginalized and occulted in Todorov-derived accounts of horror's appeal.

First, though, I want to introduce and explore Todorov's key ideas in more detail. The audience/reader emotion that Todorov removes from his analysis is not defined as rigorously and specifically as the cognitivists' version of 'emotion', and actually seems more akin to both 'affect' and 'emotion' as these are discussed by cognitivists. Regardless of terminological differences, the fact remains that Todorov's account minimizes emotional response, which is judged to be too subjective to be of any use to a theory of the literary 'fantastic':

> This sentiment of fear or perplexity is often invoked by theoreticians of the fantastic ... [as] ... the necessary condition of the genre ... It is surprising to find such judgements offered by serious critics. If we take their declarations literally – that the sentiment of fear must occur in the reader – we should have to conclude that a work's genre depends on the *sang-froid* of its reader. (Todorov 1975, p. 35)

Although, as I have mentioned, the 'fantastic' and the horror genre are not strictly coterminous, we can still extrapolate from Todorov's point: for the 'subjectivist' critic, if a text inspires fear in its reader then it can be counted as part of the horror genre, but if another reader is not at all afraid in response to the same text, then it must seemingly lack the necessary conditions to be counted as a horror fiction (see also Vorobej 1997). Genre attribution thus appears to depend on the emotional disposition of the specific reader/viewer. However, this logic misses the fact that audiences (and critics, for that matter) may evaluate entirely non-scary horror texts as 'bad' or 'failed' horror, but as horror nonetheless. On the basis of such a flawed argument, Todorov is rather quick to rule out audience affect as an important aspect of the fantastic, and the horror genre. As a result, his discussion of readers' pleasures becomes overly rationalist.

If Todorov's definition of the fantastic is not to hinge on audience emotion, then how does he go about defining this type of text? It is important to note that his definition is a 'theoretical' rather than a 'historical' one (Todorov 1975, pp. 13–14); that is, 'the fantastic' as discussed by Todorov is not a genre that has historically existed as such; it is, instead, an analytical category defined in Todorov's theory. The 'fantastic' is, then, famously defined as follows:

First, the text must oblige the reader to consider the world of the characters as a world of living persons and to hesitate between a natural and a supernatural explanation of the events described. Second, this hesitation may also be experienced by a character; ... Third, the reader must adopt a certain attitude with regard to the text: he will reject allegorical as well as 'poetic' interpretations. These three requirements do not have an equal value. The first and the third actually constitute the genre; the second may not be fulfilled. (Todorov 1975, p. 33)

The fantastic thus 'occupies the duration of this uncertainty' as to whether diegetic events are natural or supernatural (1975, p. 25). It can now be seen why this work has been of value in theorizing horror: many horror texts, whether or not they 'scare' their audience, nevertheless require the audience to intellectually hesitate over 'realistic' (i.e. non-poetic or allegorical) narrative events, considering whether these are natural/supernatural (although see Lem 1985, pp. 218–19 for a challenge to the separation of naive realism and poetry/ allegory).

In Todorov's model, the 'pure' fantastic occurs in a text where readerly indecision is generalized; this type of text can never be closed down or resolved as a matter of 'natural' or 'supernatural' diegetic events (1975, pp. 43–4). The moment of the 'fantastic' thus occupies the duration of the entire text. By contrast, where the 'fantastic' occupies only part of a text's duration, being resolved midway through a narrative, or at the narrative's conclusion, then the text concerned branches into other subgenres. For example, in the 'fantastic-uncanny' compound 'events that seem supernatural throughout a story receive a rational explanation at its end' (1975, p. 44). This could be labelled, not entirely facetiously, a 'Scooby-Doo style narrative', since in the cult cartoon Scooby Doo 'ghosts' are formulaically revealed to be human characters trying to trick others into believing in the supernatural.

By contrast, in the 'fantastic-marvellous' compound, we find that 'class of narratives that are presented as fantastic and that end with an acceptance of the supernatural' (1975, p. 52). Such fictions can be thought of as 'conventional horror', since most texts that are generically marketed and classified (by producers and consumers) as horror are of this type; seemingly supernatural monsters or forces are narratively introduced and eventually confirmed as supernatural. (And to complicate my reference above, the movie version of Scooby-Doo (2002, dr: Raja Gosnell) is 'fantastic-marvellous' rather than 'fantastic-uncanny'; in a reflexive variation on the original TV cartoon's formula, it eventually introduces supernatural events that are narratively accepted as supernatural.)

Todorov's final theoretical genres are 'the uncanny' and 'the marvellous'. Lacking any fantastic hesitation, these are characterized as follows:

[In the pure uncanny] events are related which may be readily accounted for by the laws of reason, but which are ... incredible, extraordinary, shocking, singular, disturbing or unexpected ... In the case of the marvelous, supernatural elements provoke no particular reaction either in the characters or in the implicit reader. (1975, p. 46)

Having outlined these subgenres, it is worth noting that Todorov's definitions of the fantastic-uncanny and the fantastic-marvellous both refer to diegetic explanations that are given at the *end* of narratives. In this account, an intellectual(ized) pleasure of horror emerges through hesitation being resolved. This neglects the possibility that fantastic hesitation may not only appear at the beginning of a narrative. Contra Todorov, the fantastic may in fact only emerge for the first time at the end of a narrative, meaning that the 'uncanny-fantastic' must also be considered. Slasher films such as *Friday the 13th* (1980, dr: Sean S. Cunningham) and *Halloween* (1978, dr: John Carpenter) appear to work in this way, since uncanny, 'shocking' events that have a rational explanation (multiple murders) are given a final, potentially supernatural twist (Jason's appearance at the end of *Friday the 13th*; Michael Myers's disappearance at the end of *Halloween*). In each case, the supernatural interpretation is not entirely confirmed; Jason's appearance could be part of a dream sequence, especially given the ambiguously coded *mise-en-scène*, and Michael's disappearance could be a matter of extreme good fortune for the character. We are thus only thrown into fantastic hesitation at the very end of these films, rather than prior hesitation being resolved at the narratives' end.

Logically, the 'marvellous-fantastic' could also exist; this would involve a narrative where the supernatural is matter-of-factly accepted by characters, until a concluding narrative event occurs that appears to (meta-paranormally) violate the already supernatural rules of the diegetic world. Empirical examples of this are difficult to produce, although arguably *The Frighteners* (1996, dr: Peter Jackson) comes close to being marvellous-fantastic. Its lead character can communicate with ghosts, and the film very rapidly takes this for granted before confronting a further supernatural threat, a ghostly serial killer, that acts as a source of shock and singularity rather than provoking 'no particular reaction either in the characters or in the implicit reader' as the pure marvellous should (Todorov 1975:54). Since *The Frighteners* both matter-of-factly accepts the supernatural and presents 'events which are ... incredible, shocking, singular, disturbing or unexpected' to its characters and implicit reader (that is, it recontextualizes the slasher movie as 'marvellous') it could perhaps be suggested that this film is actually an uncanny-marvellous hybrid without any fantastic hesitation. Marvellous in its diegetic acceptance of ghosts, it is also uncanny by virtue of representing ghostly happenings that, although following the laws of reason of the diegesis, remain non-marvellous by virtue of being 'shocking' and 'singular', akin to killings in non-supernatural slasher movies. In any case, *The*

Frighteners is a film that, like *Friday the 13th* and *Halloween*, causes difficulties for any easy application of Todorov's work.

Given that Todorov's model has been much applied to horror texts, it has also been much criticized. Questioning Todorov's work on the basis that the 'pure' fantastic is not numerically frequent – there are very few 'pure fantastic' films – and suggesting that the concept therefore has a 'limited range of empirical applicability' misses the point that Todorov is not attempting to explain a vast corpus of texts; his interest lies in a 'theoretical' rather than 'historical' genre (see Donald 1989, p. 18). Further criticisms of Todorov have focused on his argument that a text can shift subgenres (from fantastic to uncanny or marvellous) at its conclusion (Hume 1984, p. 14). Quite why this should be taken as an 'inescapable drawback' (ibid.) is, however, unclear; Todorov's account of genre is, if anything, more sensitive than 'historical' genre-based accounts, since it does not globally ascribe generic classifications (text A = horror), but rather relates the dynamics of narrative unfolding to genre classification.

Other critiques and developments of Todorov's work have sought to significantly historicize his account. Rosemary Jackson argues that the 'problem (and problematization) of the perception/vision/knowledge of the protagonist and narrator and reader of the fantastic text is not considered by Todorov in any historical perspective' (1981, p. 31). For Jackson, questions of seeing and knowing that are raised by the fantastic should be considered as a specific part of 'Romantic and post-Romantic thought' (ibid.), in which scientific knowledge and rationality are themselves problematized.

And José Monleón picks up on Todorov's emphasis that fantastic hesitation is produced when 'a [diegetic] world which is indeed our world, the one we know, a world without devils ... or vampires' (1975, p. 25) is narratively disrupted by 'an event which cannot be explained by the laws of this same familiar world' (ibid.). Hesitation is hence produced between a rational explanation – the event is a character's delusion, and 'the laws of the [diegetic] world then remain as they are' in actuality (ibid.) – and a supernatural one, where 'the event has indeed taken place ... but then this [diegetic] reality is controlled by laws unknown to us' in actuality (ibid.). Monleón points out that this definition presupposes that 'the laws of our world' are known, fixed and static, whereas such 'laws' actually change sociohistorically over time. For example, contemporary Western society no longer believes in witches or devils:

> But what must we understand by the laws of our world? Should a story written in the Middle Ages be considered according to the concept of nature upheld in those times or according to our current understanding of reality? Should the genre of a work change as the history of humanity modifies the idea of nature? (Monleón 1990, pp. 4–5)

Therefore, Rosemary Jackson (1981) raises the question of how epistemology can shift historically, while Monleón (1990) implies that our very ontologies, what we take to essentially exist 'in reality', can also be historically mutable. Despite emphasizing historical shifts, both of these critiques can actually be reformulated as synchronic and social critiques: how 'seeing/knowing' is approached may be thought of differently by different but contemporaneous audiences (a Romantic poet and a scientist), just as the laws of 'our world' may be different for specific contemporaneous audiences (a Catholic who believes in the Devil, and a secular humanist who does not). Fantastic hesitation may therefore be experienced differently according to cultural differences in the audience; would a devout Catholic experience *The Exorcist* (1973, dr: William Friedkin) as fantastic-marvellous, for example, or would their interpretation lack any 'fantastic' hesitation due to their religious view of the 'laws of the world'? Just as Carroll's (1990) philosophy of horror cannot tell us whether actual audiences cognitively experience fear or disgust, Todorov's model cannot tell us whether actual audiences experience 'fantastic' hesitation.

It is also worth recalling that Todorov (1975) is concerned solely with analysing literature. Although critics have continued to explore the fantastic in this literary vein (e.g. Cornwell 1990 and Heller 1987), others have considered how 'some of ... [Todorov's] ... observations can ... be extended to the discussion of cinema in several ways' (Carroll 1990, p. 151; see also Donald 1989). Indeed, Noël Carroll has outlined a number of cinematic devices that provoke or sustain fantastic hesitation:

- Unreliable or untrustworthy point-of-view shots, where a character is represented as mentally unstable (1990, p. 152).
- '[F]orms of visual interference like overexposure ... or ... shadows' (1990, p. 154). Here, the audience has to infer supernatural events rather than having the 'eyewitness certainty' of most realist film representations (ibid.).
- Use of off-screen sound (1990, p. 154), again so that the audience infers supernatural events.
- '[U]nassigned camera movement' (1990, p. 155) can cause audiences hesitantly to interpret the camera's 'objective' gaze as 'subjective', that is, is there a supernatural force watching the characters, or is the camera simply calling attention to itself through such movement?
- The 'ambiguity of certain Hollywood codes' (1990, p. 155) such as over-lighting to indicate an apparitional figure, or indicating a dream sequence through non-naturalistic lighting, etc. This can be exploited so that audiences are unsure whether an event should be interpreted as natural or supernatural.

Although he doesn't follow up on the consequences of his own observation, Carroll also notes that '[i]nitially, *Nightmare on Elm Street* [1984, dr: Wes Craven] may have benefited from ... [the] ambiguity ... [of its codings] ... though by now informed viewers know that Freddie is "for real"' (1990, p. 156).

The unexplored problem this raises for filmic theories of fantastic 'hesitation' is the issue of extra-textual knowledge. For, unlike Todorov's theory – which presupposes a first reading (1975, pp. 89–90) of a discrete and isolated text treated as an aesthetic whole – horror films are not such isolatable or isolated texts. Indeed horror films are (quite unlike the historical, literary texts studied by Todorov) extra-textually promoted via trailers, or via online secondary texts, as well as being sequelized such that audience knowledge can be presupposed (Budra 1998).

This means that audience 'hesitation' can be thwarted by a variety of extra-textual sources; publicity intertexts (film reviews or magazine previews) may already have revealed the supernatural threat in a given film's narrative. Or, watching an 'old' horror film (e.g. *Nightmare on Elm Street*), the viewer may already possess knowledge of the diegetic supernatural threat. Or, if the specific film is a sequel, audiences may already know if a character is supernatural. Or, online spoilers may give away the fantastic-uncanny or fantastic-marvellous twists of a narrative. Where audience pre-knowledge is likely to affect a text's ability to construct fantastic hesitation, what Todorov identifies as the 'meta-reading' or re-reading of a fantastic text – 'we note the methods of the fantastic rather than falling under its spell' (1975, p. 90) – may often occur in the putatively 'first' reading of a horror film.

In the remainder of this chapter I want to suggest a counter-Todorovian model, considering how *The Sixth Sense* (1999, dr: M. Night Shyamalan), and a range of other horror films, fail to meaningfully accord with Todorov's (1975) approach. As I have outlined thus far, Todorovian readings of horror discursively restrict the genre's pleasures to those of intellectual resolution (of the narrative question 'natural or supernatural?'). But if imputed pleasures of 'fantastic' hesitation and/or resolved hesitation do not seem to wholly explicate the workings of texts such as *The Sixth Sense*, then what theoretically marginalized counter-discourses of pleasures can be brought to light and utilized?

FROM 'EPISTEMOLOGICAL HESITATION' TO 'ONTOLOGICAL SHOCK': COUNTER-TODOROVIAN HORROR

Todorov's model repeatedly implies that pleasures of the fantastic – and, by implication, horror texts that generally fit into this schema as examples of the 'fantastic-marvellous' – are intellectual and rationalizing pleasures of mastering the text. Just as cognitive theories of horror neglect their discursive and conceptual 'Other' ('affect'), what the Todorovian approach neglects is the possibility that a text may work to 'master' its audiences; that is, the audience may be deliberately misled by a text that withholds key narrative information. This process, usually culminating in a significant narrative 'twist' or 'reveal' that provokes the ideal reader to reinterpret all that they have previously perceived, cannot always be readily theorized by recourse to Todorov. For, in this instance, hesitation is not inevitably or necessarily linked to the narrative representation of 'fantastic' and art-horrifying events. Quite the contrary, the hesitation that characterizes the fantastic may be entirely absent for both characters and audiences, despite the fact that staples of the horror genre, such as ghosts, etc., are textually and diegetically dealt with. Rather than hesitating between interpretations of events, the audience may be dramatically thrown from one non-hesitating interpretation to another. For example, characters narratively assumed to be alive might be revealed diegetically as dead, but neither they nor the ideal audience would know this fact until the narrative's abrupt turning point. Or narrative events assumed to have happened may not have happened at all, again without any hesitation being incited as audiences are confronted by a sudden transformation of the diegetic rules.

This 'sudden twist' structure has been one of the major features of recent horror films such as *Cut* (2000, dr: Kimble Rendall), *Kolobos* (1999, dr: Daniel Liatowitsch and David Todd Ocvirk), *The Others* (2001, dr: Alejandro Amenábar), *The Sixth Sense* and *Soul Survivors* (2001, dr: Stephen Carpenter), as well being pre-empted and continued in playful and subversive 'slasher' movies such as *April Fool's Day* (1986, dr: Fred Walton) and *American Psycho* (2000, dr: Mary Harron; see Cardwell 2002, p. 79), and occurring in the horror-thriller likes of *Jacob's Ladder* (1990, dr: Adrian Lyne), *Fight Club* (1999, dr: David Fincher), *The Game* (1997, dr: David Fincher), *Identity* (2003, dr: James Mangold), *Memento* (2000, dr: Christopher Nolan) and *Vanilla Sky* (2001, dr: Cameron Crowe).

In this type of film, fantastic hesitation is generally *not* experienced in relation to a specific natural/supernatural narrative shift: Dr Malcolm Crowe (Bruce Willis) in *The Sixth Sense* is a ghost, but the diegesis (or rather, the film's *sjuzhet* – how it structures narrative events for the audience) leads us to suppose that he is alive. Likewise, Grace (Nicole Kidman) and her children in *The Others* are represented as living characters, until a narrative twist reveals them to be the ghosts of the house. In a reversal of the previous interpretive framework that the film has put into play, 'ghostly' intruders are in fact the diegetically living characters. *Cut* also shifts from a natural to supernatural explanation of events, but without ever having generated hesitation over the nature of the killer. Interpreting the film as intertextually indebted to *Scream* leads the audience to suppose that the killer will be one of the cast of characters, and that talk of a 'curse' should be dismissed. But this assumed natural explanation and game of 'guess the killer' is then matter-of-factly transformed into a supernatural explanation (diegetically, the killer is a manifestation of 'creative energies' that have leaked out of an unfinished 1980s slasher movie entitled 'Hot-Blooded'). Characters do not hesitate over such an explanation; it is suddenly introduced and immediately acted upon, leaving the heroine to destroy the film stock of 'Hot-Blooded' and thus melt the celluloid-inspired stalker.

Unlike *The Sixth Sense*, *The Others* and *Cut*, other films of this broad type do not specifically invoke the supernatural, but rather play with different levels of diegetic reality, that is, is this narrative event 'real' or is it a dream/delusion/hallucination? Such films use the devices of realism to portray subjective states of mind and perceptions as if they are objective, then abruptly reveal that what the audience has taken as objective (without hesitation) has actually been diegetically subjective. *Fight Club* arrives at its gothic personality-disintegration twist via this route, and *Vanilla Sky* also plays with the conventions of film-narrative-as-objective. Likewise, *Identity* shifts its diegetic frame of reality (see Leyland 2003); events we have assumed are diegetically 'real' (following the conventions of realist film and its 'eyewitness certainty') are recontextualized as one character's interior mindscape (and another post-*Scream* stalker movie *Kolobos* plays a similar trick on its audience). Similarly, *Soul Survivors* suddenly shifts the status of one character from 'dead' to 'alive' via a psychological rather than ghostly explanation. In this case, events shown 'as real' (utilizing the conventions of realist film as an objective representation of diegetic reality) are revealed to have been part of one character's dream state.

Textbook applications of Todorov's model fail to consider such non-supernatural-based forms of 'hesitation': as Terry Heller argues, some fictions can 'take advantage of the possibilities of the fantastic in arousing horror ... [by provoking] ... a hesitation between two or more ways of understanding events ... [where] ... all the suggested interpretations are natural' (1987, p. 40). Furthermore, by focusing on questions of epistemology, the Todorovian model fails to capture entirely the sudden, startling narrative twists that can be achieved through ontological horror – that is, the shock and disorientation that can be provoked in characters and audiences alike (although again, characters need not be startled) when an accepted/interpreted narrative 'reality' is instantaneously revealed to be either one 'subjective' level nested within an alternative, 'objective' reality (*Identity*; *Soul Survivors*), or a radical misinterpretation of diegetic ontology (*The Sixth Sense*; *The Others*).

Brian McHale captures the distinctiveness of such fictions when he writes that 'a poetics based on the principle of hesitation, but not, as in the "classic" fantastic described by Todorov, hesitation between alternative explanatory hypotheses (natural or supernatural)' needs to be considered (1992, p. 208). For McHale, this non- or neo-Todorovian fiction is characterized 'rather, [by] hesitation between alternative *worlds* (levels of reality, orders of being)' (ibid.). And, I would argue as a supplement to this, such neo-Todorovian 'ontological hesitation' (ibid.) can also operate as a form of narrative twist or counter-Todorovian ontological shock whereby:

the whole cognitive universe of the novel needs to be replaced ... This is a thorough frame replacement ... a large-scale belief switch applied to the whole narrative perspective, which is thoroughgoing enough to be regarded as a frame replacement. It is a sort of paradigm-shift in comprehension ... (Stockwell 2000, p. 165)

Such texts thus seek to misdirect their audiences by generating fantastic (or non-fantastic) hesitation at one level of narrative 'reality' before revealing that events require a radically different interpretation at a different level of diegetic reality. Hesitation thus may be incited for the ideal reader, but it is then ultimately overwritten by a shift in interpretive framework that is forcefully immediate (from diegetic 'dream/delusion' to 'reality', or from natural to supernatural) rather than occurring as the result of resolved hesitation. Characteristics of the fantastic are thus reflexively and deceptively invoked by these texts; we hesitate over whether *The Sixth Sense*'s Cole Sear (Haley Joel Osment) can see dead people, just as we hesitate over the issue of whether the house in *The Others* is haunted – but such hesitations are distractions from the impact of the final narrative twist. The epistemological hesitation of the fantastic – where it is even evoked – falls rapid, stunning prey to the ontological shock of a 'paradigm-shift in comprehension'.

The 'strictly regulated dispersal of textual information' (Austin 2002, p. 99) that surrounds texts of this type generally means that reviews, and even online cinephiles' discussions, refrain from divulging 'spoilers'. Revealing 'the twist' would, of course, 'spoil' potential viewers' pleasure, depriving them of an aesthetic experience of shock in response to the text's manipulations and ontological playfulness. Thus, just as epistemological hesitation falls victim to textual knowledge – recall that the second reading of a 'fantastic' text cannot help but be a metareading – so too does ontological shock succumb to knowledge of the 'twist' ending. As Thomas Austin has noted, films such as *The Sixth Sense* work, socially and culturally, by 'recruiting reviewers and, subsequently, viewers into a privileged group who know the secret, and who are relied upon to talk about the film without giving too much away' (ibid.).

This 'code of conduct' is as evident in professional film reviews, for example Philip Strick's account of *The Sixth Sense* in *Sight And Sound* (see Strick 2002, pp. 257–8) as it is in amateur reviews, such as those available at the Internet Movie Database (imdb.com). Strick is minimalist in his account of *The Sixth Sense*'s closing twist, noting that the film is a 'mass of disquieting details ... [that] ... takes a number of detours toward a final reversal that throws everything open to question' (2002, p. 257). As for amateur reviews, one imdb review for the ontological-shocker-cum-reflexive-slasher *Kolobos* is headed '*SPOILER ALERT* *SPOILER ALERT*' (Dr Gore, 21 May 2003), while another reinforces even more hyperbolically that it will not discuss plot details unannounced, beginning with the phrase 'SPOILERS' six times (letrias, 18 October 2002). Other *Kolobos* posters refuse to discuss the film's plot twist in detail, commenting only that 'All is revealed in a suitably ambiguous final scene' (spoodie, 3 September 2002), and promising 'the twist at the end ... I'll not give anything away' (DeVip, 26 April 2002), or even urging readers to 'Read another review for the plot cause I wouldn't want to give anything away' (Kolobos85, 5 November 2001). And yet others tease the potential viewer by saying 'Wait till the end – it is a BIG surprise' (vicky.power, 18 November 2000) or offer interpretative assistance:

'And as for those of you that cannot figure it out, e-mail me to find out, because this is not the place to spoil the movie' (Ludovico W. Yanto Jr, 23 March 2000). By promising to 'explain' the twist if asked, or by refusing to discuss it online, these posters precisely confirm their status as part of a 'privileged group who know the secret'. By remaining suitably vague, reviewers such as Philip Strick similarly confirm their status within this type of in-group.

Marguerite La Caze has noted of *The Sixth Sense* that 'it interweaves the natural and supernatural, and invites two very distinct readings' (2002, p. 111). For La Caze, the film's 'twist' means that audiences can respond to it as 'a conventional horror film, where the main puzzle is: what is frightening the little boy?'; and also, once the secret has been divulged, audiences can then reflect back on their memories of the film, recontextualizing it as 'a meditation on the nature of mourning and death through its emotional realism' (2002, p. 113). The notion of 'two readings' fits with my argument here that fantastic hesitation can be used as a distraction from, or a blind for, the further textual device of ontological shock. However, by focusing on how the audience can reinterpret narrative events once they have undergone a 'paradigm-shift' in understanding, La Caze neglects to analyse the affects of shock linked to the twist itself. As a result, her analysis focuses on 'normal' or paradigmatic conditions of interpretation, that is how we interpret when we master/understand the pre-secret text, versus how we interpret when we have mastered/understood the post-secret text. What goes missing in such an account is the dislocating, transformative moment of the twist itself and its pleasures for (non-academic) audiences.

Such an absence should not surprise us; academic subculture has typically betrayed a lack of concern with the affective impact of the plot twist. Such twists are subordinated to the cognitive mastery of analysis in academic material, which thus adamantly reserves the right to 'spoil' narratives for potential viewers. 'SPOILER ALERTs' may be common on imdb, but they rarely, if ever, turn up in academic studies! (See Hills 2002, Chapter 1, for more on fans versus academics, and consider the contrasting discourses of horror's pleasures examined in Parts I and II of this book.) Even critics such as Noël Carroll, who have devoted much attention to horror's plotting, have had little to say about the pleasures of a good narrative 'twist', perhaps on the assumption that such twists are, like the very different 'shock' of the startle reflex, in no way restricted to (or thus indicative of) horror as a genre. Yet the type of twist I am discussing here – the diegetic shifting from one 'level of reality' or 'order of being' to another, often interweaving the natural and supernatural and evoking a (distracting but related) element of hesitation – remains significant across horror/thriller/science-fiction/fantasy genre texts, given its abilities to problematize, destabilize and recontextualize the narrative 'real'.

What I am terming 'ontological shock' provokes an extreme awareness of the horror text as a constructed artefact (Tan 1996, p. 65); we have been duped, the text has withheld information and tricked us. Hence the ideal audience–text relation here is not one of cognitive or epistemological mastery. Quite the reverse; such texts inspire a sense of their artful ability to act on (and deceive) the audience, whose beliefs in the conventions of realist film are played upon. Horror of this type, which does not only or centrally rely on 'fantastic' hesitation, ever more strongly implies an underlying authorial agency. It should therefore come as little surprise that *The Sixth Sense* and its bravura 'twist' – La Caze notes that 'repeated viewings ... make ... it seem astonishing that evidence [of Crowe's ontological status] could have been overlooked' (2002, p. 113) – have been so insistently linked to accounts of M. Night Shyamalan, the film's writer and director, as an *auteur*. Indeed, for Reynold Humphries, the 'clues' of *The Sixth Sense*, especially '[Crowe] having lunch with his wife who takes no notice of him for the simple reason he's dead' are exactly a sign of Shyamalan's 'daring' (2002, p. 192) to hint at the 'twist' so that it is in full view of the audience all along. The impact of *The Sixth Sense* on its audiences is thus read as indexical of authorial agency, supporting the notion that Shyamalan, as an *auteur*, has succeeded in affecting the film's audiences.

By introducing a discourse of horror's pleasures as linked to 'ontological shock' rather than epistemological hesitation, we can consider the possibility that audiences do not always cognitively 'master' or intellectually 'resolve' a text. Instead, they may be 'mastered' by a text, that is, allowing themselves to be open to the knowing, game-playing manipulations of an aesthetic artefact. Both cognitive and Todorovian approaches to horror have definitionally and discursively restricted the genre's pleasures to types of cognitively construed 'emotion' or rationalizing 'hesitation'. Each theoretical approach has thus generated its own occulted 'Other' or counter-discourse of pleasure: the 'affective' dimensions of horror for cognitivism, and the 'ontological shock' of horror/fantasy texts in the case of Todorovian accounts. Each approach has thus offered a highly selective and orthodox explanation of what is to be counted as 'horror', and how this horror is said to operate on and for audiences.

Developing a counter-Todorovian perspective on horror has meant analysing popular horror texts that narratively hesitate between different natural explanations before suddenly shifting the narrative level of reality, as well as addressing infamously tricky films such as *The Sixth Sense* which hesitate between supernatural/natural explanations before abruptly transforming the diegetically 'natural' into the 'supernatural'. Such massive, instantaneous narrative 'twists', their associated shock, and the sense of having been outwitted by an artful *auteur*, cannot be explained via textbook Todorovian accounts of 'fantastic' hesitation.

Throughout this chapter I have developed the argument that horror's pleasures are more varied than any single theoretical framework, and its concomitant assumptions, seem to allow for. Single-theory approaches result in theoretical foreclosures of horror's pleasures, as each theory finds its own characteristic pleasures at work in horror texts, and thus validates its own foundational, definitional assumptions ('hesitation' is important, not 'shock'; or, as we have already seen, 'emotion' is important, not 'affect'). In the next chapter I will move on to consider how the horror genre has been subjected to varieties of psychoanalytic interpretation, raising the question of 'repression' and its own theoretically marginalized counter-discourses of horror's pleasures.

Chapter 3

Psychoanalysing Horror:
Restoration ... and Repetition

In this chapter I want to consider psychoanalytic approaches to the horror genre, and how these have constructed and circulated specific discourses of horror's pleasures, in line with the foundational assumptions of applied psychoanalysis (see Turvey 2004, p. 73). We might suppose that psychoanalysis would give us a way to think about potential ambivalences of horror, whereby pleasures may be tinged with anxiety (Urbano 2004, pp. 28–9). In fact, as I will argue here, the psychoanalysis of horror has often been rather more interested in defusing ambivalence and enacting a type of splitting, dividing horror texts into (bad) 'reactionary' and (good) 'progressive' instances (as in the work of Wood 1986). The psychoanalysis of horror has also sought to validate the genre by linking it to specific theoretical tenets (such as 'repression' and 'abjection'), sometimes even treating films as if they are dream-works rather than approaching horror texts as texts (see Wood 1986, pp. 77–8; Rank 1989; Pinedo 1997, pp. 39–40; Gabbard 2001). Psychoanalytic approaches have thus tended to discursively police and categorize horror texts while also bidding for horror's cultural value as a sign of allegedly transhistorical, psychical processes (e.g. 'the unconscious', 'the Oedipal complex'), and thus as a validation of psychoanalytic theory itself.

Insofar as any coherent 'pleasures of horror' can be read as implied and constructed across different schools of Freudian and post-Freudian psycho-analytic thought on horror, I would argue that these can be identified as 'pleasures of restoration'. That is, *horror is said to narratively restore repressed material, before finally restoring repression itself* via its narrative closures, or its textual boundedness (see, e.g., Tony Williams 1996). Alternatively, horror restores pre-Oedipal pleasures of 'the abject', in Julia Kristeva's (1982) terms, before restoring the pleasurable structures and orders of the Symbolic. Or to return to Freud, horror restores what is familiar within what, at first, appears to be unfamiliar and threatening, representing 'the uncanny' in fiction (see Arnzen (ed.) 1997 and Stern 1997).

In what follows I will survey these broad approaches to what I am terming 'the pleasures of restoration'. As in the two previous chapters, my overview should not be taken as a disinterested survey of the field, but rather as an active intervention, stressing how psychoanalytic theory has specifically viewed and discursively constructed the pleasures of horror. I will go on to argue that such approaches contain the seeds of an alternative narrative concerning horror and pleasure. This theoretical road-not-taken concerns pleasures of 'repetition' rather than those of 'restoration'. Before reaching this point, however, I shall introduce and work through a range of Freudian and post-Freudian approaches to the horror genre's texts and their discursively constructed/implied pleasures.

THE CULTURAL POLITICS OF THE 'RETURN OF THE REPRESSED'

As Andrew Tudor has commented, '[b]y far the most common accounts of the appeal of horror are grounded in concepts from Freudian theory' (1997, p. 446). Jonathan Lake Crane similarly observes, in his overview of genre criticism and the horror film, that 'Freud ... constitutes the lingua franca of horror ... criticism' (1994, p. 24). Given that this is arguably so, I will focus on how Freudian work has been taken up in academic analyses of horror (this necessarily neglects Jungian approaches to horror, see for example Kaminsky with Mahan 1985; Lucanio 1987; Iaccino 1994; and on Jungian film theory more generally, see Hockley 2001).

Freud's essay on 'The Uncanny' (originally written in 1919; see Freud 1990a) has been the primary source for much psychoanalytic work on horror (see the pro- and anti-Freudian debate staged between Schneider 2001 and Freeland 2001), as well as fascinating many commentators in its own right (Cixous 1976; Kofman 1991; Rand and Torok 1994; Weber 2000; Royle 2003). For example, both Carol J. Clover (1992, p. 48) and Barbara Creed (1993, pp. 53–4) – Andrew Tudor's exemplars of 'structural psychoanalysis' rather than the 'simple repression model' (1997, p. 446) – quote the same section from Freud's essay on 'The Uncanny' when discussing horror texts' diegetically dark, damp, dank, terrible places as symbolically 'intra-uterine'. Fear of such bad places is, for each critic, a type of womb fantasy. Without reaching this precise psychoanalytic argument, Jack Morgan (2002, p. 183) also cites Freud on 'the uncanny' at the beginning of a discussion of horror's 'sinister loci'.

Freud discusses a wide range of impressions that are capable of arousing a sense of 'the uncanny' or, in German, *das unheimlich* (literally, the unhomely): 'The ... "uncanny" ... is undoubtedly related to what is frightening – to what arouses dread and horror ... we may expect that a special core of feeling is present which justifies the use of a special conceptual term' (Freud 1990a, p. 339). And Freud's discussion specifies what is 'special' about the uncanny. It is 'that class of the frightening which leads back to what is known of old and long familiar' (1990a, p. 340). This intuition, supported by etymological detective work in the first section of 'The Uncanny' (1990a, pp. 341–7), is then developed by Freud into the more precise conclusion that the uncanny is 'one class [of frightening things] in which the frightening element can be shown to be something repressed which *recurs*' (1990a, p. 363). And more precisely again, Freud subdivides his assessment of 'the uncanny' into:

(1)   instances where it 'proceeds from repressed infantile complexes, from the castration complex, womb phantasies, etc.' (1990a, p. 371); and
(2)   instances where 'primitive beliefs which have been surmounted seem once more to be confirmed' (1990a, p. 372).

Thus Freud's notion of 'The Uncanny' can be said to involve the (temporary or momentary) restoration of repressed material or the apparent restoration of 'surmounted' beliefs. The first type of 'the uncanny' is taken up and discussed in Robin Wood's work. Linda Badley points out that Wood's (1978) *Film Comment* article 'provided an influential application of Freud's essay on "The Uncanny" to horror' (Badley 1995, p. 160, n. 2). Wood's perspective successfully popularized the 'return of the repressed' thesis on uncanny horror – indeed this phrase formed the title of his (1978) article, being reiterated as a subheader in 'The American Nightmare ...' chapter of *Hollywood From Vietnam to Reagan* (1986, p. 77). That the 'return of the repressed' thesis has become so influential is also attested to by the fact that introductory textbooks casually throw in horror film examples when discussing the return of the repressed (as in Easthope 1999, pp. 32–3). The phrase has also recurred as a book title (Clemens 1999), though the book concerned does not solely rely on Freudian psychoanalysis.

By contrast, the second type of 'the uncanny' has been less frequently discussed in academic work on horror. In this case, it is 'surmounted' and *not* repressed beliefs that give rise to the uncanny; beliefs such as the 'omnipotence of thoughts, ... the prompt fulfilment of wishes, ... secret injurious powers and ... the return of the dead' (Freud 1990a, p. 370). Such beliefs, held consciously by 'primitive' cultures, or by the ('primitive') young child, are not repressed over time. Rather, they are surrendered as mistaken. But these beliefs are never wholly done away with, and can *seem* to be reconfirmed by actual or aesthetic experiences in which a 'conflict of judgement' is generated over 'whether things which have been "surmounted" and are regarded as incredible may not, after all, be possible' (Freud 1990a, p. 373).

This neglected aspect of the uncanny forms the central part of Steven Jay Schneider's (2000a) corrective return to Robin Wood's work. In fact, Schneider criticizes both Noël Carroll (1990) and Wood (1986) for their reliance on the 'return of the repressed' argument alone. As Schneider rather pertinently puts it: 'by identifying repressed infantile complexes as the sole source of uncanniness/horror in psychoanalytic theory, Carroll is ... [perhaps] guilty of the same mistake as ... Robin Wood' (Schneider 2000a, pp. 173 and 178).

What, then, are the discursively constructed pleasures of 'restoration' alluded to in the work of Wood (on the Freudian 'return of the repressed') and Schneider (on the Freudian 'reconfirmation of the surmounted')? I will discuss Wood's work, and critiques of it, in some detail before moving on to consider Schneider's contribution to the horror/uncanny/repression debate.

Wood's argument may be broadly Freudian, but it also departs from Freud by introducing the 'basic repression/surplus repression' distinction suggested by Herbert Marcuse (1987). 'Basic repression' is 'universal, necessary, and inescapable. It is what makes possible our development from an uncoordinated animal capable of little beyond screaming . . . into a human being' (Wood 1986, p. 70). By contrast, 'surplus repression':

> is specific to a . . . culture and is the process whereby people are conditioned from earliest infancy to take on predetermined roles within that culture . . . *surplus* repression makes us into monogamous heterosexual bourgeois patriarchal capitalists . . . that is, *if* it works. (Wood 1986, p. 71)

If horror deals with 'something repressed which recurs' then, for Wood, this is not merely 'universal' basic repression involving the Oedipal complex, etc. It is also, and more importantly, surplus repression, so that what recurs is necessarily politicized and constitutes a challenge to the dominant order of society:

> central to . . . [the horror film] . . . is the actual . . . dramatization of the . . . repressed . . . in the figure of the Monster. One might say that the true subject of the horror genre is the struggle for recognition of all that our civilization represses or oppresses, its re-emergence dramatized . . . as an object of horror . . . and *the happy ending (when it exists) typically signifying the restoration of repression.* (Wood 1986, p. 75, my italics)

The monster, so conceived, becomes a 'meaning machine' (Halberstam 1995, p. 21) coded to represent a variety of repressed and oppressed groups in society (cf. Schneider 2000a, p. 185; see also Becker 1999, p. 80 on horror as representing 'repressed fears of . . . the feminist movement'). Wood lists groups of repressed/ oppressed 'Others' that he argues are marginalized by the dominant social order and frequently represented as monstrous in horror texts (Wood 1986, pp. 74–6): women and female sexuality (e.g. *Cat People* 1942, dr: Jacques Tourneur); the proletariat (*Texas Chainsaw Massacre* 1974, dr: Tobe Hooper); other cultures (as in *The Manitou* 1978, dr: William Girdler); ethnic groups within the culture (e.g. *The Possession of Joel Delaney* 1972, dr: Waris Hussein); alternative ideologies or political systems (*Invasion of the Bodysnatchers* 1956, dr: Don Siegel); bisexuality and homosexuality (*The Bride of Frankenstein* 1935, dr: James Whale); and children (e.g. *The Exorcist* 1973, dr: William Friedkin). Alongside much excellent work on depictions of femininity in 'classic' 1930s horror (e.g. Berenstein 1996) through to 1990s film (Young 2001), the genre's often reactionary representations of homosexuality – 'the Queer monster' – have also been productively analysed in related work (see Benshoff 1997; Saunders 1998), and so too has the representation of the 'monstrous child' (Aguirre 1990, p. 213–5; Büssing 1987).

While many have followed in Wood's (1978 and 1986) footsteps, other critics have contested his formulation of horror, suggesting that it is simply too general to explain the genre's variety, and also arguing that horror's monsters are as often 'repressive' as they are a symbolic coding of 'the (return of the) repressed' (Jancovich 1992, p. 16). Wood himself has addressed this latter point in a discussion of 1980s horror (1986, p. 195), arguing that the genre's 'Reactionary Wing' (1986, p. 191) represents the monster not as an id-like figure disrupting social order (and temporarily lifting surplus repression), but rather as a type of superego figure 'avenging itself on liberated female sexuality or the sexual freedom of the young' (1986, p. 195). This results in a shift in horror's cultural politics:

> Where the traditional horror film invited, however ambiguously, an identification with the return of the repressed [i.e. the audience had sympathy for the monster – MH] the contemporary horror film invites an identification (either sadistically or masochistically) with punishment. (1986, p. 195)

Thus, Wood defines horror as either 'progressive' or 'reactionary'. Radical horror has the monster representing oppressed and repressed forces, while reactionary horror depicts its monsters as 'simply evil' and 'totally nonhuman' (1986, p. 192), where 'what is repressed ... must always return as a threat, perceived by the consciousness as ugly, terrible, obscene. Horror films, it might be said, are progressive precisely to the degree that they refuse to be satisfied with this simple designation' (1986, p. 192).

Quite unlike Noël Carroll's definition of the monster (see Chapter 1), Wood posits horror monsters as either sustaining audience identification/sympathy, or as being totally dehumanized, repulsive and threatening (Carroll, of course, would tend to see only the latter type of 'monster' as meriting the designation: see Carroll 1990, pp. 160 and 172 for attacks on Wood's approach). Wood filters Freud (1990a) on 'the uncanny' through the work of Marcuse (1987) to construct a way of reading horror that stresses the cultural politics of its representations. This places a certain implicit demand on horror's audiences, namely that any pleasures taken in horror can (and should) also be recognized and classified as either 'progressive' or 'reactionary'. On Wood's account, such pleasures can be deemed progressive where the audience revels in the monster's threat to dominant social/cultural norms (norms that are themselves ideological), and reactionary where audiences take pleasure in the monster's narrative destruction, and hence the restoration of social/cultural order. For Wood, this signals the 'restoration of repression', and so is not *really* a 'happy ending' at all (1986, p. 75).

In Woodian terms, then, horror fictions typically enact a doubled restoration: progressive restoration, via the monster, of all 'that our civilization represses or oppresses' followed by the reactionary restoration of repression/suppression. Horror's implied pleasures are thus necessarily contrapuntal; they involve opposing and reinforcing repression/oppression (for repetitions of this psycho-analytic-formalist 'formula' on horror see Craft 1984; Heller 1987, pp. 83–6; Robert D. Newman 1993, pp. 62–3). However, rather than this apparent ambivalence – where pleasure and repression/oppression are interwoven – being fully reflected in Wood's work, it actually leads to his splitting apart of 'progressive' and 'reactionary' horror. Thus some of horror's pleasures become more globally suspect (reinforcing repression/oppression), while others can be readily applauded by the Marxian-Freudian critic for challenging the dominant, ideological social/cultural order.

This view of horror converts a textual-narrative struggle against monstrosity into a cultural struggle against 'monstrous' oppression or ideology (for more on this discursive bleeding from pop-cultural text to theory, see Chapter 8 on 'theory-horror'). Like Carroll, Wood is not concerned with actual audiences for horror, and how they react to narrative closure or to 'progressive' monsters. His audiences are, once more, 'ideal' readers who can be projected out of the seemingly all-powerful horror text and its narrative/formal structures. Thus horror's pleasures are theoretically imagined or projected by Wood, in line with his project to validate and legitimate horror as a deadly serious business. Horror is not just trivially about rampaging monsters; it returns to the centres of social/cultural power, being a challenge to, or an operation of, cultural power.

This theoretical narrative appears somewhat aggrandizing of horror texts; it grants them a fixed meaning and an exaggerated symbolic potency, via the notion of repression, that we might well want to challenge. By using the concept of repression, and especially Marcuse's (1987) notion of 'surplus repression', Wood codes horror as both the servant and disruption of ideological forces at large in society. In Robin Wood's work psychoanalysis thus operates performatively to convert horror, often a devalued or disreputable genre, into the site of theoretically and politically crucial processes (see Hills 2004e). Horror's pleasures are not discursively constructed here in terms of a variety of affects or emotions; instead they are written into, and disciplined within, a specific cultural-political framework. Pleasure is always a priori related to *surplus* repression, and its lifting or its restoration, with the result that no pleasures of horror seem to escape a totalizing 'progressive/reactionary' grid of meaning.

Thus, although Wood supplements Freud, making horror's pleasures less a matter of timeless processes of repression essential to civilization, and more a matter of socio-historically located surplus repressions, this supplement itself calls for historicization. As Anthony Elliott has remarked:

> The Freudian-inspired social theory developed by ... Marcuse did much to bring the insights of psychoanalysis to a wider public; such ideas were

especially suggestive in the context of the political demands of sexual radicals' and students' movements in the late 1960s and early 1970s. Yet the ideas of ... Marcuse are not greatly debated today, and it is interesting to reflect on why this is so. The short answer is that the psychoanalytic theorem which equates modern culture with high levels of sexual repression ... seems misguided at best and simply wrong at worst. (Elliott 2001, pp. 70–1)

Elliott's argument points out that sexuality has hardly been repressed in modern culture; rather, sexualized imagery and discussions of sexual identities have discursively proliferated in the modern period (this argument is akin to Foucault's (1990) infamous challenge to the Freudian 'repressive hypothesis'). Linda Badley's assessment of psychoanalytic approaches to horror resonates with Elliott's view of Marcuse's datedness, since Badley, again following Foucauldian perspectives, suggests that many recent horror movies:

> do not testify to repressed sexuality but instead reflect our saturation with sexual images and options, a state of cultural hyperconsciousness and confusion ... The horror genre as traditionally defined, as the expression of repressed sexuality, is defunct, and ... horror has been energized by something else. Sexual terror has become part of a much larger anxiety about gender, identity, mortality, power, and loss of control. (1995, pp. 13 and 14)

These arguments lead to the suggestion that Wood's work on horror in the 1970s and 1980s was very much formed by and within its own (sub)cultural context, drawing on Marxian-Freudian syntheses that were influential at the time in radical, academic politics, but which have now been called into question by the rise of Foucauldian paradigms. In an essay whose title – 'Eros and Syphilization' – refers to Marcuse's (1987) *Eros and Civilisation*, Dana Polan has argued that theoretical bids for horror's 'progressiveness' can only be problematic:

> any nomination of the horror film as a progressive genre, simply because it depicts certain limitations of dominant society, would be wrong in missing the ways a critique of certain aspects of domination may itself derive from ... other equally dominating aspects of that same society. (1997, p. 126)

In other words, Wood's project appears to perform a vast semiotic fixing of horror's meanings. Repression is used conceptually to elevate the horror genre as a timeless re-enactment of psychological processes, while surplus repression is used to elevate horror to the timely status of a grand cultural-political struggle. The type of ambivalence raised by Polan's commentary is itself seemingly 'repressed' or silenced in Wood's categorizing 'reactionary'/'progressive' account of horror. Polan argues that cultural power acts through so many different channels and forces that there can be no definitive restoration of repressed material without this allegedly pleasurable restoration *simultaneously* implying other dimensions of repression/oppression. For example, horror films may critique aspects of contemporary culture – such as the zombie-consumers of *Dawn of the Dead* (1978, dr: George A. Romero) – while still potentially reinforcing ideological notions of 'might is right' via a militaristic response to monstrosity. I would suggest that whether 'the return of the repressed' and repression itself can be clearly separated, either by narrative phase or across discrete texts, is *the* question raised by Wood's approach. His own Freudian-indebted theoretical machinery implies that such separations or splittings are clearly possible, and indeed Wood's critics have contributed to this tendency by counter-reading horror as being about 'repressive' monsters rather than viewing monsters as 'returns of the repressed' (as in Jancovich 1992, p. 16). Yet an alternative theoretical path, put forward by Andrew Britton, lies in the argument that 'the return of the repressed isn't clearly distinguished from the return of repression' (cited in Polan 1997, p. 126).

Psychoanalytically derived, scholarly readings of horror that celebrate its progressiveness or condemn its 'reactionary wing' seem bent on elevating horror as a priori culturally 'important' within political struggle. And as Wood himself has recently noted, within a staunch defence of the 'return of the repressed' thesis:

> What was crucially determinant of *The American Nightmare* was our political commitment – leftist, radical, with at least an interest in Marxist ideology and especially in the confluence of Marx and Freud in '70s thought. That commitment was vastly more important to us than any desire to tell 'the whole truth and nothing but the truth' about the horror film ... Criticism of *The American Nightmares* approach has in fact concentrated not on politics but on *psychoanalysis, which to us was a valuable weapon that could be used politically*. Relatively speaking, our radical political commitment has been generally ignored, despite the fact that it embodies the foundation of our arguments. (Wood 2004, p. xiv, my italics)

Rather than attacking Wood's position for its somehow inaccurate or problematic use of Freud-via-Marcuse (Carroll 1990; Jancovich 1992; Schneider 2000a), what I have sought to excavate here so far – in line with Wood's own comments on the slanted reception of his ideas – is precisely how Freudian psychoanalysis is put in the service of a specific cultural politics in Wood's work. But by making politics more important than telling 'the whole truth and nothing but the truth' about horror film, Wood substitutes what he has framed as a quasi-legalistic demand for horror's 'truth' for a different, Marxist and cultural-political demand. It is this demand for cultural-political legibility (where is the monster of ideology and how can it be combated by 'heroic' diegetic monsters?) that prematurely does away with horror's semiotic instabilities, and its doubled but indistinguishable restorations of repression and repressed material. Whereas horror's pleasures require categorization on Wood's account – as progressive/disruptive of social norms, or as conservative/ reactionary and reinforcing such norms – I am suggesting here that horror's pleasures may be discursively counter-constructed as confusing political systems of thought and destabilizing systems of psychoanalytic theory (being at once representations of restored repression and restored repressed material). By contrast, applications of psychoanalysis, especially when used as a 'political weapon', consistently seek to categorize, reduce and contain horror's pleasures within prescribed, pre-given theoretical discourses.

We have travelled some distance from the Freudian 'uncanny', but I now want to return to this by considering Steven Jay Schneider's (2000a) re-reading of Freud's landmark (1919) essay.

UNCANNY HORROR AS THE 'RECONFIRMATION OF SURMOUNTED BELIEFS'

Where Robin Wood seizes on Freud's first definition of the uncanny to support his 'return of the repressed' argument, Schneider (2000a) reopens Freud's second definition: the 'reconfirmation of surmounted beliefs'. This means that Schneider's account of uncanny horror somewhat sidesteps issues raised by 'repression' as a concept, and whether repression is a myth or a trope 'now tainted by cliché, nostalgia ... parody, or satire' (Badley 1995, p. 17). Similarly, by focusing on surmounted beliefs, Schneider avoids Andrew Tudor's warning to the effect that:

> [A]n account of horror in terms of the 'return of the repressed' may appear to relate certain features of horror texts illuminatingly to our presumed psycho-sexual constitution, [but] it does not directly address the question of the attraction of horror. Indeed, one might argue that bringing such fearful things to the surface is likely to be far from pleasurable. (Tudor 1997, p. 449)

Schneider's account of the uncanny is thus useful in a number of ways:

- It allows us to account for why it is that the same 'monster' (e.g. Dracula) may be frightening when represented through certain aesthetic devices and codes of realism, but not at all frightening in old horror films, or if represented via different aesthetic techniques. That is, despite being based on a supposedly 'universalizing' psychoanalytic account, Schneider's work can potentially account for socio-historical and aesthetic variations in horror texts and their monsters' 'effectiveness'. This is so because the 'reconfirmation of surmounted beliefs' requires a 'conflict of judgement' on the part of audiences, meaning that monsters must be aesthetically convincing – via codes of realism – in order to provoke such a conflict, and hence an experience of the uncanny (Schneider 2000a, p. 184).

- It allows us to account for a wide range of different monsters via the notion that monsters are metaphors for different surmounted beliefs, such as that the dead can return to life (reincarnated monsters); the omnipotence of thought (psychic monsters); the existence of doubles (dyadic monsters) (Schneider 2000a, p. 182).

Unlike Wood's 'return of the repressed' thesis, Schneider's account does not require us to accept that horror's attraction relates to, or calls upon, unconscious processes; in fact one might characterize Schneider's work here as a 'psycho-analytic account of horror without the unconscious'. In this it is certainly unusual, moving closer to cognitive accounts of horror than other psychoanalytic theories (although see Schneider's arguments against Noël Carroll's 'neo-Jentschian' position, 2000a, p. 178). Schneider attempts to square universalizing with particularistic accounts of horror (2000a, pp. 186–7), meaning that his work can be considered as theoretically liminal, or as a monstrous category violation that is neither entirely 'cognitive' nor entirely 'psychoanalytic' despite being based on a detailed re-reading of Freud. Nor is Schneider's work here either clearly transhistorical or socio-historical in its outlook. It muddles attempts that have been made to map work on horror (such as Tudor 1997).

And given that my argument thus far in this first part of *The Pleasures of Horror* has been that different schools of thought on the genre discursively and theoretically imply certain types of 'pleasure' for ideal audiences, then we may expect the question of pleasure to be raised even more acutely by Schneider's metatheoretical blurring of theoretical categories. In fact, Schneider's account implies that the pleasures of horror are akin to those already recounted as being discursively dominant in Chapters 1 and 2 (that is, cognitivists' definitions of 'emotion' and cognitive/intellectual 'hesitation'). By temporarily repressing the concept of repression, Schneider returns to the languages of cognition and hesitation since audiences experience the fictionalized/depicted uncanny only when a 'conflict of judgement' is aesthetically evoked, that is, they are led to hesitate over whether an incredible event is indeed possible. This 'conflict of judgement' scenario is almost entirely in line with the traditional Todorovian approach to horror outlined in Chapter 2. And at the same time, audiences' hesitation is based on processes of cognition, partly aligning Schneider's account with Carroll's (1990) argumentative position. By displacing repression with 'reconfirmation' Schneider actually minimizes any distinctively psychoanalytic construct or narrative of pleasure (e.g. what I am terming 'restoration'). Surmounted beliefs do not require the operation of the unconscious or mechanisms of repression, thus denuding this ostensibly psychoanalytic explanation of horror of psychodynamic processes, as well as contra Wood (but pro-Carroll), making horror's monsters a matter of metaphor and aesthetics rather than a matter of monstrous ideology.

Schneider's return to Freud is sufficiently faithful that it accepts certain distinctions made, rather hesitantly or insecurely, in 'The Uncanny' (1990a). For example, Schneider recapitulates Freud's point that the uncanny based on repressed material (type 1) is equally uncanny when experienced in fiction and reality, whereas the 'reconfirmation of surmounted beliefs' (type 2) can entirely lack an uncanny effect in fiction depending on how it is presented (Schneider 2000a, p. 175; see Freud 1990a, p. 374).

Yet by repeating this established Freudian wisdom, Schneider does not consider the way in which Freud immediately contradicts his own point by observing that a specific aesthetic representation of a severed hand (which should give rise to the uncanny by returning a repressed infantile fear of castration) is, after all, not uncanny (1990a, p. 375). Freud's solution to this problem is to suggest that the reader does not put him/herself in the place of the specific hand-losing character. But this alleged 'one exception' (1990a, p. 374) reintroduces what Freud has already supposedly banished – the possibility that narrativized, aesthetic 'returns of the repressed' do *not or need not* operate in the same way as actual returns of the repressed. In Freud's example, for instance, the reader is said to be (presumably pleasurably) focused on the 'superior cunning' of another character rather than experiencing an uncanny effect (1990a, p. 375).

Why, then, should Freud insist on the continuity of fictional and real experiences of the uncanny where repression is concerned, but happily discuss the aesthetic transformation, or withholding, of uncanny effects based on the 'reconfirmation of the surmounted'? It is striking that his 'one exception' to the argument that repressed complexes generate the uncanny equally in fiction and real experience occurs in a single paragraph at the very end of 'The Uncanny', whereas by contrast he devotes a full two pages to discussing how the 'reconfirmation of the surmounted' can be differently rendered aesthetically (1990a, pp. 373–4; it is this discussion that predominantly informs Schneider's work).

What Freud appears unduly anxious to close down – and hence what goes missing in Schneider's re-reading to-the-letter – is the possibility that the uncanny based on restoring repressed material might also be open to aestheticized interventions and stagings. For Freud, the 'return of the repressed' does not (or rather, definitionally *cannot*) hinge on a 'conflict of judgement' since this would again place audience cognition centre-stage, rather than viewing the return of the repressed as unconsciously driven and thus as beyond the self's conscious control. In short, for the theory of the 'return of the repressed' to hold, this type of 'uncanny' experience actually *has* to be denied the aesthetic malleability of the 'reconfirmation of the surmounted' type. It is out of conceptual and theoretical necessity that Freud seeks to bury his counter-example. For if the 'return of the repressed' can be warded off by aesthetic devices or representations then it cannot operate entirely as an unconscious process, but must also involve cognitive dimensions. What Freud is protecting here is his 'under-cognitive' account of uncanny horror, just as cognitive theorists and Todorovians work logically and discursively to protect their 'over-cognitive' and intellectualizing discourses of horror.

Psychoanalytically influenced accounts of horror have not been limited to Freud's narrative of 'The Uncanny', despite this forming my central focus so far in this chapter. Rival accounts have variously drawn on Lacanian work (Copjec 2000; Žižek 2000), focused on or challenged a Mulveyan analysis of the sadistic male gaze (Clover 1992; Linda Williams 1996; Berenstein 1996), considered horror as generating masochistic pleasure or fetishistic seeing/not-seeing (Neale 1980; Giles 1984; Neale 1996; Pinedo 1997), linked horror to theories of hysteria (Newman 1993; Bronfen 1998), made use of Laplanche and Pontalis's rethinking of fantasy (Creed 1993; Linda Williams 1999), and focused on Kristeva's notion of 'abjection' (Creed 1993). Picking a way through this terrain would probably require a book of its own (see Schneider (ed.) 2004b and Sabbadini (ed.) 2003). In any case, many of the debates in this domain are already well mapped (see also Donald 1989; Thornham 1997; Wells 2000; Schneider 2000a). That being the case, in the next section I will restrict myself to considering the pleasures of restoration implied in work on horror and abjection (Creed 1993).

HORROR AS THE 'PURIFICATION OF THE ABJECT'

Although more clearly post-Freudian than Robin Wood's Freudian-Marcusean approach to horror, Barbara Creed's (1993) *The Monstrous-Feminine* continues to imply structurally similar pleasures of horror. Rather than repression being the key trope, it is 'abjection', a concept borrowed from Julia Kristeva's (1982) *Powers of Horror*, that is used to integrate and unify horror texts as an object of analysis.

Like the uncanny, abjection is very much not a concept with a singular referent. And where the uncanny has two main lines of Freudian definition, abjection (as glossed by Creed) is similarly doubled. It is defined via rituals concerning bodily wastes, emissions and biological processes, and via religious rituals/taboos. In the first instance, it is the protection of the self's 'clean and proper body' (Kristeva 1982, p. 72) that is crucial. This means that bodily wastes, etc. classified as not-self must be excluded from the self, being cast out across the self/not-self boundary that demarcates the clean and proper body. As Creed puts it:

> The place of the abject is ... the place where 'I' am not. The abject threatens life; it must be 'radically excluded' (Kristeva 1982, p. 2) from the place of the living subject, propelled away from the body and deposited on the other side of an imaginary border which separates the self from that which threatens the self ... Further, the activity of exclusion is necessary to guarantee that the

subject take up his/her proper place in relation to the symbolic. (Creed 1993, p. 9)

Horror 'abounds in images of abjection' (Creed 1993, p. 10) of this first type, representing the violent expulsion of vomit (*The Exorcist* 1973, dr: William Friedkin), pus (*Demons* 1985, dr: Lamberto Bava), menstrual blood (*Carrie* 1976, dr: Brian De Palma), and so on (see Mendik 1998; Reich 2001; Bell-Metereau 2004). And it also returns repeatedly to the figure of the corpse, which for Kristeva is the ultimate in abjection:

> If dung signifies the other side of the border, the place where I am not and which permits me to be, the corpse, the most sickening of wastes, is a border which has encroached on everything. It is no longer I who expel [bodily wastes]. 'I' is expelled. (Kristeva 1982, pp. 3–4)

Horror also relates closely to the second type of abjection discussed by Creed: religious categories. Cannibalism, a tabooed 'food loathing' (Creed 1993, p. 9), is central to an entire subgenre of horror; Creed lists films such as *Blood Feast* (1963, dr: Herschell Gordon Lewis), *Motel Hell* (1980, dr: Kevin Connor), and *The Hills Have Eyes* (1977, dr: Wes Craven) (ibid.), and we might add Hannibal Lecter's film appearances as well as the many zombie movies that are narratively preoccupied with the eating of flesh, not least of which would be the rather self-explanatory *Zombie Flesh-Eaters* (1979, dr: Lucio Fulci).

Abjection is concerned, then, with the ritualistic, cultural construction of borders; the border separating self and not-self; the border separating tabooed foods or substances; even the borders of cultural categories and 'laws' (Creed 1993, pp. 10–11; Cavallaro 2002, pp. 199–206). This means that the abject, category-violating monster of Creed's account closely resembles the monster as defined by Noël Carroll (1990). But abjection does not just violate fragile laws or categories; crucially, it 'opens up' the represented self, creating both the monstrous-feminine (Creed 1993, pp. 12–13) and the monstrous-masculine (Linda Ruth Williams 1999). By challenging cultural norms of the bounded self and body, abjection depicts selves in states of physical disintegration and mental/spiritual 'possession' (see Clover 1992, p. 78). However, Graham Ward's reading of *Stigmata* (1999, dr: Rupert Wainwright) versus *The Exorcist* raises an interesting point: a 'spiritualized' opening up of the self may be depicted, theologically, as a positive counterpart to more negative and threatening connotations of bodily abjection (2003, pp. 145–53). Ward suggests that while *The Exorcist* deals with 'fear of penetration' (2003, p. 148) and abjection, in the film *Stigmata* 'fear of penetration is ... overcome ... a pleasure is involved in being penetrated ... In this relationality there is a transcendence and ecstasy' (2003, p. 149). Ward argues that despite its emphasis on the gendered body of Frankie Paige (Patricia Arquette), who is diegetically possessed by the 'spirit of God in Christ' (2003, p. 149), *Stigmata* ultimately constructs a soul/body opposition, overwriting its imaginary bodily abjections with a narrative of transcendent (soulful) Oneness-through-loss-of-self. Of course, in *The Exorcist* it is Regan's possession by demonic forces that compounds bodily abjection with a theological loss-of-self (see Mäyrä 1999, pp. 150–2), whereas in *Stigmata* it is Frankie's possession by Godly forces that opposes bodily abjection with spiritual transcendence rather than a demonic invasion and swamping of the self. Specific horror narratives, and their invocations of good/evil, can therefore configure abjection as an uneasy blend of narratively represented pleasure-pain. The abject can connote pleasurable self-transcendence and/or painful self-annihilation, depending on how this is mapped across mind/body or soul/body binaries.

Rather like the contrapuntal rhythm of repression/the uncanny, in which repressed material is restored prior to repression itself being restored, abjection tends to follow a similar narrative arc in horror texts, giving raise to ambiguous pleasures of attraction/repulsion that are cyclically replayed:

> [T]he subject is constantly beset by abjection which fascinates desire but which must be repelled for fear of self-annihilation. A crucial point is that abjection is always ambiguous. (Creed 1993, p. 10)

However, as I have argued, if repression/the return of the repressed is also always ambiguous, academic approaches have nevertheless typically closed down such ambiguity. Abjection is no different, typically being split into non-ambiguous moments of horror. For Wood (1986), recall that horror temporarily lifts repression, only to restore it in the putative 'happy' ending. For Barbara Creed (1993), the 'popular horror film' works likewise to 'bring about a confrontation with the abject (the corpse, bodily wastes, the monstrous-feminine) *in order finally to separate out the symbolic order from all that threatens its stability*' (Creed 1993, p. 14, my italics). It is hence the 'purification of the abject' that forms the 'ideological project' par excellence of the horror genre in Creed's terms (ibid.). This accounts very well for films such as *The Exorcist*, but following Ward (2003), it might seem to make less sense of the abject-related ambiguities of *Stigmata*.

Graham Ward has not been alone in pointing out the need to consider precisely how abjection is narratively framed in horror. Jason Jacobs, for example, has sought to distinguish horror's abjection from that present in 'body trauma TV', arguing that here 'the meaning of such butchery ... is firmly closed, directed to positive healing rather than violent destruction' (Jacobs 2003, p. 69). However, such a clear 'horror'/'medical drama' contrast may be premature. For, as with Jacobs's reading of TV hospital dramas, horror also moves through representations of abjection towards a positive sense of the enduring, clean and proper self (that is to say, remarkably few popular horror films conclude with every character becoming abject; usually a key figure of identification survives the abjection that has surrounded him/her). The key generic difference is thus perhaps less one of abjection as spectacular pay-off versus abjection as a narrative stage towards healing (Jacobs 2003, pp. 69–70), and more formally one of whether stages of abjection and restoration are centred around the same body (as in hospital dramas), or narratively dispersed across different actants (as in much horror), or even contrasted through a soul/body or mind/body dualism in relation to one actant (as in some 'theological' horror).

Creed notes that abjection's fascination is related to the subject's development from a 'pre-symbolic' stage of maternal authority to an affiliation with the (paternal, post-Oedipal) symbolic order of civilized society. As such, representations of abjection can allow for the return of archaic, socially tabooed pleasures:

> On the one hand, ... images of bodily wastes threaten a subject that is already constituted, in relation to the symbolic, as 'whole and proper'. Consequently, they fill the subject – both the protagonist ... and the spectator ... – with disgust and loathing. On the other hand they also point back to a time when a 'fusion between mother and nature' existed; when bodily wastes ... were not seen as objects of embarrassment and shame ... [A]t a more archaic level the representation of bodily wastes may invoke pleasure in breaking the taboo on filth ... and a pleasure in returning to that time when the mother–child relationship was marked by an untrammelled pleasure in 'playing' with the body and its wastes. (Creed 1993, p. 13)

At this point it is worth once more reiterating the slogans that encapsulate seemingly very different psychoanalytic approaches to horror:

'Return of the (surplus) repressed' (Freud 1990a; Wood 1986)
'Reconfirmation of the surmounted' (Freud 1990a; Schneider 2000a)
'Purification of the abject' (Creed 1993).

Each psychoanalytically informed account, despite differences in their readings of Freud, and their post-Freudian developments or Freudian/post-Freudian tensions, conforms to the same basic narrative structure of restoration. Indeed, Paul Wells even goes so far as to describe Kristevan abjection as 'a particular model of "the return of the repressed"' (2000, p. 16). And Jack Morgan discusses 'Stephen King's analysis in *Danse Macabre* [1982] as ... cognate to Kristeva's' (2002, p. 226). Abjection is a type of represented disintegration that 'is therapeutic in that it impels towards reintegration' says Morgan, just as for King 'the melodies of the horror tale ... are melodies of disestablishment and disintegration ... bring[ing] things back to a more stable and constructive state again' (cited in Morgan 2002, p. 226).

These various psychoanalytic accounts of horror are structurally similar iterations of one master narrative:

(1) 'X' is lost via civilizing processes (whether repressed Oedipal complexes, repressed fears of castration, primitive animistic beliefs or the pleasures of revelling in filth and muck).

(2) This 'X' is restored temporarily and narratively via horror texts.

(3) 'X' is then expelled again, returning us to our starting point, and ritualistically restoring civilized society (repression/the mature cognitive self/the symbolic order).

Via loss, restoration and civilized restoration, each account acts as an almost pure figure of narrativity itself. Horror's implied pleasures of restoration thus persist across otherwise very different theoretical, psychoanalytic frames. Horror is consistently taken to represent the cultural site of a contained regression, a to-and-fro of present and archaic selves, and a limited opening on to gothic counter-selves. And whether through Freudian or Kristevan gambits, horror is transported from the realm of the trivial (fictional monsters and representations of vomit) to the elevated terrain of (timeless or transhistorical) civilization and its malcontents. Such accounts of horror and its pleasures thus work to performatively valorize horror by chaining it to imputed psychological and socio-cultural processes, while also discursively fixing horror as non-ambivalent. Pleasures that should, theoretically, be ambivalent and undistinguishably fascinating/repulsive are repeatedly separated out into categories or distinct narrative moments or types of texts. Psychoanalytic theories cannot, seemingly, tolerate horror's own thorough-going category violations. As Charles Weigl has argued, 'horror operates by blurring categories ... How could we hope to understand the genre by keeping those categories [return of the repressed/ repression itself; pre-symbolic/symbolic] intact?' (2002, p. 704).

Is it possible to put forward a psychoanalytically derived account of horror that respects horror's category blurring? In the remainder of this chapter I will attempt to put forward just such a counter-discourse of horror's pleasures. Of course, it could be argued that I have constructed a structurally coherent 'master narrative' across different psychoanalytic approaches to horror by focusing only on those approaches especially amenable to such a contextualization, while writing out the full range of other theoretical options (Lacanian; gaze-based accounts; hysteria-based accounts, etc.). Against such an accusation I would note three things:

(1) Other psychoanalytic accounts I have not covered here are, I would suggest, equally open to the suggestion that they valorize horror by linking it to grand schemes of cultural 'order' or transhistorical totalities.

(2) Similarly, other accounts of horror (based on alternative readings of Freud, readings of Jung, Lacan, or Laplanche and Pontalis) tend to imply non-ambiguous and theoretically predetermined pleasures of horror, whether these are primarily sadistic, fetishistic pleasures, or disguised reactivations of (repressed) primary fantasies. Horror, in such approaches, remains a

mirror in which psychoanalytic theory can narcissistically identify itself and imagine itself as all-seeing/not-lacking.

(3)   Other psychoanalytic accounts, particularly those of the Lacanian 'uncanny' or what has been termed 'extimacy' (Bronfen 1998, p. 385), are no less prone than Freudian-based interpretations to accusations that they neglect horror's precise aesthetics and varied pleasures.

My interest in the next section therefore lies in sketching out a psychoanalytic theory of horror through which generic and theoretical narratives/structures can dialectically interact, with genre working to destabilize 'Theory', rather than pop culture becoming merely a token or an instance of fantastically all-possessing and all-powerful psychoanalytic thinking. What might horror's pleasures come to look like within such a counter-discursive approach?

REPETITION, REPETITION, REPETITION

Following Steven Jay Schneider's (2000a) useful intervention, it is possible to once more re-read Freud on 'The Uncanny'. While repeating Freud's insistence on the art/reality continuity of uncanny experiences based on repressed complexes, Schneider passes over Freud's note on repetition:

> How exactly we can trace back to infantile psychology the uncanny effect of ... similar recurrences is a question I can only lightly touch on in these pages ... For it is possible to recognise the dominance in the unconscious mind of a 'compulsion to repeat' proceeding from the instinctual impulses ... a compulsion ... lending to certain aspects of the mind their daemonic character ... [W]hatever reminds us of this inner 'compulsion to repeat' is perceived as uncanny. (Freud 1990a, pp. 360–1)

Freud's linking of the uncanny to repetition-compulsion is rarely built upon significantly in psychoanalytic work on horror. Unlike the master trope of repression, one might say that repetition-compulsion has languished as a forgotten marker of the uncanny. Cynthia Freeland (2001, p. 37) notes Freud's point on the matter, but then moves on to critically discuss the 'return of the repressed' thesis. Robert D. Newman (1993, p. 67) similarly discusses repetition-compulsion only in passing, before moving rapidly to the question of castration anxiety. Schneider (2000a) and Wood (1986 and 2004) have little to say on horror and repetition-compulsion, and Noël Carroll's interlude on Freud and the uncanny (1990, pp. 174–5) also absents repetition-compulsion in favour of interrogating the 'repression hypothesis' (1990, p. 177).

Readers of Freud's 'The Uncanny' are referred to 'Beyond the Pleasure Principle' for more on repetition-compulsion (Freud 1990a, p. 360). And it is here that Freud famously discusses repetition-compulsion in relation to child's play and the 'fort-da' game, 'the first game played by a little boy of one and half and invented by himself' (Freud 1990b, p. 283). This game involved the child throwing away a wooden reel attached to a piece of string while announcing 'fort' ('gone'), and then retrieving the reel with 'a joyful "da" ["there"]' (Freud 1990b, p. 284). Freud interprets this game as the child's symbolic restaging of his mother's going away, through which he is able 'to revenge himself on his mother' by symbolically sending her (the reel) away himself. Freud thus concludes that this repetition-in-play works to convert passive experience into active mastery:

> At the outset he was in a *passive* situation – he was overpowered by the experience; but, by repeating it, unpleasurable though it was, he took on an *active* part. These efforts might be put down to an instinct for mastery. (Freud 1990b, p. 285)

Yet Freud rules that the pleasures taken in aesthetic artefacts are irrelevant to his concern with repetition-compulsion (1990b, p. 287), suggesting that these require 'some system of aesthetics with an economic approach to its subject matter'. In view of his consideration that uncanny experiences in real life can remind us of repetition-compulsion, for example in the 'factor of involuntary repetition which ... forces upon us the idea of something fateful and inescapable' (1990a, pp. 359–60), Freud appears to prematurely rule out – in both 'Beyond the Pleasure Principle' and 'The Uncanny' – the possibility that 'uncannily' pan-deterministic repetitions can also occur aesthetically in fiction. This absence is partly contradicted by Freud's own example in 'Beyond the Pleasure Principle', where he uses a 'romantic epic *Gerusalemme Liberata*' (1990b, p. 293) to exemplify repetition-compulsion that appears, within the transference, as a passive experience of 'perpetual recurrence of the same thing' (1990b, p. 292). Indeed, Freud even discusses how:

> what psychoanalysis reveals in the transference phenomena of neurotics can also be observed in the lives of some normal people. The impression they give is of being pursued by a malignant fate or possessed by some 'daemonic' power; but psychoanalysis has always taken the view that their fate is for the most part arranged by themselves and determined by early infantile experiences ... We are ... more impressed by cases where the subject appears to have a *passive* experience, over which he has no influence, but in which he meets with a repetition of the same fatality. (Freud 1990b, pp. 292–3)

We might well ponder whether people who appear to be 'possessed by a "daemonic power"', and who are thus seemingly involuntarily caught up in repetition, can act as a source of the uncanny in both fact and fiction. For horror, it can be argued, resembles both child's play and aesthetic depictions/

representations of psychoanalytic transference (cf. Paul 2004). Like play, it contains unpleasure for its audiences, converting passive, negative affects/ emotions into active experiences (i.e. aesthetic choices on the part of consumers). And the genre frequently depicts characters repeating actions in such a way as to (arguably) become uncanny – often being diegetically rather than metaphorically possessed by daemonic forces. Furthermore, even where characters do not repeat actions within an atmosphere of uncanny or 'possessed' pan-determinism, horror narratives are still frequently marked by other forms of uncanny narrative repetition. These can be identified as 'themed' types of killings; supernatural or ghostly repetitions; apparent coincidences revealed as motivated acts (super-natural or otherwise); repetitions of violence, suffering and catastrophe. The centrality of repetition across horror's texts is amply testified to by any and all general theories (of which Carroll 1990 remains probably the leading instance), as well as by the fact that repression and abjection models stress the need for such processes to return over and over again (Wood 1986, p. 80; Creed 1993, p. 10). Horror's repetitions have also been discussed by Roger B. Salomon, drawing on a piece entitled 'Horror for Pleasure' by Geoffrey O'Brien:

> O'Brien notes a curious quality of repetition, calling ... [horror] 'a genre that seems to define itself by constantly recapitulating everything it has been ... we always seem to wind up where we started ... It is an eternal return to the site of unmodulated shock'. (in Salomon 2002, p. 8)

Elsewhere in *Mazes of the Serpent: An Anatomy of Horror Narrative*, Salomon explains his choice of title: 'mazes of the serpent' is a 'metaphor of labyrinth' (2002, p. 98) that both evokes and reflects horror narratives' general reliance on redundancy and repetition (Salomon 2002, pp. 96–101). In Salomon's account, horror works narratively, or rather does not work, by leading 'away from meaning rather than encouraging its generation ... Horror narrative can only dramatize one paradigmatic experience or multiply meaningless events toward no other end than random death' (2002, pp. 98–9).

This emphasis on nihilistic repetition is not viewed negatively by Salomon; rather, the staging of absence is one of horror's virtues in his reading. However, I would argue that Salomon's blanket pronouncement neglects to consider the different types of repetition that generically mark out horror. For example, slasher narratives typically imply some psychological 'repetition' or restaging on the part of their diegetic killers (Dika 1990). This is captured especially well in the film *Deep in the Woods* (2000, dr: Lionel Delplanque), where repetition-compulsion becomes the self-referential focus of the film's narrative. Such repetition, contra Salomon, is not concerned with meaninglessness. Rather, it comes to represent the pop-Freudian patterns, meaningfulness and exaggerated transparency or legibility of the diegetic slasher's psyche. One of the potential pleasures of horror here is, then, a pleasure taken in psychical legibility, with the killer's bizarre repetitions becoming a narrative puzzle to be solved, and a circuit of meaning to be reconstructed.

Other types of repetition, apart from the staging of horror's 'numbers' (Freeland 2000, p. 255), can concern textual mirrorings between diegetically 'real' and 'unreal' events. This is a standard device of much 'media horror' (horror texts that treat mediation as a theme, and/or which self-reflexively consider horror's 'powers' as a media product). For example, it occurs in *Demons* and *Demons 2* (1986, dr: Lamberto Bava), in *Cut* (2000, dr: Kimble Rendall) and *Popcorn* (1991, dr: Mark Herrier), as well as most famously in *Scream* (1996, dr: Wes Craven). In *Popcorn*, diegetic dreams are replayed at the level of diegetic reality, and also films-within-the-film such as the glorious *Them!* (1954, dr: Gordon Douglas) pastiche, 'Mosquito', are lethally restaged via gimmicks in the Dreamland theatre's auditorium. In fact this device gives rise to very similar effects of *mise-en-abyme* as are encountered in *Deep in the Woods*; there it is a theatrical play that is re-enacted lethally at the level of diegetic reality; here it is a series of films which are repeated and thus translated across diegetic levels of 'image' and 'reality'. Rather than rendering one character's psyche transparent, this form of uncanny repetition suggests the meaningfulness and supra-legibility of pan-determinism: somehow 'real' events are prefigured and predetermined by aesthetic representations-within-representations. A saturation or excess of meaning structures these repetitions.

Such repetitions, at the level of character psychology or diegetic fiction/ reality, create the impression of a 'determinist pattern ... so intense that the fictional world is portrayed as containing nothing that is unique or the product of free will' (Leffler 2000, p. 191). Killers are driven by their own repetition-compulsions (serial killer fiction can almost be considered as a dramatisation *tout court* of repetition-compulsion, partly deriving its own brand of uncanniness from this). And fictions repeat in 'the (diegetic) real'. Horror's pan-determinism offers completely controlled – and thus completely and precisely meaningful – fictional repetitions. According to this argument the horror genre, at least in its subgeneric strands of 'media horror' and slasher flicks, is concerned with the symbolic annihilation of semiotic excess. Rather than horror's monsters being over-coded and over-determined (Halberstam 1995, p. 21), I am suggesting here that much of horror's appeal lies in its textual attempts to represent fictional worlds and monstrous killers as carriers of transparent meaning. Horror hypersignifies.

The oft-used psychoanalytic comparison of horror films and dreams is thus, I suspect, greatly misguided. As the product of psychical primary processes, dreams are indeed radically over-determined. By contrast, the aesthetic constructions of horror might even be thought of as 'nightmares-in-reverse', being attempts at foreclosing primary processes of condensation and displacement via fantasized worlds of total meaning where horrific events/acts/monsters are converted into symbolic equations (or allegories/hypersignifications).

Rather than chaos, randomness and contingency nihilistically driving horror narrative, in this view the horror genre potentially works to obliterate threats of randomness and loss of meaning. Horror's uncanny dramatization of repetition-compulsion, in which acts and events insistently replay themselves, implies an aesthetic staging of psychoanalytic transference, as well as a narrative reconstruction of the process of child's play.

Freud's work on child's play has given rise to general theories of reading as play (Calinescu 1993). And cultural theory, in the form of Harvie Ferguson's work, has linked repetition to pleasure not as its consequence ('X' is enjoyable, therefore I repeat it) but rather as its anxiety-carrying precursor: 'The play impulse ... underlies *both* the repetition of pleasure *and* the persistence of anxiety' (Ferguson 1996, p. 154). Both approaches could profitably be related to horror as a specific genre, given its characteristic repetitions and its ambiguous mingling of anxiety/pleasure. Furthermore, Isabel Pinedo's work on horror's 'bounded experience of fear' (1997, p. 38) emphasizes, somewhat akin to Freud's account of play, how 'the element of control ... [experienced by horror's audiences] turns stress/arousal ... into a pleasurable experience' (1997, p. 39). Indeed, this playfulness is captured in Pinedo's (1997) notion of 'recreational terror'.

However, play theories of horror such as Pinedo's that read horror as 'an exercise in mastery, in which controlled loss substitutes for loss of control' (1997, p. 41) hardly serve to ambiguate horror's pleasures. Instead, a further rhetoric is substituted for that of the 'repression model' (Tudor 1997, p. 447), a rhetoric where pleasure is a potential substitute for lost, absent and preceding trauma rather than stemming from the 'return of the repressed'. In terms of the master narrative already identified, play theories of the loosely or vaguely Freudian type put forward by Pinedo could thus be added under the rubric 'substitute for (traumatic) loss of control'. All the elements of the previously identified psychoanalytic master narrative remain present: an initial loss; a re-presentation or restoration of that loss in disguised form; and a restoration of civilization/culture (through the necessary boundedness of horror).

Instead, if we are to ambiguate horror's pleasures as category-violating combinations or compounds of play/transference and pleasure/anxiety – the counter-discourse that I am aiming to develop here – then it may help to hold on to Harvie Ferguson's point, as well as considering yet another re-reading of Freud, this time André Green's return to 'Beyond the Pleasure Principle' (Green 2002 and 2003):

> having pointed out how the manner in which repetition-compulsion is expressed is often felt to be uncanny, Freud then discovered that this uncanniness was related to what is most familiar to us ... The reversal into the contrary ... is not enough in itself – it is the mutual relationship between the terms that determines their intelligibility. (Green 2003, p. 114)

Repetition-compulsion's uncanny reversal of what is familiar into the unfamiliar is thus a matter of essential symbolization ('wooden reel' for 'mother') and intelligibility in Green's reading, and more than this, such intelligibility is present only for an observer, not for the player him/herself:

> The Other, who is a necessary witness of the game – the position occupied by Freud – can perceive the meaning of it from where he is standing, through the product of what he has generated ... This ... movement, however, is already present in the binding process of the game, which, as it is constituted, is self-reflecting ... [I]ts emergence in reality brings about a new distribution of functions which puts the reflective position in a zone of extraterritoriality where the observer can position himself. (Green 2003, pp. 106–7)

Here, Green usefully emphasizes that child's play requires an audience to grant it meaning, and that it effectively requires the Other to determine its intelligibility. The function of meaning-making is separated off from the player. This is shared by the matter of transference, where the intelligibility of 'acting out' also separates the subject from the meaning of his/her activities, calling up an extraterritoriality where intelligibility can be reconstructed or witnessed. Green interprets play as if it is proto-transference when he argues that 'the present captivating effect of the game ... erases the historical dimension of the past' (2003, p. 107).

Play, then, is not readily separable from transference in this reading; both attempt to 'abolish time' (2003, p. 71) by an act of 'realization' that crushes 'the polysemic value of action through the urgency of its effectivity' (2002, p. 79). But such a seeming 'automatism' (ibid.) also constructs its own absent position of intelligibility. Green argues that the 'object between trauma and play' (2002, p. 126) needs to be thought through, suggesting that:

> in the compulsion to repeat, the transference-object is like a hypothetical transitional intermediary. The object is apprehended according to a gradient which varies from the threatening situation experienced repeatedly in transference neurosis ... to the situation that can be observed in the play – which is hypersignifying ... as an inaugural form of minimal symbolisation. (Green 2002, p. 127)

Transference objects can be seen as part-play and part-trauma, seeming to be at once 'hypersignifying' and 'threatening'. Here I am arguing that we can productively view horror texts, and their dramatizations of traumatic and playful repetition-compulsion, as *aesthetic representations of hypersignifying and threatening transference objects*. That is, horror can be theorized through a collision of play-metaphors and transference-metaphors rather than being discursively positioned as a dream-metaphor. Horror can be interpreted as represented play/transference both in its projection of a position of intelligibility (so that the viewer is placed in the position of Freud witnessing the fort-da game, and struck by the uncanniness of representations of repetition-compulsion) and in its invocation of 'daemonic' or pan-deterministic forces that generally exceed characters' awareness (again, uncannily reminding 'us of this inner "compulsion to repeat"').

Note that such an approach to horror, attempting to excavate psychoanalysis for counter-discourses of horror's pleasures, does not simply apply psychoanalytic theory. Instead it destabilizes and violates psychoanalytic categories of 'play' versus 'transference', constructing and construing horror's pleasures as an aesthetic blurring of these phenomena rather than as 'cognitive' violations of cultural categories such as life/death, man/beast. In much psychoanalytic work to date pleasures of 'restoration' have been centrally implied in otherwise very different accounts of uncanny horror (Freud 1990a; Wood 1996; Schneider 2000a; Creed 1993). Uncanniness as a pleasure of repetition has been curiously repressed and marginalized as an alternative counter-discourse of horror's pleasures. Perhaps critics have been afraid of noting horror's immense textual and intertextual machineries of repetition for fear of reproducing a narrative of horror-as-devalued-genre. It is possible that 'repetition' lacks the heroic and textually valorizing potential of 'repression' as a trope.

In Part I of *The Pleasures of Horror* I have argued that different theoretical approaches to horror have constructed discourses of 'pleasure' that work to validate their own frameworks, definitions and a priori assumptions. In Chapter 1 I suggested that cognitivists identify the pleasures of horror as 'object-directed' emotions and narrative suspense. They thus appear to overrationalize horror, refusing to consider the role of anxiety and affect within horror's pleasures. Chapter 2 considered Todorovian approaches to horror. Again, these appeared to be overintellectualizing accounts, construing horror as an epistemological challenge for/to its consumers, and marginalizing counter-discourses of pleasures of diegetic ontological shock. And in this chapter I have argued that psychoanalysis, despite its diverse schools, has usually implied that horror's pleasures are those of 'restoration'. A very much 'under-cognitive' master narrative of pleasure has thus underpinned various psychoanalytic theories of horror. Contra such arguments and their concerns with return/reconfirmation/purification/substitution, I have suggested here that horror might not only violate cognitive cultural categories, but that it may also violate the analytical categories of psychoanalysis itself. In each chapter I have thus argued that theories of horror discursively construct limited models of pleasure, suppressing and marginalizing what become theoretically 'Othered' ways of thinking about horror's pleasure (such as 'affect'/'shock'/'repetition'). And I have hence sought to excavate or redevelop these counter-discourses, suggesting from the outset that it is impossible to access extra-discursive 'pleasures of horror' through which we might ontologically adjudicate competing theoretical discourses. Rather than judging certain theories of horror to be 'right' and others 'wrong', then, I have instead attempted to open up a broader range of discourses on horror's pleasures, paying particular attention to counter-discourses that have been occulted and occluded in line with theoretical orthodoxies.

In Part II I will supplement these theoretical concerns with a focus on the pleasures that horror fan audiences claim for themselves. Rather than taking a naively empiricist viewpoint – which would suggest that horror's pleasures are 'real' when discussed by fans, but that they remain a 'construct' in the ideal, theoretical speculations of cognitive philosophy and psychoanalysis alike – I will continue my emphasis on pleasure as performative and discursively constructed. To this end I will go on to argue that horror's fans draw on dominant, limited and restrictive discourses of pleasure in much the same way as horror's philosophers.

Part II

The Pleasures of Horror in Fan Practices

Most of the time, flesh-and-blood genre communities remain beyond reach. Though we may have intermittent contact with others fond of the same genre, we are usually reduced to only imagining their presence and activity ... *Instead of regular participation in an actual group, genre spectatorship more often involves constructing an image of such a group* out of fragments gleaned from every possible field. Not only industry discourse, but critical language, passing comments and chance encounters provide the reference points that permit genre fans to imagine ... the absent community with which they share a particular taste. Though genre viewing in some cases leads to contact with actual community members, and though the meaning of genre viewing may be fundamentally caught up in nostalgia for a specific absent community, most genre spectators maintain only an imagined contact with the broader generic community. (Rick Altman 1999, p. 161, my italics)

Chapter 4

Displaying Connoisseurship, Recognizing Craftsmanship

With much work on horror fandom now occurring (see, for example, Kermode 1997; Cherry 1999 and 2002; Bolin 2000; Hoxter 2000; Jancovich 2000; Sanjek 2000; Williamson 2001; Kimber 2002) comments that the audience has been neglected in studies of horror (e.g. Gelder 2000, p. 6) have begun to seem strained. On the contrary, one might conclude that the horror fan has been theorized to death of late. In this chapter I will argue that alongside the 'aestheticization' of horror there are a range of ways in which horror's pleasures are narrated and constructed by fans. Fan accounts of horror and pleasure have tended to centre on self-mythologized 'first encounters' between fan and genre, as well as on how 'being a horror fan' shifts its experiential meaning between childhood and adulthood. For many horror fans the pleasures of horror are discursively constructed through micro-narratives of biography as well as through notions of belonging to a fan culture and through notions of horror-as-art. Yet in each case fan accounts of the horror genre and its pleasures circle around a discourse of connoisseurship. It is this that I will now turn my attention to.

CONNOISSEURSHIP IN HORROR FAN CULTURES AND FAN BIOGRAPHIES

Fan cultural distinctions tend to mark out some horror texts as 'visionary' and dismiss others as 'inauthentic' horror (Jancovich 2000, pp. 29–31; Sanjek 2000, p. 317). As Mark Jancovich has observed: 'while some horror fans embrace Freddy Kruger [sic] ... as a cult hero, others seek to disassociate themselves from these fans through an association with cult "auteurs" such as Dario Argento' (2000, p. 28). Discourses of aestheticization and authentication – 'underground' horror-as-art versus 'mainstream', commercial horror – allow fans to pleasurably imagine and demarcate the boundaries of horror fan culture, indicating the knowledge that one must share in order to 'properly' be a horror fan. Such discourses do not only work to culturally separate out fans and non-fans, or long-term fans and inauthentic (new) teen fans (Jancovich 2000, p. 30). They also allow horror fans to bid for the wider cultural value of their texts by tactically aligning 'horror-as-art' discourses with discourses of 'legitimate' aesthetics. Horror-as-art is thus an over-determined interpretative tactic, allowing fans to position themselves against a range of imagined Others (state censors/moral campaigners/critics of horror).

Within such multi-stranded struggles over horror and cultural distinction, 'connoisseurship' emerges as *the* master trope in fan struggles against other 'inauthentic' consumers and policing authorities. The pleasures of connoisseurship are thus pleasures of social and cultural distinction/belonging, as well as allowing fans to perform their (constrained) cultural agency via the specific interpretation and contextualization of pop-cultural texts. Such agency is exhibited in Mark Kermode's (1997) account of being a horror fan. Kermode repeatedly emphasizes fans' knowledge: 'Here were people who *knew* what they were talking about, grown-up people who had been doing this for *years*, who actually *understood* what these movies were about' (1997, p. 58).

In Kermode's account, horror fans are divided from non-fans, since the latter group lack detailed information about any horror film they see, and are simply 'scared by it, then wander[. . . ing] out of the cinema and back into the mundanity of their everyday lives' (1997, p. 59). Non-fans 'cringed' at *The Fly* (1986, dr: David Cronenberg) and its gory abortion scene, while Kermode and a fellow aficionado 'chuckled smugly' at their recognition that the onscreen doctor was Cronenberg in a cameo role (1997, p. 60). The act of being scared is predominantly located on the side of non-fandom (or casual horror film viewing):

> The horror fan . . . is . . . not only able but positively compelled to 'read' rather than merely 'watch' such movies. The novice, however, sees only the dismembered bodies, hears only the screams and groans, reacts only with revulsion or contempt. Being unable to differentiate between the real and the surreal, they consistently misinterpret horror fans' interaction with texts that mean nothing to them. (1997, p. 61)

Horror fans are knowledgeable, and seemingly not scared by horror, given their 'educated', metaphorical, and allegorical rather than literalist readings. Aware of horror's conventions and representations, fans actively 'read' aesthetically and thematically, whereas for Kermode, non-fans appear to watch naively, as if what is represented onscreen is somehow affectively 'real'. On one of the rare occasions when Kermode links fear to the position of the horror fan, this is not a fear of any horror film but is instead, tellingly, a fear of not knowing enough about the genre (1997, p. 58).

The possibility consistently discursively warded off is that the fan may actually experience fear in response to a horror text. Shockers can be 'groundbreaking' when experienced (1997, p. 58), but what they *do not* (or must not, in this account) provide for fans are 'a test of machismo [or] passing scares' (1997, p. 60). We are told that fans get 'more out of the movies than' this, 'watching them again and again, learning them, studying them' (ibid.). Kermode thus aligns the fan with the figure of the scholar: fans, unafraid and triumphant, master their beloved horror texts through repeated viewing and aesthetic *study*. His account hence works to construct an image of the generic community (Altman 1999, p. 161), and a sense of what it means to be a horror fan, discursively privileging knowledge over affect. In this regard, it fits with Julian Hoxter's (2000) work on 'cult learning' and horror film: 'Those [fans] who use an accumulation of knowledge to evade the emotional experience of ... [horror films] ... may in their own right be taking possession ... [of these films] ... in making ... [them] ... their own area of expertise' (2000, p. 185). Although Kermode attributes the 'test of machismo' only to inauthentic fans or casual consumers, his own discursive substitution of fan knowledge for affect actually has the result of portraying fans as 'tough' or 'hard'. Fans do not 'cringe'. They get the in-joke rather than being grossed-out:

> horror fans often deny that horror films frighten them. Within certain circles, the very value of watching these films, or at least the value of saying certain things about that viewing experience, is to assert that they do not frighten but only amuse ... within certain contexts, it would be inappropriate (other than in exceptional circumstances) to admit to being frightened by horror films. (Jancovich 2000, p. 32)

I will return to the question of 'exceptional circumstances', but here I am arguing that Kermode's account attempts to valorize horror fan practices via discourses of fan 'literacy' and knowledge rather than affect or emotion. A further instance of fan knowledge and cultural/generic discrimination is recounted in Brigid Cherry's survey and analysis of female horror fans (1999). Whereas Mark Kermode's masculinist, subcultural account (Hollows 2003) centres on the metaphorical/allegorical artistry of gore effects, Cherry's female fans favoured 'subtle' horror:

> Viewers preferred to watch films they took to be imaginative, intelligent, literary or thought-provoking. Dislike was often expressed for films that revolved around excessive or gratuitous displays of violence, gore or other effects used to evoke revulsion in the audience. (Cherry 1999, p. 195)

Other markers of 'quality' favoured by these female fans were 'high production values in art direction, set design and costumes, [a]cting' and 'plot and characters' (1999, p. 194). These 'aestheticizing' criteria, it should also be noted, fly in the face of those used by the (predominantly male) 'Film Swappers' studied by Göran Bolin (2000), who favoured extreme gore in the texts they canonized, moving closer to the aesthetic criteria endorsed by Kermode (1997).

This provides some evidence for gendered interpretative communities within horror fan subculture, but before overly reifying gender differences it is important to recall the similarities as well as differences across such inter-pretations; Cherry's (1999) female fans may favour 'subtle' horror, while Bolin's (2000) 'underground' male fans favour 'splatter', but both groups nevertheless continue to demarcate and valorize their preferences via debates over horror's aesthetics.

These various analyses and expressions of horror fandom indicate that pleasure is narrated and discursively constructed in specific ways by horror fan cultures. Contra many theorists' text-derived focus on horror as 'scary', cognitively challenging or 'uncanny' (see Part I), fans' expressed pleasures typically appear to be those of connoisseurship rather than fear, disgust, intellectual hesitation or ideological subversion/reaffirmation. Connoisseurship secures the distinctiveness of fan subcultural identities, also allowing for differential bids for (sub)cultural value, as well as contesting the authority over horror's circulation that is exercised legally by State censors (see the following chapter).

But how do fans deal with their experiences of the horror genre which cannot, by definition, be discursively constructed as 'knowledgeable', that is, their first encounters with horror? The beginning of Mark Kermode's 'becoming-a-fan' story runs as follows:

> I ... sensed from the very beginning that there was something incompre-hensibly significant about the actions being played out on-screen, something which spoke to me in a language I didn't quite understand ... I felt from the outset that beyond the gothic trappings these movies had something to say to *me* about *my* life. I just didn't have any idea what. (1997, p. 57)

Kermode's initial experience of becoming a fan, prior to his adopting a social role within fan culture, is romanticized and shrouded in mystery in this self-description. It is 'self-absent' because Kermode seemingly cannot provide reasons for his liking of horror at this biographical point (the horror-as-art discourse does not emerge until he is discussing the fan community's shared interpretations and valorizations of horror, e.g. 1997, p. 61). Instead, Kermode's account stresses the powerful impact that late-night horror films had on his child-self:

> At around 11.00, when everyone else was in bed, I would sneak down into the family living room and sit entranced by a selection of creaky ... horror flicks, usually from the Hammer or Amicus stable. No matter that I had to have the volume turned down so far that it was impossible to hear anything that was being said: what was captivating was the electrifying atmosphere, the sense of watching something that was forbidden, secretive, taboo. It was, indeed, my first real experience of discovering something that was uniquely *mine*,

something that existed outside the domain of my parents' control and authority. (1997, p. 57)

In a description otherwise powerfully marked by the insistent repetition of knowingness and readerly competence, Kermode positions his movement into fandom as a transformation that is beyond self-control or self-mastery. Horror might uniquely 'belong' to him, being outside parental jurisdiction, but its textual significance is dimly 'sensed', not fully understood. It could be argued that this is a discourse of Romantic excess that works to valorize the fan by aligning them culturally and narratively with a discourse of 'the lover swept away by their passion'. This is indeed the paradigmatic discourse of affect that Kermode draws on; not that of being scared or fearful, but rather a notion of horror's Romantic 'intensities', and of being overwhelmed by something outside the self that cannot be fully articulated or comprehended at the time (LaFollette 1996, pp. 61–2; Illouz 1997, pp. 173–4). Horror is thus doubly revalued here; it is both part of an artistic lineage/tradition for its community of adult fans, and it is akin to an intensely cherished (and 'possessed') love object for its individual child fan.

This Romantic excess or intensity recurs as a 'discourse of affect' in Charles E. Weigl's academically published self-account of being a horror fan (2002). Again, Weigl links this experience of affective excess to his childhood love of horror:

a childhood fascination sanctioned in recent years, cloaked in the respectable robes of academic research. Truth be told, it has always been more of an obsession than a fascination. When he was a boy [Weigl is writing about his child-self in the third person – MH], from the moment he was able to read the television listings in the newspaper, he spent almost every Saturday afternoon glued to the set for that afternoon's line-up of old horror films. (2002, p. 707)

For both Kermode (1997) and Weigl (2002), knowledge displaces affect, but within a narrative of self rather than as part of an account of horror fan subculture. The discursive problem addressed by 'becoming a horror fan' stories is that while knowledge and 'literacy' can be used to distinguish and revalue the adult, 'tutored' horror fan – the reader of horror's niche magazines and participant in fan cultural activities (Heffernan 2004, p. 226) – such discourses cannot logically or readily account for why horror so affected or inspired the proto-fan in the first place. 'Fascination' or sitting 'entranced' are thus called upon to do this discursive work, without necessarily raising the culturally feminizing spectre of horror as fear provoking. But such 'obsession/fascination' also has to be held partly at bay from the current, rational (and especially academic) self. By conferring this status on the child-self of the past, a discursive distanciation is safely effected.

What such micro-narratives achieve is the discursive production of a contemporary valued self, aligned with cultural norms of rationality and literacy, while aporias in this self-account (how to explain becoming a fan?) are dealt with via performative citation of Romantic intensities, attributed to the past/child self. The fact that this micro-narrative so economically works to position the (masculine) horror fan as beyond cultural reproach may account for its widespread circulation across horror fan cultures. For, as I will now go on to show, it is not at all restricted to academic self-accounts of horror fandom. Versions of this 'before' and 'after' micro-narrative – 'Romantic-intensity-turned-to-cool-knowledgeability' – crop up across a number of horror fan online message boards.

Of course, the recurrence of this structured self-narrative may indicate that horror fans all share a basic (ontological) experience of horror, but I want to suspend that question here. Rather my interest lies, performatively, in *what such an account can do for horror fans*. Kermode (1997) and Weigl (2002) use this style of account to displace the question of adult, male fans being scared by horror. Similar micro-narratives can also be appropriated to allow horror's scares to be discussed without the fan concerned coming to resemble a non-fan, and without cultural codes of masculinity or rational subjectivity being transgressed. In other words horror fans can use this type of self-account to explain what it means to be a horror fan, and/or how they became a fan, while warding off the taint of 'pathologized' horror fandom. Such micro-narratives work partly in the service of hegemonic masculinity (and/or performatively rational subjectivity) by constructing 'anti-effeminate' affective responses to pop-cultural narratives (Warhol 2003, p. 88). However, these self-accounts simultaneously challenge dominant, hegemonic cultural representations of 'weird' horror fans (Jenkins 1992; Jensen 1992; Tudor 1997) by stressing fans' media literacy, education, and knowledge of the genre (Hunt 2003). And they work in the service of fan/non-fan cultural distinctions, separating the intensely affected, diachronic fan from the synchronically scared but non-diachronically affected and more casual moviegoer (for more on non-fans' memories of watching horror films as children, see Kuhn 2002, Chapter 4).

Since I want to move on to discuss a range of online horror fans' postings, it is important to consider the specificity of these as texts (Hills 2002, pp. 175–7). Given that fans are posting to genre-specific message boards, we should not assume that fans' sentiments simply reflect or mirror the offline 'reality' of other fan activities (Bird 2003, p. 81). Postings need to be analysed instead as a specific textual production of fan identity, one that is aimed at a readership assumed to be made up of other horror fans, and also, importantly, a readership that can rapidly indicate its approval or disapproval of any given posting by virtue of the message board's status as asynchronous computer-mediated communication. This degree of interactivity (Flew 2002, pp. 21–2; Burnett and Marshall 2003, p. 52) in relation to 'internal communication' (Bolin 2000,

p. 62) within a fan culture means that it is important to address how subcultural assumptions are drawn on, reinforced and activated by online fans.

As Henry Jenkins has recently put it, rather 'than talking about interactive technologies, we should document the interactions that occur among media consumers' (2002, p. 157). This means treating interactivity not merely as an ideological '"value-added" characteristic ... of new media' (Lister *et al.* 2003, p. 20) but rather as part of a 'user flow' (Caldwell 2003, pp. 135–41) or 'overflow' (Brooker 2003, p. 323) from proprietary texts (e.g. horror films) to different ranges of official/unofficial websites or message boards involving audience-to-audience interactions (see also Altman 1999; Fleming 2000; Skal 2002, pp. 180–1). Analysing such audience interaction, Jenkins uses the work of Pierre Lévy, *Collective Intelligence: Mankind's Emerging World in Cyberspace* (1999), to argue that:

> Online fan communities are the most fully realized versions of Lévy's cosmopedia. They are expansive self-organizing groups focused around the collective production, debate, and circulation of meanings, interpretations and fantasies in response to various artifacts of contemporary popular culture. (Henry Jenkins 2002, p. 158)

Lévy's 'cosmopedia' (1999, pp. 214–20) is a vast knowledge space divorced from territorialization, a collective intelligence made 'accessible to us through computer technology for the representation and dynamic management of knowledge' (1999, p. 216). Lévy uses the image of knowledge as a patchwork quilt 'in which each point can be folded over on any other' so that the cosmopedia 'dematerializes the boundaries between different types of knowledge. It dissolves the differences between specializations' (1999, p. 217; see also Bird 2003, pp. 51–85 on the image of the 'cyber-quilt'). However, it remains important to consider the ways in which online fan cultures do not *always* 'dissolve differences between specializations'. Quite to the contrary, they may enact their own forms of specialized fan knowledge. For example, if a horror message board posting does not resonate with subcultural knowledge then it is likely to become the subject of flaming and abuse, or to languish unanswered (Hodkinson 2002, p. 180). The skill that posters are required to display when initiating threads of discussion is thus that of articulating shared assumptions within the fan culture. Within the context of new media use, then, those fans who post to horror-related message boards are necessarily involved in more or less successfully articulating textualized subcultural identities. The more productive a thread is in prompting positive or affirming responses, the more readily it can be interpreted as a successful subcultural performative – a successful 'doing' of being a horror fan, which other fans iterate in their responses. And the more a posting receives abusive or querying responses, then the more it can serve to demarcate the boundaries to appropriate fan cultural identity. The 'knowledge space' or cosmopedia of online horror fandom is thus collective and interactive, but it is also collectively and interactively *constrained*, limited to bounded performances of fan subcultural identity. The connoisseurship that online fans display is thus always a badge of appropriate belonging, and an articulation of subculturally defended norms concerning 'what it means to be a horror fan'.

To take one example of this process, the now-defunct Horrorentertainment.com message board contained a section headed 'deep discussion', this being separated from news and reviews. One thread, headed 'Is it possible for a film to scare hardcore horror fans?', enacted the discursive separation of horror's 'scariness' from reactions of 'real' horror fans. The very fact that such a question made sense to a number of respondents indicated that 'adult' horror fandom was being constructed here *not* as a matter of textually provoked affect or emotion, but rather as the absence of such affect. The range of responses also indicated that this poster had successfully articulated a fan cultural identity premised on shared subcultural norms. The thread begins: 'one member stated that no horror film had truly scared him since he was a child', with the poster going on to observe that:

> Nowadays the scares are rare. Granted I do still jump on occasion. But how long has it been since a new movie rocked my world? I honestly cannot say ... Perhaps it's part growing up, and part absence of a truly horrifying picture released in recent years? (Sulla, 1 April 2002, 10:25pm)

This post positions the fan's openness to the text as a childhood experience, implying that to be scared or horrified by horror is inappropriate for the 'hardcore' and grown-up fan. But at the same time a desire is indicated for horror to return to its scariness of old, implying that openness to the text is not univocally disavowed, but is also a potentially positive experience that inferior horror films cannot deliver. The fan's loss of self is hence both discursively absented and valued. This is a version of the 'Romantic-intensity-turned-cool-knowledgeability' self-account in which Romantic intensity remains desired even while it is both nostalgically cast into the past and simultaneously related to an adult connoisseurship, being 'part absence of a truly horrifying picture released in recent years'.

Not all the responses to this thread on Horrorentertainment.com drew so directly on a series of 'child' versus 'adult' and 'affected' versus 'detached' oppositions. One poster simply asserted that they 'have never been scared by any movie', thus contrasting 'real' scares ('when my daughter ran away from home' – Borgosi, 4 April 2002, 05:37pm) to film's unreality. This also blocks out fan affect, challenging fan stereotypes (Jenkins 1992) by drawing on a binary of fantasy/reality and aligning the fan with 'the real'. However, it is worth noting that this response remains a micro-narrative of self; horror is still given meaning here as non-scary in relation to a significant event in the poster's life as a parent (for this, read 'adult'), just as Sulla invokes 'growing up' as one reason for a relative lack of scary movies. It could thus be argued that this response emphasizes 'cool' knowingness rather than desired or nostalgic Romantic intensity, while continuing to assert the poster's adult identity.

Further responses on this message board accepted that fans could be scared by horror films, but differentiated between the degrees of fear that horror may inspire:

> I do believe that it is possible to scare horror fans but I do not think that it is applicable for a horror fan to be scared to the point where he or she cannot get to sleep for days on end. I think the scares only come in minor increments. (Gothic, 11 June 2002, 12:08am)

As in Kermode's (1997) account, this respondent goes on to emphasize fans' awareness of 'all of the genre flicks in the world', suggesting that generic knowledge works to reduce the possibility of an affective/fearful response. And once again, the issue of temporality is discursively introduced, although this is a reversal of Kermode's differentiation between non-fans who are momentarily scared and fans who are not scared but who are moved and affected by horror so that the genre becomes a part of their ongoing project of self. Gothic's posting maintains the distinction between fans and non-fans that Kermode's account demarcates, but reframes this as a distinction between non-fans who cannot sleep for days versus fans who might be scared, but only in far more contained, momentary ways. What this discursive manoeuvre achieves is a binary opposition that confers irrationality on non-fans of horror – what is the matter with these people that they cannot sleep for days? – while conferring rational subjectivity on the fan who is scared, but only in 'minor increments'. What could threaten fan identity as an excessive or 'effeminate' affective reaction (Warhol 2003) is again recuperated as rational and culturally normative in this fan's discursive construction of horror's pleasures. Being too scared, where pleasure tips into displeasure, is discursively demarcated as the typical lot of non-fans rather than knowledgeable fan-connoisseurs.

In contrast to these discussions, fans posting to the newsgroup alt.horror were seemingly happier to make a conventional link between horror films and their affective power. In two specific threads, fans discussed what made a 'good' and scary horror movie. In this case, scariness is variously equated with the 'medium' ('16 mm or grainy colour film' is scary, whereas 32 mm 'would not look as frightening' – Robert Aveberry 2002-06-16 20:39:18 PST), with the 'substance' of a horror film (^Tool^, 2002-06-17 02:16:22 PST), or with the pop-cultural context ('it's not scary now – it's so ingrained as a part of pop culture that it's about as scary as the Hamburgler in a home invasion' – blowup, 2002-06-17 08:54:27 PST). Although at first appearing to value horror film as scary, what this different set of definitions achieves is a semiotic and cognitive dispersal, rather than blockage, of fans' openness to the text. That is to say, even where the horrifying nature of horror is supposedly accepted, this itself becomes the subject matter for detailed fan debate and expressions of knowledgeability. Fan mastery is then enacted through the argumentative turn-taking of a newsgroup thread, with horror texts' affective power being variously contested by fans who once more assert their *knowledge*, although this time it is a knowledge *of* the mechanics and aesthetics of fear production rather than 'knowledge' explicitly and discursively opposed to 'emotion'.

Debates over horror's affects and aesthetics are also carried out by online fans via the substitution of 'disturbing' for 'scary'. In this case, fans discuss which horror films or scenes have most disturbed them, as in the thread 'What movie disturbed you the most when watching it' (Calico, 10 August 2003) on the diabolical-dominion.com message board, or the thread 'Most disturbing scenes ever' (pfloyd, 20 July 2003) on the 'Creature Corner' message board (www.chud.com). In each of these instances fans debate the effectiveness of horror films and/or specific scenes without direct reference to these being 'scary'. 'Disturbing' horror is defined by both of these fan groups as something clearly distinct from scariness:

> What movie disturbed you the most when watching it. It doesn't even have to be bloody or scary. (Calico, 10 August 2003)

> I almost posted my list of most disgusting scenes, but that's not the same as most disturbing, right? And that's different from scary, too. (Mad Dog Mike, 21 July 2003)

'Disturbing' horror appears to be discursively constructed by these fans as a textual aesthetics that deals with extreme and unsettling representations, without necessarily showing gore (hence it is not 'disgusting' horror) or necessarily scaring the fan. To be disturbed is hence figured as an imaginative, conceptual response; horror is once again treated here as at least partially non-affective or disembodied. It is contextualized and valorized as a 'mind genre' of aesthetic extremes and devices rather than an a priori 'body genre' that possesses any sensationalist or literalist effectivity.

Despite these variations, fan cultural norms concerning micro-narratives of child/adult and fan/non-fan distinctions are most insistently reiterated in online displays of connoisseurship, occurring across a wide range of horror message boards. For instance, long-term fandom is displayed by the vast majority of posters on the 'Freddy vs. Jason' message forum (www.fridaythe13thforum.com) responding to a thread entitled 'How old were you when you first got into horror?' Again, there is a certain discourse of fan subcultural-authenticity-turned-life-story structured into the very heading, which presupposes a 'first' moment of horror fandom existing at some distance from the implied adult fan self. 'How old ...?' can thus be read as 'How young ...?' The question provokes fans to performatively display their subcultural identity by indicating the duration of their fandom, and its typically adolescent or pre-adolescent beginnings. Even fans who report that they are in their teens tend to locate the 'origin story' of their fandom many years in the past:

> I'm turning 15 at the start of september and I was brought into horror when I was 7 and my bro brought home Noes, I go hook on those and I soon got hooked on Friday movies when I was 9. (bertskarzi196, 14 July 2003)

> I'm currently 18, and I got into it, probably around 5 years old, with Friday the 13th: The Final Chapter. (James M, 16 July 2003)

> I started loving horror at the age of 4 and I'm 14 now. (RekeHavok, 17 July 2003)

This thread allows fans to construct the 'moment' at which their fandom began, and this is usually located in childhood or adolescence, positioned in contrast to their current age. Duration of fandom is iterated and insistently emphasized, as well as an initiating Romantic intensity that is fixed as a childhood experience. This allows fan to distinguish between when they first got into horror (i.e. when they were not knowledgeable fans, but were affected children), and their later fandom, as well as distinguishing them from casual consumers of horror by stressing their 'enduring fandom' (Kuhn 1999). This subcultural assumption that horror fandom is enduring and has its roots in the fan's childhood is reproduced in a questionnaire posted to the horror message board at horror.net ('Can you fill in my horror survey?', Cathy, 16 October 2001). This asked 'What was the first film that ever scared you?' as well as 'What is the most recent film that scared you?', thus allowing fans to micro-narrate differences between their younger and current selves. One respondent's distinction between 'first' and 'most recent' scary films offered up a particularly instructive, implicit micro-narrative of self; his first scary film was *When a Stranger Calls* (1979, dr: Fred Walton), about which he notes 'I was alone at home … and the first twenty minutes properly freaked me out … I kept staring at the phone on top of the tv, waiting for the psycho to call me up' (Mikael, 17 October 2001). Thus, while the younger self is 'properly freaked out', and appears to display a modality confusion (switching between real and fictional modalities, as in 'waiting for the psycho to call me up'), the current, rational fan-self appreciates the aesthetics or 'moodscape', writing very articulately and expressively about *Requiem for a Dream* (2000, dr: Darren Aronofsky), and expertly selecting specific scenes as especially 'scary'.

In fact, Mikael's emphasis on specific scenes is an act of discerning connoisseurship that is often repeated on other horror message boards. Though fans generally display an interest in discussing their favourite films (e.g. a thread on Horrorfind.com, 'Favourite Horror Movie?', Zombie_Child, 29 May 2003), this connoisseurship is often more precisely located around effective scenes rather than dealing with films treated as wholes. In this regard, horror fans display a tendency to fracture and fragment films, combining auteurist readings with types of reflexively affect-focused interpretation where moments are grouped together across discrete texts on the basis of their power or intensity. The thread 'Last movie that actually made you jump in your seat?' (Evil Ash, 13 August 2003) on the upcominghorrormovies.com message board rapidly becomes concerned with scenes rather than with 'whole' films, while on terroraustralis.net another popular thread deals with the issue of 'Scenes that Scare' (Drexl, 11 June 2003). This classification of horror texts thus hinges not so much on an 'author-function' (Foucault 1979) as on a type of 'affect-function', but one where fan knowledgeability again comes into play in terms of fans' ability to list particular scenes within films. That is, rather than simply picking out 'scary movies', the identification of key scenes again allows for a clearer performance of fan knowledge and connoisseurship. Affect is invoked, but knowledge once more offers an insulation from horror's scare stories by virtue of the very form of the debate, where fans construct detailed links between a network of genre texts, for example:

(1)   The Changeling – the playback of the tape recording.
(2)   Ringu – you know the one, I do not need to tell you.
(3)   The Eye (2 points) – the elevator scene and the corridor scene.
(4)   The Shining – those creepy twins.

Opinions? (Drexl, 11 June 2003.)

However, even these lists of 'scary scenes' also continue to present versions of 'child' versus 'adult', and 'affected' versus 'detached' micro-narratives of self. Reply 2 on the terroraustralis.net thread comments that:

> This has no effect on me anymore, because I've seen it a zillion times, but it's what got me into horror in the first place; all the scenes when Michael Myers jumps into sudden attack in Halloween 2. (Pando, 11 June 2003)

Similarly, the upcoming horrormovies.com thread is introduced as follows:

> I've come to the sad realization that I have over exposed myself to horror movies and almost nothing creeps me out or startles me in movies anymore. I remember when I was younger I would dwell on a movie for days after watching it and still be freaked out. Sadly not anymore. (Evil Ash, 13 August 2003)

Both posts activate versions of what I have termed the 'Romantic-Intensity-turned-cool-knowledgeability' self-account, nostalgically lamenting the loss of horror's powerful affects while distancing the knowing, adult fan from their former child-self. My argument here is that this style of account occurs repeatedly across horror message boards due to the fact that it offers a skeletal or minimalist construction of fan identity that fans can subscribe to in order to demonstrate their distinctiveness from non-fans, while also discursively managing the 'problem' of horror's affects and pleasures so that fans do not self-represent as displaying 'effeminate' affects (Warhol 2003) or irrational behaviours within their media consumption.

So far in this chapter I have used a range of online fan postings to analyse how fans produce a sense of their subcultural distinctiveness. One way in which this is achieved is through reading horror as art, but another route into fan distinction occurs via the construction of fan autobiography, typically narrated as an indicator of long-term and authentic fandom, but also produced as a performative construction of adult detachment versus inspiring childhood intensities. Fans thus intently theorize and discursively construct the pleasures of horror, both in relation to 'subcultural' and 'autobiographical' levels of valorization. It is not only the case that horror's pleasures are debated and discursively restricted in academic arguments: online horror fan culture is no less restrictive than academia in its construction of specific narratives and discourses of pleasure. Where academic accounts use psychoanalysis or cognitive philosophy to explore, and discursively fix, horror's pleasures, online fans rely on recurrent, iterated micro-narratives of the genre and their knowing involvements with it. And where academic accounts of horror have seemingly taken for granted its status as 'scary' (e.g. Carroll 1990), online fans variously narrate their subcultural, knowledgeable identities in discursive opposition to 'scariness', or treat horror's scares reflexively, as something to be catalogued, dissected and debated within further displays of fan expertise. In the next section I will explore another set of fan practices through which texts are aestheticized, addressing interpretations of horror's special effects (SFX).

RECOGNIZING HORROR'S SFX CRAFTSMANSHIP

Appreciating the craftsmanship of SFX works yet again to position horror as artful, but it also simultaneously decentres fans' approaches to auteurism. Reading horror via its SFX creates a network of author functions: rather than entirely classifying a film through its director as *the* 'source' of meaning, horror films can also be classified by fans according to their lead SFX designers and creators. It therefore makes sense for books target-marketed at horror fans to discuss the SFX work of Dick Smith, Rick Baker, Rob Bottin, Steve Johnson and Stan Winston (as in Salisbury and Hedgcock 1994), as well as, say, analysing the films of Wes Craven and David Cronenberg. This multiple classification of different authorships (the director-as-*auteur* alongside the SFX technician-as-craftsman) appears to broadly distinguish fan from academic interpretative communities. As Pamela Church Gibson has written of H.R. Giger's work on *Alien* (1979, dr: Ridley Scott):

in all the mass of critical literature, there are only very brief references to ...
[Giger's] work ... It is within the non-academic [i.e. fan and industry/
promotional] work centred around the series that Giger receives his due
recognition. But why should he be acknowledged and discussed only within
the pages of magazines devoted to special effects ... ? (2001, p. 45)

In the case of academia, horror continues to be valued rather more uni-
dimensionally through institutionalized norms of auteurism. SFX are typically
studied thematically rather than in relation to specific SFX creators: compare
Salisbury and Hedgcock (1994) with Pierson (2002). And where academic work
does argue that 'cinematic style (as well as authorial consistency) can be located
in the fields of ... effects-direction' (Bukatman 2003, p. 82; see also Gallardo C.
and Smith 2004, pp. 23–7) then this brand of argument tends to be produced by
scholars drawing on fan classifications within their academic work (or drawing
on their own subcultural identities as fans as well as academics).

The academic study of special effects has also tended to approach SFX through
the assumption 'that effects are virtually synonymous with science fiction'
(Barker with Austin 2000, p. 82). For Michele Pierson, SFX have a privileged
place in the genres (horror/fantasy/science fiction) that make up 'the ...
cinefantastique' (2002, p. 106), but it remains the case that science fiction is the
space for 'special' SFX. Horror's effects 'bear repetition' as markers of genre, but
supposedly do not function as markers of SFX development or novelty (2002, p.
102). Science fiction's SFX, by contrast, are the more pioneering and groundbreaking, arriving ahead of their time and before they have grown 'familiar'.
There is an aesthetic valorization at work here: where science fiction film
innovates, horror merely reiterates. Such a narrative has been contested by
horror's fans and scholar-fans:

John McCarty says that *Blood Feast* by Herschell Gordon Lewis (1963) was
the 'first of the gore films' – and he should know, since he coined the term
'splatter film' ... Another gore landmark was George Romero's *Night of the
Living Dead* (1968), which became a hit on the midnight cult film circuit.
Gore crossed over into mainstream cinema in 1973 with *The Exorcist* ... The
growth of gore is obviously tied to the development of new methods and
technologies for creating special effects in films ... Specialty books about
horror masters emphasize the industrywide effect of advances made in
particular films, such as the Oscar-winning special effects by Rick Baker ...
in *An American Werewolf in London* (1981). (Freeland 2000, pp. 241 and 243)

Special effects, I would argue, are 'special' (that is, novel) in some horror films
just as they are in some science fiction movies, and it makes little sense to a
priori prioritize one genre over the other. Thankfully, not all recent scholarly
work has dismissed horror fans' appreciation of SFX as somehow deficient,
trivial, or wholly complicit with industry/promotional discourses (see Church

Gibson 2001; Hunt 2003; and on fan interest in SFX as 'commodified' knowledge, see Klinger 1991). Martin Barker and Kate Brooks, for example, have put forward the notion of 'doubled attention' to explain how horror's fan audiences make use of special effects:

> It seems that in watching horror ... we frequently manage the experience by insisting on the separation of experiencing and experiencing-as-effects. If we can do this, there is always a place to retreat to, saying to ourselves 'They made that scary, by doing that'. We are frightened, or disturbed, or jumpy, or startled. But that experience can be, sometimes but not always, made manageable, even pleasurable, by the doubled attention of knowing that this is an effect of an 'effect'. If we cannot maintain the distinction, then the pleasure goes. We are simply scared ... *It is of course possible to specialise in one half of the double attention. This is what horror fans in effect do.* (Barker and Brooks 1998, pp. 284–5, my italics)

The notion of 'doubled attention' is also somewhat prefigured in Isabel Pinedo's discussion of horror's SFX:

> Awareness of artifice ... is ... an essential ingredient of recreational terror. The combination of realism and artifice in special-effects violence allows the bored viewer who needs to spike the experience to focus on the realism ('pretend it's real') while simultaneously allowing the overstimulated viewer verging on terror to focus on the artifice without abandoning a sense of realism ('pretend it's fake'). Recreational terror ... depends on the tension between special-effects realism and awareness of its artifice. (Pinedo 1997, p. 55)

Where Barker and Brooks suggest straightforwardly that 'horror fans' specialize in one half of doubled attention – treating effects as effects – Pinedo offers a more sensitively gendered reading of this process, arguing that:

> culturally, males are expected to display bravado and unflinching vision, whereas females are expected to cower and look away. The instruction that these magazines provide about special-effects technology allows the fan viewer to distance him or herself from depictions of violence by looking for the trick, for example, the cut from the actor to the prosthetic device ... Looking for ruptures in realism is the counterpart to not-seeing or looking away. (Pinedo 1997, p. 57)

Despite the generic 'him or herself' in this account, it seems clear that Pinedo associates 'looking for the trick' with a masculinized reading strategy. Where females are supposed to perform their femininity by looking away, male fans can supposedly shield themselves from horror's affects by focusing on the techniques of SFX. Although empirical work on horror's audiences has notably disputed the idea that 'looking away' is an inevitable feminine response (see Cherry 1999), work on female horror fans has reinforced the sense that such fans are far less interested in SFX than their male *Fangoria*-reading counterparts. As Brigid Cherry puts it, the 'emphasis on gore as the reason for disliking most horror magazines reflected the tastes of the participants [female horror fans – MH], and, in particular, the dislike of gory, special-effects driven horror films' (Cherry 2002, p. 50).

Thus, despite Pinedo's relatively simplistic equation of 'looking away' with the female audience and 'looking for ruptures in realism' with the male audience, it appears to be the case that female horror fans do not quite read horror's SFX in the same way that many male fans do. Accounts of horror fandom which claim to represent horror fan subculture, such as that of Mark Kermode (1997), can thus again be read as falsely generalizing accounts that reflect on the experience of sections of anti-effeminate (Warhol 2003) and masculinized horror fandom:

> Directors, writers, actors, even special effects men, all become recognisable to devotees who provide the hard-core fan-base for the genre. Through the pages of *Fangoria* – and later *Gore Zone* – we had met these people in their natural surroundings, seen photographs of them goofing around with severed latex heads, and read their behind-the-scenes accounts of how the movies got made. (Kermode 1997, p. 60)

Kermode's 'we' does not seem to include the female fans analysed by Pinedo (1997) and Cherry (1999 and 2002). Although Kermode's account backs up Barker and Brooks's notion of one-sided double attention (indeed Barker and Brooks 1998, p. 285 cite it to support their argument), Kermode also places an emphasis on the technical artistry of SFX, stressing – as many fans do – the importance of SFX designers and technicians such as Tom Savini and Dick Smith. These SFX men are clearly treated as *auteurs* of a sort within sections of horror fandom and in associated magazines such as *Cinefex* (see Pierson 2002, pp. 133–4), *Fangoria* (Conrich 2000), *The Dark Side* (Jancovich 2000, pp. 28–9) and *Cinefantastique* (Sanjek 2000, p. 316). It is therefore important to amend Barker and Brooks's (1998) emphasis on horror fans as displaying a type of 'one-sided double attention' by noting the following:

- One section or faction of male horror fandom forms an interpretative community that reads horror through its SFX as effects, but we should not be overly generalizing about this reading practice, since it tends to exclude many female horror fans and other sections of male horror fandom (Jancovich 2000, pp. 28–9).
- Those male horror fans who do read effects primarily as effects do so by viewing certain effects as authored, relating them to discourses of horror-as-art. 'One-sided double attention' is thus not only about managing the

line between tolerable fear and unacceptable scariness (contra Barker), or about performing a version of 'good' and unflinching masculinity (contra Pinedo); it is also about some 'fans' desire to have the craft of effects ... treated as a legitimate (i.e. authored and hence authorized) form of aesthetic expression' (Pierson 2002, p. 73).

By arguing that horror's special effects are self-reflexively used by sections of horror fandom to sustain and generate a reading of horror-as-art, I am thus suggesting here that film aesthetics do not only precede and 'cause'/incite/invoke audience 'emotions' or 'affects' (contra cognitivist and psychoanalytic assumptions). Fan 'interpretative communities' tend to nominate specific scenes or special effects as particularly noteworthy and artfully achieved, referring these back to directors and to SFX craftsmen. They are not simply reacting to filmic aesthetics here, for their discourses and interpretations are also, in a sense, constructing and framing (hence 'aestheticizing' or multiply 'author-izing') the 'object' itself. However, it is worth remembering that not all horror's SFX are construed as authored, even within SFX-focused fan communities. Certain effects are repeatedly prioritized in fan accounts and 'speciality books' as *special* special effects as opposed to unremarkable or reiterated special effects. Not all FX are equally special. Some sequences, which take on a life of their own outside of their original textual framing via fan histories of horror film and other forms of cultural circulation, become key markers of and for SFX technology – for example, Screaming Mad George and *Society* (1989, dr: Brian Yuzna), Dick Smith and *The Exorcist* (1973, dr: William Friedkin) and *Scanners* (1981, dr: David Cronenberg); Rick Baker and *An American Werewolf in London* (1981, dr: John Landis); and Rob Bottin and *The Thing* (1982, dr: John Carpenter). This extra-textual circulation of SFX stills/images therefore partly reflects and partly sustains fans' aestheticizing of horror. In this manner, fan audience investments in horror-as-art are not experienced simply in relation to 'the text itself' (a limitation of Carroll's (1990) account; cf. also Part IV). They are, rather, layered and reinforced through extra-textual 'floating signifiers' such as SFX images extracted from their original narrative frames (and here I am drawing on Bennett and Woollacott's (1987) account of 'popular heroes', but applying this to SFX imagery rather than iconic characters).

Fan practices of aestheticization – indicating a desire for horror to be taken seriously as art – have repeatedly worked to frame horror's pleasures within discourses of fan agency, discrimination and expertise. This discursive splitting between 'active', agentive, genre-educated fans working to read horror-as-art, and 'passive' non-fan consumers subjected to horror's textual affects produces a fan-cultural narrative of horror's pleasures that is strikingly unlike the discourses of pleasure used by cognitive philosophers, literary scholars and psychoanalytic critics (see Part I). For this discursively framed version of horror and pleasure is one in which horror does not act upon the audience. Rather, the audience acts upon horror. Fans' multiply 'author-izing' aestheticizations of horror and its SFX, their displays of knowledge rather than 'emotion', and their discursive constructions of Romantic 'intensities' restricted nostalgically to childhood fan-selves, all suggest that the pleasures of horror cannot be discursively restricted to notions of fear and disgust, or to approaches that conceptualize horror's pleasures as emerging through the relationship between a singular text and audience member (single-text approaches such as that of Todorov (1975) are considered in Chapter 2). Instead, fans' constructed and construed pleasures of horror hinge on imagined versions of their 'generic community' (Altman 1999), or subculture, and its distinctions.

To reiterate, I am not contrasting fan discourses of pleasure – somehow assumed to reflect 'real' pleasures – to scholarly discourses that would then be assumed to be idealized, speculative or somehow 'unreal'. Taking a thorough-going performative approach, neither fan nor academic discourses of horror's pleasures have any greater ontological claim: both are precisely constructions, occurring within different (sub)cultural contexts and doing different things for their respective producers. It may hence be no accident that the majority of academic and fan accounts of horror's pleasures are so radically disconnected from one another: where academics all too frequently assume that horror's pleasures are a 'paradox' that they alone can heroically and logically resolve, fans assume that horror's pleasures are produced through their own discernment, activity/agency and subcultural knowledge. Both academic and fan subcultures hence performatively claim agency for themselves while denying it to imagined Others. Academics assume that they can actively explain horror texts while its audiences are passively and emotionally subjected to the genre's products (either due to 'under-cognitive' psychoanalytic mechanisms or 'over-cognitive' emotional responses). By contrast, fans assume that they can actively explain horror – using notions of genre history, production history and aesthetics rather than theoretical terminologies – whereas non-fans or casual consumers of the genre are passively subjected to its scares. Horror's fans and professional philosophers may well share one thing, then: unshakeable faith in their subculture's ability to legitimate and make sense of the horror genre.

But what are the discursive and cultural limits to the powers *over* horror that fans discursively claim in opposition to the 'powers *of* horror' which are assumed elsewhere in much academic discussion and in media effects reportage? This takes us into the concerns of the next chapter: censorship, and fan practices of 'rebelliousness' in the face of State legal powers. I will argue that such practices – bootlegging and illicit film swapping (Bolin 2000) – need to be addressed as highly constrained and situated fan performances of 'activity'. Without a system of censorship to oppose, the distinctiveness of horror fans' subcultural identity would be greatly reduced, as would connotations of 'subversion', masculinized 'daring', and foreign 'exoticism' that have become attached to the horror genre by virtue of various, nationally specific censorship systems.

Chapter 5

Challenging Censorship

So far in this part I have argued that horror fans discursively construct the pleasures of horror in relation to their own life stories, via forms of connoisseurship, and through the aestheticization of horror and its SFX. All these narratives of horror's pleasure revolve around emphasizing the agency and activity of the specific fan or fan culture. I have therefore suggested that in fan practices, horror is viewed as pleasurable not so much for the way that it scares fans – this affective reaction is typically attributed to non-fans by those self-identifying within horror fandom – but rather for the way that horror texts can be used to perform and display types of agency, whether this is a knowledge of narrative worlds, of specific aesthetics, or of production and genre histories. Through a range of practices, horror fans enact their fan-cultural distinctiveness, and perform their ability to do things with horror, rather than discursively framing their encounter with the horror genre as one of being affected by it. And where horror *is* viewed as affective, then this is very much contextualized within an ongoing and reflexive, subcultural project of the self, rather than as a matter of specific, momentary or irrational 'scares'.

Such fan practices resemble, but are not identical to, the 'textual poaching' (Jenkins 1992) that has been said to characterize media fandom (although Jenkins's focus is really on cult TV and telefantasy fans). Fans viewed as textual poachers take certain meanings from texts or, more recently, they have been able to produce their own digital texts that support readings of an originating text (see Brooker 2002; Jenkins 2003). By contrast, horror fans' agency performed and displayed through interpretations and aestheticizations of horror texts – 'textual agency' rather than 'textual poaching' – does not seek to appropriate characters or shift textual meanings *per se*. Instead, it is concerned with discursively positioning horror within temporal frameworks (both personal and generic) in order to discursively convert affective responses into knowledgeable reactions. It is hence concerned with constructing horror fandom as a matter of knowledge/literacy rather than as emerging through a purely or predominantly affective response. This discursive 'warding off' of affect can be viewed partly in relation to cultural norms of gender and masculinity (Warhol 2003), but it is also partly a matter of warding off horror's attribution as a low or 'body genre' (Linda Williams 1999) and hence bidding for its cultural value (Hills 2004e).

Where notions of 'textual poaching' broadly engage with debates over audience activity, forming part of what has been termed 'active audience theory', what I am terming horror fans' 'textual agency' needs to be viewed as thoroughly performative rather than ontological; that is, horror fan audiences tend to discursively produce their fan identities *as* active. The specific (sub)cultural need for horror fans to produce their fan identities as agentive also emerges in the light of the cultural debates (on 'effects') that have sought to contextualize the genre as powerfully, if not dangerously, affecting. Fans therefore have to 'resist' dominant, culturally preferred meanings of horror not so much at the level of specific horror texts, but rather in relation to the discourses that circulate around horror (in much academic work, as well as in journalistic reportage). Discourses of pleasure constituted in fan practices therefore do not tally with discourses of horror's pleasure as these are constituted in other cultural sites, for example media coverage, much academic work and censorship debates. Where moral panics discursively frame audiences as passive, vulnerable and potentially open to being corrupted or depraved by media content, horror fan interpretative communities consistently position their pleasures as the result of 'active' and knowledgeable spectatorship.

Now, to conclude that such audiences really *are* 'passive' or 'active' would miss the very point that these are positions, and representations, that are fought over within cultural politics, rather than ontologies to be decided between. (Academic debate over the 'active' audience thus tends to mask its own performativity, and its own participation in cultural politics, as a reflection of 'the facts'.) In what follows, then, I will not argue for or against the 'truth' (McKee 2003b, p. 17) of fan audiences' agency. Instead I want to consider how horror fans' discursive performance of textual agency relies, in part, on what it seeks to dispel, that is, the counter-narrative of horror's pleasures as dangerous and in need of regulation/censorship. My argument will therefore be that despite horror fans' frequent opposition to forms of censorship, the distinctiveness of their subcultural identity – particularly its connotations of 'transgression' and 'rebellion' – depends on those meanings that censorship and effects debates confer on the horror genre. Horror fans may well oppose censorship, but they are also semiotically and subculturally indebted to it.

By 'censorship' I am referring to what Shaun Kimber, following Jansen (1990), terms 'regulative censorship': 'With respect to British film censorship this is taken to refer to the collective actions of ... Local Authorities, the British Board of Film Classification, Trading Standards, the Police and Customs' (Kimber 2002, p. 1). Various studies have traced institutional and cultural histories of censorship in this sense (Kuhn 1988; Dewe Mathews 1994; Petley 2000). However, the term censorship is sometimes used in a rather more metaphorical vein: Steffen Hantke has compared 'conventional censorship' to 'academic censorship', with the latter referring to an academic failure to engage with horror's embodiment (2002, p. 6). And displaying a substantive variant on the concept of censorship rather than a metaphorical twist, Annette Hill discusses 'self-censorship', by which is meant 'methods of [personal] choice in relation to watching/not watching violent movies' (1997, p. 51). My discussion of censorship here should be taken to refer only to regulative or 'conventional' censorship. In the first section of this chapter I will consider how UK horror fans' attacks on censorship construct horror's pleasures as a matter of cultural politics and agency, positioning fans as cultural critics, and partly replaying the terms of the academic 'active' audience debate (see, e.g., Fiske 1989 and the commentary of Silverstone 1994, pp. 152–8). I will then move on to consider cultural (and subcultural) citizenship, and how these more recent academic discourses may have begun to supersede discussions of fan 'activity' while operating in a similar way; that is, allowing academics to romanticize and ontologize fans' practices and circumventions of censorship.

CENSORSHIP AS THE ENEMY OF HORROR FANDOM: AN ESSENTIALLY 'ACTIVE' AUDIENCE?

Fans of the horror genre have not always been well represented in academic debates on media censorship, as Shaun Kimber (2002) has pointed out. Kimber interviewed UK 'genre fans', defined as 'people who derive pleasure from the consumption of films which ... transgress established boundaries of taste and decency' (2002, p. 1). However, these fans' pleasures in 'genre' films were taken as an established fact rather than something requiring discursive construction by fan respondents. Pleasure is hence ontologized in Kimber's framework – it is treated as an experience that occurs *to* fans, rather than a theoretically inaccessible experience that is worked over and worked through *by* fans, via discourses of pleasure. Take, for example, comments made by Gordon and quoted in Kimber's audience research:

> I agree with film censorship for social protection only. Like most of today's true horror fans I've managed to see uncut many of the movies that the ... [British Board of Film Classification] deem unfit for general release. I agree with the censors on most of these cuts and exclusions for the general viewing audience. But I also believe some how these titles must be legally available to those who wish to see [them] ... in their intended uncut format. (2002, p. 9)

Kimber discusses the way that fans argue about the 'rights and responsibilities related to the form that film censorship should take' (2002, p. 9). Adopting a seemingly contradictory stance on censorship, fans such as Gordon recognize a need for film regulation while also attacking censorship for its infringement of individual freedoms. Yet Gordon also discursively constructs a specific pleasure of horror viewing in his account when he notes that 'like most of today's true horror fans' he has managed to circumvent BBFC censorship. This fan respondent thus frames 'true' horror fandom as being about a type of transgression: namely, the act of viewing what one should not otherwise legally have access to. Fan pleasures, in this case, are not simply taken in relation to a given horror text. Rather, such pleasures take on a *discursive* existence in relation to the cultural history of the text concerned, and the discursive repertoires within which it has been placed, as well as the material history of its circulation (or lack thereof). Thomas Austin's (2002) work on audiences for Oliver Stone's controversial *Natural Born Killers* (1994) reaches similar conclusions. Austin notes that:

> Viewers could appear 'hip', 'in the know' and/or socially transgressive by watching *Natural Born Killers* ... the statements of respondents attesting to enjoyment of the film could be seen to contribute to their own self-perceptions as beyond the cultural 'mainstream' ... In addition, the film's 'outlaw' status was effectively certified by the BBFC delay in certification, often recalled by respondents as a 'ban'. The film could appear to some as a subcultural artefact which had been misunderstood and interfered with by 'mainstream' institutions such as 'ignorant journalism' and the BBFC. Hence, watching and enjoying *Natural Born Killers* could become a symbolic act of social transgression in itself: a defiance of authority, a message to 'fuck the censors', a rejection of media disapproval. (2002, p. 186)

For 'cult' audiences (Austin 2002, pp. 178–9) of the film, such as those viewing it at a special one-off screening at the independent Prince Charles cinema, London, this discursive construction of textual agency enabled fans to separate themselves out from 'the general viewing audience' as well as from the pathologized 'dangerous' audience that media coverage suggested could be drawn to the film (Austin 2002, p. 180). The act of 'enjoying' films that have been censored, denied a classification, or had their general release delayed, therefore needs to be viewed symbolically and performatively – as in Austin's (2002) work – rather than ontologically, as in Kimber's research (2002). 'Watching and enjoying' *Natural Born Killers* affords fans a route to communicate their subcultural difference and their valued, subcultural transgression of 'mainstream' tastes.

Although Kimber's research usefully cautions us from assuming that horror or genre fans will automatically be opposed to censorship in all forms and instances, it nevertheless retains an emphasis on fans' opposition to the censorship of fictional film violence:

> I think that the censorship of film violence is artistically and morally wrong, oppressive, fascistic, and just plain illogical. Special effects artists like Tom Savini are artists, as are the directors ... who incorporate these crafts into their movies. Censoring their work is like going into an art gallery and

putting stickers onto bits of paintings so that we do not get the full picture. (Dario, quoted in Kimber 2002, p. 5)

This comment returns us to debates considered towards the end of the previous chapter (SFX being mobilized within an aestheticization of horror), but it also indicates an investment in a specific and 'defended' subject position (Hollway and Jefferson 2000, p. 59) – here, that of the 'discerning' and agentive fan. Both Gordon and Dario discursively display their agency as fans by calling censorship practices into question; either fans' subcultural difference should be recognized by the State – 'I also believe some how these titles must be legally available to those who wish to see [them] . . . in their intended uncut format' (Gordon) – or State practices of censorship should be condemned and fought as 'just plainly illogical' (Dario).

Various studies of audiences for violent/controversial films have discussed the 'activity' of appreciative viewers (see Hill 1997, pp. 27–37 and 107–8) rather than explicitly discussing fandom. For example, Martin Barker *et al.*'s excellent study, *The Crash Controversy: Censorship Campaigns and Film Reception* (2001), devotes two chapters (5 and 6) to 'positive' audience responses to the film *Crash* (1996, dr: David Cronenberg), considering in detail how four women and four men valued it (although some of these respondents, e.g. Lindsey, Kelly, Michael and Philip, could be viewed as Cronenberg fans, since they used his other films as an intertextual frame through which to interpret *Crash* (2001, pp. 65 and 93–4)). There is an apparent correlation in these interviews between anti-censorship discourses and 'enjoyment' or appreciation of the film (see 2001, pp. 65–6 and 93–4). Barker *et al.*'s positive respondents variously talk about being 'against censorship of any kind' (Nicola, quoted 2001, p. 65), suggesting that they 'do not want to be dictated to' over what media texts or images they can and can not access (Lindsey, quoted 2001, p. 65), or referring to the 'utterly ludicrous decision to ban the film' (Philip, quoted 2001, p. 94). Michael and Philip, respondents analysed by Barker *et al.*, echo the discourses of Shaun Kimber's (2002) interviewees, articulating 'an overarching political response to the question of censorship' (2001, p. 96) in which it is depicted as 'essentially an irrational process' (2001, p. 98). Michael and Philip offer fan critiques of censorship that share the terms of academic criticisms (e.g. Gauntlett 1995; Barker and Petley (eds) 1997 and 2001; Kermode 1997 and 2002; Fowles 1999, pp. 56–8). Censorship is considered by these fans to be based on ill-informed and unfounded fears, to operate as a form of class-based paternalism, and to derive from discredited, or at best unsubstantiated, behaviouralist assumptions (see Kimber 2002, pp. 6–7).

What such audiences are enacting is a discourse, a performance, of critical agency. It should therefore come as no surprise that such a discourse is, in this instance, shared by fan audiences and academics studying censorship debates. However, unlike fans' argumentative positions, academic work at least has the potential of feeding into 'policy recommendations' (Hill 1997, p. 105) by depicting horror's audiences as 'active', discerning, reflexive, and so on. Such work seeks to challenge representations of horror fans as 'dangerous', 'depraved' or as otherwise culturally pathologized. Arguing that audiences are actively critical of censorship, work in film and cultural studies can then go on to champion or defend such audiences as an extension of its own cultural politics. In such instances, academia appears to argue for and on behalf of fans' subcultural difference. By contrast, censors tend to argue for and on behalf of non-fan cultural groups. Of course, censors are seeking to protectively restrict media access while liberal academics are opposed to this. But the discursive mechanisms at work are strikingly similar – audience groups are discursively ontologized as 'passive' (by censors) or as 'active' (by a range of cultural studies academics), with cultural policy then being argued over on the basis of these moralizing depictions. As Roger Silverstone has put it: 'One can enquire into the ideological force behind the insistence that the audience is active' (1994, p. 153).

How audiences discursively represent their own practices, and how those representations are negated or appropriated in mass media coverage and across regulatory cultural sites, all feed into the morality of cultural 'common sense', and from there (potentially) into cultural policy-making. Thus the active/passive audience debate remains far from being merely a matter of academic nostalgia (Garnham 2000, p. 114). It is itself part of the discursive production of audiences as objects calling for, or refuting, mechanisms of governmental and social control.

Rather than perceiving 'active audience' theory as somehow validated by fans' performances of textual agency, we might instead judge fans' agentive claims as spurious and excessively individualistic. In the case of horror fans, we could conclude that claims to agency are unreal or illusory, being constrained by more powerful strategies of State censorship. This adjudication of 'unreality' would allow our cultural studies perspective the luxury of critical detachment, and the role of ob-scene critique. In line with my previous work on fandom (2002), I would suggest that we must refute any such ontologizing either/or. The allure of the ontological – where academics, and other (sub)cultural groups decide the active or passive 'reality' of a given cultural phenomenon – works to iterate and reinforce deep-rooted cultural distinctions between who 'has' power and who does not, as well as between who is 'rational' and who is not, who is 'critical' and who is not, who is morally sound and who is not, who arbitrates 'true' meaning and who does not.

Refuting an ontology of horror's pleasures in relation to 'active'/'passive' fandom means considering horror's fan audiences within the agenda of 'third generation' audience studies, which has been broadly characterized as 'a constructionist view' (Alasuutari 1999, p. 6). Within this perspective, it is how audiences are discursively constructed, and how audiencehood is performed, that become the central objects of investigation (1999, p. 6). This involves a focus on the '(meta-)discourses within which both media consumption and media scholarship itself are constituted' (Morley 1999, p. 204), and has also increasingly invoked moral questions and discourses (Morley 1999, p. 199; Bird 2003, p. 166). However, the moralities discussed here have largely been restricted to audience performances of citizenship in relation to factual/news media content (Höijer 1999, pp. 183–91), while media fictions have been relegated, by audiences, to the status of 'guilty' pleasures (Morley 1999, p. 201).

As I have already argued, horror fans specifically seek to morally elevate the consumption of horror fiction in order to avoid the pleasures of horror being depicted as dangerously or pathologically self-absent. Such fans are thus somewhat unusual in terms of performing and claiming textual agency via culturally pathologized fictional forms, while also discursively refuting the notion of 'pleasure' as self-absent or as a matter of being acted upon by texts. Taking a 'third-generation' audience studies approach to such claims, we can suggest that horror fans are out of sync with surrounding, 'common-sense' discourses of audience agency/pleasure (Höijer 1999; Morley 1999). For horror fans, 'agency' and 'pleasure' are discursively articulated as agency-pleasure, whereas these terms otherwise tend to be morally opposed by media consumers as (moral) 'agency' versus 'pleasure'; that is, watching the news is what one 'must' do as a cultural agent, or good citizen, before being able to more pleasurably relax and unwind in front of a TV soap (Höijer 1999, p. 183).

Horror fans' articulation of agency-pleasure is, however, closer to academic notions of media consumption and pleasure as essentially active, just as fans' opposition to censorship links them discursively to academic arguments. Where both fans and academics are concerned with discursively revaluing the consumption of popular culture, both subcultures will tend to deploy similar 'meta-' discourses of moral valorization: academics ontologize the 'active' audience, while fans perform textual agency.

In the face of claims and counter-claims over different audiences' 'activity' and 'passivity', to assume that the active/passive audience debate could ever resolve whether audiences really are one thing or the other remains, I am suggesting, a mistaken venture into ontology. 'Activity' and 'passivity' are terms loaded with moral freight, and are reflexively activated by fans and academics alike for their 'ideological force'. For non-academic audiences, 'passive' pleasures are recurrently 'guilty' and are taken in relation to texts that are accepted as culturally devalued or culturally inappropriate to one's performed cultural identity (gender, age, etc.). 'Active' media consumption, by contrast, tends to be discursively claimed by audiences for texts that are accepted as culturally valorized or assumed to be appropriate to one's cultural identity (Morley 1999). These dominant relations are subculturally transgressed by horror fans precisely because the dominant cultural status and value of texts is being challenged here – the otherwise devalued horror genre is revalued, and thus treated as a site for textual agency rather than a source of 'guilty' pleasure.

The problem for fans is not simply that censors definitively have 'strategic' power that they can only oppose by 'tactically' seeking out bootlegs or foreign copies of uncut horror films (de Certeau 1988; Hills 2004d). It is rather that the censors' position of expertise and discernment – their own legally enforced enactment of textual agency, if you like – does not accord with the textual agency performed within horror fan subculture. Máire Messenger-Davis (2001, p. 162) refers to the 'cultural elitism' that horror fans represent in censorship debates, and although we may consider censors to be a more obviously 'elitist' group of readers than fans (given their legal and professional status), Messenger-Davis's accusation does, I think, capture something of the curious homology that pertains between censors and fans. The semiotic and material struggle between fans and censors can be interpreted as one that concerns forms of expertise and what counts as a valid reading of the horror genre – dangerous pop culture, or valorized popular art? Well-educated fans, very high in cultural and subcultural capital (i.e., official level of education and level of fan, subcultural knowledge: see Thornton 1995), will therefore tend to be extremely critical of censors' readings of horror. Censors are attacked for their 'clumsy bludgeoning' of films and their 'genre-illiterate' approach (Kermode 1997, p. 65), as well as for having presided over a 'hundred-year reign of terror' (Kermode 2002, p. 22) by butchering and cutting horror films that fans, as auteurists, feel should be seen in their authorially 'intended' form.

By performing textual agency through horror fictions, fans raise an intriguing possibility: that cultural citizenship may not only occur through the textual agency of news consumption and 'being informed', but may also be enacted through other types of media consumption such as horror fandom. Media fandom in general may have been much analysed in cultural studies (Jenkins 1992; Hills 2002; Gray 2003), but for all that it has rarely been explicitly linked to discussions of citizenship. This relative absence of work on fans-as-citizens is puzzling, especially given the 'cultural turn' in citizenship debates whereby the figure of the 'consumer-citizen' and the notion of 'cultural citizenship' have moved to the fore (see Miller 1993; Isin and Wood 1999; Cronin 2000; García Canclini 2001; Stevenson 2001). In the next section I will therefore consider how horror fans' opposition to, and transgression of, censorship regulations can be theoretically linked to notions of cultural citizenship rather than to notions of audience 'activity'.

CENSORSHIP AS THE ENGINE OF HORROR FANDOM: A DISTINCTIVELY 'TRANSGRESSIVE' AUDIENCE?

Notable exceptions to the absence of work on fan-citizens are the interventions of Joke Hermes (1998) and John Hartley (1999). Hermes examines how the consumption of feminist detective fiction can contribute to 'cultural citizenship':

> The political value of popular culture is to be found in its contribution to citizenship ... First of all, citizenship should be redefined as sets (plural) of practices that constitute individuals as competent members of sets of different

and sometimes overlapping communities one of which should ideally constitute the national (political) culture. (1998, pp. 158–9)

Hermes then goes on to argue that popular culture can provide the 'grounding for a citizen identity' despite existing outside the domain of 'administrative politics' (voting, etc.) (1998, p. 160). Her assumption is that:

> a set of texts will invite its readers to rethink and possibly revalue moral issues and, by implication, the public interest … Reading fiction may … sharpen our democratic abilities and appetite and constitute us as worthy partakers in debates that are vital for democracy. (1998, p. 160)

This view of 'cultural citizenship' and fandom (1998, p. 161) is clearly opposed to more traditional or 'modernist' notions of citizenship, in which the practices of citizenship are assumed to occur through, and in relation to, factual material such as news, and via the terrain of 'administrative politics'. Citizenship, within such discourses, is assumed to operate only as democratic membership of a Nation State, thus depending on an idealized (if not fantasized) 'unified' public sphere and on civic participation. Like Joke Hermes (1998), John Hartley (1999) has also narrated a shift from 'civic' and 'political' citizenship to new, pluralized citizenships based around 'rights of identity', which he terms 'cultural citizenship' and 'DIY citizenship', these being based around 'subcultural identities … taste or fanship of various kinds' (1999, pp. 178–9). Hartley's account very much ontologizes and emphasizes the agency of such audience citizenships:

> The point is, 'citizenship' is no longer simply a matter of a social contract between state and subject, no longer even a matter of acculturation to the heritage of a given community; DIY citizenship is a choice people can make for themselves … there's an increasing emphasis on *self*-determination as the foundation of citizenship. (1999, p. 178)

As with prior active audience theory, this type of approach seeks to equate audience activity with agency (see Silverstone 1994, p. 152) as the 'reality' of what audiences do. However, my 'third-generation' audience studies, interest in cultural citizenship and 'DIY citizenship' – where media texts and the mediasphere provide ways for plural audiences to articulate 'social cohesion based not on sameness but on difference' (Hartley 1999, p. 181) – lies in how discourses of citizenship can be used, academically, to confer moral worth on fans of devalued texts, as well being drawn on by fans to valorize their fan practices. When fans criticize censorship regulations (Barker *et al.* 2001; Kimber 2002) then they perform the role that Hermes' concept of 'cultural citizenship' allocates to readers of popular fiction, developing what can be identified as 'a critical stance' (1998, p. 160). Notions of cultural or subcultural citizenship thus morally elevate media audiences, in effect working as the pedagogic and theoretical inheritors of 'active audience' ideologies.

We might expect the horror fan – as a dedicated and transgressive consumer of censored texts – to show up in discussions of consumer, cultural or audience-citizenship. Horror fan subculture poses questions that could rightfully be viewed as a part of public sphere debate: who has the right to restrict media access, and should subcultures have any right to the cultural expression of their subcultural difference? However, it seems that fans' subcultural identities are not often recognized as a significant form of cultural difference. Although feminist and class-based reworkings of public sphere theory (Fraser 1992; Negt and Kluge 1993) have been significant, with Habermasian work on the public sphere being critiqued for its focus on a singular, unified public sphere rather than a range of public spheres (see Dahlgren 1995, p. 17), considerations of fan identity-politics have by and large failed to address the issue of subcultural citizenship, and whether a fan-based public sphere might exist alongside Habermas's (1989) bourgeois public sphere.

A limited range of scholarly texts have explored this direction; Göran Bolin's article 'Film Swapping in the Public Sphere: Youth Audiences and Alternative Cultural Publicities' draws on Fraser (1992), Negt and Kluge (1993) and Hansen (1990; 1991; 1993) to argue that Swedish horror fans display their own 'alternative cultural public sphere' (2000, p. 57). This concept takes off from Jürgen Habermas's discussion of the literary public sphere:

> Habermas did not use the concept of the cultural public sphere in his *Structural Transformation of the Public Sphere*. When he discussed questions related to other areas than the political, he used the concept of the literary public sphere. This sphere he considered as an early form of the political publicity, the 'training ground for critical public reflection' (Habermas ... 1989, 29). (Bolin 2000, p. 59)

Rosa Eberly's *Citizen Critics: Literary Public Spheres* (2000) also makes use of this Habermasian discussion, analysing how contemporary fiction such as Bret Easton Ellis's novel *American Psycho* (Eberly 2000, pp. 104–32) has provoked and sustained 'critical public reflection' over issues of censorship, art versus popular culture, and 'dangerous' media coverage/publicity. These 'critical' media and public debates all closely replay arguments made by horror fans as to whether censorship is useful, desirable or justifiable, although Eberly (2000) does not focus on fans specifically. Her analysis refers to the 'citizen critic' as a person who 'produces discourses about issues of common concern from an ethos of citizen first and foremost – not as expert or spokesperson for a workplace or as member of a club or organization', thus ruling out experts such as public intellectuals as well as fan experts. Unlike Bolin (2000), Hermes (1998) and Hartley (1999), who view cultural citizenship as emerging through subcultural fan communities, Eberly (2000) appears to oppose citizenship interests, discourses and concerns to specialized interest groups such as fan/academic subcultures; her work thus implicitly returns to the Habermasian (1989) ideal of a unified polity and citizenry that these other writers seek to fracture.

Beyond literary public spheres, there are other proto-publics discussed by Habermas that might also be profitably related to the notion of subcultural citizenship. For example, Jodi Dean (2002) has drawn attention to Habermas's discussion of secret societies:

> Although Jürgen Habermas's theory of the bourgeois public sphere is widely read for its account of publicity as the rational achievement of Enlightenment universality, it also, and perhaps surprisingly, acknowledges the constitutive place of the secret. Taking up the practices out of which the sense of a public sphere emerged, Habermas includes in his account of salons and coffee-houses the secret societies typical of Freemasonry. (Dean 2002, p. 29)

Dean then goes on to cite Habermas's relevant analysis:

> The decisive element was not so much the political equality of the members but their exclusiveness in relation to the political realm of absolutism as such: social equality was possible at first only as equality outside the state. *The coming together of private people into a public was therefore anticipated in secret, as a public sphere still largely existing behind closed doors.* (Habermas 1989, p. 35, my italics)

Pointing out that the 'usual emphasis on Habermas's discussion of the family and the literary public thus needs to be complicated' (2002, p. 30), Dean's emphasis on secret proto-publics, gathered 'outside' the State and in private, resonates with notions of 'underground' horror fan subculture and its 'Film-Swappers' (Bolin 2000, p. 61). Resembling the Habermasian literary public sphere, horror fans gather together to performatively activate and debate the aesthetics of horror 'through which an audience-oriented (*publikumsbezogen*) subjectivity [can] communicate ... with itself' (Habermas 1989, p. 29). Simultaneously resembling the secret societies of the Freemasons, underground horror fan subculture occurs 'behind closed doors', as it were, partly by virtue of the technical illegality of viewing censored texts uncut, and partly because the subculture is, of course, disarticulated from the State while simultaneously stressing its 'distance' from the norms, tastes and decencies of the 'mainstream'. Although not a secret society, horror fandom – specifically at the 'underground' end of the spectrum of horror fan identities – nevertheless positions itself as transgressive, and thus reflexively participates in connotations of secrecy, illegality, extremism (of representation) and deviance. To an extent, then, the cultural pathologization of horror audiences that tends to be opposed by fans closer to the 'mainstreamed' field of horror (and academics studying horror, e.g. Tudor 1997), may in fact be welcomed and embraced by 'transgressive' fans. For these fans, textual agency becomes linked not just to the critique of censorship regulations, or to the aestheticization of horror, but also to the evasion of State censorship policies and the performance of masculinized, transgressive 'toughness'. There is thus an investment in horror's lack of respectability and cultural marginality here, an investment that, on occasion, discursively migrates from fan practices to those of academics studying horror (see Hantke 2002, p. 8 and Read 2003).

Stressing the marginality and 'secrecy' of horror fan subculture – its self-identified 'underground' nature – may link these subcultural practices by analogy to Habermas's proto-public of the 'Secret Society'. However, we should consider that the conceptual splitting between 'literary', 'proto-', and 'public spheres' is a significant theoretical problem. Habermas refers to the 'political public sphere (as distinguished from a literary one, for instance)' as occurring 'when ... public discussions concern objects connected with the practice of the state' (1989, p. 231). But any demarcation of 'literary' (or cultural) versus 'political' public spheres can only succeed in reifying 'politics' as something that exists in some imagined or idealized sphere and not in others. Any such approach would fail to note that the 'political public sphere ... is not so much a physical place as it is an occurrence: any time two or more individuals come together to discuss matters of politics the public sphere takes place' (McAfee 2000, p. 83). And if this is so, then horror fans' discussions of censorship, for instance via fanzines' cataloguing of different film edits or via the 'summarizing [of] a restricted film's plot' (Kermode 1997, p. 64; Sanjek 2000, p. 317) are simultaneously both cultural and political. Contra Habermas's (1989) conceptual separation of terms, horror fan discussions frequently both 'concern objects connected with the practice of the state' (censorship) and approximate to literary/proto-public sphere discussions by virtue of appreciating and dissecting media texts 'behind closed ["underground", subcultural] doors'.

This subcultural investment in the 'underground' and its transgressiveness can lead us to view horror's 'subcultural citizenship' in a very specific way; that is, as a reflexive attempt to violate norms and regulations of the dominant, national culture. Although the State and its institutional representatives thus figure in horror fans' own 'imagined communities' (Anderson 1991) or 'generic communities' (Altman 1999) as an enemy to be fought and evaded, these same representatives also allow fans to construct their subcultural difference from and against the 'mainstream'. The 'enemy' of censorship that is so frequently railed against simultaneously allows for the validation of 'true' horror fandom and its distinctiveness. As Mark Jancovich has noted:

> information and inaccessibility need to be carefully regulated and balanced. For example, many publications present themselves as guides to an inaccessible 'underground' where knowledge is not only essential to appreciation and the making of distinctions, but as such, operates as a precious emblem of *insider* status ... inaccessibility is maintained

throughout the scene not only through the selection of materials – they are not for everybody – but also through their virtual unobtainability. (2002c, pp. 318–19)

'Underground' horror fandom, like 'underground' cult movie fandom, depends on its treasured texts not being readily accessible outside the fan subculture. Censorship thus partly works to secure and protect the subcultural difference of 'true' horror fandom, meaning that fans can demarcate the 'authenticity' of their fan practices by referring to having seen 'uncut' films, or films that were banned in the UK as 'video nasties'. Kate Egan has analysed how online horror fans discuss the 'video nasties' phenomenon, often seeking to 'demonstrate … active participation in such a time, and the dangerous and illicit activities they took part in, in order to obtain and watch the object that fascinated them' (Egan 2003). Egan analyses one particular website, *Hysteria/Slasher/Nasties* (http:// www.south-over.demon.co.uk/Hysteria/slasher_nasties_1.html), discussing how the site's creator

> not only demonstrates how the 'nasties' phenomenon provided the background to his generation, and how he felt a sense of attachment to the 'nasties', but also, notably, how he got involved himself, responding positively to the 'nasties'' connotations of danger, illicitness and scarcity, taking his parents' video card into the video shop, and watching 'nasties' on friends' VCRs. (Egan 2003)

In this case, censorship is not just opposed, it is also celebrated by virtue of the fact that it makes certain media texts scarce, hard to find and thus subculturally desirable and distinctive. Subcultural citizenship is hence not only about critiquing censorship in community or public debates; it is also about a discourse of 'daring' and 'excitement' as the fan illicitly or illegally acquires valorized 'uncut'/rare horror. It is in order to facilitate such acquisitions that the 'film-swapping' analysed by Göran Bolin (2000, p. 61) and referred to by Peter Hutchings takes place:

> During the 1980s and 1990s, [Dario] Argento fandom tended to be based on the obtaining (usually from other fans) of video versions of otherwise hard-to-see Argento films, with these samizdat third- or fourth-generation copies, sometimes with Dutch or Japanese subtitles, offering the opportunity to view the elusive uncut versions denied to the market either by censors or by distributors … In Britain, this concern with the depredations of censorship was, and continues to be, intertwined with a critique of the state-imposed censorship embodied in the Video Recordings Act [1984]. (Hutchings 2003, p. 131)

This critique – again, censorship being depicted as the enemy of horror fandom – is captured in fan statements such as 'Let's put an end to film censorship and let the adult viewer decide' (the website *Dario Argento: Master of the Macabre*, www.jazzman59.freeserve.co.uk, quoted in Hutchings 2003, p. 132). But the situation Hutchings describes is one that is clearly marked by a type of quest narrative as well as by appeals to 'rational' critique. Acquiring 'uncut' Argento, or other uncut horror texts, means circumventing 'state-imposed' censorship by trading with other members of the subculture and importing foreign versions of films, resulting in an Italian *giallo* (Needham 2003) possibly being viewed 'with Dutch or Japanese subtitles'.

The horror fan's quest to track down 'hard-to-find rarities' is testified to in discourses of pleasure such as the following: 'It's great fun being a horror fan in the UK. It's exciting trying to track down uncut horror films' (Adam, quoted in Kerekes and Slater 2000, p. 287). And this quest narrative also appears in fan discourses that do not explicitly refer to 'excitement' or fun, but which nevertheless convey an excess of detail, as if the fan concerned is reliving or re-experiencing his discovery of long-sought-after horror films:

> I came across an antiques shop in a country village which doubled as the local video store ... I went in and entered a veritable Aladdin's Cave. Standing in neat rows on a polished wood writing bureau were numerous videos. The first to catch my attention was *Cannibal Ferox* – [1981, dr: Umberto Lenzi] both versions, the 18 rated and the XX uncut print. Immediately behind it was *Snuff* [1976, drs: Michael and Roberta Findlay and Carter Stevens], the first time I'd seen it since its nationwide disappearance many months ago ... I got the best part of my collection from this one shop. Pretty much all the tapes were in excellent condition. The cases were a bit grubby – the shop owner was a heavy smoker and a yellow film coated the protective plastic sleeve. There was a musty smell to the videos, too. Not an unpleasant odour – just what became an associative 'video nasty aroma'. I still have the films after almost fifteen years. (Kevin, quoted in Kerekes and Slater 2000, p. 288)

These accounts occur in a section of David Kerekes and David Slater's book *See No Evil* entitled 'Crime' (see 2000, p. 4). The technical illegality of black market trading in uncut horror is emphasized by Kerekes and Slater, who report that 'the Video Recordings Act [VRA] made it an offence for anyone to supply a videocassette without a classification certificate' (2000, p. 296). And the fact that horror films imported to Britain have been rather haphazardly seized by HM Customs is also discussed (2000, p. 306). This focus on the policing of 'video nasties' depicts fans as authentic members of an 'underground' horror subculture by virtue of their transgressions, while State institutions are represented as operating arbitrarily and as lacking textual/generic knowledge (2000, p. 306). There is certainly a critique of the 1984 VRA carried in such work, thus also positioning horror fans as subcultural *citizens* engaged in debate over State

policies and public media coverage. But as *subcultural* citizens, fans' transgressions are also produced by, and in relation to, the very censorship discourses
and regulations that they oppose. Such performatively enacted transgression:

> does not deny limits or boundaries, rather it exceeds them and thus completes
> them. Every rule, limit, boundary or edge carries with it its own fracture,
> penetration or impulse to disobey. The transgression is a component of the
> rule. (Jenks 2003, p. 7)

There is thus an inescapable contradiction carried at the heart of academically
depicting and morally elevating horror fans as 'active audiences' or (latterly)
'subcultural citizens'. Fan expertise and genre 'literacy' means that fans will tend
to display and perform critiques of State institutions that lack such knowledge,
thus potentially contributing to public debate, even if fan voices are rarely heard
outside of niche, subcultural media. Yet horror fan subculture is partly given a
sense of imagined subcultural homogeneity, and hence an image of its existence
as a 'generic community' (Altman 1999), through: (a) opposing censorship and
(b) searching for 'banned' or 'uncut' material. As Kerekes and Slater note, there
was a 'sense of community that came with collecting' films banned as 'video
nasties' (2000, p. 294). This means that horror fans convert the very pre-
conditions for their subcultural distinctions (consuming horror that is too
distasteful/obscene for the 'mainstream') into a force to be opposed and done
away with. If horror fans were heard more widely in public debate, and
championed ever more effectively by academic and other cultural groups, then
arguably part of their subcultural investment in 'transgression' would be eroded.
More adequate recognition as part of a pluralized public sphere would result in a
loss of 'the aura of "forbidden fruit"' ... something ... [promising] a meaning
different from that handed down or sanctioned by society and its privileged
institutions' (Telotte 1991, p. 12). It is an alluringly 'forbidden cinema' (see
Conrich and Petley (eds) 2000), that sustains many horror fans' discourses of
pleasurable textual agency and subcultural difference. Censorship thus operates,
culturally and discursively, as *the enemy and the engine of horror fandom*. Fan
subculture is highly critical of State practices while also performing subcultural
distinction through connotations of 'secrecy' and 'illicitness'.

Although it may be tempting to morally elevate horror fandom via the notion
of 'subcultural citizenship', following the lineage of 'active' audience theory, this
move presents some difficulties. We may be able to avoid ontologizing fan
practices and pleasures, instead considering that fans make discursive,
performative claims of textual agency and 'transgression'. But the notion of
(sub)cultural citizenship (developing out of Hermes 1998, Hartley 1999 and
Bolin 2000) nevertheless threatens to ontologize 'active' fan audiences. And it
threatens to erase contradictions between fans' subcultural or 'alternative public
sphere' appreciations of 'uncut' horror and their 'political public sphere'
criticisms of State censorship. Championing fans' rights to access uncensored

texts would, furthermore, mean dispelling the 'daring' and 'subversive' connotations that surround horror fan practices (Sanjek 2000, p. 317). And it would also mean undermining and countering discourses of fan pleasure that hinge on performing textual agency, and on working to 'find' texts that have been withheld from 'mainstream' consumers.

In this chapter I have considered how censorship debates are subculturally engaged in by horror fans. This has taken me far from the type of academic discussion of horror and pleasure that I began with in Chapter 1. Whereas cognitive philosophies of horror's pleasure assume that violations of cultural categories exist within the genre's texts (e.g. Carroll 1990), the discursive framings of horror and pleasure I have considered here concern fans' violations of cultural categories. Censorship establishes that specific texts are tabooed or prohibited, and subcultural fan practices then seek to transgress/violate this cultural category of 'censored' or restricted material. The pleasure-agency that is discursively articulated is thus one of boundary crossing in relation to how texts are culturally classified, rather than being a response to textual content *per se* (and this suggests, yet again, that 'single-text approaches' focused purely on horror's textual operations such as Carroll (1990) and Todorov (1975) are somewhat flawed). Unlike Carroll's (1990) arguments, then, these pleasures of horror are performed through and in relation to the genre's wider cultural status. It is not being scared that is important in these fan discourses; rather, it is once again knowledge and agency that are iterated as the key discursive components of fan practices and pleasures. Affect, where it even occurs discursively, relates to the 'excitement' of viewing uncut horror. Steffen Hantke (2002, p. 6) has alleged that academic criticism tends to lose sight of horror's embodiments and affects, but it seems that fans also discursively 'screen' these dimensions, or more specifically, discursively displace 'affect derived from the text' with 'affect accompanying the discovery of an uncut text' as a material artefact (cf. Kevin cited earlier). By doing so, fans construct themselves as active agents pursuing a quest for uncut horror in the face of State-imposed rules rather than passive subjects affected by media texts. Textual agency is a vitally important concept, then, not for what it can tell us about the ontology of fan pleasures – I have argued that we can never have critical, theoretical access to these pleasures – but for the way that it can illuminate how audiences and academics seek to discursively position media consumption and its pleasures. The pleasures of horror, as these are performatively enacted in a range of fan practices of connoisseurship (Chapter 4) and censorship-critique (this chapter), have generally either been inverted in academic work (so that horror's audiences are, by definition, affected by specific texts, or such that horror is essentially viewed as a 'body genre') or ontologized (so that horror audiences simply *are* critics, experts and subcultural agents). In contrast, I have sought to argue here that horror's pleasures are discursively constructed in various ways in fan practices, typically as a function of the genre's ascribed (sub)cultural value. Fans discursively construct pleasure in ways that are very much disconnected from the dominant academic theorizing explored in Part I of *The Pleasures of Horror*.

In the next part I want to shift focus and consider how pleasures are not only discursively restricted in relation to something identified by fans and scholars as 'the horror genre', but are also discursively denied in relation to areas and arenas cognate to horror fiction as a generic tradition/body of texts. I will argue that cultural work is done to keep 'horror', as a genre nomination and cultural category, in its place. Para-sites – that is, cultural locations beyond those where 'horror' is 'naturally' assumed to belong, for example 'the horror genre = horror *film* and horror *fiction*' – are typically exnominated or disavowed as 'improper', 'inauthentic' instances of (not-quite) horror. I am using the term 'exnominated' here not to refer to naturalized, ideological representations that remain unspoken or unmarked (McKee 2003b, pp. 106–7) but rather to refer to ideological, cultural processes whereby specific discourses of genre (Mittell 2004) are consistently written-out or over-written by dominant, common-sense generic attributions. This shares connotations of 'naturalized absence' and 'structuring absence' with Roland Barthes's infamous use of the term (1972), but I am more concerned with how naturalized cultural constructions of generic ascription can work to block out and displace culturally threatening alternatives. Horror and its pleasures are thus culturally policed not only in relation to what it means to be a part of horror's audiences, but also in terms of a denial that horror has any reach, relevance or circulation in para-sites beyond its dominant cultural locations: sites such as television (Chapter 6), factual media reportage (Chapter 7), and cultural theory itself (Chapter 8). Thus far I have examined discursive constructions of the pleasures of horror, exploring marginalized academic counter-discourses (Part I) and considering how fans perform specific versions of pleasure-as-agency in order to challenge their pathologized portrayals or embrace connotations of transgressive, masculinized 'deviance' (this part). I will now move on to consider the borders and boundaries of 'the horror genre', analysing how cultural constructions of such borders relate to discourses of pleasure.

Part III

Para-sites: Beyond 'Generic' Horror

[G]enres develop over time dialectically through their interactions with other kinds of writing [and cultural production] ... Derrida's famous passage from 'The Law of Genre' [Derrida 1992, p. 230] ... puts this with ... succinctness: 'Every text participates in one or several genres, there is no genreless text, there is always a genre and genres, yet such participation never amounts to belonging.' ... [Yet] *texts both bring to bear and have borne upon them multiple genres* ... Derrida's formulation by itself is incomplete for our purposes because it does not attempt to theorize how texts operate economically and politically. (Michael Gamer 2000, pp. 45–6, my italics)

Chapter 6

TV Horror

Studies of horror seem to assume that film is the genre's 'natural' home; even when horror's transmedia presence is alluded to (as in Carroll 1990 and Leffler 2000) examples still tend to be drawn from either film or novelistic fiction (see also Jones 2002). TV's material role in the mediation and construction of the horror genre (Carroll 1990, p. 3) has thus been rendered relatively invisible. Television has been treated as a para-site for horror; a cultural site that is assumed to be alien to the genre and a space where horror supposedly does not belong. In this chapter I will argue that the assumption that horror has no place on the small screen hinges on fixed discourses of TV as a 'cultural form' and 'industry', while also prejudging and essentializing the medium's mode of reception (see Hills and Williams forthcoming). As Peter Hutchings has commented, by focusing on '"cutting edge" developments in the genre' (invariably, that is, 'cutting edge' developments in horror film) many academic accounts miss the fact 'that horror films persist in our culture long after their production, via TV, repertory schedules and, most recently, video and DVD, and that at any one time there are different entrance points into the genre' (2001, p. 2; see also Dresser 1989, pp. 80–100).

In Part III of *The Pleasures of Horror* my interest lies not in asking the common question 'why horror?' (posed by Carroll 1990 and Tudor 1997) and instead in exploring 'where is horror?', or more exactly, 'Where is the horror genre *assumed* to exist?' This might be considered rather tangential to addressing the pleasures of horror. However, by analysing how/where the horror genre is discursively positioned, it becomes possible to consider how 'authentic' horror is related to certain discourses of pleasure, 'pleasures' that become allegedly impossible to sustain via 'inauthentic' horror. Arguments over where horror does and does not belong culturally are therefore always also arguments about what its pleasures are assumed to be.

Gregory A. Waller's work (1986 and 1987) represents one of the most sensitive explorations of horror and TV to date (see also Kaminsky with Mahan 1985; Wheatley 2002). But even Waller is tempted to conclude that 'made-for-television horror would seem to be by definition impossible' (1987, p. 159; see also Muir 2000, p. 1). Despite cataloguing the ways in which horror and its supposed affects are attenuated, dissipated and disrupted by television as form and technology, Waller nevertheless concedes, '[y]et the genre exists, throwing motion-picture horror into high relief' (1987, p. 159).

Looking at more recent academic surveys of television and genre, one could still be forgiven for assuming that 'Horror TV' (Ono 2000, p. 163) does not meaningfully exist as a category. For example, horror makes no appearance in *The Television Genre Book* (Creeber (ed.) 2001). Nor does it appear in *Television Studies* (Miller (ed.) 2002), despite the fact that an image from *Buffy the Vampire Slayer* (USA, WB 1997–2001, UPN 2001–3) occupies the cover of the latter book, while an image from *The X-Files* (USA, Fox 1993–2002) appears on the cover of Creeber (2001). *The Television Genre Book* does indeed discuss *The X-Files*, but it nominates the programme generically under the heading of 'science fiction TV', despite observing that by '[m]anipulating the generic fluidity of science fiction television, the series attempted to integrate the basic structure of the detective genre ... with elements of horror and science fiction' (Johnson 2001a, p. 30). Other possible candidates for the status of TV horror are also generically nominated in ways that render horror relatively invisible: *Twin Peaks* (USA, ABC 1990–1) is discussed as 'postmodern drama' (Page 2001, p. 44), while *Buffy the Vampire Slayer* is considered as one of the 'teen dramas ... [that] ... reflects the American networks' growing interest over the 1990s in the adolescent market as a valuable niche demographic' (Johnson 2001b, p. 42). And elsewhere, M. Keith Booker has analysed *Twin Peaks* and *The X-Files* as instances of what he terms 'strange TV' (2002). Horror as a generic ascription is rendered structurally absent in these discourses, or *academically exnominated*. TV series, all of which draw intertextually on horror in significant ways, are instead made extra-textually to bear a variety of alternative genre categories (Gamer 2000, pp. 45–6). We obviously cannot expect *The Television Genre Book* (2001) to include every TV genre, and editorial judgements had to be made as to what should be included/excluded. But it is striking that where TV is concerned, horror appears to be conceptually and generically dispensable. By contrast, it is difficult to imagine an overview of film genres that would ignore horror – see chapters in, for example, Browne (ed.) (1998); Dixon (ed.) (2000); Neale (2000) and Neale (ed.) (2002).

Why, then, might TV Studies have marginalized the horror genre? One possible answer lies in early distinctions made between film and TV, and with what came to be known as 'glance theory'. This was introduced by John Ellis in his (1982) study of television, *Visible Fictions*. Ellis argued that the TV spectator 'glances rather than gazes at the screen; attention is sporadic rather than sustained' (Ellis 1982, p. 24). In defence of such a position, Ellis cites TV's place within the 'distracted' domestic sphere, contrasting this to the sustained and concentrated 'gaze' of the theatrical cinema spectator. This film/TV binary opposition of gaze/glance has become part of the history of TV Studies, and Ellis has refused to revise his position (John Ellis 2000, p. 100) in the light of strong critique from John Thornton Caldwell (1995). Joan Hawkins (2000) argues that 'glance theory' works by discursively fixing television as culturally inferior to film:

> The 'discursive rules' of glance theory essentialize performance and exhibition space, privileging and sacralizing certain spaces while expressing anxiety about others. But they also serve to essentialize and fetishize media – where a certain value inheres in the medium itself (irrespective of content), such that one can somehow 'disrespect' a film simply by consuming it within an unsacralized space [i.e. on TV], and where TV constructs not only the way we watch television programs but the way we watch anything ... transmitted or projected via TV. (Hawkins 2000, p. 40–1)

Ellis's argument, Hawkins suggests, works simplistically and discursively to position TV as always determining its viewers' responses. In 'glance theory' it seems impossible to credit the viewer with any motivation to watch TV, concentratedly, as part of a focus on discrete texts and textual affects. The a priori assumptions of glance theory can thus lead us towards one explanation as to why horror on TV might be considered, discursively, to be inauthentic (and as undeserving of academic theorization). Where horror film can supposedly assume a focused viewer, watching attentively and being caught up in a film's structure as an 'emotion machine' (Tan 1996), horror on TV appears to contrastively assume a distracted, disengaged viewer, and one who is *not* caught up in the 'dialectic between seeing and not seeing [that] is played out in horror cinema' (Kavka 2002, p. 227). Instead, in this account, horror on TV appears to lose all affective/emotional intensity simply by virtue of being televised and received within the distracted, sociable domestic sphere.

Such an assumption can be challenged in a variety of ways. One recent interrogation, based on empirical research, appears in the work of Geraldine Bloustien (2002). Bloustien argues that young female fans of *Buffy the Vampire Slayer* often prefer watching the programme in their bedrooms:

> In these locales ... the programme may be engaged with very differently from the way it is watched in the lounge or living room. A high proportion of the respondents in my ... research stressed that they preferred to watch *Buffy* at home, either alone or with close friends in their bedrooms. ... It would seem that in the more intimate context of the bedroom, the television ... can become an even more powerful forum for exploring fantasies, desires and dreams. (Bloustien 2002, p. 434)

Contra the accounts of 'glance theory', Bloustien's work suggests that what she terms the 'Gothic' or '(neo-)Gothic' textuality of *Buffy the Vampire Slayer* (ibid.) can sustain intense viewer–text engagements, which fans pursue via highly motivated uses of domestic space (and see also Bloustien (2004) on fans' motivated, focused TV viewing in public spaces). Fans typically watch in their private spaces precisely in order to sustain the type of uninterrupted 'gaze' that glance theory suggests cannot be articulated to television as a domestic medium also characterized by its interruptible 'flow' (Williams 1975; for more on this, see the next chapter).

Glance theory is not alone in its attack on TV as a medium incapable of sustaining the intense textual affects/emotions presumed to characterize 'authentic' horror, and assumed to give rise to its characteristic pleasures. A variety of other discursive positionings of TV have worked to imply that horror on TV must, by definition, be 'inauthentic', and it is to these that I will now turn.

CENSORSHIP AND SCHEDULING: CHALLENGES TO CULTURAL PRODUCERS' TEXTUAL AGENCY

Horror's seeming invisibility as a TV genre should not be viewed entirely as the fault of academics who have, historically, theorized television in limited ways. The absence of 'TV horror' can also be considered as a matter of TV's own industry practices, suggesting that the genre's academic absence partly replays its intertextual marginalization in TV publicity, as well as its textual marginalization on TV. In what follows I will consider issues of censorship and scheduling by examining the complaints of horror's practitioners – professional (screen)writers – with regard to these factors. First, I will address Stephen King's (1982) discussion of horror and US TV, before analysing British horror-thriller writer Stephen Gallagher's indictment of British TV with regard to fantasy/horror genres.

King focuses his ire on censorship, suggesting that it is network 'Broadcast Standards and Practices' and 'federal regulation' that operate to neuter TV horror, thus rendering it inauthentic. King makes direct use of the metaphor of 'neutering', writing in *Danse Macabre* that 'television has become ... like a fat old spayed tomcat dedicated to the preservation of the status quo and to the concept of LOP – Least Objectionable Programming' (1982, p. 252). King's analysis of horror shown on, and made for, television repeatedly positions TV horror as a watered-down, attenuated version of authentic horror (which, for King, is found in horror novels; 1982, p. 281).

Television's industrial practices of censorship operate, as far as King is concerned, as an obstacle to the aesthetics and affects of horror, where 'the bedrock of horror fiction ... is ...: you gotta scare the audience. Sooner or later you gotta put on the gruesome mask and go booga-booga' (1982, p. 253). Television as an industry and television drama as a form thus restrict writers from achieving the affects and pleasures that discursively define 'true' horror:

> For the writer, the most galling thing about TV must be that he or she is
> forbidden from bringing all of his or her powers to bear ... [A]lways keep

> this fact somewhere near to hand: television has really asked the impossible of
> its handful of horror programs – ... to horrify without really horrifying, to
> sell audiences a lot of sizzle and no steak. (King 1982, pp. 252 and 254)

King argues that television denies what I would term 'textual agency' to horror's
writers. It would seem that textual agency is highly significant for creators of
horror, involving an imagined capacity to 'do things' to horror's audiences.
Situated power – performed through the textual production or consumption of
horror – thus emerges as a theme for both the genre's producers and its fans (see
the previous chapter), as both perform cultural agency via the genre. When the
capacity for textual agency-pleasure to be performed is reduced, then horror
becomes positioned as 'inauthentic'. Mainstream, commercial horror may be
devalued as 'inauthentic' by fractions of horror fandom (Jancovich 2000 and
2002c) not only because of 'commerce'/'art' or 'feminine'/'masculine' binary
oppositions (although these clearly remain relevant), but also because – as
opposed to 'underground' horror – 'mainstream' texts do not allow for such
exaggerated performances of textual agency. Fans cannot claim cultural
distinctions of 'ownership' and 'discovery' over a mainstream text in the way
that they can with underground or more clearly subculturally validated horror
(Tudor 1974, p. 183).

Likewise, where horror's creators cannot claim textual agency, then they too
will seemingly tend to devalue the texts and the medium concerned. Comparing
television with books, Stephen King's authenticating emphasis on authorial
'freedom' (i.e. his discursive performance of textual agency) is writ large:

> Let's ... turn to the bookshelf; I want us to talk about some stories where all
> the artificial boundaries are removed – both those of visual set and of network
> restriction – and the author is free to 'get you' in any way he can. (King 1982,
> p. 281, leading into a discussion of 'Horror Fiction')

In other words, in 'authentic' horror, anything goes. The author is aesthetically
'free', according to the discourses mobilized by King. By contrast, TV horror is
not 'really' horror precisely because it cannot go all-out to scare audiences: types
of graphic 'splatter' horror that are possible in novels and films are generally less
permissible in made-for-TV horror (although I will complicate this contention
later).

Gregory A. Waller's (1987) examination of TV horror echoes many of
Stephen King's thoughts, as Waller also stresses the significant 'influence of
network censorship codes' on the aesthetics of televisual horror (1987, p. 148).
Unlike King, however, Waller does not automatically conclude that the
restrictions of censorship – enforced via networks' internal 'Broadcast Standards
and Practices' monitoring – result in 'inauthentic' horror that simply isn't
horrifying. For Waller, horror on TV can be linked to a distinct aesthetic

tradition within the history of horror fiction, thus being discursively repositioned and valorized:

> [T]he same powerful network censorship restrictions that separate telefilms from the mainstream of contemporary theatrical horror films put made-for-television horror in the position of carrying on what ... S.S. Prawer, and other commentators praise as the 'restrained' tradition of horror that is based on suggestion and indirection ... In principle, if not in practice, ... made-for-television horror ... is the heir to Victorian ghost stories, Val Lewton's RKO productions in the 1940s, and classics of 'indirect' horror. (ibid.)

This bid for the revalorization of TV horror remains hesitant, but suggests one direction that can be taken by attempts to validate television horror. A virtue is made out of the fact that TV drama (due to regulation, censorship, its imagined audiences and its domestic reception) cannot always show the monster or the gore that characterizes 'art-horror' (according to Carroll 1990, p. 53).

By linking TV horror to a specific aesthetic tradition, Waller in fact places it closer to what Noël Carroll has termed 'art-dread' rather than 'art-horror' (cf. Freeland 2004). Where art-horror seeks to induce emotions of repulsion and disgust in audiences (alongside suspense and fearful tension), art-dread is, according to Carroll, a distinguishable emotional experience: 'Where art-horror involves disgust as a central feature, what might be called art-dread does not' (Carroll 1990, p. 42). It is striking that Carroll – who, to reiterate, pays no sustained attention to media specificity in *The Philosophy of Horror* (1990) – really only makes explicit mention of horror on TV when discussing what he terms 'art-dread': 'Many of the episodes on the old TV series *The Twilight Zone* [US, CBS 1959–64] are of this sort ... I do think that there is an important distinction between this type of story ... *tales of dread* ... and horror stories' (ibid.; for more on this specific series as 'TV horror' see Hills 2004c).

Such commentary forces us to consider the way in which different discursive positionings of TV horror can draw on similar, empirical observations. Empiricism is no object to differential discursive framing, or so it would seem. Hence, while Waller (1987) tentatively links TV horror's alleged lack of monsters and disgust to a valued and historical generic lineage of 'restrained' horror, Stephen King (1982) narratively frames the same textual 'fact' as a matter of horror's neutering, while Noël Carroll rules such texts out of his theory of 'art-horror' altogether.

TV censorship may have raised questions as to the authenticity and pleasures of TV horror, but this has not been the only aspect of the television industry to draw complaints from horror's critics and creators. Screenwriter, TV director and horror novelist Stephen Gallagher (see www.stephengallagher.co.uk), writing in the commercial UK horror/sf niche magazine *Dreamwatch*, has suggested that horror on TV is as much a victim of scheduling practices as it is of censorship. Gallagher contrasts 'producer-led' and 'scheduler-led' TV (2000, p. 82). He argues that British TV of the 1950s and 1960s was relatively awash with telefantasy – TV drama drawing on the codes and conventions of horror and science fiction genres – but that, more recently, TV schedules have lacked such diversity. Like King, Gallagher draws on discourses of agency to account for this shift; previously, he argues, TV producers would 'find material they felt a personal enthusiasm for, develop it, fight its corner, and do their best to get it through the system ... Once it was made, the schedulers scheduled it' (Gallagher 2000, p. 82). However, the contemporary British TV industry is characterized quite differently:

> The Broadcasting Bill introduced a decade ago ... essentially remov[ed] the individual autonomy of the ITV companies and requir[ed] them to create and fund one centralised body – the ITV Network Centre – to determine the overall content of the channel ... The BBC under John Birt has largely aped that model, with the result that everything we now see is the result of a 'rationalised' system in which the schedulers tell the producers what they want made in order best to serve their schedules. (Gallagher 2000, p. 82)

Textual agency is, as in King's account of US TV, denied to horror's creators (producers as much as writers). TV horror does not merely become 'inauthentic' through this process; it is rendered almost entirely absent from schedules, especially in UK-originated formats. The 'personal enthusiasm' of the industry professional, thus implicitly figured as fan-like in this account, is displaced by an affectless and 'rationalized' system. This system, for Gallagher, powerfully restricts horror on TV. His argument is that:

> The only bets being made are the safe ones ... (and even if you get a one-off through the system, you'll still be urged – as I was during the shooting of *Oktober* – to 'remember the grannies'). The more that banal and sunny naturalism gets its grip on the schedules, the harder it's going to be for the rest of us to find that darker-textured 'thrill of the unnatural'. (Gallagher 2000, p. 82)

Gallagher directed and adapted a three-part, prime-time version of his own bestselling UK horror novel *Oktober* (1988) for the ITV Network in 1997 (Carnival Films; sold as a one-off telefilm to the US market, 1998) and draws on his own experiences in this account, which is written for a target market of genre fans. It is striking that both King and Gallagher align themselves with notions of 'authentic' horror, seemingly writing as much as fans as media professionals. In each case, their discursively framed 'authentic' horror, whether it is 'go[ing] booga-booga' (King) or crafting a 'darker-textured "thrill"' (Gallagher), is represented as alien to industry practices of TV censorship and scheduling. In each case the horror writer – like the horror fan – is preoccupied by textual agency; either desiring to create horror without 'artificial boundaries' (King) or contrasting fan-like enthusiasm with the 'bean-counter's way of dealing with the products of the imagination' (Gallagher 2000, p. 82; and see Gallagher 2004, p. 82). An 'art'/'commerce' binary thus continues to play out through such accounts, with 'authentic' horror being described as unrestricted, freely creative, and as aesthetically championed and defended by TV producers.

Stephen Gallagher's (2000) account is not simply important for the way that it structurally iterates the terms of Stephen King's (1982) survey of TV horror. Gallagher also restores to fan and critical vision an aspect of the TV industry that has been little analysed. For, as Graeme Turner has noted:

> The component that is often left out of the conventional ... industry/text/ audience triangle is the programmer or scheduler: the person who places the programme within the channel or network schedule. There has been very little academic attention paid to the work of the programmer, but it would seem logical to assume that their practices – and thus TV schedules – are influenced by their understanding of genre. (Turner 2001, p. 5)

Following Turner and Gallagher's leads, we can suggest that the genre of horror has had a major impact on the work of TV schedulers: largely, a negative one. That is, the genre has been perceived by schedulers as a threat to TV's cultural operation as a 'family' and domestic medium, where audiences cannot be regulated, and where 'it can be said that all programs are for children ... because of the accessibility of the medium, its ease of use, ... lack of parental supervision, and global reach' (Schneider with Pullen 2001, p. 74). In such a context, horror is conceptualized as a genre that calls for non-prime-time scheduling, generally having to be positioned in late-night, or post-watershed schedules, and thus automatically being excluded from attracting a mass audience despite the popularity of the genre in other media. As Gill Branston and Roy Stafford have observed:

> UK television channels do not perceive ... series involving horror ... as suitable for prime-time programming at 8 or 9 pm, partly owing to the so-called Family Viewing Policy before the 9 pm watershed ... Clearly ... the domestic context of viewing does not make ... [TV] ... ideal as a vehicle for full 'body horror', and the resulting possibility of nightmares for the younger 'family audience' has to be borne in mind by ... schedulers. (2003, p. 87)

It may be reasonable to say, as Andrew Tolson has, that 'television uses generic categories – or ... that a "generic system" has been "institutionalised" in television' (1996, p. 97). However, Tolson's study of one UK TV listings guide, *The Radio Times*, which aims to explore 'the relevance of generic distinction ... to both the process of production, and ... the generation of publicity' (Tolson 1996, p. 98) neglects to consider the point that some generic classifications may be unwelcome in the intertextual activation of meaning carried out by listings and publicity. If 'generic definition is one way of attracting potential viewers' (Tolson 1996, p. 99) then it is also one way of losing viewers, or of threatening viewers' culturally constituted sense of what is 'appropriate' for television schedules. Genres, as 'cultural categories' constituted through discursive practices (Mittell 2004, p. 13), can be mobilized in a variety of ways, but their circulation in discourse can also be exonominated or culturally restricted. Hence what Jason Mittell (2004, p. 15) refers to as the 'generic function' (adapting Foucault 1979) can be as much about how certain genres, that is horror, are rendered relatively invisible in specific cultural sites as about how genres are positively discursively produced in others. 'TV horror' tends to be a dangerous, difficult generic or cultural category for broadcasters, threatening television's deep-rooted discursive links to the safety of hearth and home. It is seemingly a problematic collision of genre and medium not only for critics and cultural producers, but also for schedulers and broadcasters.

I will now go on to consider ways in which a variety of TV texts have drawn on the traditions of the horror genre. If there is an 'orthodoxy' surrounding TV horror then it is that television drama does not or cannot 'show' and 'imagine' as much as film and fiction – this is why the discursively constructed pleasures of horror identified in Part I seem to belong more comfortably to horror film and novelistic fiction rather than to TV. By contrast, television has not, discursively and culturally, been constructed as a site of intense emotion/affect, or of depicted monstrosity, or of the subversive lifting of repression.

SHOWING THE PAST, SHOWING LESS: 'GOTHIC TV'

If horror and television have endured a difficult relationship, then one exonominating strategy that can be used to ameliorate horror's cultural threat (as something 'inappropriate' for TV and its domestic, family audiences) is the displacing category of 'Gothic TV' (Davenport-Hines 1999, p. 376). There has never been a convincing definition of 'the gothic' that definitively separates it out from 'horror' (see Kavka 2002, p. 227 for one attempt), and it remains the case that 'there is often a slippage' in many critics' work on the horror genre 'between the term "horror" and terms such as "fantasy", "the Gothic", and "the tale of terror", terms which are not commensurate with one another but through which differences can be elided' (Jancovich 2002a, pp. 7–8). However, as well as eliding differences by slipping from 'horror' to the 'gothic', those producing, publicizing and writing about television can also produce cultural distinctions, suggesting that 'Gothic TV' is superior to devalued (or culturally inappropriate) TV horror. Mark Jancovich has observed a similar process at work in publicity surrounding *The Silence of the Lambs* (1991, dr: Jonathan Demme):

> [T]he terms 'Gothic' and 'terror', rather than 'horror' ... engage a familiar set of distinctions by which 'the Gothic novel' and 'the tale of terror' are not constructed as other to legitimate culture ... but rather are associated with legitimate culture through a series of distinctions in which 'horror' is constructed as their own other. (Jancovich 2002b, p. 159)

These same performative acts of generic (re)classification have occurred around horror on TV, with 'Gothic TV' functioning as a discursive other to TV horror – the latter being associated with gore and low culture, and the former carrying connotations of historical tradition, and 'restrained' suggestion or implication rather than graphic monstrosity and splatter. Peter Hutchings has put forward a concise evaluation of this 'gothic'/'horror' opposition in relation to film, commenting that a 'fairly widespread approach identifies horror as a vulgarised, exploitative version of Gothic ... [T]he term "Gothic horror" ... usually refers to a specific type of horror film, one which has a period setting' (1996, p. 89).

'Gothic TV' therefore offers the generic possibility of intertextually associating television with high(er) cultural versions of horror *literature*, meaning that TV horror can be safely contained within TV schedules and publicity by virtue of being discursively approximated to period drama or literary adaptation. As Stephen Gallagher has commented, '*Gormenghast* [UK, BBC 2000] is a one-off that gets through on the Great Books ticket, and it's a conspicuous rarity' (2000, p. 82). Writing about the late 1960s ITV horror anthology, *Mystery and Imagination* (UK, ITV 1966–70), Helen Wheatley indicates the enduring importance of this 'Great Books' ticket, also considering how this series was intertextually linked to gothic literature in its attendant publicity: 'the act of television viewing ... [is] ... given a sense of cultural kudos here when compared to the reading of literary fiction' (Wheatley 2002, p. 168; see also Delasara 2000, p. 163 for a discussion of *Buffy* and *The X-Files* as 'Lovecraftian'). Ur-texts of gothic literature thus occupy privileged places in relation to TV horror, as they can work intertextually to separate out such TV from the generic classification of horror-as-low-cultural-threat. 'Gothic tradition' (Tonkin 2001, p. 49) hence re-genrifies and exnominates horror, transforming it discursively from an alleged 'body genre' focused on intense emotion/affect and recontextualizing it within a more genteel paradigm of period drama. By showing less gore and being diegetically cast back in time 'Gothic TV' not only takes on a literariness or worthy wordiness, it also overwrites the culturally dangerous category of 'TV horror'.

The safety of 'the Gothic' for TV producers, schedulers and publicists lies partly in the fact that its texts are often highly familiar to audiences, being effectively pre-sold through audience recognition. Even critics and writers who aim harsh words at the failure of TV horror (usually via essentialized accounts and discourses of what TV 'is' as a medium) appear to uphold the culturally elevated status of 'Gothic TV'. Both Stephen King (1982) and Gregory Waller (1986) praise the BBC/PBS 1977 production *Count Dracula: A Gothic romance based on Bram Stoker's Dracula*. King describes it as 'moody and romantic' (1982, p. 280), while Waller approvingly analyses how its representations of Dracula disrupt the '"realistic" (conventional, illusionary)' representations of other, human characters (1986, p. 166). Waller also renders explicit the bid for cultural value that is carried by this 'gothic' TV programme:

> *Count Dracula* [Philip Saville, 1977] ... relies heavily on interior sets that look very much like elaborately detailed stage sets, befitting the emphasis on bravura performances ... and on ensemble acting ...; and it presents itself as an adaptation of literature ... that demonstrates a serious respect for its source, a preference for adult themes and situations, and a great dependence on the word. (Waller 1986, p. 156)

Count Dracula was released commercially in 2002 under the 'BBC Learning' label, indicating that it should be viewed as 'TV art' and as a text suitable for educational (i.e., official/legitimate cultural) purposes. It shares this marketing and genre-discourse recontextualization (Mittell 2004) as a culturally valued text with a range of TV dramas available under the British Film Institute's 'Archive TV' label: *A Warning to the Curious* (UK, BBC 1972), *The Signalman* (UK, BBC 1976), *The Stone Tape* (UK, BBC 1972), *Whistle and I'll Come To You* (UK, BBC 1968), and *Ghostwatch* (UK, BBC 1992). There is a doubled appeal to history and tradition as markers of cultural value here; such texts are often adaptations of gothic, Victorian literature in the first instance (*A Warning to the Curious* and *Whistle and I'll Come To You* are adaptations of M.R. James short stories, and *The Signalman* adapts a Charles Dickens story) or they are potentially marked by 'qualities' of the gothic, such as suggestion in the case of *Ghostwatch*. And by way of further cultural valorization, these texts are secondly valued as markers of televisual history via notions of 'the archive'. Appeals to legitimating 'history' are hence compounded, being worked diegetically into the original texts *and* activated through the positioning of these texts within video/DVD marketing discourses. Even *Ghostwatch* takes on the distancing patina of 'TV history', having been commercially released 'ten years on' (Volk 2003, p. 36) from its first and only BBC broadcast.

'Gothic TV' does not only introduce history and historicization as markers of cultural value; it also specifically activates connotations of 'historical distance' as a way of tempering the affective intensifications assumed to characterize horror as a genre. 'Gothic TV' thus insulates itself from horror's allegedly powerful emotions/affects, textually internalizing, as an aesthetic device, the 'out-of-timeness' and anachronism of TV reruns or reshowings of 'old horror movies' (Weigl 2002, p. 707; see also Kermode 1997, p. 57 and Lembo 2000, pp. 2–3). Such 'programmed anachronism', as I would term it, works by constructing a distancing sense that the time-frame of diegetic representations is out of joint with broadcast time, as well as relying on the operation of this (assumed) affect-dampening mechanism at the level of 'exhibition', that is via the showing of reruns or old films. There is a diegetic and discursive 'textuality of memory' (Grainge 2003, p. 217) at work in 'Gothic TV' that seeks to pre-reduce horror's affects on behalf of television audiences via an historicizing defence. As Geraldine Bloustien has argued, 'the classic stories and Gothic legends retold in the late 20th century are also, importantly, one step removed from the originals, being refracted through the ironic distancing of contemporary folklore' (Bloustien 2002, p. 432). That is, gothic 'classics' are not always retold straight in contemporary popular culture; they are also textually invoked as cultural memories, and as knowing constructions of 'pastness'. Hence '[t]elevision series like *The Addams Family* [USA, ABC 1964–6) and *The Munsters* (USA, CBS 1964–6], with their … inversion of everyday American family life, use a composite of figures from literary and visual Gothic texts' (Botting 1996, p. 168) but they use these figures comedically and as 'out of time' rather than as a directly 'present' horrifying/monstrous threat. Such shows may not, after all, carry the cultural prestige of 'Gothic TV'-as-literary-adaptation, but they still carry programmed anachronism, allowing the safe conversion of horror's monsters into familiar figures of fun (see also Greenberg 2004). Probably the most spectacular example of this process, focused on trash horror rather than literary adaptation, has been carried out by *Mystery Science Theater 3000* (USA, Comedy Channel/Comedy Central/Sci-Fi 1989–99), which deconstructs 'old low-budget … horror films' (Caldwell 1995, p. 23). As Henry Krips has commented, '*MST3K* … encourages viewers to act upon their knowledge that the movie's special effects are crass, its plot unbelievable, and so on, thus undermining any attempt to engage with it realistically' (1999, p. 167). By textually pre-reading old horror films for media-savvy audiences, *MST3K* converts horror into comedy, knowingly marking out these films' aesthetic obsolescence and rendering them unproblematic in relation to discursive and cultural constructions of TV as a domestic, family medium.

Programmed anachronism is also, arguably, what occurs when the figure of Dracula is introduced into *Buffy the Vampire Slayer*. The episode 'Buffy vs. Dracula' (5–01) initially suggests that Dracula is a serious threat to Buffy, but ultimately represents the Count as overly familiar, and as reduced in (narrative and affective) potency: 'In "Buffy vs. Dracula" Buffy is fighting not only the manifestation of the character Dracula, she also fights the Hollywood narrative tradition that would have a woman succumb to the power of Dracula' (Millard Daugherty 2001, p. 163). Of course, our heroine does not succumb. Dracula's affects and his gothic narrative are textually construed as obsolete within the Buffyverse; his power is no match for the Slayer's determination. The episode concludes by self-reflexively 'refracting' Dracula-the-character through Dracula-the-media-texts, as 'when Dracula's dust reassembles, Buffy is right there to stake him, again and again. "You think I don't watch your movies?" she asks. "You always come back"' (Millard Daugherty 2001, p. 162).

This line and its ironic distancing perfectly capture the programmed anachronism of 'Gothic TV' where it veers into diegetically 'contemporary' narratives. Classic horror monsters retain just enough monstrosity to act as a narrative threat in present-day settings, but their power to disgust and repulse is reduced, and they ultimately come to connote 'pastness'. Where contemporary gothic literature often proceeds through forms of 'counterfictional horror' (see Chapter 9), critiquing the gothic by converting its subtexts into texts, 'Gothic TV' is less obviously counterfictional. Instead it uses the gothic as an intertextual marker of cultural value (often replaying rather than criticizing the cultural politics of the gothic) and/or as an intertextual marker of cultural memory. In this second case, the gothic is either valued (in period dramas) or dismissed (in contemporary dramas) as dated *per se*. Although it could be argued that 'Buffy vs. Dracula' ideologically challenges gender representations, it achieves this through its semiotic harnessing of Dracula and 'pastness', thus constructing an (ideologically limited) utopian 'present' in which feminism has magically triumphed over the dark forces of patriarchy.

As well as triumphing over Dracula, Buffy also tackled the gothic threat of Frankenstein's monster, which was intertextually activated in Season 4 (Rose 2002). Gothic 'pastness' has been similarly coded into *The X-Files* as a form of programmed anachronism, most obviously in the '1997 episode, "The Post-Modern Prometheus" (5–6; 1997), broadcast in black and white [which] drew on figures and the iconography of *Frankenstein*' (Kellner 2003, p. 135). Although an unusual episode of the series, particularly given its use of black and white, this again captured the logic of 'Gothic TV' as a 'textuality of memory' (Grainge 2003, p. 217). Previous media representations of monstrosity are called up by the episode, working to distance the (industrially imagined or ideal) viewer from those emotions and realisms that generally characterize horror's monsters in contemporary film.

The intertextual, media-saturated knowingness of the likes of *Buffy* and *The X-Files* has been critically commented upon, and this type of textuality has typically been viewed as a way of maintaining a realist sense of 'the contemporary' (Krzywinska 2002b, p. 189–90; Kellner 2003, p. 133). Such arguments reasonably stress textual effects of the 'contemporary', but what they neglect to consider is that any construction of the contemporary, and of contemporary 'realism', depends on self-consciously exposing previous aesthetic strategies, realisms and narratives as defunct or unconvincing. Such a manoeuvre occurs via programmed anachronism, and via a textual and aesthetic distancing of certain gothic monsters that are represented as non-threatening, misunderstood, misguided or quite simply as lacking in affective power. 'Hoary figures' (Kellner 2003, p. 133) are thus not only reappropriated and made relevant, they are also simultaneously undermined and precisely displayed as 'hoary'.

Following the narrative of TV and censorship that I examined in the previous section, critics have often viewed televisual horror as 'Gothic TV' due to its reliance on 'suggestion'. TV's supposed inability properly to show horror has recurred as a theme here, and not only thanks to censorship, but also via essentializing discussions of TV's poor image resolution and small image size when compared to film. S.S. Prawer (1980, p. 20) picks up this point, and Waller (1987, pp. 147–8) and Branston and Stafford (2003, p. 87) follow suit. However, this 'showing less' school of thought fails to consider the importance of connoted 'pastness' within 'Gothic TV'. A singular emphasis on television's purported inability to 'show the monster' fails to consider that the relative safety of 'the gothic' as a re-genrifying cultural category for TV horror lies not only in its indirectness, but also in the manner in which it *can* show the monster, but only as textually/representationally distanced (diegetically in time, and metaphorically as 'obsolete', comedic or lacking in affective power). 'Showing less' does not, therefore, account entirely convincingly for much TV horror that has been branded and discussed as 'Gothic' (Bloustien 2002, p. 435; see also Wheatley 2002, pp. 177–8). Such an account also fails to consider the ways in which 1990s popular/cult TV horror such as *Buffy* and *The X-Files* is produced within a qualitatively different TV industry to the one criticized by Waller (1987) and King (1982) in the 1980s. Shows such as *Buffy*, *The X-Files*, *The Kingdom* (Denmark, DR 1994) and *Urban Gothic* (UK, Channel 5 2000–1) may, in part, use programmed anachronism, but they still 'show more' than earlier critical approaches to horror and TV would suggest is possible.

It is thus the changing nature of US and UK TV industries that I want to examine next, arguing that graphic horror has taken up a more significant place within TV programming over the past decade.

SHOWING MORE: *AUTEURS* TARGETING FANS

Mark Jancovich's work on 'authentic' horror and cultural distinction (2000, 2002b) has not explored the role of different media in bids for horror's 'authenticity'. Despite this, Jancovich has been one of the few critics writing on horror to take seriously the possibilities of TV horror (1996, p. 303). And in his recent cultural history of the horror genre (2002a), he makes a bold statement of horror TV's importance: '[B]y the mid-1990s, it was on television that the really interesting developments in horror were taking place in shows like *The X-Files* and *Buffy the Vampire Slayer*' (Jancovich 2002a, p. 7).

Even here, though, the way in which television can function as a marker of horror's supposed inauthenticity remains discursively potent. It is 'teen TV' that acts as horror's Other for some fans. As horror films become culturally and discursively proximate to teen TV – for example, sharing star actors with shows such as *Dawson's Creek* (USA, WB 1998–2003) or *Buffy the Vampire Slayer* – so they supposedly become 'bland', 'mainstream' and unscary, at least in the eyes of specific factions of 'underground' horror fans (see Jancovich 2000 and 2002a, p. 7). Contra such fan lore, Jancovich asserts that 1990s TV is where 'developments' in the genre can be identified (see also Jancovich and Lyons 2003). Such a critical stance is worlds away from Waller's late-1980s assertion that 'there are few, if any ... masterworks or cultural milestones to be found in the sprawling and often monotonous landscape of made-for-television horror' (Waller 1987, p. 147). Waller positions TV horror as a shadow of developments happening elsewhere, such that horror's 'evolution' is said to happen in film and novels, while television simply imitates horror film, or produces degraded made-for-TV sequels (1987, p. 146).

What has changed? What altered cultural, industrial contexts might underpin Jancovich's revaluation of TV horror? The most significant, I would argue, is the shift towards targeting fans as niche markets. This movement can be linked to the rise of new networks (or even 'post-network' TV: McKee 2002, p. 69) in the US, and to the decentring of terrestrial channels by satellite/cable TV in the UK (see Hills 2002, pp. 36–41). In each instance, broadcasters can no longer readily assume a mass audience for their programming, and as audience share threatens to dwindle then key demographics and 'avid fans' (Reeves *et al.* 1996, p. 31) become more significant to TV producers, as do notions of 'quality/ authored TV' that can be distinguished from textual competitors by virtue of aesthetic and diegetic 'uniqueness' (see Hills 2004a and 2004b). Within such industry realignments, established genres that sustain dedicated fan cultures become far more attractive possibilities. Genre fans can be channelled into new media platforms by discrete, targeted programming: these are viewers who do indeed attend to TV programmes as 'eventful'. Fans can thus be courted as the lifeblood of specialist, niche channels, since they are likely to operate as predictable, dedicated consumers (Hills 2002, p. 36). It is within this context that shows such as *Buffy the Vampire Slayer* make sense, as do their pronounced intertextual uses of the codes and conventions of the horror genre. Reeves *et al.* have usefully encapsulated what is at stake in this type of popular cult TV:

> By the 1990s, two general types of cult television shows had emerged. The first type, in the tradition of *Star Trek*, is comprised of prime-time network programs that failed to generate large ratings numbers but succeeded in attracting substantial numbers of avid fans ... By contrast, shows of the second type first appear on cable or in fringe timeslots and are narrowly targeted at a niche audience. (Reeves *et al.* 1996, p. 31)

The X-Files, like *Buffy the Vampire Slayer*, is thus aimed at a cross-over audience composed of avid fans and more casual but committed viewers; it was not programmed or treated as a prime-time show that had to sustain 'hit' ratings. Likewise, the ratings for later *Star Trek* franchises (which arguably also began to address fans more directly, as well as drawing more obviously on horror intertexts in many Brannon Braga-scripted shows) and for *Buffy* are not in the bracket that would be expected for prime-time, mass-audience shows. Such shows, as examples of what Reeves *et al.* term 'TV II' (1996, p. 29), target multiple fan cultures via their generic hybridities:

> *The X-Files* has been especially canny in courting ... pre-existing fan
> cultures. [T]he show's generic migrations allow it to appeal to a variety of
> subgroups within sci-fi fandom ... The frequent plots dealing with serial
> killers and/or the supernatural draw in fans from the horror/dark fantasy fan
> groups that exist on the margins of sci-fi fandom. (Reeves *et al.* 1996, p. 32)

As designed cult TV, this type of US television drama has to textually negotiate
residual and emergent logics of imagined audiencing. Residual 'imagined
audiencing' invokes the figure of the mass, domestic audience that cannot be
regulated, and which has to be assumed to include vulnerable child-viewers.
However, a contrastive and emergent logic of imagined audiencing invokes the
figure of the expert fan audience, complete with media/genre competencies and
subcultural fan knowledge. Such contradictory logics lead to a confusion of
textual strategies, as the generic hybridity of *The X-Files* and *Buffy* partly
qualifies horror's intertexts via programmed anachronism or comedic distancing,
while also drawing on the conventions of graphic horror in order to target
'horror/dark fantasy' fans. Thus *Buffy*, for example, has been subjected to 'a cache
of ratings and parental advisories on the screen during each episode. Most ...
episodes are classified as TV14 ... and are labelled with DSLV warnings' while
also displaying marked 'tonal variation' as it cuts rapidly from 'serious' to 'ironic'
moments of horror genre intertextuality (Parks 2003, pp. 118 and 123; see also
Lake Crane 2004, p. 148).

The emergent logic of 'quality popular TV' (Jancovich and Lyons 2003)
aimed at fan audiences and promoted via industry narratives of televisual
authorship clashes discursively with residual – but still powerful – discourses of
TV censorship and regulation. Generic hybridity becomes not just a way to
interpellate fan audience coalitions; more than that, it is a way of managing the
discursive hybridity or confusion that underpins the multiple positionings and
'imagined audiencings' at work around contemporary TV horror.

Texts such as *Buffy* and *The X-Files* hence become notable for their move
towards 'showing more' of graphic horror's monstrosities while simultaneously
claiming a culturally valued status as 'authored' TV and/or targeting niche fan
audiences rather than mass audiences. Such textual manoeuvres in dark fantasy
are not restricted to the decentred US TV industry; similar responses have
occurred in the UK and in Denmark, through anthology series such as *Urban
Gothic* and serials such as *The Kingdom*.

The Kingdom (1994), directed by film *auteur* Lars von Trier, pushed at
televisual boundaries in its representations of horror. Far from 'showing less',
this example of 'quality/authored horror TV' concluded with 'its most notorious
scene ... [where] a nurse gives birth to a fully grown man, his head coming first
as he graphically spits and screams his way into the world' (Creeber 2002, p.
388). As with the cases of *Buffy* and *The X-Files*, this is TV horror partly
legitimated by discourses of authorship. However, unlike these US popular/cult
shows, *The Kingdom* was a serial rather than an ongoing series, its four-and-a-

half-hour running time being broadcast in five parts in the UK, where it was shown late at night on the specialist public service channel BBC2. *The Kingdom's* horror-genre-based representations were partly licensed by its textual structure – its most graphic horror appearing at the narrative climax of the final part – and partly by reference to von Trier's authorial vision. This auteurism was textually reinforced via the unusual device of having Lars von Trier himself appear onscreen at the end of each episode, speaking directly to camera:

> von Trier ... implies ... [a] ... duality at the end of each episode when he bizarrely addresses the audience: 'Should you want to spend more time with us at the Kingdom,' he warns, 'be prepared to take the good with the evil.' (Creeber 2002, p. 403)

This placing of the *auteur* within his own TV text can be considered as a variation on the strategy of programmed anachronism. In this case, it is 'programmed auteurism' that is produced, as *The Kingdom* anxiously attempts to textually prop up and sustain its legitimacy as authored TV. Just as programmed anachronism converts extra-textual discourses, readings and experiences of 'old horror' into a textual strategy aimed at cueing certain (detached, distanciated) responses to TV horror, so too does 'programmed auteurism' convert extra-textual discourses – this time of authorship – into textual strategies. In this instance, it is not a temporal distance from horror's allegedly powerful emotions that is sought, but rather a self-consciously aestheticized distance. In his work on *The Kingdom*, Glen Creeber suggests that '[p]erhaps its generic familiarity as a piece of television drama was able to "centre" its more unusual, unexpected and outrageous dimensions' (2002, p. 389). However, given the massively bizarre and episode-framing appearances made onscreen by von Trier (alongside rolling credits), I would suggest that it was this figure of the *auteur* that acted more significantly, not only to 'centre' but also to aestheticize (and thus make culturally 'safe') this drama as TV horror. Notably, the US remake of *The Kingdom* also drew heavily on discourses of authorship by using 'Stephen King' as a 'brand name' (see Fiedler 1987; Badley 2004). Entitled *Stephen King's The Kingdom Hospital* (ABC 2004), it featured writer and executive producer King onscreen in a cameo role as character Johnny B. Goode. Although not fully comparable to von Trier's 'programmed auteurism' in *The Kingdom*, this was nevertheless an attempt at reinforcing discourses of authorship directly within the text itself, rather than leaving them as extra-textual bids for cultural value.

If TV horror developed across the 1990s, and in different national contexts, towards 'showing more', it therefore did so via generic and discursive hybridity, with 'horror' and 'TV' being brought together via the pursuit of niche, fan audiences while remaining problematically disarticulated in relation to mass, domestic audiences. This tension between different 'imagined audiencings' has resulted in unusual textual strategies such as von Trier's liminal – inside-and-outside the text – address to camera, as well as 'gothic' classifications of graphic horror (*Urban Gothic*) and textual moments of programmed anachronism (e.g. in *The X-Files* and *Buffy*). TV horror has not yet entirely evaded the discursive positionings of television which suggest that horror, and the affective pleasures of horror, cannot belong on TV.

One major development, I have argued here, has been towards a conflictual discursive hybridity, in which 'showing more' exists uneasily alongside both discourses of TV censorship and 'imagined audiencings' that construct television's audiences as in need of protection from TV horror. Horror has indeed evolved on television. But it remains caught in transition between different discourses of television as a 'mass' and 'niche' medium. Horror on TV is still generally constructed as 'inauthentic', 'unscary', 'old/dated horror', as well as ironic or comedic, with all these attributions implicitly operating in contrast to discourses of the contemporary horror film as 'graphic', 'frightening' and 'cutting edge' (Hutchings 2001, p. 2). And the 'cultural category' of TV horror is still typically exnominated in favour of 'Gothic TV' in industry and academic discourses (Mittell 2004). Horror texts thus 'bring to bear and have borne upon them multiple genres' (Gamer 2000, p. 46). Such a view cannot be wholly totalizing, however, given industrial shifts towards construing 'quality popular' TV as authored, and towards targeting 'cult' fans of horror as a niche market.

In the next chapter I want to consider another of horror's para-sites: 'true horror'. Pleasures of horror have been recurrently analysed as responses to the *aesthetics* of art-horror fictions (Carroll 1990; Leffler 2000), while fan discourses have also, but differently and somewhat more selectively, emphasized the concept of horror-as-art (see Parts I and II). 'Art-horror' and 'horror-as-art' both assume a fixed or identifiable fact/fiction boundary, but what happens to discourses of horror's pleasures when that conceptual border is threatened?

Chapter 7

True Horror

Developing out of the arguments of the last chapter, there is a further way in which television has been discursively constructed as a threat to the pleasures of horror. Television has again become one of horror's para-sites by virtue of the fact that, potentially, it brings into proximity what can be termed 'true' (factual) horror and (fictional) 'art-horror'. So insistently are these 'factual-real' and 'fictional-entertainment' categories of horror discursively reiterated that it could be argued they form part of the fundamental, moral 'schemes of cultural categorization' that Noël Carroll discusses, following Mary Douglas's work (Carroll 1990, p. 31). TV scholars and horror writers have consistently reinforced categorical distinctions between 'true' and fictional horror. For example, Stephen King's (1982) survey of the horror genre, *Danse Macabre*, argues that:

> Horror has not fared particularly well on TV, if you except something like the six o'clock news ... [T]he reason horror has done so poorly, by and large, on TV, is ... [that] ... 'It is very difficult to write a successful horror story in a world which is so full of real horror'. (King 1982, pp. 250–1; see also Bianculli 1992, pp. 3 and 4)

King's concern appears to be primarily aesthetic rather than inherently moral; it becomes 'difficult' to create horror when one's audience has too freshly or immediately in mind the realities of 'true' horror. There is seemingly a necessary distance that has to be observed between 'reality' and 'entertainment' in order for horror fiction to function affectively, and pleasurably, as a genre. And it is television – construed as the bearer of news and a prime mediator of 'the real' – that threatens to undo this imaginative 'gap' that sustains horror as an aesthetic, narrative exercise. Television, it would seem, weakens the imaginative distance that has to be culturally and morally maintained between 'true' and 'entertainment' horror, between fact and fiction (see also Gabler 1998, p. 86; Solomon 2003, p. 250). A similar argument is also put forward by Gregory A. Waller (1987) when he relates TV horror (fiction) to TV news:

Having been to hell and back, the viewer can also proceed with life as usual, staying tuned for the 11:00 news and the never-ending stream of programs that have been advertised during the telefilm's commercial breaks. Watching in the well-lit, familiar confines of our homes, we know that television – life – goes on. (1987, p. 159)

Here, Waller also privileges TV news as horror fiction's disruptive Other. But in his account, it is not entirely clear whether 'the 11:00 news' supposedly deforms art-horror by presenting a rival and morally prioritized 'true' horror. Instead Waller seems – contra King – to position the news as a symbol of daily ordinariness and security. It is thus not just horror as a TV genre that is open to contradictory discursive bids for its status (see the previous chapter); news can be positioned as either 'horrific' or as 'calming' by different critics, yet in each case it still functions discursively as a reduction of horror fiction's effectiveness. If viewed as horrifying, TV news trumps art-horror, and if seen as a part of television's ritualistically soothing 'flow' (Williams 1975; see also Tithecott 1997, p. 119), it prematurely does away with and dissipates the (assumed) intense affects of horror fiction. In either case, news media reportage seemingly threatens to do away with the pleasures of fictional horror if 'fact' and 'fiction' stray too close together.

However, in Chapter 3 I emphasized (following Weigl 2002) that horror texts can often involve – and even potentially be defined by – category violations of a type that breach both cultural classifications ('dead'/'alive') and also theoretical binaries (e.g. the psychoanalytic 'play'/'transference' opposition). If this thoroughgoing category violation is the horror genre's very lifeblood then the question I want to pose here is, can critics' discursive separations of true horror and art-horror be sustained? What of horror texts that blur the lines between 'fact' and 'fiction'? And, more categorically challenging even than any such blurring, what of the horror genre's involvement in the 'real' reportage of 'real' events? I will argue here that fictional horror's tropes, devices and discursively assumed affects play a material and cultural role beyond their usually perceived parameters.

In what follows I will suggest that news stories can themselves be interpreted as horror texts that make use of the aesthetic structures of fictional horror. This should sensitize us to the importance of analysing horror's para-sites. For if horror operates intertextually and culturally outside the boundaries of its generically nominated texts (Winter 2000; Mittell 2004), then its cultural significance cannot be entirely captured by strictly genre-based studies. Much like 'strange TV' or 'Gothic TV', factual news texts may 'bring to bear' elements of the horror genre without having this generic attribution 'borne upon them', to return to the epigraph that frames this part of *The Pleasures of Horror* (Gamer 2000, p. 46).

In the next section I will specifically review philosophical arguments that separate out 'true' horror and 'art-horror', reconsidering Noël Carroll's (1990) work. I will then go on to analyse the fictional and journalistic representations of serial killers. As in the previous chapter, I will argue that horror's imputed and textual-affective pleasures can be highlighted and explored by considering disjunctions between where horror exists (empirically and intertextually) in our culture, and where it is common-sensically nominated as (safely and generically) existing.

KEEPING IT UNREAL

'True crime' exists alongside crime fiction as a generic category in contemporary pop culture, however controversial and hybridized its aesthetic/narrative/factual forms may be (see Biressi 2001; Brown 2003, p. 90). Yet there is no genre known as 'true horror': my chapter title is counterfactual. Presumably one could argue that occultist texts approach one possible cultural function for 'true horror', and then there is the mythic and demonized 'snuff movie' (Petley 2000; Black 2002, p. 115; Brown 2003, pp. 118–23; Carter and Weaver 2003, p. 56). It remains striking that the classification of 'horror' is culturally and discursively reserved for fictional, generic nominations. Like the notion of 'TV horror' (Chapter 6), I am suggesting that 'true horror' has been systematically and culturally exnominated. This offers us another of horror's para-sites for excavation, representing a further form of cultural common sense through which horror has been denied a textual and intertextual presence in discourses of genre.

'True horror' is seemingly a monstrous violation of basic cultural categories. Horror is not only kept unreal in ordinary language and everyday genre attributions (see Carroll 1990, p. 13). It is also kept unreal in academic studies of horror. Noël Carroll's definition of 'art-horror' is meant to mark out the (foundationally assumed) fact that:

> This kind of horror is different from the sort that one expresses in saying ...
> 'Brinksmanship in the age of nuclear arms is horrifying,' or 'What the Nazis
> did was horrible.' Call ... [this] ... usage of 'horror', *natural horror*. (1990,
> p. 12)

This is indeed 'the first of many lines' that Carroll draws in his *Philosophy of Horror* (Weigl 2002, p. 702). Carroll's choice of terms is instructive; by appearing as 'natural' such horror is supposedly unmediated, unconstructed and unpackaged. It simply *is*. What this opposition misses is that so-called 'natural' horror is often encountered precisely via mediation, narrativization, and other aesthetic devices. Natural horror remains 'natural' only in the most abstract and unhelpful of senses. This has been emphasized in John Taylor's work on photojournalism:

> While I accept Carroll's description of the visceral effects of 'art-horror', I cannot sustain his distinction between 'art-horror' and 'natural horror'. I am suggesting not that they are interchangeable, or the same, but that 'natural horror' does not exist. Some events (like floods or earthquakes) can be natural, but responses to them are cultural ... Horror is meaningful only because it is cultural and historical. What the Nazis did to the Jews ... was not 'natural horror', as Carroll claims, but a managed and organised politics of terror and extermination. (1998, p. 37)

What is notable about this critique of Carroll's work is that Taylor, too, feels the need to insist that the category separation called up by Carroll must be preserved. Even if 'natural' horror should be relabelled 'cultural horror' (testifying to its mediation, as in photographs of corpses, for example; see Taylor 1998, p. 37), the separation of cultural horror and 'art-horror' remains intact. Although Taylor observes that there 'is nothing about a text taken in isolation which infallibly distinguishes it as either documentary or fiction' (1998, p. 37), he suggests that the fact/fiction distinction lies, rather, in 'the way that viewers read the texts, what assumptions they make about them, and what they expect from them' (1998, p. 37). The 'natural' versus 'art-horror' distinction is thereby recomposed at the level of interpretative frameworks; what is usually taken as 'the horror genre' becomes distinguishable by the fact that it is to be read as fiction, regardless of whether its texts touch on, or make semiotic use of, 'real-life' threats or forms of 'natural horror', such as *The Keep* (1983, dr: Michael Mann) involving Nazi protagonists, or *Deathwatch* (2002, dr: Michael J. Bassett) and *The Bunker* (2001, dr: Rob Green) reflecting on the horrors of World War I and World War II respectively. And even where film texts such as *Dahmer* (2002, dr: David Jacobson) or *Ed Gein* (2000, dr: Chuck Parello) more directly claim to represent or 'dramatize' real serial killers' lives, according to such an 'interpretative framework' argument the 'community of understanding' for natural/cultural horror (or documentary/biopic horror) remains securely distinct from that for art-horror (see Ellis 2002, p. 198 on documentary forms and 'communities of understanding').

But this approach, useful though it may be, tends to reify such 'communities', neglecting how horror texts such as *Dahmer* may violate cultural categories of fact/fiction, thus violating their supposedly 'separable' communities of under-standing by throwing up category confusions, errors or hybrids (e.g., is *Dahmer* to be read as a biopic or a type of slasher flick, or a combination of the two?). Arguably, part of the success of *The Blair Witch Project* (1999, dr: Daniel Myrick and Eduardo Sánchez) as a 'horror mockumentary' (Rhodes 2002) lay in the fact that, regardless of whether actual viewers read it as documentary or fiction, it could be narrated in publicity and secondary discourses as an attack on the cultural categories of 'fact'/'fiction'. This almost made it, perhaps somewhat akin to the likes of *Dahmer* and *Ed Gein*, a kind of 'meta-horror' film – a film that monstrously violated cultural categories at the level of secondary, publicity intertexts rather than simply through its documentary 'look' or textual attributes (Stahl 2000, pp. 316–17; Rhodes 2002, p. 57; see also Fleming 2000, pp. 248–51). Contra Stahl (2000), it is hardly necessary to fall back on models of simulation/simulacra or postmodern theories to account for the cultural machineries surrounding *The Blair Witch Project*. What we find here, rather than some grandly exaggerated loss of 'the real', is a precise set of textual and intertextual negotiations with factual/fictional 'communities of understanding'. As Joel Black has argued, '*The Blair Witch Project* owed its success less to the finished product – the film itself – than to the unpredictable, interactive promotional process leading up to and following its release' (2002, p. 13), a process that sought to destabilize the film's status as either 'art-horror' or 'true' horror.

Noël Carroll is not alone in reinforcing the natural/art-horror distinction. In an essay entitled 'Real Horror', philosopher Robert C. Solomon also tackles the question of distinguishing art-horror from its real-life Other. Solomon invokes 11 September 2001 as an example of real horror:

> Regarding ... movies ... it is all well and good to ask what pleasure people find in the fear or horror that otherwise would seem to be a most unpleasant emotion ... But it makes no sense at all ... to ask such a question of real-life horror. (Solomon 2003, pp. 230–1; see also Levinson 1990 and 1991)

Solomon suggests that the real horror of 11 September 'was in no way pleasurable ... It did not involve any distinctive narrative ... did not involve any monsters (leaving aside the metaphors by which the terrorists would soon be described) ... did not involve epistemic uncertainty ... [and] ... [e]veryone watching was powerless to do anything' (2003, pp. 231–2). Solomon's comparison of true horror and 'art-horror' stands on the distinction that art-horror is 'by definition horror "mixed" and compromised ... by being packaged and intentionally presented ... the pleasure lies in precisely the fact that it is make-believe, that it is *not real*' (2003, p. 251).

Although Solomon's argument appears persuasive, like Carroll's (1990) construction of 'natural horror' it too lacks a focus on the *mediation* of what is termed 'real' horror. Solomon (2003) largely writes out the mediation of 11 September. He fails adequately to consider mediated narrations of the World Trade Center event (see Zelizer and Allan (eds) 2002; Jameson 2003), thus failing to address such coverage as also 'packaged and intentionally presented'. Instead, Solomon implies that 'real horror' is a form of pure disruption. If we accept this argument it then becomes necessary to note that, for Solomon, 'real horror' can only be an initial moment of unbidden catastrophe, whereas the subsequent repetitions, narrations, imagings and mediated aestheticizations of that 'moment' have no place within his schema. His argument therefore runs into difficulty when addressing the news mediation of 11 September:

> Art-horror is a good way to reiterate trauma in a safe ... way, if only because it ... is obviously not real. By contrast, real horror repeated – like the continuous repetition of television images after September 11th – can contribute to and even cause mental illness. (2003, p. 253)

Because Solomon has already defined 'real horror' in such a way that opposes it to the media constructions and aestheticizations of 'art-horror', he cannot deal with media images of 'real' horror as anything other than versions of a 'window on the world' that must, definitionally, lack any capacity for pleasurably or safely reiterating trauma. It is this that leads to Solomon's bizarre conclusion that watching images of 'real horrors' repeatedly can, unlike the repetitions of art-horror, 'cause mental illness'. Unsurprisingly, Solomon offers no evidence for this alleged 'distinction' between art-horror and real horror.

The error that produces this strangeness is, I would argue, Solomon's refusal to countenance 'real horror' that is also packaged and narrated. Like Carroll's 'natural horror', Solomon's 'real horror' is problematically defined from the outset as *not*-art-horror, as its logical opposite. This moral and categorical opposition leads both writers into a series of blind spots, since Carroll cannot account for art-horror that violates factual/fictional cultural categories, while Solomon fails to convincingly analyse the mediation of 'real horror'. What matters most for both critics is that art-horror 'cannot be *too* real' (Solomon 2003, p. 250).

Solomon addresses (and dismisses) an alternative viewpoint: 'that people use "make-believe" horror to *compensate* for real-life horrors such as those witnessed in New York on September 11th' (ibid.). This 'compensatory' view has been put forward, again in relation to 11 September, by Richard Kearney:

> The hunger for horror stories did not abate in the wake of 9/11 ... The main reason for this, I suspect, is that the terror of the Twin Towers was *so* terrible that surrogates were needed to put some kind of mask on it. Analogous or alternative horrors were desperately sought in the guise of images and stories that might take some of the harm out of the *actual* horror ... As if the narrative framing of horror, that Hollywood horror stories allowed, could afford relief from the unbearable immediacy of the event. (2003, p. 120)

Kearney's assertions seem opposed to the type of position staked out by Carroll (1990) and Solomon (2003). But like Taylor's (1998) challenge from photojournalism studies, Kearney's opposition resolves into sameness. Kearney's argument is based on assumptions similar to those that drive Solomon's work: narrative is equated only with horror film, whereas 'unbearable immediacy' marks out the 'event' of real horror. What is again philosophically denied is the possibility that 'real' horrors can be more than momentary events, that they can be mediated (over time) rather than being purely 'immediate', and that 'real' horrors can thus be journalistically and narratively-aesthetically framed.

Fortunately there is an alternative to the traditions represented by King (1982) and Waller (1987) regarding TV's monstrous over-proximity of fictional and factual horror, and Carroll (1990) and Solomon's (2003) arguments concerning real or 'natural' horror versus art-horror. Although rather more dispersed than philosophically systematic, a number of countering voices have stressed links between real and fictional horror. As Charles E. Weigl bluntly argues, 'the horror genre exists because horror exists' (2002, p. 718). Rather than viewing the relationship between 'generic' and 'true' horror as one of moral/ categorical separateness, distinguishable 'communities of understanding' or compensatory 'masking', other writers have stressed semiotic and intertextual continuities between true horror and art-horror. In *Images of Fear: How Horror Stories Helped Shape Modern Culture (1818–1918)*, Martin Tropp suggests that:

> Horror stories, when they work, construct a fictional edifice of fear and deconstruct it simultaneously, dissipating terror in the act of creating it. And real horrors are filtered through the expectations of readers trained in responding to popular fiction, familiar with a set of images, a language, and pattern of development. Horror fiction gives the reader the tools to 'read' experiences that would otherwise, like nightmares, be incommunicable. In that way, the inexpressible ... becomes understandable and communal. (1990, p. 5)

True horror, in this argument, can only be perceived as such by virtue of the meaning-makings of horror's generic templates and narrative structures. Fact and fiction can never be as clearly separated out as moral arguments – discursively denying pleasure to 'true' horror – would dictate (see Malcolm 1991, p. 154). Rather than the 'events' of true horror exceeding or escaping narrative, they are culturally placed within narrative schemes taken from horror fiction according to Tropp (1990). This genre-'reality' linkage is seconded by Nick Bingham (2002) in a study of Frankenstein-like narratives in journalistic coverage of genetically modified food. Bingham suggests that:

> Far from being abstract 'mind-sets' ... located safely (or otherwise) within the heads of a marginalized fandom, the 'expectations, conventions, and interpretative codes' ... that constitute the genre have helped shape our contemporary surroundings. (2002, p. 182)

Like Tropp (1990), Bingham (2002) identifies how the horror genre's narratives offer 'us a way of navigating our way through an unfamiliar landscape' (2002, p. 185) by making sense of scientific developments and cultural, moral challenges. Factual 'events' are thus narrativized within a more general process of cultural meaning-making, rendering fact/fiction boundaries permeable if not abjected (see also Knox 1998, pp. 27–8). I would argue that it is no accident that Timothy Murray opens his fascinating study *Like a Film: Ideological Fantasy on*

Screen, Camera and Canvas (1993) with the words '[i]magine a script for a horror movie' (1993, p. 1). This first line eventually discloses its meaning; what Murray is describing as a horror movie is in fact 'a docudrama of an event that shocked New York City on ... April 23rd, 1992', a car accident in Washington Square (Murray 1993, pp. 1–4). Murray's point in invoking the horror genre here is that docudrama and fiction can share codes of meaning. More than this, Murray argues that 'the specialized codes of cinema can themselves become ... "naturalized" or cultural' (1993, p. 3). Rather than there being absolute dividing lines between cinematic fictions and news-based codes of representation, mediation can fold back into contemporary culture, meaning that real people, and real journalists, can comprehend or decode 'true'/'real' experiences as being 'like a movie' (Murray 1993, p. 4). Returning to the example of 'true horror' offered by both Solomon and Kearney, 11 September, it should be recalled that early sense-making attempts on the part of journalists involved exactly this linkage:

> Some news reports likened the unfolding tragedy to a Hollywood disaster epic – 'It looks like a movie', said NBC's Katie Couric – although as time moved on comparisons with real events in history came to the fore. (Zelizer and Allan 2002, p. 4; see Branston and Stafford 2003, pp. 74–7)

Such connections are more than merely rhetorical, more than convenient similes. They are moments and linkages in which horror fiction escapes its fictional, generic frames in order to prop up narratives and meanings surrounding 'true' horror. They are moments in which the horror genre is not where it is, instead circulating intertextually in cultural spaces, para-sites, that are generally and discursively constructed as alien to 'art-horror' (see Cohl 1997, p. 15).

Michael Thomas Carroll (2000) has also argued that horror fiction's interpretative codes can move outside its generic boundaries: 'slippage ... between the texts of horror and other texts is based on the extension of ... primal disgust to the symbolic boundaries of the self as reflected in the ideologies of nation, race, and gender' (2000, p. 105). For Carroll (2000), horror's chief ideological importance lies not in the possibility that its own fictional texts are ideologically 'progressive' or 'reactionary' (see Chapter 3), but rather that explicitly 'Political' (with a capital 'P') and factual ideologies can function as extensions of horror's thematics, disgusts and Otherings. Carroll's proffered example is, in fact, fascism, which he analyses as 'cognate to the horror literature' of H.P. Lovecraft in the 1920s (2000, p. 101). If this argument does indeed hold, then studies of the horror genre which overpolice, and powerfully erect boundaries between 'fact' and 'fiction' (Carroll 1990; Leffler 2000; Jones 2002; etc.) can only fail to discern the multiple cultural lives of horror fiction's meaning-making, both within 'Political' ideologies and within the journalistic narration of true horror and its tragedies.

In order to further explore these possibilities, often excluded in definitions and studies of discursively constituted 'generic' horror, in the next section I will consider serial-killer narratives. How might 'true horror' and 'art-horror' intersect here?

SERIALITY AND DISCOURSES OF PLEASURE, CLICHÉ AND DEADLY DEFERRAL

Serial-killer narratives have arguably provided one privileged interface for 'true' horror and fictional art-horror since it is here that cultural narratives of both 'fact' and 'fiction' are forced to deal with 'realist horror' in which 'the monster is a true-to-life rather than supernatural being' (Freeland 1995, p. 130). Unlike vampires, zombies, werewolves *et al.*, the figure of the serial killer-as-monster can readily travel between fact and fiction, requiring no ontologically reconstructed 'fictional worlds' to harbour its existence. Such 'realist horror' has been described by Cynthia Freeland as thwarting 'the initial assumption that we can draw a clear distinction between artistic imitations and reality' (1995, p. 133). This apparent ontological insecurity of the 'fact'/'fiction' boundary has been attested to in many recent studies of the serial killer. These routinely track the serial-killer image through reportage and fictions, often moving unannounced between the two spheres (Duclos 1998; Seltzer 1998; Newitz 1999), using chapter structures to demarcate the fragile borders of fact and fiction (Jenkins 1994), or discussing the blurring of fact and fiction in a preface prior to focusing purely on serial-killer 'fictions' (see Simpson 2000, pp. xiv–xv).

As in Roger Stahl's (2000) reading of *The Blair Witch Project*, 'postmodernism' is again invoked by Freeland as the theoretical classification that can make sense of such fact–fiction blurring (1995, p. 133; see also Conrath cited in Simpson 2000, p. xiv). But this manoeuvre does little to help us consider exactly what is at stake when fictional and factual narratives of the serial killer begin to interpenetrate. Nor does it allow us to consider, in a more nuanced manner, how 'factual' and 'fictional' narratives and their aesthetic structures may come to resemble one another while also, perhaps, differing in crucial ways.

In this discussion, then, I will avoid citing 'postmodernism' as an apparent explanation, especially since it also appears to fix 'the real' in place by virtue of claiming that this is precisely what has been lost within media culture. In other words, 'reality' has to be discursively, ontologically and argumentatively fixed in place in order for the theorist-critic to suggest that 'reality' and 'fiction' have begun to bleed, via the postmodern, irredeemably into one another. Any such philosophical argument is thus self-absenting, if you like; the critic is positioned outside or above that which she or he surveys, being able to nostalgically lament *and define* the very 'real' that is supposedly under threat. Such arguments are often also profoundly 'presentist' in tone, lacking a wider sense of cultural history and implying that the 'postmodern' collapse of fact/fiction begins with

TV 'infotainment' in the 1990s (Tithecott 1997, p. 118), or even with the apparent novelty of *The Blair Witch Project* (Stahl 2000).

Challenging such grand-theoretical presentism, Karen Halttunen's (1998) study *Murder Most Foul: The Killer and the American Gothic Imagination* traces the shift towards 'gothic narrative' in factual accounts and explanations of actual crimes, arguing that this began to occur in America in the eighteenth century:

> emerging secular literature organized the popular response to murder within a set of narrative conventions that are most usefully characterized as Gothic ... The first of these conventions was horror, which employed inflated language and graphic treatments of violence and its aftermath in order to shock the reader into an emotional state that mingled fear with hatred and disgust. The new murder stories explicitly instructed readers to experience horror in the face of the crime. (1998, p. 3; compare this with Ingebretsen 2001, p. 20)

These news stories formed part of what Halttunen identifies as 'the cult of horror that was beginning to shape popular murder literature' (1998, p. 49). She dates the first 'full-blown horror account in American murder literature' to 1783 (1998, p. 51), arguing that gothic narration replaced the 'condemned criminal as moral exemplum ... [of] ... a sinful humanity' with the 'murderer as moral alien' (1998, p. 57). Halttunen also suggests that gothic narrative served a dual purpose in crime reporting; it allowed readers to confirm their own normalcy 'in the face of the morally alien', while simultaneously 'Gothic-horror affirmed the ultimate incomprehensibility of any given crime of murder' (1998, p. 4). This failure 'to assign meaning' to crime meant that gothic narratives were compelled to fall back on 'Gothic conventions of the fundamental mystery of murder – its intrinsic unknowability' (1998, p. 4).

Halttunen's historicizing perspective indicates that for as long as 'the gothic' has existed as a fictional genre its narrative framings have leaked out into 'true'/ factual reportage. This argument reinforces my own concern here with the category-violating narratives and discursively constructed pleasures of 'true' horror. Whereas Cameron and Frazer (1987) argue that 'horror ... belongs to the domain of the aesthetic' (cited in Tithecott 1997, p. 130), marking out the same moral boundaries as Robert Solomon (2003) and alleging that any pleasure taken in 'true' horror can only be inappropriate, Richard Tithecott's (1997) study of Jeffrey Dahmer and the media's construction of the serial killer strongly suggests otherwise:

> now we can rush live, without leaving our homes, to a scene of a crime or a disaster via a television camera strapped to an ambulance or police car. The sense of inappropriateness has disappeared. *The pleasure of horror, that which was deemed appropriate only in a recognizable world of fiction, is now something one can experience (without fear of condemnation) on television framed as reality.* In our

creation and consumption of infotainment *we have sprung the aesthetics of horror from fiction*. (1997, p. 130, my italics; see also Black 1991, pp. 9–10)

Reading Tithecott (1997) alongside Halttunen (1998), we can suggest that horror's movement beyond fiction is not entirely culturally novel (although its presence outside fiction clearly remains moralistically overruled, contested, and/ or rendered discursively invisible by critics concerned to reinforce the fact/fiction boundary). But precisely what 'pleasures of horror' have escaped the bounds of the fictional and come to rest, sometimes exnominated or rendered critically invisible, in the para-site of 'true' horror?

It has become a commonplace in cultural theories of the serial killer for critics to argue that actual serial killers' actions tend to lack narrative structures. Theorists such as Denis Duclos (1998), Cynthia Freeland (1995) and Mark Seltzer (1998) have all posited that twentieth-century serial killers' crimes are, in the first instance, either under-narrativized or un-narratable by the standards of classical narrative, indicating a private and a cultural 'death of meaning' (Duclos 1998, p. 166). Other writers have gone on to argue that it is gothic narrative which ultimately supplies an aestheticized intelligibility to these crimes (see, for example, Biressi 2001, pp. 178–81 and Jenkins 1994, p. 108). Pursuing this line of argument, Nicola Nixon claims that '[serial] killers' actions, in their abject plotlessness, are intrinsically bereft of any narrative potential to proffer comprehensibility' (1998, p. 222). She argues that it is this 'representational vacuum' (1998, p. 223) which calls literary solutions into being: 'gothic figures flesh out with fiction what is otherwise unavailable in the real, and, in turn, make "story" possible – although true crime generally fails to acknowledge the debt' (1998, p. 224).

The question of meaninglessness versus meaningfulness appears to be crucial here, as it is in discursive oppositions between 'real' and art-horror (e.g. Solomon 2003). For Nixon (1998), pleasures of horror encountered in true horror are the formal pleasures of a tale well told. However, literary-gothic attempts at narrativizing actual serial killers' actions have been repeatedly counter-positioned not as the achievement of secure meaning (and narrative pleasure taken in comprehensibility), but rather as semiotic failures:

> our fascination with such monsters persists in the face of a basic frustration to understand or explain them. If the monster is given any motives at all, they are formulaic sexual ones. But such clichéd horror film explanations are similarly trotted out in news accounts of real cases ... Plots in realist horror, like stories on the nightly news, are dominated by the three r's: random, reductive, repetitious. (Freeland 1995, pp. 131 and 134)

Motives and narrative explanations are said to be 'formulaic' and 'clichéd' (Freeland), or again they 'have a transparently perfunctory character ... take the form of pop-psychology and cliché ... [and] ... are *experienced as unconvincing*'

(Seltzer 1998, p. 255) by the reader. In this orthodoxy, the seriality and repetition of serial-killer representations vis-à-vis motivation allegedly undermine narrative pleasures of meaning-making. Efforts to supply (gothic) narrative structure, and intelligibility, themselves become overly serialized and thus excessively artificial/unreal in the eyes of these critics.

By contrast, Nixon's argument – along with that of Biressi (2001), Jenkins (1994) and Tithecott (1997) – is that horror's narrative, aesthetic frames and conventions can produce pleasures of true horror that are akin to those theorized for art-horror (Carroll 1990), and in which the serial-killer figure, in factual and fictional texts, is placed within similarly hypersignifying narratives of repressed childhood trauma, or constructed as part of a narrative that emphasizes the serial killer's (fantasized/mythic) omnipotence and transgression of moral values (e.g., see Staiger (1993, p. 145) and Tasker (2002) on the appeal of Hannibal Lecter).

Perhaps unsurprisingly, 'seriality' remains the master trope here. On one side of this debate seriality is harnessed to discourses of displeasure and dissatisfaction: this is the seriality of the 'cliché', or the seriality of 'interminable chapters ... to keep one waiting for an ever deferred conclusion' (Halberstam 1995, p. 172). And set against these variously frustrating versions of seriality there remains the seriality of narrative, carrying implied pleasures of 'good' aesthetic form. If the pleasures of art-horror have indeed found a home-from-home in true horror, then this argument suggests that it is pleasures of narrative structure which are paramount in both fact and fiction (Gomel 2003, p. xiv). Indeed, Richard Dyer (2002) has suggested that conventions of narrative structure considerably delimit exactly which stories can be told about real serial killers. Dyer argues, somewhat provocatively, that it is not a serial killer's crimes *per se* that are un-narratable, but rather these crimes viewed from the victim's perspective:

> You could in principle devote a whole book or film to the victim's life up to the murder, but it would ... be pretty boring and in any case have nothing to do with the murder, because that is just what erupts into the narrative and ends it. On the other hand, if you just told the story of the victim *as* victim, then there'd be next to no story and it'd be over too soon. And we cannot dwell on any individual victim too much anyway, because the point is the repetition, the next episode/victim, in short, the seriality .... [This] is merely a function of our pleasure in being told stories, in the satisfaction of our delight in the forms of narrative. (2002, p. 116)

Dyer concludes that 'in this age of seriality' good stories must 'give us the narrative hooks and repetitions we have learnt to crave' (2002, p. 116). Although restricting the type of accounts that can be given of serial killers, this alleged cultural need for the solace of narrative form once more positions art-horror and 'true' horror as twinned performances of hypersignification (see Chapter 3 on repetition-compulsion and purely fictional serial killers/slashers). Both types of horror are called upon to deliver the specific rhythms and pacings of 'good' narrative, being neither over too soon nor infinitely delayed. In a sense, then, a serial killer's actions offer a type of pre-seriality, where an actual series of crimes can then be made meaningful via aesthetic, hypersignifying post-serialization. Or to put it another way, what serial killer narratives do, in both fact and fiction, is work to produce an aesthetically satisfying sense of seriality and certainty/ legibility through 'their stock characters ... [and] behavioral profiles' (Fuss 1993, p. 199; see also Indiana 1999, pp. xiv–xv and Roscoe and Hight 2001, p. 178).

However, the 'serial' in the term 'serial killer' has also been discursively linked to a deadly version of narrative dissatisfaction (i.e. the infinite provocation of further desire). This linkage is contained within the derivation/etymology of the phrase itself. As Mark Seltzer recounts, Robert Ressler – the FBI agent who has been credited with coining the term 'serial killer' – did so partly by referring to movie serials:

> in my mind were the serial adventures we used to see on Saturday at the movies ... Each week you'd be lured back to see another episode, because at the end of each one was a cliff-hanger. In dramatic terms, this wasn't a satisfactory ending, because it increased, not lessened the tension. The same dissatisfaction occurs in the mind of serial killers. (Ressler cited in Seltzer 1998, p. 64)

As Seltzer goes on to argue, this 'would seem to posit something like an equation between acts of killing and an addiction to representations' (1998, p. 65). Serial killers' murderous repetition-compulsions have thus been foundationally, definitionally and discursively linked to the role of media audiences whose desires are held in thrall to unresolved serial narratives. This discursive articulation has, of course, proved extremely tempting to critical media scholars, since its logic can be taken up within moral critiques of the media. For example, Mark S. Roberts discusses what he terms the 'media-addict-murderer' (2003, p. 353) in which specific types of true crime can supposedly be linked to media addiction and the 'dissolution of television and media in general into life' (ibid.). The point, in this argument, is that subject/object divisions have (allegedly) disastrously collapsed for some individuals, along with the 'media'/'reality' distinction, such that:

> There is only a 'hybrid monster' forged by the fragmented extensions of a self absorbed into the blinding speed of electronic media. A self that reveals itself only by taking on and speaking through, that is monitoring, the very form of the media to which it owes that existence. (2003, p. 352)

This weakened subject, who feels their existence only in relation to the media, is also attested to in Joel Black's (1991) discussion of 'media-mediated murder', where 'in the world of the hyperreal, identity is contingent upon image' (1991, p. 135). Again, Black links specific types of true crime, including the serial killer (1991, p. 142), to a 'quest for identity' that seemingly only the media can deliver within a hyperreal scene. Mimetic addiction to media, especially the media perceived as a (or *the*) source of self-identity, is therefore harnessed to the figure of the serial killer within a generalized critique of hyper-reality. The serial killer's moral transgression and crime become synecdochally figurable as the crime of a society in which media and reality are not successfully kept apart, and thus in which the art-horror/true horror category is violated. Seriality is linked to a discourse of deadly deferral in this theoretical narrative due to the fact that 'the media' (but especially television) and 'the serial killer' are made part of a semiotic equivalence. Both mirror the other's loss of reality. Other critics have not used the powerfully morally transgressive figure of the serial killer to validate a moral critique of contemporary mediation *per se*, but have instead focused more precisely on the linkage in Ressler's 'serial killer' definition between himself-as-dissatisfied-media-audience and the fantasizing killer:

> What is interesting here is the way Ressler, who studies serial killers, is himself participating in the same type of serialized, unsatisfying fantasy. When he came up with the name 'serial killer,' it was he who was thinking about adventure serials like *The Phantom*. Along these same lines, we may postulate that the pleasure an American audience gets out of consuming serial killer narratives is in the way serialized homicidal crimes seem so well-adapted to the mass cultural form. (Newitz 1999, p. 76)

Like Annalee Newitz, Mark Pizzato (1999) also embraces the discursive link between serial audiences and serial killers, but unlike Newitz he does so in order to condemn possible audience pleasures in the seriality of serial-killer narratives: 'we are in danger of becoming more and more "addicted" to television and movies, like [Jeffrey] Dahmer to his violent fantasies and rituals' (1999, pp. 97 and 88–9). Here, Ressler's blurring of himself-as-audience and the serial killer is again opened out into an all-purpose condemnation of media seriality and generalized 'addiction'. Once more, the serial killer functions less as an object of study, and more as a metaphor that can be used to cast moral disapprobation across an anonymous 'mass' of consumers construed, rather bizarrely, as serial-killers-*manqué*.

Given this discursive reliance on seriality as a kind of deadly deferral or unsatisfying, compelling 'media addiction' that mirrors the serial killer's unsatisfying fantasies, we should consider that Richard Tithecott's (1997, p. 130) conclusions cited above – that the pleasures of art-horror can supposedly now be enjoyed in relation to true horror without moral condemnation – may appear excessively optimistic. Indeed, what I have been tracing here is precisely the way in which many theorists either deny or exnominate pleasure altogether in relation to true horror, or view any such pleasure as 'sick' and morally inappropriate (Solomon 2003, p. 231), using the figure of the serial killer to mirror an imputed moral 'sickness' in media society *tout court*, and/or in media audiences (Pizzato 1999; Roberts 2003).

However, Mark Seltzer's (1998, p. 255) dismissal of explanatory clichés in serial-killer narratives raises a different version of serial displeasure; not infinitely deferred satisfaction and media addiction, but instead a repetition-too-far, a serial iteration of terms that collapses desire into boredom and dissipates narrative involvement or identification via a breaking of the aesthetic frame. Seltzer positions his ideal reader (and by implication, himself as an academic, psychoanalytic reader) in the role of detached sceptic, unconvinced by narrative clichés and not at all captivated by seriality. This should caution us that seriality can be, and has been, claimed for a variety of discursive positions. As I have demonstrated here, it can be used:

(1)   to discursively secure or fix the pleasures of horror across 'true' horror and art-horror;
(2)   to pathologize all mediated seriality, via the 'serial' killer, as a type of compulsion/addiction; and
(3)   to underpin moral arguments that deny narrative pleasure altogether in relation to what are characterized as 'real' serial-killer non-narratives or failed/clichéd attempts to narrativize resistant, brute reality.

The first position is what I have broadly argued for across this chapter, while the second and third stances both play a role in seeking, I would say prematurely and simplistically, to culturally fix distinctions in place between true or 'real' horror and art-horror. The second position, often linked to a generalized 'postmodern' lament (see Black 2002, p. 15), views true horror and art-horror as bleeding together while the theorist-critic is simultaneously placed outside this scene rather than being implicated within it. This critic hence plays the role of detached seer and moralist wishing for 'fact' and 'fiction' to be (re-)purified. Although the third position may initially seem very much opposed to 'postmodern loss of the real' arguments, it actually shares their focus on moralistically cleaving 'fact' from 'fiction' in the face of challenges to this binary. Here, discursive work is done – foundationally and repeatedly – to maintain the fact/fiction division, primarily through the denial of pleasure, narrative and mediation in relation to 'true' horror, which is figured as raw, immediate and narrative-less. As Julia Hallam and Margaret Marshment (2000) have remarked, 'the ethical and moral concern of "blurring the boundaries" between fiction and fact is a discursive property of different academic practices' (2000, p. 237). That is, academic practices and discourses *work on texts to produce them as meaningful within ethical/moral frameworks* which are concerned with fact/fiction 'blurring', either identifying and decrying such category violation, or ruling it out a priori.

I have argued in this chapter that 'fact'/'fiction' can bleed together as an expression of the horror genre's thoroughgoing and textual mixing of cultural categories, a specific violation that is curiously opposed by critics such as Carroll (1990) who have otherwise championed horror texts' abilities to challenge cultural categories. As I suggested at the beginning of Chapter 6, by considering *where* (not why) horror's affects and pleasures are culturally and discursively assumed to exist – in art-horror but not true horror – we can highlight assumptions which have been made about the pleasures of horror; that they definitionally relate to narrative structure, legibility and a safe distance from 'the real', for example. We can also examine horror's 'para-sites' to indicate how such pleasures are culturally constituted and policed, such that even philosophers of horror are at pains to condemn or deny 'pleasures' taken in 'real' horror via a marginalizing of the aestheticization, mediation and narration of true horror.

In the next chapter I will move on to consider a further para-site for horror's pleasures, and thus another cultural site that has been defined as alien to horror: the terrain of cultural theory itself. Theories of horror (as well as other, influential social/cultural theories) may not, after all, be entirely and categorically separable from the horror genre and its supposed affects and pleasures. Indeed, 'Theory' may actually work through various codes and conventions of the horror genre in order to attempt to shock, outrage and affect its readers.

Chapter 8

Theory-horror

So far in this part of *The Pleasures of Horror* I have suggested that the codes, conventions and assumed pleasures of the horror genre have typically been discursively restricted within the terrain of TV drama and in relation to the factual reportage/mediation of 'true' horror. Horror 'naturally' (i.e. culturally) belongs instead to film and fiction. Its intertexts are critically negated or neglected in relation to other para-sites, being rendered relatively invisible in the academic literature on horror. Exnomination is the order of the day, with 'TV horror' becoming somehow oxymoronic (or subordinated to 'Gothic TV'), while 'true crime' displaces true horror as a culturally viable classification. In each case, the horror genre's empirical, intertextual presence beyond its archetypal and safely fixed cultural locations is glossed over, both outside and inside the academy. Yet horror's supposedly 'invisible' intertexts persist in their cultural overflow and in their challenge to categorical distinctions such as fact/ fiction. As Ken Gelder has eloquently observed, 'the rhetorics of horror circulate more broadly ... They provide ways of defining ... what is evil ... and ... good in societies, what is monstrous ... and ... "normal" ... and so on. These rhetorics are put to use routinely not just in horror texts themselves' (2000, p. 1).

In this chapter I will argue that the texts of social/cultural theory form a further para-site where the tropes and narrative structures of the horror genre have circulated, and where 'what is evil ... and ... good in societies' have been defined through the rhetorics of horror (Rickels 1999, p. x). Horror fictions, I am suggesting, have a reach that extends not only beyond fiction and into 'fact', but also into the hallowed, jargon-heavy pages of 'Theory' (Cunningham 2002, pp. 16–19). These 'other kinds of writing' (Gamer 2000, p. 45) are intertextually and dialectically indebted to the horror genre, which displays a role and a presence beyond its 'generic' boundaries as a cultural category (Mittell 2004).

It is common for social and cultural theory to be considered within academic subculture via a series of powerfully structuring oppositions or 'moral dualisms' (Hills 2002, pp. 8–9). As Ann Game has argued of sociology:

the discipline is defined through the oppositions, fact-fiction and theory-fiction; and, with the negation of fiction, the dualism, fact and theory, remains. Social reality is taken as determinant; theory is a reflection. But, this reflection is privileged as adequate correspondence to social reality, as opposed to fictional reflection. (1991, p. 3)

This 'repression of fiction' (1991, p. 7) through theory seen as correspondence-to-the-real, blocks any view of social (and cultural) theory as 'a writing practice' (ibid.) and as a form of textuality in its own right (see also Greig 2004). It is as if theory presents ideas in a neutral register, without using narrative strategies, rhetorics, tropes and discourses drawn from outside the properly 'theoretical' sphere. Any allegation that a given theory is narrativizing, or using some rhetorical/affective devices thus becomes a challenge to the 'properly' theoretical identity of the given text. This appears to remain the case as much in relation to deconstructionist philosophy as sociology, given that Jacques Derrida's response to readings of his *Specters of Marx* (1994) is to point out how critics have devalued his work by reading it as an affective, narrative text rather than as 'good' theory:

> But I am naturally no longer in agreement with him [Aijaz Ahmad] when he reduces this … to the 'performance' of a 'literary text' … in its turn reduced to conventional, confused notions of 'form of rhetoric', 'affectivity', 'tone', and so forth. Who would deny that there are rhetoric, affect and tone in *Specters of Marx*? I certainly would not, but I lay a different kind of claim to them, and relate them differently to the performativity of the analysis. Does Aijaz Ahmad think his text is so very atonal? Does he think that what he writes has been purged of all affectivity, all rhetoric …? (Derrida 1999, p. 230, see also pp. 234–5 and 247 where Derrida is responding to Jameson 1999, Lewis 1999 and Ahmad 1999 among others)

I will return to the question of theory's 'performative' status below. Here I want to note only, with Derrida, that such questions of whether, and when, theory is read as 'aesthetic' remain questions of 'how one writes or argues, of what the norms that apply here are (especially the academic norms). This question is anything but "aesthetic"; it is particularly, and perhaps above all, political' (1999, p. 248). That is, reading theory *as* aesthetic (narrative/affective/tonal) remains a cultural-political practice of disqualification within academic arguments. It represents an attempt to position rival theories as improper and monstrous forms of non-theory. The way in which specific theories have been discursively positioned as art-horror in order to disqualify them as 'improper' scholarship can be made readily apparent by considering a few examples drawn from TV Studies:

Poltergeist [1982, dr: Tobe Hooper] ... and *Videodrome* [1983, dr: David Cronenberg] ..., for example, picture the television set itself as a source of horror – a notion less imaginatively pursued by certain opponents of television, like Jerry Mander. Mander's *Four Arguments for the Elimination of Television* can be read as something of a horror story in which television is an evil, *Caligari*-like monster that insidiously isolates and manipulates viewers, transforming them into mindless, enslaved zombies. (Waller 1987, p. 146)

Here, a critical position that Gregory Waller wishes to rhetorically devalue – Mander's work – is not dismissed via detailed argument. It is, rather, dispatched by discursively aligning Mander's work with art-horror, then characterizing Mander's theory as 'less imaginative' than horror fictions! A similar manoeuvre occurs in Joan Hawkins's study of art-horror *Cutting Edge* (2000). Hawkins condenses her alignment of John Ellis's (1982) 'glance theory' and *Videodrome*'s art-horror into a single adjective, 'Cronenbergian':

In Cronenbergian fashion, TV takes on a kind of viral aspect here, such that not only TV programs but the apparatus itself seems empowered to infect and transform the viewer, to literally change the way the viewer looks (or doesn't look) at images. (Hawkins 2000, pp. 40–1, my italics)

These instances concern critics who are explicitly activating and reading theories *as* horror, very much in order to devalue said theories as 'inauthentic' and 'bad' theory-fictions (for further examples concerning feminist work read/devalued as horror stories, see the account of 'gothic feminism' in Meyers 2001, pp. 4–7). Such interpretative activations of theory-as-horror work, morally, to maintain the separation of theory and horror, implying that theory forfeits its value (and identity) as theory when it can be read as Cronenbergian, or as 'a constant flow of horror stories' (Christina Hoff Sommers cited in Meyers 2001, p. 5).

Contra such activations of theory-as-horror, my argument in this chapter is emphatically not aimed at devaluing some monstrous hybrid to be termed 'theory horror'. Rather, I want to highlight how 'academic norms' render empirically evident intertexts (such as horror's narratives) invisible in theoretical texts via a dominant subcultural view of 'theory' as opposed to 'fiction' (Game 1991, p. 3). As long as describing any given theory as 'aesthetic' remains only a term of abuse or disqualification (as in Waller 1987 and Hawkins 2000), then we will be strangely incapable of taking seriously the ways in which theory seeks to persuade, startle and even affect its readers. While horror is generally discursively positioned as a 'sensationalist' genre working on its readers'/audiences' bodies (Linda Williams 1999), academic work tends to be discursively counter-positioned by scholars as occurring within a resolutely non-affective cocoon of pure, disembodied 'rationality' and 'logic' (see Hills 2002, p. 3). Given that fact/fiction boundaries have been tenaciously reinforced in influential work on art-horror (Carroll 1990), and given the politics of 'academic norms' referred to by Derrida (1999), perhaps we should have expected 'theory horror', as another of horror's para-sites, to be discursively ruled out and warded off by conventional, communal academic framings of 'Theory':

> Of course, to some, the desire to juxtapose the name of Jacques Derrida with that of Stephen King, Peter Straub, George Romero, and even Count Dracula might seem monstrous in itself but then, as Donna Haraway suggests, 'monsters have always defined the limits of community in Western imaginations'. (Castricano 2001, p. 13; on a possible 'aesthetic' of the Derridean text see Derrida 1999, p. 248)

My interest here lies in challenging this view of 'Theory' (whether deconstructionist or sociological, psychoanalytic or cognitive) as made up of disembodied, Olympian and philosophically rational-logical texts. Forms of cultural theory have become institutionally and academically successful, I will argue, precisely because they seek to horrify, shock and affect their readers. Freudianism, Marxism and post-structuralism have not succeeded mimetically by dint of mere logic, but rather by affectively provoking their readers. Given this argument, the separation of 'text' and 'experience' that has marred not only cultural studies and its persistent text/audience binary, but also psychoanalysis with its Lacanian/object-relations binary, therefore needs to be carefully reconsidered (see Minsky 1998; Campbell 2000). Theoretical texts are always an experience for their readers, as well as being merely textual 'arguments' (see Coen 1994 and Ekegren 1999). Cultural theory, as much as horror fiction, thus needs to be addressed as an affective and cognitive experience, moving through what D.A. Miller (1988, p. 190) has fleetingly referred to as 'the somatics of writing' and towards what Terry Threadgold (1997, p. 31) has discussed as the 'associative' logic of reading: 'Other ideas, other significations, other texts are associated with the text as we read. It is a corporeal process and a game.' It is hence to *experiencing theory* as a material, corporeal process, and not 'reading' it as an abstraction-on-the-page, that this discussion will turn (see also Barrett 1999, pp. 202–3).

I have argued elsewhere (Hills 2004e) that theories of horror (and social/cultural theory more generally) tend to be treated as 'constative' – that is, as disclosing facts about, or conceptual structures of, real states of affairs. Contesting such a position, I have suggested that theory should instead be considered as significantly performative:

> the habitual orientation of the truth-seeking theorist [implies that] a given theory should be, either scientifically or hermeneutically, more adequate than its rivals, and should thus refer to a state of affairs outside its own model of these affairs. And yet, even while pursuing a constative or referential view of theoretical work, theorists continue to do things with theory, that is, they continue to perform cultural identities, [and] (de)value objects of study ...

Thinking about theories of horror as performative does not mean entirely bracketing off all questions of truth ... It does, however, mean (temporarily) shifting our focus away from the referential claims of different theories. *Performative theorization* is the cultural work that theory performs as a persuasive, legitimating, affective, and valorizing form. (Hills 2004e, pp. 205–6)

Considered performatively, theory does not merely tell us about the world, or even about the world of media texts. Rather, social/cultural theory (and I am including media, literary and film theories under this rubric) does things with texts, challenging the wider cultural devaluation of the horror genre, for example (Hills 2004e), or endeavouring to jolt and morally agitate audiences into ways of thinking and feeling critically about media culture (see Barcan 2003, pp. 368–9). When viewed as performative, theory has to be taken as an effort to influence and persuade, affect and move its experiencing, embodied readers.

As José López has recently pointed out, social theory is typically approached in textbooks via 'the visual metaphor ... asking students to consider what is excluded from the conceptual vistas opened up by particular theoretical positions' (2003, p. 2), or via 'the notion that ... theories are conceptual maps ... [where] ... theorizing is represented as an attempt to produce a logical and coherent network of concepts that can be used to map ... reality' (2003, p. 3). However, such rigorously constative approaches – the theoretical 'vision' and 'map' of reality – 'miss something so obvious that it is easily overlooked: the fact that ... theory is a language-borne practice. As such, it is ontologically more than just a logical structure' (ibid.). As language borne, theory cannot escape being constructed through metaphors, imagery, and indeed, narrative force (Gibson 1996, Chapter 1; Smith 2000, p. 150). Although it is often treated as 'pure' conceptuality or logic, theory cannot – by definition – be adequately examined through such approaches. In *Passionate Sociology*, Ann Game and Andrew Metcalfe make a similar argument, noting that:

> although sociology [and for this, we could just as well substitute psychoanalysis, philosophy or cultural studies – MH] is proud of its studies of artistic convention and genre, it pays almost no heed to its own narrative conventions: sociologists tell stories as if they weren't storytellers, and as if storytelling were a less rigorous and honest pursuit than theirs. These topics are absent from almost all introductory ... textbooks. (1996, p. 65)

Such absented narrative conventions include the 'horror story' (Game and Metcalfe 1996, p. 64), given that sociology has 'been traditionally motivated by a horror of disorder. Social analysis is often a story of the heroic quest into chaos from which the analyst emerges with order' (1996, p. 85). This very much resembles the 'restoration' narrative structure posited for horror by psychoanalytic theories (see Chapter 3), lending credence to my argument that theory might be *written* through the conventions of horror, rather than being merely 'activated' or read-as-horror within an interpretive and discursive framework intent on disqualifying specific academic work as non-theory.

If at least some theory, some of the time, is written using the codes and conventions of horror, then it might follow that the discursively constructed pleasures of theory could resemble those of horror, rather than horror existing as a type of 'popular' narrative, and theory as a type of 'pure' conceptual logic. Of course, discursive resonances between 'pleasures of horror' and 'pleasures of theory' might strike us as highly unlikely; if one 'criterion for horror fiction is that we are compelled to read it swiftly, with a rising sense of dread ... [where] ... we can see no way out except to go forward' (Oates 1997, p. 35), then it seems improbable that this particular discourse of pleasure would or could be related to the reading of cultural theory, where a slow and iterated engagement between masterful text and readerly disciple is usually recommended by scholars (see López 2003, pp. 146–7; Steinert 2003, pp. 41–2). Clearly, even where theory uses the devices of horror fiction, it does not thereby magically or discursively *become* horror; rather, it draws intertextually on horror's narrative and affective structures.

What discourses of horror's pleasures might migrate, then, along with horror's intertextual presence, into 'theory horror'? If horror fiction is allegedly a quick, immersive read, while theory is a gradual, difficult non-page-turner, then it would seem also that horror is always discursively a 'body genre' aiming to 'portray and affect the sensational body' (Linda Williams 1999, p. 270) while theory is a counter-discursive 'mind genre', lacking such portrayals and affects. However, this opposition is excessively tidy, as well as reinforcing cultural hierarchies that associate 'low' culture with the body and 'high(er)' cultures with the mind. In the next section I will demonstrate how influential psychoanalytic, sociological and philosophical theories in the humanities have recurrently used 'horror stories' in order to mobilize discourses of pleasure relating to disgust, ontological shock and restoration/repetition (cf. Chapters 1, 2 and 3 respectively). Theory horror is thus partly a body genre. Although it may not portray the body as pornography, melodrama and horror variously do, it nevertheless seeks to affect readers' bodies. And as Anna Dacre has argued: 'many recent studies seek to rescue the popular from the trash can ... But if art is to be acknowledged in the popular, perhaps the popular needs also to be seen in art, or in the traditional haunts of high culture' such as the 'academic essay' (1998, p. 3; see also Pitkin 1998, pp. 4–5).

DISCOURSES OF PLEASURE IN RELATION TO THEORY
AS GOTHIC-HORROR: REFRAMING AND REFAMILIARIZATION

Given that the gothic is discursively positioned as an 'affective form' (Haggerty 1989, pp. 1–14), as is horror (and following Cavallaro 2002, I am collapsing the terms 'gothic' and 'horror' together here rather than attempting to uphold a binary that legitimates one at the expense of the other), then the intertextual presence of Gothic-horror in theory should raise the question of theory's affects. The gothic somehow comes to infect or pollute theory, but at the same time this category violation, this transgression, animates theory.

Interpretations of Sigmund Freud's writings have begun to stress the possibility not of reading the gothic (and horror) psychoanalytically, but rather of reading psychoanalysis as a version of gothic narrative (although Rickels (2002) associatively short-circuits psychoanalysis with science fiction rather than the gothic, while Farrell (1996, p. 116) reads psychoanalysis as 'Quixotic satire universalized in the language of science'). However, I would argue that readings of Freud-as-gothic carry an illicit charge and an awareness that 'academic norms' are being broken here. This hesitancy and assumed transgressiveness is evident in the fact that such readings are typically contained in the closing pages of book-length studies of the gothic, as in Day (1985, pp. 177–90), Kilgour (1995, p. 220) and Williams (1995, pp. 239–48). They are thus presented as if separate (and safely separable) from their respective main bodies of gothic research, these being textual components that continue to respect the academically dominant 'theory'/'fiction' binary. Alternatively, readings of Freud-as-gothic become deliberately playful exercises, as in Robert J. C. Young's piece, 'Freud's secret: *The Interpretation of Dreams* was a Gothic novel' (1999).

Some of these readings of Freud (especially Williams 1995) work in the same way as other accusations of theory-as-horror: they imply that Freud's work should not be taken entirely seriously as theory, suggesting instead that his theoretical works may have achieved some of their historical and cultural resonance as 'stories', precisely by virtue of using narrative and affective structures drawn from the gothic:

> *The Interpretation of Dreams* conforms to the tenets of the Gothic genre in a number of ... ways. In the first place, its mode is performative: while ostensibly offering the reader knowledge ... its real project is to produce theatrical effects during the reading process ... [just as] ... the project of the Gothic novel is ... to make the reader undergo an experience – typically a frisson of horror. (Young 1999, p. 217)

This performative, aesthetic dimension of Freud's theory is then discussed by Robert J. C. Young in a section headed 'Shock Horror' (1999, pp. 220–5). Young's argument is that Freud both:

analyses the formal structures of dreams ... [and] ... presents us with a procession of Gothic horrors [in the form of recounted dreams] whose cumulative effect is increased by our attention being ostensibly focused on the concomitant technical descriptions of how dreams operate. (1999, p. 223)

There is thus allegedly an oscillation between horrific images and their containing, framing rationalizations built into Freud's work (Freud 1974[1900]), creating a gothic doubling or fragmenting of narrative levels (Sage 1988, pp. 207–10; Cavallaro 2002, p. 113). A tension is created between enlightenment rationality and its excessive, mysterious Other. Elsewhere, Anne Williams (1995, p. 239) discusses 'Dr Freud's Gothic Novel' in terms of the narrator's role rather than the rhythmic pacing/intensification of horrifying narrative:

> Freud's characteristic rhetorical stance casts the doctor/narrator as a Dr. Van Helsing, convincing his skeptical audience, who ignore at their mortal peril the reality of the power he proclaims (though Freud proclaims the improbable reality of the unconscious, not of the vampire). (1995, p. 245)

Williams's scepticism is apparent in the phrase 'improbable reality', and in her discursive articulation of the unconscious with Dracula (1995, p. 245); a key concept of psychoanalysis is re-contextualized as an enduring Gothic-horror character, thus rendering it as fantastic rather than as a 'good-theoretical' reflection of reality. Freud's work on the unconscious is Van Helsing's struggle with Dracula: psychoanalysis is a 'bad' horror story (complete with 'improbable' and unreal monsters) rather than a 'good' theory.

Taking a less sceptical approach to psychoanalysis than Williams (1995), and a less playful stance than Robert J. C. Young, William Patrick Day argues (akin to Young 1999, p. 207) that Freud's 'popularity and power is ... founded on much the same basis as the popularity and power of the Gothic' (Day 1985, p. 179). Day's argument hinges on a number of factors: that the gothic prepares readers to accept that dreams should be interpreted symbolically, making Freud's work generically legible or comprehensible (1985, p. 180); that the gothic affirms and investigates characters' inner lives, again generically paving the way for psychoanalytic inquiry as a sense-making practice (ibid.; Smith 2000, p. 72); and that Freud's work echoes the 'attitudes toward [sexual] pleasure that fill the Gothic fantasy' (1985, p. 183). This last point attributes a combination of 'fear and desire' to Freud's approach to sexuality, with sexual behaviour supposedly being figured by Freud as 'animal' and 'degrading' (1985, p. 183).

The discursively construed pleasures of psychoanalytic theory are hence, in this reading, pleasures of *safely contained fear and disgust* (cf. Carroll 1990 and Chapter 1). Alien forces are unleashed ('the unconscious'), and horrific dreams are recounted, but both dreamwork and the unconscious can be ultimately understood and contained by psychoanalysis as a gothic-dependent 'science of fear' (Day 1985, p. 177). It is not 'unreality' that renders fear, desire and disgust safe in this instance, of course (unlike the horror fictions discussed in Chapter 1); rather it is psychoanalysis as a 'science' and technique for controlling unruly forces of the id. Unreality or fictionality can offer no defence against horror's affects here, given that psychoanalysis converts monstrous gothic fantasy into 'the substance of reality' (Day 1985, p. 186). However, this conversion process – with its gothicized 'basic conceptual metaphors' (Williams 1995, p. 244) – means that theory written like horror fiction possesses a cultural familiarity, even as it purports to introduce paradigm-shattering concepts such as the unconscious.

Freudian psychoanalysis is, in this sense, a writing technique based powerfully on refamiliarization, and on framing what appears, conceptually, to be unfamiliar and threatening as something already long-known (within the Gothic-horror genre's template). Thus, when horror texts draw reflexively on psychoanalytic theory (Carroll 2004; Creed 2004), it can be argued that they are participating in an ongoing circuit or dialectic of theory/fiction semiotic appropriation (Gamer 2000, p. 45) by restoring psychoanalysis to one of its own sources. Lines between theory and horror fiction are, on this argument, discursively permeable, with both cultural theories and cultural fictions co-responding to ontological questions that confront a culture (e.g. self-identity/ gender differences).

But if 'theory horror' traffics in the semiotic containments and pleasure-discourses of generic refamiliarization (testified to in the examples drawn from Day 1985, Williams 1995 and Young 1999) it also participates in discourses of pleasure such as 'ontological shock' (Chapter 2). It does so by virtue of stressing, in the first instance, its *reframing of common (or non-theoretical) understandings*, and its disruption of lay theories. For theory horror to function as such, it has to successfully negotiate two moments: it must be sufficiently disruptive of pre-theoretical expectations and understandings in order to attain the status of 'Theory' (let us call this 'reframing'), but it must not stray too far from pre-theoretical, cultural understandings, or it risks illegibility and excessive alienation/detachment from the very realms of culture that it seeks to act upon (this represents the formal, narrative and cultural-political need for refamiliarization). Theory-horror is hence called upon to enact a skilful balancing of semio-conceptual proximity and distance from its surrounding (popular) culture. Its performative, affective power lies in offering a shocking reframing of pre-theoretical and pop-cultural sense-making – for example the monstrosity of 'the unconscious' – allied to a safely generic reframing of this very disruption, for example 'the unconscious as Dracula' (Williams 1995, p. 245) or even the death instinct as Dracula (Day 1985, p. 183).

Opposing 'theory' to 'fiction' installs a culturally one-dimensional model that emphasizes only theory's detachment from the sense-makings of storytelling and popular culture. Such an approach stresses theory's distinctiveness and its reframing 'ontological shock', rendering it radically discontinuous with surrounding cultural memes and semes. This fails to consider that affective and effective theory must also remain connected to wider cultural currents of meaning-making if it is to circulate mimetically, affecting its professional academic readers as well as lay readers and students. Rather than contrasting theory to fiction, then, we might utilize similar discourses of pleasure in relation to each: theory, like 'generic' fiction, seeks to refamiliarize the world that it depicts, and may intertextually use horror as a generic template to effect this refamiliarization. Both theory and horror could thus be framed via discourses of 'restoration', although where horror multiply restores repressed material and repression itself (in psychoanalytic accounts of the genre – Chapter 3), theory restores 'order' from 'chaos' (Game and Metcalfe 1996), likewise producing a sense of narrative closure and the refinement/purification of concept categories (Greig 2004). Cognitivists (as in Chapter 1) could also approach both theory and horror via discourses of emotion, since theory achieves its distinctiveness as a cultural category by discursively presuming to shock its readers into a new ('critical') view of the world and seeking to 'reframe' cultural common sense. Horror's pleasures constructed discursively as cognitive processes of 'fear and disgust' therefore also become relevant to 'theory horror', along with the counter-discourse of 'ontological shock'.

Other historically influential systems of social/cultural thought have displayed the same interactions of reframing and refamiliarization as occur in Freud's (1974) work. Just as Day (1985, p. 186) argues that Freud converted gothic fantasy/fiction into 'the substance of reality', so Chris Baldick argues that in Karl Marx's writings 'the myth of Frankenstein has become the great fact of nineteenth-century life' (1987, p. 140). In terms of formally sustained narrative pleasures, Marx and Freud are not so far apart. Like Freudianism, Marxism makes use of the figures of Gothic-horror fiction, making it difficult to univocally and unambivalently argue that Marx and Freud represent counter-currents to the horror genre where this is depicted as anti-Enlightenment critique (Jones 2000, pp. 258 and 267–8).

As Ghislaine McDayter has observed, critics need to address why the 'gothic language of monstrosity is picked up by Marx for his own political purposes' (1999, p. 51). McDayter's question, implying that the gothic can be put to radical as well as conservative political aims (see Moretti 1988), has been amply investigated of late. Perhaps this is partly thanks to Jean-François Lyotard's injunction that '[w]e must *come to take Marx as if he were a writer, an author full of affects*' (1994, p. 95, my italics), but it is more specifically due to bursts of Derridean interest in the Marxist gothic following the book *Specters of Marx* (Derrida 1994; see also Maley 1999; Parkin-Gounelas 1999; Luckhurst 2002; Wolfreys 2002). As Mike Wayne puts it:

> Marx famously invoked the 'spectre of communism' ... which, he argued, was haunting the bourgeoisie. Marx wanted to stress how frightened the

bourgeoisie were of something that had yet to materialise. With the spectre, Marx 'announces and calls for a presence to come' (Derrida 1994:101) anticipating a future yet to happen rather than, as ghosts usually are, the trace of something already past. (2003, p. 201; see Thomas 1998, p. 211)

Drawing on Derrida, Wayne emphasizes that Marx's use of a gothic figure (in Marx and Engels 1998[1848]), the spectre or ghost, reverses a usual or expected generic logic.

This rhetorical 'montage' (Osborne 1998, pp. 195–6 and 2000, p. 72) thus condenses moments of reframing and refamiliarization into one manifestation; the imagery of the spectre both reverses and calls upon a narrative framing drawn from 'the gothic tale' (Osborne 2000, p. 72). This achieves the result of 'transferring the rhetorical power of an image which he [Marx] is actually setting out to "demystify" onto the process of demystification itself' (Osborne 2000, p. 73). A similar argument is put forward by José Monleón, who notes that when 'Marx adopted an image of the fantastic to depict a concrete political phenomenon, he was both using dominant discourse as well as deconstructing a cultural metaphor' (1990, p. 60). The discursive reorientation of theory-horror – deconstructing/demystifying – is hence pleasurably connected to the 'power' of dominant discourse, albeit in a fictional/generic guise.

Baldick recognizes this cementing of rhetoric and analysis – performative and constative theory – when he remarks in 'Karl Marx's Grave-Diggers and Vampires' that:

> ghosts, vampires, ghouls, werewolves, alchemists, and reanimated corpses continue to haunt the bourgeois world [in Marx's writing]. I shall argue that this apparent anomaly in Marx's presentation of bourgeois society is more than a decorative trick of style ... Rather, it follows from and reinforces certain major elements within Marx's understanding of capitalism. (1987, p. 121)

The Marxist appropriation of Gothic-horror, then, lends an affective charge to the manifesto as well as to many of Marx's other writings. Capital and capitalism become sources of horror for Marx, repeatedly figured as 'vampire-like' (Baldick 1987, p. 130). Moreover, the concept of alienation, where 'the surrender of your vital capacities to an "alien" force ... ensures that your own powers are turned against you', works to reframe 'the Frankenstein myth' (Baldick 1987, pp. 131–2) while drawing on what I would term its *retributive* 'structure of feeling' (Williams 1965, p. 64).

Raymond Williams's concept of 'structure of feeling' is concerned with a generalized cultural experience 'as firm and definite as "structure" suggests, yet ... [which] operates in the most delicate and least tangible parts of our activity' (ibid.), as well as operating in and across the literary texts of a given period. Structures of feeling are considered to permeate cultural fields, and although

Williams does not weave together 'theoretical' and 'literary' productions, I am arguing here, following Day (1985) and Baldick (1987), that theoretical texts and 'fictions' may share characteristic structures of feeling. Williams's discussion of the seeming cultural automatism of a structure of feeling is instructive:

> The point of the deliberately contradictory phrase ... is that it was a structure in the sense that you could perceive it operating in one work after another which weren't otherwise connected – people weren't learning it from each other; yet it was one of feeling much more than of thought – a pattern of impulses, restraints, tones, for which the best evidence was often the actual conventions of literary ... [and theoretical – MH] writing. (Williams 1979, p. 159)

As Ien Ang has noted, it 'is emotions which count in a structure of feeling' (1985, p. 45). Her analysis famously goes on to analyse a 'tragic structure of feeling' in soap opera: 'tragic because of the idea that happiness can never last for ever but ... is precarious. In the tragic structure of feeling emotional ups and downs occupy a central place' in the text, and in its fans' recounted pleasures of the text (Ang 1985, p. 46). 'Structure of feeling' is thus useful, despite its seemingly 'contradictory' phrasing, for the way that it implies a narrative structure or micro-narrative ('emotional ups and downs') that can carry an affective charge for readers, also spilling over across otherwise unconnected texts.

In Marx's writing, as in the Gothic-horror of 'the Frankenstein myth', I would suggest that there is a shared structure of feeling. This is 'retributive' rather than tragic; it is persistently concerned not with emotional ups and downs but rather with the moralizing narrative of a monstrosity or evil that returns to punish its creator (arguably, such a structure of feeling is also present in contemporary sociological 'risk theory'; see Beck 1992). Hence the feeling carried by this structure is one of retribution as a type of natural and inevitable justice: the guilty will be dealt with, but they will in fact punish themselves; their own powers will be turned against them. The persistence over time of this powerfully moralizing structure of feeling is suggested by Mike Wayne's observation that:

> In *The Communist Manifesto* we have the basic template [or structure of feeling – MH] of many ghostly apparitions in contemporary cinema today. A dominant and often complacent social order repressing that which challenges its existence and values ... and the appearance of some spirit crying out for past injustices to be recognised ... for good old-fashioned bloody vengeance. (Wayne 2003, pp. 201 and 210)

Derrida, too, links discursively assumed affects of horror to *The Communist Manifesto*, noting that since 'it [the spectre of communism] is neither real nor legendary, some "Thing" will have frightened and continues to frighten in the equivocation of this event ... To make fear ... To cause fear in the enemies of the *Manifesto*, but perhaps also in … the Marxists themselves' (1994, p. 104). From a performative perspective it is perhaps unsurprising that critical theory should seek to discursively 'make fear', given that its aim is to portray the failings, inequities and evils of existent social orders, and to provoke the ideal reader to a state of shock, horror and moral outrage. Of course, some Marxists may still be horrified to consider that Marxist writings iterate structures of feeling drawn from Gothic-horror. The notion that Marxism displays a characteristic 'structure of feeling' may also offend Marxist critics via its emphasis on narrative and affect rather than on the constative/reflective aspects of Marxist theory. However, it might fairly be suggested that Marxism's cultural history cannot be disengaged from the 'performative mode' of Marxist theory (Derrida 1994, p. 103; Osborne 2000, p. 72) in which moving, horrifying and persuading readers by producing 'theatrical effects' assumed to characterize the horror genre is as culturally-politically important as Marxism's constative dimensions, and is in fact thoroughly integrated with them. Such integration extends to the iteration of retributive structures of feeling, since this specific narrative and emotive structure is replayed both at the level of social problems identified by Marxism and at the level of salvation hoped for. The theory-narrative of Marxism is hence one of forces constantly being monstrously torn from the self and turned back against it; this structure of feeling pervades Marxist commentary on the horror of 'commodity fetishism' (see, e.g., Wayne 2003, pp. 189–90) where 'human agents … have lost control of their world' (Baldick 1987, p. 126). And this same structure of feeling pervades Marxist accounts of capitalism's systemic collapse: 'The bourgeoisie has assembled … a creature whose power will crush its creator' (Baldick 1987, p. 127).

Basic concepts such as fetishism and alienation are thoroughly gothicized, and it is this collision of the conceptual and the narrated that makes Marx's use of ghostly metaphors far more than 'mere' metaphors or rhetorics. It could be said that the Marxist historical dialectic is nothing less than a gothic retributive structure of feeling elevated to philosophical-theoretical dignity; a narrative of essential, inevitable and bloody vengeance. However, this 'conversion' process, as with that enacted by Freud's theory, does not imply that theory and horror fiction become entirely one and the same. Rather, both Freudian and Marxist 'theory-horror' interact intertextually with 'other kinds of writing' (Gamer 2000, p. 45) such as the gothic. There is an ontological shock presupposed via the monstrous concept of the unconscious, just as there is in relation to concepts such as commodity fetishism and alienation. Anthony Woodiwiss (2001) discursively calls up the 'pleasure' of this shock in Marx's writing when he notes 'the pleasure that Marx [and by implication, the ideal reader – MH] takes in the form of volume one of *Capital* where the first six chapters follow the narrative structure of a conjuring act: first we are reassured that everything is as normal but suddenly a rabbit is produced – Marx's version of the labour theory of value' (2001, p. 36).

The 'conjuring acts' of Marxism (Marx and Engels 1998) and psychoanalysis (Freud 1974) present their readers with theoretical frameworks that urge an altered or reframed view of 'the real', but they nevertheless do so within refamiliarizing 'generic' moral, narrative and emotive coordinates drawn from the horror genre. Both Marx and Freud seek to appropriate the discursively assumed powers of gothic fiction to shock and 'make fear' (McGinn 1997, p. 176). Although I do not have space here to analyse other instances of theory-horror in any detail, I would suggest that processes of reframing and refamiliarization can be excavated across a range of influential theoretical texts other than those of Freud and Marx and Engels. For example, the academic popularity of post-structuralism has been linked to its gothicism by Mark Edmundson:

> the fin-de-siècle academic world has a gothic mode of its own. Much, though surely not all, of what is called theory draws on Gothic idioms. Its subject is haunting. In the language of theory the virtuous villain, the monster of morality, gets renamed ... Jacques Derrida's antagonist is the metaphysics of presence ... But the most intriguing exponent of Gothic theory is surely Michel Foucault ... His haunting agency, which is everywhere and nowhere, as evanescent and insistent as a resourceful spook, is called Power. (Edmundson 1997, pp. 40–1; and see Kilgour 1998, p. 51)

Edmundson's first target here is Derrida. And indeed, the gothic narratives of deconstruction have been investigated in a fascinating book-length study by Jodey Castricano, *Cryptomimesis* (2001; see also Wigley 1993). Drawing on Noël Carroll's (1990) work, Castricano argues that Derrida's writing is akin to 'Gothic-horror in popular culture':

> cryptomimesis [Castricano's term for Derrida's mode of writing – MH] approaches abjection because it concerns itself with the collapse, or the permeability, of the border between inside and outside, between attraction and repulsion ... cryptomimesis is a writing practice that is characterized by disintegration, by the breaking-up of language into its elements or constituents. Decomposition ... might ... be thought of as the aesthetic principle behind cryptomimesis which, because it sets up a challenge to 'taste', has its affinity with Gothic 'horror'. (2001, p. 32)

Castricano goes on to argue that Derrida's writing practices also provoke disgust via their abject decomposition (ibid.). Although this application of Noël Carroll's *The Philosophy of Horror* to the philosophy of Derrida is provocative, ultimately Castricano's abject collapsing together of theory and horror (2001, p. 26) is purified and contained by her reading of Stephen King's *Pet Sematary* (1983) as an 'allegory of cryptomimesis' (2001, p. 67; see also 2001, pp. 59 and 65). In this relation, Gothic-horror is finally subordinated to the lessons of

Derridean thought, with deconstructionism being discovered and thus validated in King's work. Popular cultural texts are made to carry and mirror 'Theory' that is guaranteed a primary and originating place, unchallenged and settled in its 'proper' (authoritative) position (and for painful examples of this symbolic domination of popular cultural texts by 'Theory' that always remains in the right, see Žižek (1997) and the apposite remarks of Carroll 2004, p. 267 and Beard 2001, p. 125).

As well as characterizing post-structuralism as 'gothic theory', Mark Edmundson also argues that Frankfurt School theorists, feminists, Freud and Slavoj Žižek all inscribe a 'Gothic antagonist' (1997, p. 40) in their theoretical writings. And to this list we could add Robin Wood's (1986) opposition to the 'ideology' embodied in horror's 'reactionary' monsters. What this points up is the extent to which much theory writing relies on refamiliarizing and morally legible narratives of good and evil, in which a 'monster' has to be located or named via the conceptual, terminological work of 'reframing', yet is also rendered dislocatable or generalizable as an ideological system or social order to be fought by the theorist and their supportive readers. Hence theory and its work become 'interminable' and the monstrous antagonist 'always reappears elsewhere' (Edmundson 1997, p. 40). On this argument, cultural theory may be as marked by repetition-compulsion as the horror genre itself (see Chapter 3).

Another of Mark Edmundson's (1997) targets is Michel Foucault, the theorist of discursive practices whose work, to an extent, underpins my approach to the horror genre and pleasure across this study (see the Preface and Foucault 1977, p. 199). The notion that discourses of the horror genre are exnominated, and that the genre spills out beyond its culturally nominated boundaries, is itself a rather gothic theory/image/narrative of the horror genre. Self-reflexively, then, this book can be considered as an example of what I have termed 'theory-horror' in that it too draws on horror's tropes and narrative devices. Despite taking a broadly performative and 'meta-theoretical' stance (Ritzer 2001, p. 15), I cannot evade the terms of this chapter's debate and implicitly position myself outside an 'object' of study. Studying discourses of horror's pleasure and the genre's attributions, nominations and structuring absences remains a gothicized narrative of cultural power, in which dominant forms of meaning and practice work to fix 'horror' in certain places while rendering its broader intertextual operations relatively invisible and marginalized. The 'horror genre' cannot be considered merely as a set of texts that explicitly carry this label, nor as an objectively identifiable corpus of films and fictions. Where horror and its pleasures are to be 'authentically' and 'properly' discerned remains an operation of cultural power and cultural reproduction, one that intersects with powerfully loaded, moral discourses.

By considering 'TV horror', 'true horror' and 'theory-horror' across the last few chapters, my aim has been to indicate how cultural assumptions have discursively framed horror, and its pleasures, as somehow 'naturally' (i.e. culturally) belonging to film and fiction. Thus, although horror circulates textually and intertextually in what I have termed horror's para-sites, *the genre's presence beyond film and fiction has been approached through a variety of inauthenticating and moralizing (critical) discourses*: TV horror is not 'really' horror; 'true' horror allegedly has no narrative and cannot be pleasurable; and theory-as-horror is allegedly 'bad' or failed theory. In place of these exnominating discourses that seek to fix horror securely within its 'generic' boundaries as a cultural category (Mittell 2004), I have sought to bring together and synthesize otherwise marginal or dispersed counter-discourses, arguing that TV horror cannot be defined solely as 'that which cannot show the monster'; that mediated true horror and its narrative pleasures need to be theorized more adequately rather than being dismissed; and that influential cultural/social theories can be approached non-pejoratively as forms of 'theory-horror'. I have thus attempted to restore horror's range of (sometimes 'invisible', neglected or devalued) intertexts to critical centrality and visibility. In the next and final part I proceed to investigate a very different type of relationship between horror and intertextuality, one that again involves and invokes discourses of fan pleasure related to intertextual recognition/knowledge (see Part II). Chapters 9 and 10 will address how the pleasures of horror may, in part, be critically and discursively constructed as 'postmodern' pleasures of intertextual referencing and citation, something that is hardly alien to the practices of academic theory-building. Having explored horror beyond its usual 'generic' borders, I will focus more conventionally on horror fiction and film in what follows. Although I will deploy a type of textual analysis, this will not constitute close readings of specific texts so much as an attempt to map the place of fictions within 'the field of horror' (Gelder 2000, p. 1).

Part IV

Scare Quotes: Beyond 'Postmodern' Horror

[P]ostmodern horror ... drifts back and forth between scares and laughs without warning. Sick humor and sickening violence, coupled with narrative and affective incoherence, define ... horror ...'s final incarnation ... *Oftentimes trading on 'insider knowledge,' a fan's familiarity with the rules of the game, these efforts underline their status as neither genre creations nor genre malcontents. Obeying some conventions and shattering others*, the most successful of these bipolar amalgamations manage to be both funny and scary simultaneously ... [T]hese productions may be so openly self-conscious about their status as productions that they cannot be sent up. For this genre, all parody is homage. (Jonathan Lake Crane 2004, pp. 147–8, my italics)

Chapter 9

Intertextuality in the Contemporary Field of Horror (I)

The 'Postmodern' Fictions of Kim Newman

My focus on the work of one author occurs here because the fiction of Kim Newman, as I will go on to demonstrate, can be taken to exemplify a specific type of intertextuality within 'the field of horror' (Gelder 2000, pp. 1 and 6, 1996, p. 30). The next chapter will then use a different case study, returning to horror film, in order to explore horror's range of intertextualities. I will argue that the 'scare quotes' of different types of horror – intertextualities that sustain horror as a knowingly self-referential genre (Brophy 1986) – form bids for textual position-taking within the field of horror and its 'space of possible' subgeneric, distinctive factions (Bourdieu 1993, p. 30). Texts seek to link themselves to preceding traditions/movements in the cultural history of the horror genre, and distinguish themselves relationally from other generic productions. The 'field of horror' is thus a cultural space in which texts – and by implication, authors – seek distinction from their rivals at the same time as seeking recognition within horror's explicitly and discursively identified 'field of cultural production' (Bourdieu 1993; see Morrison 1996).

My broad aim in this part of the book, then, is to analyse how different types of intertextuality can be displayed in different horror texts, meaning that to merely label such horror films and fictions as 'postmodern' unhelpfully lumps together and academically abstracts very different intertextual strategies. Rather than considering intertextuality as an attribute of allegedly or automatically 'postmodern' horror (as in the epigraph that frames this part: Lake Crane 2004, pp. 147–8), I will instead address those distinctions in cultural value that can be constructed through horror texts' varied intertextual strategies. First, though, I want to consider how the term 'postmodern' could be applied to Kim Newman's horror fictions, addressing difficulties with this application of postmodern theory.

'POSTMODERN' HORROR FICTIONS?

Kim Newman's horror novels, novellas and short stories tend to repeatedly define themselves through and against their textual predecessors. *Anno Dracula* (Newman 1993) is a reworking of Bram Stoker's *Dracula* (1994[1897]) where the Count has become head of the British Empire, while the novella 'Further Developments in the Strange Case of Dr Jekyll and Mr Hyde' (Newman 2000a) rewrites Robert Louis Stevenson's original novella (1979[1886]) by suggesting that Jekyll and Hyde were, after all, two different people rather than aspects of one personality. Both rewritings (Newman 1993 and 2000a) appropriate the tone, language, style and form of their gothic originals: *Anno Dracula* features Jack Seward recording his spoken thoughts via a phonograph, drawing on *Dracula's* testimonial and epistolary form, while 'Further Developments' offers further written confessions from Dr Jekyll, and repeats the shifting subjective viewpoints of Stevenson's 'Strange Case'. We might therefore suppose that Newman's work could be analysed as postmodern in a variety of ways.

First, it might be thought of as a form of pastiche, where the styles, forms and narratives of 'classic' gothic texts are imitated by way of homage rather than critique (Hoesterey 2001, p. 95). Newman's texts are very much *not* parodies, seeming to concur with Jonathan Lake Crane's (2004) argument that postmodern horror, especially, is immune to parody by virtue of its extreme self-consciousness, as well as resonating with Fredric Jameson's famous (1985) discussion of postmodernism as characterized by 'blank parody':

> That is the moment at which pastiche appears and parody has become impossible. Pastiche is, like parody, the imitation of a peculiar or unique style, the wearing of a stylistic mask, speech in a dead language: but it is a neutral practice of such mimicry, without parody's ulterior motive, without the satirical impulse ... Pastiche is blank parody. (Jameson 1985, p. 114)

Secondly, although shifting between humour and horror due to their literary and media self-referentiality, Newman's counterfictions (rewritings of previous fictional, diegetic worlds) nevertheless remain works of horror: their almost constant citation of other horror texts ensures that they display 'a fan's familiarity with the rules of the game' (Lake Crane 2004, p. 148) rather than becoming 'genre malcontents' (ibid.) and forfeiting their generic identity. Such 'rampant' intertextuality (Latham 2002, p. 104) seems almost enough to characterize Newman's work as 'postmodern' in and of itself, since as Graham Allen has observed, 'any discussion of ... intertextuality ... leads us towards the issue of Postmodernism' (2000, p. 181). Indeed, it is precisely such proliferating intertextuality that leads Gary Wilkinson (2000, pp. 15–17) to identify Newman's fictions as 'postmodern'. Wilkinson argues that Newman's fictions are profoundly self-referential in terms of revolving around gothic horror's foundational texts, while simultaneously citing more contemporary horror films. They 'step ... through the silver screen' (Wilkinson 2000, p. 15) to become simulations of simulated realities, or what Jean Baudrillard (1994) would term 'simulacra'. On this account, Newman's fictions have 'no relation to any reality whatsoever' (Baudrillard 1994, p. 6): they are postmodern phantoms, horror fictions chasing previous horror fictions.

Thirdly, Newman's fictions can be addressed as 'postmodern' violations of the 'popular culture' versus 'high culture' binary, as they return intertextually to 'classic' gothic texts: 'postmodern intertextuality ... challenges the separation between high and low culture' (Bignell 2000, p. 86). This line of thinking has also been very much characteristic of theoretical narratives and discourses regarding 'the postmodern'. To cite Fredric Jameson again: 'one fundamental feature of all the postmodernisms enumerated above [in music, philosophy, film, literature and architecture – MH] ... [is] the effacement in them of the ... frontier between high culture and so-called mass or commercial culture' (Jameson 1991, p. 2).

However, such accounts tend to focus on selective attributes of 'the postmodern', reading fiction as a reflection of theoretical assumptions and definitions (much as the discourses of pleasure analysed in Chapters 1, 2 and 3 work to prioritize and reflect related theoretical orthodoxies). Such 'po-mo' accounts thus produce a univocal sense of 'the postmodern' that subsequently reduces empirical instances of culture to one manically iterated master narrative. Such an approach ultimately installs sameness across instances of popular culture. Contra such a theoretical discourse (and see the useful critique of Bignell 2000, p. 62), I am concerned here not with reading horror's 'intertextuality' as an automatic signifier of 'the postmodern', but rather with considering *a range of textually and sociologically distinctive types of intertextuality*. It therefore makes little sense to merely read the intertextual as 'the postmodern', unless differential modes, aesthetics and cultural politics of this postmodernity can then be distinguished.

In pursuit and exemplification of a more sensitive account of intertextuality – one that *is* capable of analysing intertextual distinctions – I will argue here that Newman's work is not univocally 'postmodern' in the sense of emptying politics out in favour of literary self-referentiality or 'blank parody' (Wilkinson 2000, p. 15). Rather, Newman's texts often represent didactic forms of cultural politics via pastiche, such as the queer reading of Jekyll and Hyde (2000a) or the anti-tabloid-moral-panic stance of 'Where the Bodies Are Buried 3: Black and White and Red All Over' (2000c). Nor are Newman's fictional works simply 'postmodern' in the sense of blurring fact and fiction in a dizzying regress of playful simulacra, since even where 'fact' and 'fiction' are interlinked this is done, again, in order to achieve specific textual effects such as contesting the cultural power of mainstreamed, heterosexualized adaptations of the Jekyll and Hyde mythos (Hogan 1988, p. 32). And nor are Newman's counter-fictions 'postmodern' in the sense of eroding the boundaries between 'high' and 'low' or 'popular' and 'academic' cultures, since the appropriation of literary theory in

Newman's first rereading/rewriting of Jekyll and Hyde (2000a) remains marginalized in that novella's subtext, testifying to continued lines of difference and distinction between 'Theory' and 'popular culture', as does the rather fleeting reference to the work of Martin Barker and Julian Petley (1997) in 'Where the Bodies Are Buried 2020' (Newman 2000c). Newman's fictions may draw on the languages of 'Theory', as I will go on to show, but they generally enact a populist distance from, or disavowal of, theoretical terminology.

Against academic narratives and discourses that characterize postmodern textuality as a destabilization *tout court* of 'the binary division of high and popular culture' (Bignell 2000, p. 86; McGuigan 1999, p. 68), I will argue that it is important to consider exactly how 'popular' culture intertextually plays with 'high' culture in order to bid for its own cultural value or to signal the seriousness of its (sub)cultural politics. Kim Newman's use of 'high(er)' culture – gothic literature and literary/cultural theory – works not to disqualify his fictions as popular culture, but rather to performatively bid for value *within* the terrain of popular horror fiction. To flesh out these claims, I will examine how the work of influential French sociologist Pierre Bourdieu might enable a more nuanced analysis of intertextuality that goes beyond simply identifying formal and a priori 'postmodern' characteristics, and which is therefore capable of identifying and exploring different types of intertextualities in horror.

BOURDIEUIAN READINGS OF HORROR AND PLEASURES OF INTERTEXTUALITY

Discussing the 'field of horror', Ken Gelder (2000) concedes that he is using the notion of 'field' 'somewhat loosely' (2000, p. 1). Elsewhere, however, he has undertaken a more detailed application of the term to horror's cultural production (1996). The concept is, as he notes, taken from Bourdieu, whose work on cultural distinctions has been much drawn upon in studies of material culture (see Harker *et al.* (eds) 1990; Hills 2002 and Richard Jenkins 2002). Bourdieu argues that artists, authors and cultural producers take up (and also generate) certain positions within their respective 'fields', where by field is meant 'an area, a playing field, a field of objective relations among individuals or institutions competing for the same stakes' (Harker *et al.* 1990, pp. 8–10; Bourdieu 1993, p. 133; Gelder 1996; see also Parker 2000, p. 44; Sconce 2002, p. 353 and Inglis and Hughson 2003, pp. 170–1). Those stakes might be recognition, as well as economic power and (sub)cultural legitimacy. I will follow Toril Moi's argument that 'the only way to understand the concept of symbolic capital is to link it to a specific cultural field. Only a field can grant symbolic capital' (1999, p. 309), where by 'symbolic capital' is meant the prestige and reputation – the honour, if you like – that is accorded to specific cultural producers in their relevant fields. I want to therefore focus on how symbolic capital is at stake in the 'field of horror', and how it can be accrued via ostentatiously intertextual displays of 'cultural capital' *and* 'subcultural capital' (Thornton 1995). The latter is defined as conferring:

> status on its owner in the eyes of the relevant beholder [i.e the fellow members of a subculture – MH] ... [It] ... can be *objectified* or *embodied*. Just as books and paintings display cultural capital in the family home, so subcultural capital [for rave subculture in this example – MH] is objectified in the form of fashionable haircuts and well-assembled record collections ... Just as cultural capital is personified in 'good' manners and urbane conversation [being 'official', legitimate cultural knowledge/education/ schooling – MH], so subcultural capital is embodied in the form of being 'in the know'. (Thornton 1995, p. 11; see Hills 2002)

Chapter 10 will then focus comparatively on intertextualities that centre on horror fans' 'subcultural capital' alone (Jancovich 2000), neglecting to display culturally legitimating 'cultural capital' at the same time (this linkage of 'cultural capital' with legitimate, high cultural education/knowledge follows the concept's 'dominant interpretation' in sociological study: see Lareau and Weininger 2003, p. 568). My approach will be predominantly text based, despite the fact that 'as Moi asserts, a purely Bourdieuian interpretation of texts is "unthinkable"' (Hipsky 2000, p. 186). Bourdieuian theory is not commonly used to interpret media/cultural texts: it is frequently deployed, instead, to address the 'particular social practices surrounding the production, distribution, and reception (or consumption)' of cultural works (Hipsky 2000, p. 186; see Harbord 2002). Where texts *are* dealt with in a Bourdieuian framework, these texts are typically not novels or films themselves, but are rather press reviews or fan letters/websites (see, for example, Jancovich 2000 and 2002b). Bourdieuian theory thus, contra Marty Hipsky's quotation of Moi, clearly allows for a *type* of textual analysis, but seemingly not primary textual analysis involving encounters with horror novels or films. However, Hipsky neglects a passage from Moi's appropriation of Bourdieu where she notes that:

> What ... [Bourdieu's] analyses may be able to help us see, however, is the way in which certain texts enter into *field-related intertextual relations with other texts*. Once we have perceived these relations, we can go on to produce new readings of the texts in question. (Moi 1999, p. 296, my italics)

Moi, then, does not rule out a Bourdieuian theory of primary texts after all: she outlines one such theory based on *intertextual* reading. Bourdieu himself has also undertaken primary textual analysis on occasions; *The Rules of Art*, for example, begins with a 'Prologue' (1992, pp. 3–43) analysing the work of Gustave Flaubert. Bourdieu addresses literary texts as 'closed system[s]' (Robbins 2000, p. 77; see Bourdieu 1992, p. 14 and 1993, p. 151), which work to map possible position-takings and social trajectories via their characters, viewing such texts as an aestheticized parallel to his own theories. Fortunately, Moi's proposal lacks such an emphasis on the mirroring of culture and sociological theory, and her appropriative 'reading with Bourdieu' (Moi 1999, p. 296) is hence not concerned with slavishly reading as Bourdieu. In fact, the form of analysis favoured by Pierre Bourdieu himself (1993, pp. 9–10 and 179–80) offers a number of difficulties that I want to summarize before suggesting ways to circumnavigate these via appropriative Bourdieuian 'readings' of the field of horror.

First, Bourdieu can be accused of excessively objectifying the 'fields' that he studies (Leledakis 1995, p. 91). In other words, he assumes that fields have an autonomy from surrounding fields, and that they therefore possess a logic of their own, acting as a kind of game apart from other social and cultural terrains (although see Bourdieu and Wacquant 1992, pp. 114–15 and Couldry 2003, pp. 667–9). As Nick Prior has commented, 'Bourdieu's use of the [field] concept is clearly most effective when dealing with those relatively developed fields, education, art, literature, in a state of high autonomy' (Prior 2000, p. 144). However, the autonomy of fields examined in Bourdieu's socio-historical analyses (Lash 1993, p. 198) can no longer be assumed in relation to contemporary cultural production (Cook 2000).

Contemporary fields no longer appear to be autonomous, as in Bourdieu's analysis of Flaubert's work: exchanges between 'impure' fields, mediated via forces of journalism, capital and television, are increasingly becoming the norm (see Bourdieu 1992, p. 344 and 1998; Earle 1999, pp. 180–1; and see Gelder 1996, p. 35 for an argument that considers interfield transgressions between literary and filmic fields of cultural production). Imposing the field concept (Robbins 2000, p. 197) on horror as a genre, it is therefore important to consider that the 'field of horror' may not exist as a 'pure' or highly autonomous field, but may powerfully intersect with other fields, for example journalism, academic subcultural production, literary, television and film production, and fan subcultural production. Thus, insofar as a 'field of horror' can be identified, its multiple interactions with other fields would render it less a game apart from other social terrains and more a game played through, and in relation to, other fields and media/cultural forces (see Couldry 2003). As Scott Lash has usefully put it, we need to analyse the 'de-differentiation of fields' (1990, p. 263) through which 'the partial collapse of some fields into other fields' (1990, p. 252) can be observed. Therefore, *the field concept requires that inter-fields be more adequately considered than is the case in Bourdieu's work* (see also Bennett *et al.* 1999, p. 261; Richard Jenkins 2002, p. 89).

Secondly, analysing horror texts for their 'intertextual relations' may tell us only part of the story of the 'field' of horror. It can allow us to consider how horror texts' 'scare quotes' place them in field-related positions with other preceding texts (see Jancovich 2002a, p. 6). But it seems to tell us nothing about the pleasures of horror that can be discursively constructed in relation to reading intertextually – the pleasures of displaying an awareness of horror as a field of possible bids for (sub)cultural value rather than viewing the genre merely as a contingent succession of 'repetitive' texts. As John Guillory has pithily understated, 'the concept of pleasure is undertheorized in Bourdieu' (2000, p. 42; Thomas 2002, p. 17) since it appears to be reduced to a competition over levels of different types of capital.

One response to the problem of pleasure in Bourdieuian readings could begin by considering that the field of cultural production is divided into 'autonomous' and 'heteronomous' poles in Bourdieu's work (1993). Autonomous, artistic products occur within a 'restricted field' of cultural production recognized by specialists in that 'field', whereas heteronomous, commercial products are generated 'in the field of large-scale cultural production' (Robbins 1991, p. 122), and are thus made for a large market of consumers who do not need to possess special competencies or skills in order to understand such products. In Bourdieu's terms, 'popular art' becomes seemingly oxymoronic as autonomous (consecrated/avant-garde) and heteronomous (deconsecrated/mass-commercial) poles are kept apart through social and cultural practices of distinction. For Bourdieu, large-scale cultural production is either directly 'commercial' (e.g. advertisements) or 'popular' (i.e., 'committed to satisfying pre-established audiences': Webb *et al.* 2002, p. 169). The socio-cultural result is that 'work done under the heteronomous principle of production is often coded as being not "real" art … This consecration belongs most obviously at the "autonomous" pole of the field, the site of "art for art's sake"' (Webb *et al.* 2002, p. 160).

However, this division is one major component of Bourdieu's theory of the field of the cultural production that has been called into question. Paul Lopes argues that there is a need to 'incorporate a restricted subfield of popular art into … [Bourdieu's] … two-pole field of cultural production' (Lopes 2000, p. 180), while Bridget Fowler has similarly argued:

> there are particular difficulties with … [Bourdieu's] division of culture into the field of *large-scale commercial production* and that of restricted production. I shall suggest that he has underestimated the capacity for work of artistic power to arise in the large-scale field. Bourdieu's conception of popular art is particularly disparaging. (Fowler 1997, p. 65)

Relatedly, it has been argued that Bourdieu's two-pole model of cultural production fails adequately to consider hybridizations of 'autonomous' and 'heteronomous' production (see Webb *et al.* 2002, p. 161). This debate gives us a way to think about horror's intertextualities and discursively constructed pleasures, since it suggests that we can view the 'field of horror' as existing *between* 'restricted' and 'large-scale' cultural production. In other words, horror novels are written, and films are made, in part to satisfy pre-existing audiences/ readers, but some of these readers do not merely constitute a pre-existent market, they are also subculturally knowledgeable fans. As Webb *et al.* note of restricted production:

the expected audiences for work produced under this set of values is the *cognoscenti* – ... those who have acquired the specialised education that will allow them to understand the 'in'-jokes, the intertextual references and the self-referentiality of the works. And the rewards in this part of the field are symbolic capital. (2002, pp. 160–1)

Horror is thus not only commercial or 'heteronomous', it also has its own 'autonomous'/subcultural pole of cultural production and consumption (see Bacon-Smith (2000, pp. 241–66) for a related argument dealing with 'science fiction culture'). Different types of intertextuality may therefore position texts relationally in the field of horror, calling on distinctive levels of audience knowledge (subcultural capital/cultural capital) and situating at least some horror texts as 'popular art' (Fowler 1997; Lopes 2000). Horror texts may be more or less imbued with intertextual cultural capital and intertextual subcultural capital, allowing 'officially', 'legitimately' educated and subculturally knowledgeable readers to exercise their discriminatory powers and thus receive the honour of 'symbolic capital' along with pleasures of recognition. Or contemporary horror texts may enact a deliberate break with proliferating and 'postmodern' intertextual relations, demanding to be read as hermetic and proprietorial (i.e., 'authored') cultural productions, and allowing readers with appropriate levels of (sub)cultural capital to respond as members of an auterist interpretative community (see Chapter 10).

If pleasure is undertheorized by Bourdieu (1993), it is nevertheless narratively implied in his theoretical framework, for we cannot plausibly suppose that the exercising of cultural distinctions, and the recognition of one's 'symbolic capital' or prestigious reputation in the eyes of fellow specialists is anhedonic or affectless. What a Bourdieuian intertextual reading can thus uncover are those bids for cultural and symbolic capital that are intertextually structured into primary texts such as horror novels and films. In turn, such a reading can demonstrate how these position-takings allow different fractions of horror's audiences and fans to perform their specialist knowledges and (sub)cultural identities, with discourses of pleasure being constructed in relation to such processes of cultural reproduction.

The 'scare quotes' of horror can hence be seen as positioning texts within the field of horror while also offering possible socio-cultural trajectories for consumers to relate to: fans may favour reference-spotting over 'being scared', whereas more casual genre followers may reverse this discursively structured knowledge-affect response. Bourdieu's two-pole model of cultural production can be thought of as indicating ideal types of 'restricted/autonomous' aestheticization (treating the text as an aesthetic construct and series of in-jokes) and 'large-scale/heteronomous' literalization (treating the text as an immersive, realist narrative), with responses to horror fictions ranging across a continuum between these extremes. Indeed such a continuum of responses, where reading horror intertextually involves pleasures of knowledgeable recognition *rather than* pleasures of being scared, is attested to in Janet Staiger's (2000) analysis of reading *Texas Chainsaw Massacre* (1974, dr: Tobe Hooper) intertextually:

> my personal invoking of the intertext of *Psycho* has been a means to defend myself from the sadomasochistic fantasies I am also constructing in viewing the text. By using the intertextual frame 'Tobe Hooper has used Hitchcock's *Psycho* as an intertext for *Texas Chainsaw Massacre* and I am smart enough to see this', I am constructing for myself the role of a listener to a joke I am attributing to Hooper. Thus, I become complicit with Hooper in the mechanisms of a tendentious joke, rather than the joke's victim – the 'average' viewer of the movie. I can laugh at the intertextual jokes rather than end up assaulted by the non-stop intensity of the plot. (2000, pp. 185–6)

Staiger astutely comments that although intertextuality has been conceptualized in many ways in literary/cultural theory, its function for readers/audiences has been neglected, along with its pleasures (2000, p. 186). She goes on to articulate intertextual knowledgeability to discourses of pleasure, restoring this dimension to Bourdieu-based theorizing: 'intertextuality obviously serves affective functions, here to give me cultural capital and to let me laugh when I see the horror and humour of Hitchcock in Texas' (2000, p. 186; see also Gelder 1996, pp. 32–3). The discursive terms of Staiger's self-analysis are replayed in Mark Kermode's (1997) account of being a horror fan, which again contrasts getting the 'in-joke' to 'cringing' in fear (see Kermode 1997, p. 60: and Messenger-Davies 2001, pp. 162–3). Such self-accounts (Kermode 1997 and Staiger 2000) can be analysed as performances of 'restricted' horror fandom and 'restricted' academic subcultural expertise, as opposed to 'large-scale' genre consumption that does not hinge on the exercising of institutionally specific skills. The 'pleasures of horror' reflected on in Part I thus need to be linked to an awareness that horror's supposed automatic status as a 'body genre' (Linda Williams 1999) neglects how horror more complexly participates in, and prestructures, forms of cultural reproduction (see also Lash 1990, p. 252 on the split interpretation of texts between those using 'categories of every-day life' and those with 'specialized classificatory frameworks'). In other words, fans and scholars of horror – not always two separable groups, as the case of Kim Newman will amply demonstrate – tend to pleasurably reference-spot horror's intertextual (sub)cultural capital and thus reproduce their sense of knowledgeability, rather than being scared by horror (contra Lake Crane's (2004) reading of 'postmodern' horror as textually collapsing together horror and humour). Through this cultural reproduction, horror becomes a matter of performed cultural value – a 'mind genre' rather than a 'body genre' – for sections of its readership/audience possessing higher levels of cultural and/or subcultural capital (see Hoxter 2000, p. 185 and Hills 2002, p. 98).

Having set out these theoretical parameters, in the next section I will consider one type of 'intertextual relation' that horror texts can display in order to performatively bid for cultural value – that is, a combination of intertextual cultural and subcultural capitals. My case study will address the fictions of British horror writer and film critic, Kim Newman, responding to Ken Gelder's observation that 'the analysis of contemporary forms has focused mainly on cinema, ignoring horror novelists altogether (with one or two exceptions)' (2000, p. 6). Although Gelder perhaps exaggerates how few horror writers have been studied academically (see the work of Bloom (ed) 1993; Talbot 1995; Joshi 2001a and 2001b; Reynolds *et al.* 2001), it remains the case that Newman has not been one of the 'exceptions' treated to significant academic consecration and canonization. Such horror novelists have typically been Stephen King and Anne Rice (see, for example, Badley 1996, which covers the fictions of King, Rice and Clive Barker. Also, very much non-exhaustively, see Hodges and Doane 1991; Gelder 1994 and 1996; Haas and Haas 1996; Marcus 1997; Tomc 1997 for work on Anne Rice, and Herron 1987; Grixti 1989; Hanson 1990; Casebeer 1996; Gelder 1996; Punter 1996; Oakes 2000; Kelso 2002; Ward 2002, pp. 117–26; Magistrale 2003 for illustrative work on Stephen King).

Newman's absence in academic study is surprising given that he has not only written much horror fiction but has also edited *The BFI Companion to Horror* (1996) and *Science Fiction/Horror: A Sight and Sound Reader* (2002a), as well as writing studies of *Nightmare Movies* (1988), *Millennium Movies* (1999a) and the Lewton/Tourneur *Cat People* (1999b) and using the pseudonym 'Jack Yeovil'. In what follows I will restrict myself to studying cultural productions expressly attributed to Newman. Admittedly there have been brief academic references to Kim Newman's horror fiction in Morrison (1996, p. 17), Luckhurst (2002, p. 529), Auerbach (1995, p. 169), and Latham (2002, p. 104), and to his non-fiction in Jancovich (2002a, p. 9) and Hogle (2002, p. 205). But with the exceptions of Wilkinson (2000) and Latham (2001) there has been little scholarly discussion of Newman's work.

KIM NEWMAN'S 'LITMUS TEXT': PLAYING 'CATCH-THE-REFERENCE'

As Eugene Byrne notes in his introduction to the collection of Kim Newman's short stories and novellas *Unforgivable Stories*:

> a lot of the tales in this book are stories about stories ... Weird because they're not your conventional alternate history stories, but because they're also alternate story stories. These are as much literary constructions as historical ones. (Byrne 2000, pp. 5–6)

In Newman's 'alternate story stories', 'Sister Hyde' enters the diegesis of 'The Strange Case of Dr Jekyll and Mr Hyde' (Newman 2000a), Jekyll's transformative potion is mass-marketed after his death (Newman 2002b), and Jack Seward becomes Jack the Ripper, existing alongside Inspector Lestrade the vampire-detective in *Anno Dracula* (Newman 1993, p. 467; Kaveney 1990, p. 17; see also Hills 2003c). By ostentatiously displaying detailed knowledge of a range of classic gothic texts, Newman's short stories and novels are constructed, in large part, through their displays of intertextual cultural capital. These popular fictions objectify their author's scholarly appreciation of 'The Strange Case of Dr Jekyll and Mr Hyde' (Stevenson 1979) and *Dracula* (Stoker 1994). For example, Newman follows *Anno Dracula* with an Afterword which contains notes on 'the dating of *Dracula*':

> Stoker does not specify which year the events of the novel are supposed to take place. Frayling argues persuasively that he intended 1893, while Wolf and Haining pick 1887 ... I have plumped, as did Jimmy Sangster, Terence Fisher and Hammer Films for their 1958 *Dracula* ... for 1885, and opted to shift on to an alternate timetrack halfway through Stoker's Chapter 21, on page 249 of Wolf's annotated edition. (Newman 1993, pp. 466–7)

Citing popular culture alongside academic texts, and offering an exaggeratedly precise definition of his 'alternate timetrack', Newman conveys authorial erudition, implying that his reworkings of foundational Gothic-horror texts should be read as commentaries on the originals (Cranny-Francis 1990, p. 99; Cohen 1996, p. 5). Literary/cultural theory is mobilized by Newman within this process of writing-as-commentary, and not only in authorial Afterwords but also in subsequent commentaries, for example Newman (2001a, p. 98):

> In my own contribution to the mythos, *Anno Dracula* (1993), I chose to expand on this neglected strand [Dracula as an 'invasion fantasy' pitting the 'filthy foreigner' against 'an emblematic array of Englishness' – MH], extrapolating a late-Victorian London in which Dracula has prevailed over Van Helsing and moved from the petty conquests of the wives of solicitors to become a new Prince Consort in control of the Empire. My purpose in the novel ... is to open *Dracula* to a variety of interpretations.

'Theory' is also self-consciously drawn on in the main bodies of some of Newman's popular fictions, as well as in secondary texts, or para-texts such as Afterwords and epigraphs. For instance, one epigraph to *Dracula Cha Cha Cha* (Newman 2000b) is a quote from horror film theorist Robin Wood (1996, p. 378). 'Further Developments in the Strange Case of Dr Jekyll and Mr Hyde' (2000a) carries out a queer reading of Jekyll and Hyde's narrative, albeit in the register of popular fiction rather than as institutionally validated 'Theory' (compare Newman's rereading with the theoretical readings put forward by

Twitchell 1985, p. 241; Clemens 1999, pp. 131–2; Showalter 2000, p. 197). And 'A Drug on the Market' (2002b), Newman's second rereading/rewriting of the Jekyll and Hyde scenario, offers a further cultural-political challenge to the gothic's emphasis on individualized disintegrations of self. On this occasion, Newman rewrites Jekyll's transformation into Hyde as a thoroughly social phenomenon and links this, in turn, to the operation of capitalism. Each of Newman's rereadings/rewritings (McCracken-Flesher 1994), whether concerning Jekyll and Hyde or Dracula, are therefore situated in relation to an original Ur-text, adopting a cultural-political position of commentary and critique (just as horror 'Theory' has sought to do).

In a Foreword to *Andy Warhol's Dracula* (Newman 1999c), fellow writer F. Paul Wilson applauds Newman's gothic rewritings in *Anno Dracula* (Newman 1993) as follows:

> I was reeled through the ... book at breakneck pace, running across characters from Stoker, Doyle, Wells, Rohmer, Stevenson ... and others. Less celebrated and some downright obscure characters abounded as well ... I realized that Kim Newman had penned, in a very real sense, a literary novel. But his referential base was not the canon of English literature taught in schools, it was *our* canon, *our* literature. (Wilson 1999, p. 5)

Wilson raises an intriguing question: should Newman's many references and in-jokes – described by Rob Latham (2002, p. 104) as a 'rampantly intertextual treatment' of horror – be construed as intertextual cultural capital or as intertextual subcultural capital? Are such references, aimed at cognoscenti at the 'restricted', specialist end of horror's continuum of readers, based upon official, educational knowledge, or on subcultural fan knowledge? The separation of 'cultural capital' and 'subcultural capital' or 'popular cultural capital' (Fiske 1992) has been rigid and absolute in previous academic work (see Hills 2002). By definition, subcultural capital is only recognized as capital in the eyes of relevant subcultural beholders, and is excluded from the institutionally validated, educational knowledges of legitimate 'cultural capital'. However, Wilson's (1999) claim that Newman's work draws on the cultural knowledge of a fan subculture – 'our canon' rather than a 'school' canon – provokes me to ponder exactly where the rigidly assumed line between cultural capital and subcultural capital can actually be drawn (on the potential relativization of 'cultural capital' see Collins 2002, p. 19). Diane Reay draws on Lamont and Lareau's (1988) definition of cultural capital as 'widely shared legitimate culture made up of high status cultural signals' (in Grenfell and James with Hodkinson, Reay and Robbins 1998, p. 138). The hostages to fortune here are, of course, 'widely shared' and 'legitimate'. The various gothic novels and novellas that Newman rereads and rewrites – such as *Dracula* (Stoker 1994) and 'The Strange Case of Dr Jekyll and Mr Hyde' (Stevenson 1979) – are, after all, taught on many university courses dealing with the gothic, and there is a multitude of published academic studies dealing with them as legitimately 'canonical' literary texts (see, for example, Levine and Knoepflmacher (eds) 1982; Bann (ed.) 1994; Gelder 1994; McCracken-Flesher 1994; Hendershot 1998; Konigsberg 1998; Turney 1998; Clemens 1999; Waller 1986; Veeder and Hirsch (eds) 1988). Against this backdrop, Stephen King's assertion that such gothic texts 'live a kind of half-life outside the bright circle of English literature's acknowledged "classics"' (King 1982, p. 65), as well as F. Paul Wilson's (1999) claim that Stoker, Doyle, Wells, etc. escape the 'school' (i.e. official/legitimate) canon seem arguable. However, we could conclude that such texts are only partly but insecurely consecrated by their appearance within university-based literary and cultural studies; they are canonical, but only as a 'generic/historical' canon and not as fully fledged 'classics'. That is, their appearance within the realms of cultural capital is contested and somewhat marginal rather than being 'widely shared' and wholly legitimate. Attributions of 'classic' status may thus be institutionally shared by Gothic-horror academic specialists, yet remain relatively 'improper' in the wider field of literature (Peim 2000, pp. 24–5).

Wilson's (1999) framing of *Andy Warhol's Dracula* (Newman 1999c) thus sounds a combative note. It performs an opposition to the official 'school' canon that is not fully borne out by the interpenetration of the 'field' of Gothic-horror with the 'field' of literary studies (and which is also partly contradicted by the use of 'Theory' as a cultural-political intertext in many of Newman's fictions). Wilson focuses on how the intertextual knowledge displayed by Newman relates to horror's fan subculture, positioning Newman – via his texts' displayed intertextual (sub)cultural capital – at the apex of fan knowledgeability:

> I have also said, in private conversation and on convention panels, that ANNO DRACULA should be the litmus text for anyone applying for an editorial position in the fantasy and horror fields. A prospective editor who doesn't get it ... should be considered culturally deprived (remember this is *our* culture) and banished to the romance department. (Wilson 1999, p. 6)

Wilson's own authentic subcultural position is displayed, for he has said this 'on convention panels', and Newman's intertextual referencing of a wide range of gothic texts is explicitly converted into a marker of 'restricted' horror readership; if you 'get' the references then you display your 'true' fan status and accrue symbolic capital as a result. The logic of competition that is implied in Bourdieu's (1993) model is shared by this Foreword given that Newman's work is positioned as a kind of 'litmus text' for full membership of horror fan subculture. This 'text' is, of course, also a punning 'Newman *test*'. Failure is equated with an emasculating lack of fan knowledge and exile to the 'romance department', which is posited as radically Other to the discursively gendered field of horror. In another Foreword to one of Newman's small press collections (Newman 2000c), Peter Atkins makes a related observation about Newman's fiction:

One of the many pleasures of reading this strand of Kim's fiction is matching your own storehouse of memories against his – playing a kind of catch-the-reference-before-he-explains-it game with the author ... The bad news is you'll nearly always lose. Kim will kick your ass. He just knows more about that shit than practically anyone else. If you're lucky enough to know Kim personally and have the balls for it, you can even play the game ... in the flesh. You should be warned, in fact, that Kim is *always* playing. No starting whistle. No half-time. (Atkins in Newman 2000c, p. 10; see also Richards in Newman 2001b, pp. 7–8, which describes Newman as 'one of Britain's foremost film and television historians')

Masculinized competitiveness – the logic of Bourdieu's theories as much as the logic of this subcultural position-taking – is inscribed into Atkins's commentary, if you 'have the balls for it', much as it is in Wilson's. Newman and his fictions are repeatedly positioned as arbiters of true 'insider knowledge' (Lake Crane 2004, p. 148) and hence as the gold standard of fans' subcultural capital. This clearly indicates the symbolic capital, or prestige, that has accrued to Newman as a result of his fictions' 'rampant' intertextualities. Furthermore, since Newman's status is celebrated by the likes of F. Paul Wilson and Peter Atkins, the issue of 'social capital' is also raised here. This is Pierre Bourdieu's (1986, pp. 114–15) term for the resources and privileges that can be accrued by virtue of one's social networks or contacts. Basically, it indicates the importance of who one knows in a field, and how powerful one's contacts are in that domain (Field 2003, pp. 17–18; Schuller *et al.* 2000, pp. 3–5). However, as Nan Lin has argued, Bourdieu's model of social capital presumes closed networks of social contacts, since his focus is on the socio-cultural action of 'preserving or maintaining resources' (Lin 2001, p. 27). Lin suggests that social capital may, contra Bourdieu, operate via 'bridges' between different social networks (or, we might say, across and between fields).

In Newman's case, his exceptionally high social capital links him not only to other horror writers and cognoscenti in the field of horror but also to academics studying horror such as Julian Petley, and to commissioning editors at the British Film Institute, who are outside the field of horror and placed in separate fields of academia and publishing. Newman's range of social contacts in the horror field is also testified to by his lengthy acknowledgements (see, for example, Newman (1993, pp. 468–9), which reads like a 'Who's Who' of British horror including Clive Barker, Christopher Fowler, Stephen Gallagher, Alan Jones, Mark Kermode, Mark Morris and so on) as well as by the links on his website at http://www.johnnyalucard.com/links.html.

However, Newman's fiction is not only introduced or contextualized by fellow writers. Many of his colleagues in the field of horror also appear in his fictions; social capital is thus not only something that exists outside the realm of fiction, or in para-texts such as acknowledgements; it is also textually re-produced as part of Newman's 'rampantly intertextual treatment' (Latham 2002,

p. 104) of horror. For example, Peter Atkins appears as 'Professor Peter Atkins of Liverpool University' in Newman 2000d, p. 217, while horror anthologist Stephen Jones, listed in *The BFI Companion to Horror* (Newman (ed.) 1996, p. 177) as well as contributing to it, has a real reference work of his (Jones 1994) cited in Newman's short story 'Completist Heaven' (Newman 2000e, p. 188; see also Jones and Newman (eds) 1988). Jones also appears in the story 'Quetzalcon' concerning a fan convention dedicated to the fictional celebrity horror writer Kingston Dunstan (Newman 2000d, p. 220).

The repeated (inter)textual implication here is that Newman has extremely high levels of social capital within the field of horror as well as extremely high subcultural capital, and that these capitals are objectified intertextually in his fictions. Indeed, subcultural capital that is less fuzzily blurred with cultural capital, and hence closer to the 'pure' end of 'restricted' horror subculture, is also displayed in Newman's texts via intertextual references to contemporary horror's fields of production and consumption. A number of Newman's short stories concern themselves with directly representing horror fan subculture (2000d and 2000e) and horror's field of production, for example the *Where the Bodies Are Buried* sequence (2000c). Yet these stories do not simply display subcultural capital; they also convey a cultural politics of horror, occupying a similar position to much academic work on horror. Academics have challenged dominant, ideological accounts of 'media effects' that have plagued horror (Barker and Petley 1997 and 2001; Jones 2002), and Newman puts forward related arguments in his fictions. To take one example, 'Where the Bodies are Buried 3: Black and White and Red All Over' concerns a series of killers who all appear to have been inspired to kill by a fictional tabloid newspaper, the *Comet* (see Newman 2000c, pp. 83, 87, 91), while in each case newspaper reporters or corrupt policemen replace *Comet* newspaper cuttings found at crime scenes with copies of a fictional horror film *Where the Bodies Are Buried 3*. Newman suggests that the 'real' source of violent crime is tabloid journalism's sensationalism and amorality and statistics given for crime rises exactly match those given for the *Comet*'s rises in circulation, a trick that Newman draws to the reader's attention by adding 'The figures were creepily familiar' (2000c, p. 91). Horror is simplistically scapegoated within this fiction's diegesis, recapitulating a key argument put forward by horror fan-scholars such as Mark Kermode (1997 and 2002). Newman's narrative-aesthetic appropriation of fan subcultural politics continues in 'Where the Bodies Are Buried 2020', which features a future 'media psychologist' (2000c, p. 104) who avers that: 'My field of study is Media Influence. Genre horror is central to the discipline. The pioneer work of Martin Barker and Julian Petley in the 1990s' (2000c, p. 124 referring to Barker and Petley 1997; Petley also contributed to Newman's (1996) *BFI Companion to Horror*). Where the third story in the *Where the Bodies Are Buried* sequence focuses on the cultural 'guilt' of tabloid newspapers rather than horror fictions, the fourth entry implies that Catholicism, and not the horror genre, has nurtured and inspired insane killers, noting that 'It's all been about attributions of guilt.

It's all been about where the bodies are buried' (2000c, p. 141). Newman's own attributions of guilt, presented via narrative and character viewpoint, fall upon those cultural institutions that have ideologically vilified horror while seeking to occupy a high moral ground: journalism and religion should become the true objects of moral panic, according to these fannish, subcultural arguments represented as a cultural politics of/in horror fiction.

The intertextualities of Newman's fictions partly display subcultural capital – see, for example, the series of references and in-jokes crammed into 'Completist Heaven' (2000e), as well as invented book-jacket blurbs from the likes of Michael Marshall Smith in 'Quetzalcón' (2000d, p. 215) and the first real branching choice that is offered to the reader in *Life's Lottery* (1999d, p. 10). They also partly exhibit a fuzzy subcultural/cultural capital via rewritings of academically canonized/consecrated gothic fictions, and partly indicate more 'legitimate' cultural capital in the form of referring to academic theory (see Newman 2000a, p. 35 and 2000c, pp. 24 and 28–9). Newman's fictions thus intertextually occupy a specific 'space of possibles' in the field of horror, indicating a multiple series of bids for cultural value, not all of which are strictly embedded in a neatly 'bounded' field of horror. Newman's fictions draw intertextually on forms of knowledge, and capital, which are not securely placed within the field of horror; primarily 'Theory' but also the arguably or fuzzily (sub)cultural capital of 'classic' literary appreciation. However, Newman's work also accrues symbolic and subcultural capital within the field of horror by virtue of its detailed fan knowledge and its replaying of fan subcultural politics.

This intertextuality could simply be read as 'postmodern', relating Newman's intertextual reworking of media fictions to Baudrillard's thesis of the simulacrum as 'self-referential simulation' (see Wilkinson 2000, pp. 15–16). But any such interpretation converts intertextual strategies into a kind of 'one-size-fits-all' academic abstraction (Lake Crane 2004), and thus loses a sense of how Newman's intertextualities work within (and outside) the field of horror to bid for the cultural and subcultural value of his fictions. We thus need to more carefully consider the 'intertextual arenas' (Collins 1989, p. 44) that are constructed by horror fictions. Newman's texts such as *Anno Dracula* (1993) self-consciously define themselves in relation to their generic precursors, requiring us to pay attention 'to how texts position themselves in relation to other texts' (Collins 1989, p. 43). For it is a distinctive positioning, a claim to culturally-politically surpass 'classic' texts nevertheless linked to a claim to continue in their tradition of cultural value, that characterizes the gothic rereadings/ rewritings of Newman's horror. Newman's 'alternate story stories' locate themselves in relation to what are insecurely canonical texts, actively bidding for neo-canonical status. Given this bid for literary/cultural value, strands of Newman's writing can be said to 'engage a familiar set of distinctions by which "the Gothic novel" ... [is] ... not constructed as other to legitimate culture

... but ... [is rather] ... associated with legitimate culture' (Jancovich 2002b, p. 159).

This is very far from a 'postmodern' collapse of demarcations between 'high' and 'popular' culture. It is, in fact, quite the reverse, being a cultural reproduction of one type of popular culture that aims to distinguish itself from more 'heteronomous' generic rivals (see Dyer quoted in Bignell 2000, p. 93) while remaining generically recognizable to specialist 'autonomous' horror fan subcultures (Bourdieu 1993) as 'popular art' (Fowler 1997; Lopes 2000). Contra 'postmodern' reductions that ignore fields of cultural production in favour of theoretical discourses and meta-narratives of sameness we can therefore locate the 'intertextual relations' of Newman's work as follows:

Intertextual Cultural Capital	*Intertextual (Sub)cultural Capital*	*Intertextual Subcultural Capital*
High but partly disavowed. Drawn from outside field.	*High, but in relation to 'literary' texts that are partly claimed as subcultural and insecurely canonized outside the field.*	*Exceptionally high; hence the 'Newman test'.*

Newman is required to disavow the extent of his knowledge of theory within his fictions in order to retain a valid place within the field of horror; were these texts to more extensively display theoretical knowledge then arguably they would become less central to the field, and would begin to collapse into the field of theory production rather than literary production. Intertextual relations may move outside the field of horror, but this centrifugal interfield movement has to be counter-balanced by centripetal intertextual forces, such as the display of subcultural capital.

Although Newman's fictions perform this kind of balancing, other fictions err towards displaying intertextual cultural capital rather than intertextual subcultural capital, and hence become either self-consciously 'literary horror' or ultimately position themselves outside the (subcultural) field of horror altogether, becoming 'mainstream' or 'contemporary' fiction. Mark Z. Danielewski's *House of Leaves* (2001) is far more ostentatious than Newman's fictions in its display of theoretical and literary intertextual cultural capital, and far less concerned with displaying very high levels of subcultural capital (see also Duncker 2002). It thus constitutes one possible limit point in the field of horror in terms of bidding for cultural value (outside the field) while remaining generically linked to horror. Indeed, Kim Newman is one of the blurb-writers captured on the book's back cover (Doubleday 2001 paperback edition), hence connecting Danielewski's work to Newman's own interfield and tradition-based bids for horror's cultural value: 'There is a core of dark power in *House of Leaves* and a sense of return to the great dark matter of American literature: the haunted houses of Hawthorne, Poe and Lovecraft' (Danielewski 2001, back cover). Note also that it is 'literature' *per se* that is referred to by Newman in this quote rather than horror fiction, clearly constructing American gothic fictions as a matter of cultural capital rather than subcultural capital or a fuzzy blurring of the two. The work of other writers such as Joyce Carol Oates, Patrick McGrath and Ian McEwan (see Morrison 1996, p. 10) could be read intertextually to indicate where the delicate balancing of intertextual cultural capital and intertextual subcultural capital results in fictions that move more definitively outside the field of horror and into 'literary'/'mainstream'/'contemporary' fiction.

Furthermore, the work of Stephen King could also be productively viewed alongside that of Newman, since King shares high levels of education or 'cultural capital' and 'social capital' with Newman, and high levels of fan knowledge or subcultural capital (see Herron 1987 and Wiater 1992). Like Newman (1988), King has also written a study of horror (1982), and both writers have drawn intertextually on gothic texts in their work, in King's case, perhaps most notably in *'Salem's Lot* (1975), the novel that first made his reputation in the field of horror (Sarrantonio 1988, p. 162) and which also kick-started horror 'bestselleritis' (according to Morrison 1996, p. 12). However, there are also interesting differences in (inter)textual position-taking that do not require economic analysis (of sales, marketing, etc.) to be analytically perceived. For example, King strikes a persistent, populist 'folksiness' in his fiction (Ward 2002, p. 125; Skal 1993, p. 360) and in commentaries such as *Danse Macabre* (1982) and the later *On Writing* (2001), the 'Second Foreword' to which begins all too characteristically, 'This is a short book because most books about writing are filled with bullshit' (King 2001, p. 11; Kelso 2002). This type of assertion, buttressed by King's considerable symbolic capital as a routinized writer of horror bestsellers, proposes to cut through over-intellectualizing and hopelessly verbose expression, since 'length' or word count is here equated with 'bullshit' and since good old common sense can supposedly do away with pesky, elitist, academic gibberish. Intertextually and discursively, King-the-writer appears as the enemy of King-the-English Professor. Thus Stephen King adopts a more vigorously anti-academic stance than Newman's mild disavowal, as well as intertextually displaying a less extensive interest or investment in subcultural capital. Where Newman's fiction bids performatively to position itself across the subcultural fields of horror fan and academic, King's indicates apparent disdain for subcultural fans and academics alike. His interpellated target is rather the 'ordinary folk' of horror's 'mass, commercial' readers, whereas Newman's ideal reader is more likely to be a subculturally self-identifying horror fan who has perhaps also studied Eng. Lit. or Cultural Theory to university level. Reading King thus offers the discursive pleasures of validating a specific cultural identity and a specific ideological stance, as does reading Newman. But the ideologies and cultural identities that can be reconfirmed are significantly opposed here, with King aiming for horror's 'heteronomous' end of the continuum of readers (non-specialists), and Newman's intertextualities making more sense to the 'restricted' end of 'specialist' readers, or self-professed horror fans.

In the next chapter I will continue this process of Bourdieuian reading, moving on to consider a very different type of intertextuality that has been displayed in the contemporary field of horror film. Although Kim Newman's horror fictions have been described as 'postmodern' (Wilkinson 2000, p. 16), *Scream* (1996, dr: Wes Craven) has become an almost totemic object in arguments over postmodern horror film. I will develop the argument of this part of *The Pleasures of Horror* – that the category of 'postmodern' horror is a somewhat unhelpful abstraction – by considering how *Scream*'s forms of 'intertextual relations' and intertextual capitals differ relationally from those displayed in Newman's work. This distinction will also enable me to structurally account for the predominantly negative reception that *Scream* has received within the academy.

Chapter 10

Intertextuality in the Contemporary Field of Horror (II): The 'Postmodern' Scream Franchise

In this chapter I want to develop the preceding focus on 'the field of horror' (Gelder 2000, p. 1) by considering how recent horror films have intertextually drawn on 'insider knowledge' and 'a fan's familiarity' with the genre (Lake Crane 2004, p. 148). Titles such as *Bride of Chucky* (1998, dr: Ronny Yu), *Cherry Falls* (2000, dr: Geoffrey Wright), *The Faculty* (1998, dr: Robert Rodriguez), *New Nightmare* (1994, dr: Wes Craven), *Scream* (1996, dr: Wes Craven), *Scream 2* (1997, dr: Wes Craven), *Scream 3* (2000, dr: Wes Craven), *Urban Legend* (1998, dr: Jamie Blanks) and *Urban Legends: Final Cut* (2000, dr: John Ottman) as well as lesser-known post-*Scream* films such as *Cut* (2000, dr: Kimble Rendall) and *Scared* (2001, dr: Keith Walley) have all participated in the 1990s and 2000s trend for horror texts to display intertextual subcultural capital. Unlike the horror fictions of Kim Newman (Chapter 9), which draw intertextually on 'classic' gothic novels and 'Theory' as markers of writerly erudition – that is as intertextual subcultural capital and as intertextual cultural capital – the likes of *Scream* display a very different, and rather more limited, range of intertextualities. It is this difference between intertextual strategies that I want to focus on here, arguing that to simply characterize such fictions and films as 'postmodern' misses the fact that they occupy different spaces within horror's autonomous/heteronomous 'field'.

Films that adopt intertextual strategies of distinction closer to those of Newman's fictions are *Bram Stoker's Dracula* (1992, dr: Francis Ford Coppola), *Mary Reilly* (1996, dr: Stephen Frears), and *Mary Shelley's Frankenstein* (1994, dr: Kenneth Branagh). Jonathan Bignell (2000) concludes that the first 'is itself a rereading of the *Dracula* novel and of the culture in which it was produced' (2000, p. 106), just as Newman's *Anno Dracula* (1993) and 'Further Developments in the Strange Case of Dr Jekyll and Mr Hyde' (2000a) reread *Dracula* (Stoker 1994) and *The Strange Case of Dr. Jekyll and Mr. Hyde* (Stevenson 1979) and thereby critique Victorian society. However, the three films cited immediately above do not display entirely analogous intertextual position-takings in the field of horror to those of Newman's fictions. Unlike Newman's emphasis on intertextual subcultural capital alongside the fuzzy (sub)cultural capital of gothic rereadings/rewritings, these films focus primarily on what is assumed to be legitimate literary cultural capital at the expense of successfully interpellating self-professed horror fans. By enacting a cultural connectivity to the 'classic' works of Stoker, Shelley and Stevenson without counterbalancing subcultural intertextualities, such texts threaten to move outside the field of horror and become 'mainstream'/'contemporary' films that draw on horror's tropes and histories (just as is the case with the fictions of Ian McEwan, say, or even Danielewski's (2001) *House of Leaves*). We could therefore read *Bram Stoker's Dracula* and *Mary Shelley's Frankenstein* intertextually as performative bids for cultural capital that reach too far outside the field of horror and thus forfeit a privileged position within that field, while also remaining 'tainted' by the horror genre in the eyes of non-fans. Indeed, Mark Jancovich has described such films as 'horror … for people who do not like horror' (2000, p. 31), and it is the interfield transgressiveness of these films – the fact that they 'try too hard' to appear culturally valuable rather than subculturally 'authentic' – which arguably renders them problematic for many horror fans and non-fans alike. Thomas Austin (2002) has noted the relative box office failure of such films, construing them as a 'costume horror cycle' (2002, p. 118), and thereby recognizing their (failed or qualified) intertextual bids for cultural capital as 'quality' horror (2002, pp. 116–17) or as what Jim Collins would call 'high pop' (Collins 2002, p. 3).

Noting the 'processual' nature of the horror genre (2002, p. 118), Austin points out that the rather awkward hybridization of the 'costume horror cycle' was followed by genre-revitalizing successes such as *Scream*. However, viewing these shifts in horror cycles merely as temporal – where something that 'works' follows on from experimental 'failures' – neglects the extent to which failures and successes may also emerge through their (relational and intertextual) position-takings in the field of horror. With this in mind, rather than addressing self-reflexive 'quality' horror, it is the immensely successful intertextual position-taking of *Scream* that I want to consider. *Scream* and its ilk draw intertextually on a corpus of previous horror films, especially in the slasher subgenre, and thus display pronounced fan knowledge within their texts. Rather than these intertextual relations calling up cultural capital such as knowledge of academic theory, they typically draw upon fan expertise, or 'subcultural capital' (Thornton 1995, p. 11), being 'emblematic of Hollywood's heightened fascination with intertextuality' (Harries 2002, p. 281). But what might this 'fascination' mean for scholarly definitions of 'postmodern' horror and their 'postmodern intertextual discourse' (Harries 2000, p. 22)? In the following section I will consider definitions of the postmodern horror film in more detail, before moving on to consider intertextual subcultural capital and the strange case of *Scream*'s academic reception.

'POSTMODERN' HORROR FILMS?

Andrew Tudor has recently argued that 'there has been a proliferation in [the] use of the expression "postmodern horror" as an apparently unproblematic descriptive term ... [F]or the most part, recent horror movies have been dubbed "postmodern" with little or no discussion of what that involves or implies' (2002, p. 105). It is certainly the case that much academic discussion of *Scream* as 'postmodern' can be aligned with Tudor's lament; rather than being clearly defined, postmodern horror has instead tended to be projected on to, and exemplified through, selected film texts.

However, Tudor has also been highly critical of attempts that *have* been made to define 'postmodern horror' cinema (e.g. Pinedo 1997), since almost all the textual qualities put forward as distinctively postmodern seem to have appeared across the cultural history of horror film (although see Williams 2000 for a less text-based definition). Postmodern horror is defined by Isabel Cristina Pinedo as involving the following textual attributes:

> [U]nremitting violence in everyday life; blurred boundaries and endemic danger; rationality questioned and authority undermined; rejection of narrative closure; extreme violence which 'attests to the need to express rage and terror in the midst of postmodern social upheaval'. (Pinedo cited in Tudor 2002, p. 114)

And as Tudor acerbically concludes: 'None of them is qualitatively new' (2002, p. 114). At least two of Pinedo's markers of 'po-mo' horror (authority undermined and lack of narrative closure) seem closely related to Tudor's own distinction between 'secure' and 'paranoid' horror (Tudor 1989, pp. 211–23, 1995, pp. 34–7 and 2002, pp. 108–9). Whereas 'secure' horror typically possesses narrative closure, with horrific threats being diegetically defeated and contained by authority figures, the latter type of horror 'presupposes a thoroughly unreliable world' in which diegetic 'expertise is at best ineffectual ... established authorities are no longer credible protectors of order' (1995, p. 36) and where narrative closure is often insecure (1989, pp. 18–19). The issue of horror films' typical narrative structure is repeatedly picked up in discussions of 'postmodern' horror. For instance, in 'The Terror of Pleasure: The Contemporary Horror Film and Postmodern Theory', Tania Modleski also observes that postmodern horror films 'often delight in thwarting the audiences' expectations of closure' (1986, p. 160).

Tudor remarks that the shift from 'secure' to 'paranoid' horror movies is not total or instantaneous, rather 'the transition stretches from the late fifties into the early seventies' (1989, p. 218). This again accords with Pinedo's work, since she notes that the postmodern horror film does not emerge through a 'clean, historically definable break' (see Pinedo 1997, pp. 14–15). Although Tudor does not label 'paranoid' horror as postmodern, he accepts that the historical shift referred to could be linked to postmodernism:

> If the discourse of paranoid horror makes sense to its users ... then that is because their everyday social world has become increasingly characterized by heightened anxiety and perception of risk ... Living in a 'risk society' ... brings with it a culture of anxiety, and some part of the articulation of that culture is to be found in its characteristic conceptions of the horrific ... Indeed, it is my most general claim that the transition from secure to paranoid horror is part of the social processes that many have sought to understand as distinctively 'postmodern', though I would prefer Giddens's ... terms 'high modernity' and 'late modernity' since his related account of trust, risk and security links more directly with my conceptualization of secure and paranoid horror. (1995, p. 38)

Tudor links 'risk' horror to the idea of 'postmodern' horror, even while using the first theoretical term to displace the second (on horror and risk theory see Lupton 1999, pp. 170–1). Reflecting on this move, Tudor later addresses the 'temptation to think that in the end it may all reduce to a question of semantics. My "paranoid horror" is much the same as Pinedo's (and others') "postmodern horror", and perhaps it matters little which term is used' (2002, p. 115). His rebuttal of any such 'semantic' accusation is that it *does* matter, because to 'employ the term "postmodern" is to make claims about both the causes and consequences of the cinema ... thus described' (2002, pp. 115–16). Whatever one makes of Tudor's response, the logic of this argument demonstrates that much academic energy has been expended in determining whether or not a certain type of post-1970s horror film is 'postmodern'. Certain assumptions have structured this space of argumentative position-taking:

(1) It is assumed that 'the postmodern horror film' represents a singular conceptual entity. Curiously, no attempt is made to delimit a differentiated repertoire/taxonomy of plural horror-movie responses to the 'postmodern' social context or environment.

(2) It is assumed that films either clearly belong to this category of 'postmodern horror' or they do not. Curiously, there is a philosophical 'law of the excluded middle' at work in such discussions, which thus refuse to address the possibility that as well as 'postmodern' horror films displaying a range of differentiated attributes, texts may be qualitatively more or less 'postmodern' rather than simply 'postmodern' ... or not.

Moving beyond these argumentative restrictions, I have suggested elsewhere (Hills 2003d) that it is possible to discern different ranges of intertextualities that are drawn on or put into circulation by supposedly 'postmodern' horror films (my chief comparison was between the reflexive diegeses of *Tesis* (1996, dr:

Alejandro Amenábar) and *Scream*; see http://www.kinoeye.org/03/05/
hills05.php). This allows us to consider exactly which intertextual knowledges
are cued, assumed or facilitated for audiences of 'postmodern' horror, fracturing
monolithic attributions of 'po-mo' status into the examination of multiple
(inter)textual distinctions within what has been labelled 'postmodern horror
film'.

However, given the tendency for debates around postmodern horror to
polarize into pro/anti camps, the identitarian tendency to define postmodern
horror in limited and monolithic ways, and a critical tendency to use it as a term
without definition (see the next section), I will suspend its unhelpful
abstractions here, breaking reflexively with its usage (contra Hills 2003d).
Thus, rather than arguing for different types of postmodern horror movie, I will
retain my focus on different intertextualities and forms of textually objectified
capital. This will enable me to argue that other critics' discussions of *Scream* as
totemically 'postmodern' are a way of either celebrating or denigrating its
specific intertextual position-takings in the field of horror, and are thus a way of
taking up specific positions in the 'field of horror' *studies* by performatively
iterating academic/disciplinary cultural identities.

For example, Andrew Tudor (2002) takes up a certain position in the field, in
the 'game apart' of academic study of horror, by discussing *Scream* while alleging
that postmodernism is passé; a bid for academic (sub)cultural capital occurs here
via a mobilizing of theoretical discourses of 'risk'. Other critics, such as Steven
Jay Schneider (2000b), retain a notion of *Scream et al.* as 'postmodern' based on
these texts' disruptions of previous subgeneric binary oppositions such as 'in-
group'/'out-group' and 'normal'/'aberrant' (Dika 1990; Pollard 2000, p. 47) as
well as on their repeated character reflexivity, where characters draw on fan
'insider knowledge' to outline and evade the 'rules' of the stalker film. While
Tudor opposes 'postmodernism' in order to perform his sociological credentials
in the academic field, Schneider takes up a celebratory stance in relation to
Scream – discussing it through Kevin Williamson's situated agency as *auteur* –
thus appearing to adopt the distinctive position of a scholar-fan (Hills 2002).
Mark Jancovich (2000, pp. 29–31), meanwhile, uses a discussion of *Scream* to
problematize what counts as 'authentic' horror, adopting a Bourdieuian
reflexivity in his work in contrast to Schneider's less reflexively pro-*Scream*
stance that translates fan cultural tastes into academic theorization.

Far more pre- or even non-reflexively, the theorists whose work I will go on to
survey in the next section use discourses of postmodernism to disapprovingly
reject *Scream* as amoral/immoral and as allegedly detached from the 'real' world
by virtue of its rampant media intertextualities. In fact, these theorists use the
term 'postmodern horror film' as a term of abuse. It becomes a way of doubly
positioning themselves and their cultural distinctions: first as academics (able to
display the legitimating cultural capital of Theory), and secondly as an audience
that finds *Scream* distasteful and Other to their valued, favoured forms of
textuality (see Sconce 1993). This readership, as an interpretative community,

does not want to get the 'in-jokes' or 'scare quotes'. They refute pleasurable participation in *Scream*'s intertextual subcultural capital in favour of mobilizing their own cultural capital *against Scream*'s intertextual position-taking in the field of horror. To view academic pro/anti arguments over 'postmodern horror film' (and *Scream*'s cultural value) merely as logical debate is thus to miss the social and cultural distinctions, the field position-takings, that structure such scholarly disagreements.

In marked contrast to Kim Newman's horror fictions, the *Scream* franchise's intertextual relations could be diagrammatically represented as follows:

Intertextual Cultural Capital	Intertextual (Sub)cultural Capital	Intertextual Subcultural Capital
Low.	*Low.*	*Reasonably high, but*
Intertextual relations are predominantly field dependent.	*Few references are made to 'legitimate' or insecurely canonized Gothic horror outside the field.*	*references are usually to mainstream, commercial 1980s 'stalker cycle'. Does not presuppose 'underground' horror fan knowledge.*

Recognizing that the textual appeals and constructed pleasures of *Scream* lie in its diegetic use of specific horror fan knowledges, Steven Jay Schneider's theorization stresses that in the neo-stalker film:

> *humorous self-referentiality gives way to serious reflexivity.* The protagonists of these films ... grow (up) to attain sober recognition of their plight; there is a movement from '*Wow! This is like one of those stalker movies!*' to '*Shit! We are in one of those stalker movies!*' ... those who refuse to 'get reflexive', or who do so too late, die horribly. (2000b, p. 74)

Getting reflexive, that is, drawing on fan knowledge about the conventions of stalker films (Lake Crane 2004) therefore appears to demarcate who lives and who dies, diegetically speaking. Yet this does not always work out according to plan. As Schneider notes: 'unfortunately for Randy [Jamie Kennedy], who has been upgraded to one of the leads this time around, *Scream 2* is not just *any* stalker sequel' (2000b, p. 83) and he is unexpectedly dispatched by the killer. The importance of Randy, the nerdy horror fanboy, to the formula of the *Scream* franchise is attested to in J.K. Muir's comments (written before the release of *Scream 3*):

> Still, no matter how daring, killing Randy was a bad call. Randy is the unquestioned mouthpiece of the *Scream* saga, the character who offers viewers ... road maps to survival. Who is going to tell us the rules in *Scream 3*? In killing off Randy ... the creators of *Scream 2* have done *Scream 3* a disservice.

Unless, of course, they have a great joke in store for all of us. (Muir 1998, p. 218)

And, of course, they did: the deceased video store clerk appears on a self-recorded video to recount the 'rules' in the trilogy's concluding part. Despite being killed off, Randy's role as 'mouthpiece of the ... saga' was seemingly recognized by writer Ehren Kruger and director Wes Craven. It is thus not only textual reflexivity that recurs across the franchise; character reflexivity, especially via the figure of Randy the horror fan, remains a central part of what might be called the '*Scream* meme' (Clark 2003, p. 63; Dika 2003, p. 210). Horror fan knowledge is hence presupposed at various levels: through horror/fantasy 'films mentioned/ seen by name', of which Muir lists 21 for *Scream*, through 'names, situations alluded to', which accounts for 14 references by Muir's tally (1998, pp. 297–8), through films that are cited directly, such as the use made of *Halloween* (1978, dr: John Carpenter), and through the 'rules' that Randy shares with other characters. Such intertextual subcultural capital is the dominant type of intertexual knowledge drawn on in *Scream*, but by the time of *Scream 3* Randy's videotaped warning finds its place alongside what should accurately be addressed as 'intratextual subcultural capital'. That is, fan audience knowledge of the *Scream* franchise itself eventually comes to supplant audience knowledge of 1970s/80s stalker films. Dialogue from the first film is quoted in *Scream 3* as Sidney (Neve Campbell) sits on a film set designed to analogue her bedroom from *Scream*, while each character from the first *Scream* has an actor double involved in the (diegetic) filming of *Stab 3*. Geoff King (2002) refers to this state of affairs as 'the film-second-sequel-within-the film-second-sequel ... juxtaposing ... characters with those playing them in the second-level fictional version' (2002, p. 126).

Intertextual subcultural capital thus shifts across the franchise, as the films become less concerned with needing 'to present the [1970s] slasher movie as unselfconscious and moronic in order to establish ... [a] ... sense of superiority over it' (Jancovich 2002a, p. 8) and more concerned with taking the franchise itself as a point of reference. Whereas the first *Scream* film arguably courts a 'crossover' teen audience and 'Gen X' twentysomething or thirtysomething audience who would have seen the original 1970s/80s stalker films (Schneider 2000b, p. 85; see also Kermode 2003b), such double-coding is less obvious by the time of *Scream 3*. Pleasures of intertextual 'recognition' incited by this text are thus still based significantly around fan knowledge, but the textual knowledge presupposed for viewers to 'get the reference' is more intratextual and 'proprietary' than intertextual/generic.

Scream's alleged 'postmodernism' is thus initially premised around intertextual references to stalker films, and is latterly (in sequel films) built around intratextual references to the franchise. Its intertextual capital is thus predominantly pop cultural or fan cultural in remit (Fiske 1992). As revealed in the film's opening scene, what really counts as knowledge here is knowing who the killer was in *Friday the 13th* (1980, dr: Sean S. Cunningham). Fans are part of the narrative solution: it is by becoming a fan (using fan knowledge) that characters are empowered to fight back against killers. As Schneider notes: 'Sidney's insider knowledge of the stalker subgenre ... enables her to anticipate the killer's improbable return and break with convention by finishing him off in unambiguous fashion' (2000b, p. 83).

Contra the position-taking of Kim Newman's fictions (or even of the film *Tesis*), *Scream* does not engage with 'Theory'. Its intertextual position-taking is resolutely non-academic, if not stridently anti-academic (Hills 2003d), providing us with an indication as to why some academic readers have found that there are few pleasures to be gleaned from the film. Adopting the type of perspective I have pursued here enables us to distinguish how supposedly monolithic and 'postmodern' horror film in fact represents a specific (inter)textual position-taking in the field of horror. In the case of *Scream*, the film's position-taking is based on the extensive deployment of populist, intertextual subcultural capital. As Schneider (2003b) observes, it thus interpellates fans of the original stalker cycle along with a new generation of teen fans and 'heteronomous' horror audiences.

However, *Scream*'s rampantly intertextual treatment of horror has provoked a 'disgust that is ... "visceral"' (Bourdieu 1986, p. 486) in much academic commentary, as I will demonstrate. The franchise's predominantly intertextual subcultural capital appears to be construed as 'facile' by academic critics marking out their 'pure' and refined taste, and higher cultural capital, by refuting 'pleasures that are too immediately accessible and so discredited as "childish" or "primitive" (as opposed to the deferred pleasures of legitimate [film?] art)' (ibid.). Furthermore, *Scream*'s 'scare quotes' have been treated not as scary or as productive markers of subcultural distinction, but rather as a form of moral transgression, being discursively positioned by a number of critics as '"low", "degrading", "demeaning"' (ibid.). Issues of cultural value have not so much been analysed in these scholarly debates as enacted within them (for one useful discussion of this tendency, see Sconce 1993).

SCREAM AND 'POSTMODERNISM': ACADEMICS' DISCOURSES OF DISPLEASURE

The *Scream* franchise has undoubtedly had a vocal reception within academic commentary. Its exaggerated intertextualities have been analysed by many of horror's critics, among them Jonathan Lake Crane (2000), Paul Wells (2000), and the aforementioned Steven Jay Schneider (2000b) and Andrew Tudor (2002). Although not always linked explicitly to discussions of 'postmodern horror film' (see, e.g., Pinedo 1997, pp. 134–5 and Humphries 2002, pp. 189–90), *Scream* has nevertheless been referred to as follows:

New Nightmare, Scream ... and *I Know What You Did Last Summer* [1997, dr: Jim Gillespie] ... become knowing deconstructions of the [slasher] subgenre, and speak only limitedly about the culture that produces them. (Wells 2000, p. 97)

For Paul Wells, *Scream* is unproblematically 'postmodern' horror. And in horror of this discursively singular 'type', genre and textual 'conventions become the terms of engagement' themselves (Wells 2000, p. 97). Wells evaluates this 'postmodern' horror extremely negatively. His remark that such texts 'speak only limitedly' about their cultural context implies that by displaying marked self-referentiality, po-mo horror film abdicates its political responsibility to reflect upon, critique or challenge its surrounding (and non-generic) culture. Becoming preoccupied with genre codes and conventions rather than with external anxieties, threats or social tensions, *Scream* supposedly averts its gaze from real horrors in the world. Such horror thus apparently no longer works to code social/cultural fears, but instead reflects only on previous genre texts, becoming a series of media products that take preceding products as their reference point (and recall Gary Wilkinson's (2000) characterization of Kim Newman's fictions as 'postmodern' on these grounds, discussed in the previous chapter).

Utilizing the work of sociologist George Ritzer (1998), Wells analyses this process as part of horror's 'McDonaldisation', arguing that 'the genre that best epitomised the address of the irrational was ... rationalised for a known and committed demographic of horror fans' (2000, p. 94) in the 1980s and 1990s. According to this position, horror became target-marketed at its fans thanks to a drive towards safe and repeatable commercial successes; franchising was a part of this logic, with films such as the *Nightmare on Elm Street* and *Friday the 13th* series (merged in 2003's *Freddy Vs. Jason*, dr: Ronny Yu) being presold through audiences' familiarity with their rampaging killers. Wells thus implicitly recognizes the importance of intertextual subcultural capital – horror is targeted at its fans – but he treats this not as one position-taking in the field of horror, but rather as horror's loss of socio-cultural vitality and relevance *per se*. Such horror speaks only to the initiated, to a subculture, and not to a wider contemporary culture of fear or anxiety.

Wells' discursive construction of the po-mo horror film as a 'turning away' (from 'the real'; from moral responsibility) is shared by other commentators. Susan Crutchfield, for instance, defines *Scream* as a postmodern horror film – repeating the self-legitimating authority of Fredric Jameson in order to do so – and then lambasts it in strikingly similar terms to Wells' dismissal:

The recent blockbuster slasher *Scream* ... exemplifies the insularity of the genre's pastiche in its reliance upon the viewer's sense of mastery of the form in order to entertain. Rather than referring out, the genre refers in, and rewards its viewers for doing so ... The slasher film's scenarios and images repeat themselves in a seemingly endless circuit of visual exchange and self-legitimation ... 'Cannibalize' is a cogent term for the ways that slasher films' reflexivity operates, capturing how material bodies ... are violently subsumed, in the postmodern text, to a logic of visual exchange, repetition and representation. (1999, p. 278)

Again, horror looks 'in' intertextually upon its own visual, generic codes, rather than referring to external threats or striving to code psycho-social anxieties over sexual/gender identities. For Crutchfield, the postmodern horror film is allegedly guilty of an immoral or amoral substitution insofar as its images start to lose their indexical referentiality. That is, bodies violated representationally onscreen no longer convincingly stand in for 'actual' bodies; instead they come to figure nothing more than previous generic representations. Or as Vera Dika bluntly puts it: 'The stalker film ... is made up of dead things ... resuscitated from parts of old films' (2003, p. 207), which leaves the 'neo-stalker' film such as *Scream* (Schneider 2000b) as sub-Frankensteinian or sub-cannibalistic.

There appears to be a fixed academic discourse at work around *Scream* – evidence for an 'interpretative community' of scholars all intertextually citing theories of the 'postmodern horror film' in shared, communal ways. For it is surprising that critics working independently of one another should otherwise have produced such similar discourses in order to position *Scream* as *the* 'bad' postmodern horror object (contra Schneider 2000b). Jonathan Lake Crane reproduces the discourse of po-mo horror as inadequately indexical and hence immoral/amoral in his scathing (2000) attack on *Scream* and its intertextualities:

On this territory, in a genre defined by knowing pastiche, death is a matter of trivia [Lake Crane is referring to the opening murder of Casey Becker (Drew Barrymore) for not knowing who the killer was in *Friday the 13th* – MH] and a trivial matter ... [T]he generic representation of gory death becomes a playful game for initiates only. The trivialisation of death through the consistently arch reference to previous work in the genre, a monstrous version of cinematic homage, reaches an even more enfeebling point near the conclusion of the film ... Climactic scenes from *Halloween* (1978) play on the television as the casualties mount. Within the knowing constraints of the postmodern horror film ... film feeds upon film as the genre embraces the acquisitive logic of cannibalism. (Lake Crane 2000, p. 59)

Like Wells (2000) and Crutchfield (1999), Lake Crane (2000) is dismayed by *Scream*'s emphasis on genre codes and its apparent disregard for anguished, indexical representations. Also like his fellow critics of *Scream*, Lake Crane emphasizes that this is a film meant and designed for horror fans, a development that allegedly harbours deleterious consequences. Either the film is a 'playful game for initiates only' (Lake Crane 2000, p. 59), or it relies on the 'viewer's sense of mastery of the form' (Crutchfield 1999, p. 278), or it is 'rationalised for a ... committed demographic of ... fans' (Wells 2000, p. 94). The problem for these critics appears to be that they read *Scream* as excessively playful in its postmodernism rather than as moralistically referential or indexical. There is thus a scholarly tendency to dismiss the fan 'insider knowledge' (Lake Crane 2004, p. 148) or genre expertise mediated by *Scream*, as if the text's intertextual subcultural capital can do nothing other than incite a type of 'masquerade mastery' on the part of fan audiences:

> Given the absolute centrality of the ironic quote in the production of postmodern horror, the past is in extraordinary demand ... In *Scream*, whenever reference is made to other horror films – as it is over and again ... the reference works not as a telling allusion but as a visual or aural quip. Cinematic citation in the contemporary horror film almost always displays cultivated expertise as a form of masquerade mastery. (Lake Crane 2000, pp. 58–9)

Rather than viewing intertextual subcultural capital as a problem (moral or otherwise), I am arguing that we should actually view it as the key to horror's constructed pleasures here. While operating to shock and startle audiences, and building up the suspense of a murder mystery (who is the ghostface-masked killer?), the *Scream* franchise also offers the possibility of repeated intertexual recognitions to horror fans. By so doing it pleasurably flatters and interpellates its fan audience without alienating non-fan, genre audiences who can still participate in the ride, and who can pick up on more obviously self-reflexive aspects such as the way in which relevant clips of *Halloween* are intercut or integrated with *Scream*'s diegetic actions, for example Randy recounting the 'rules' of slasher films, and later being menaced by the killer; Sidney deciding to have sex with her boyfriend Billy Loomis (Skeet Ulrich); Stu (Matthew Lillard) ultimately being crushed by a TV set showing *Halloween*. Despite double-coding its self-reflexivity and subcultural intertextualities so that these can work differently for 'autonomous' fans and 'heteronomous' audiences (i.e. some intertextual citations are more obviously signposted textually than others), it can also be argued that *Scream* does not cease to work as a referential/indexical (i.e., realist) horror film, despite the protestations of Jonathan Lake Crane. Vera Dika (2003, p. 209), Geoff King (2002, p. 127) and Andrew Tudor have each suggested that *Scream* does not, in point of fact, break the frame. Its intertextual references are 'contained' so that it:

> keeps its reflexivity and self-consciousness firmly within the confines of the diegesis, its characters explicitly articulating genre conventions (in both dialogue and action) in such a way as to ensure that their self-consciousness remains a verisimilitudinous component of the narrative and does not therefore question the 'reality' of the film world. (Tudor 2002, p. 110)

Geoff King considers the scene in *Scream* where Randy watches *Halloween* on video, shouting at a character on the TV screen (i.e. in *Halloween*) to 'look behind you' at exactly the same time as Ghostface is standing behind him (and is, furthermore, reflected in the TV screen for the audience to see, thus literally superimposing diegetic and intertextual levels in one shot). Reaching analogous conclusions to Tudor (2002), King suggests that this intertextuality:

> invites the viewer to experience the sequence as a multi-layered ... game rather than part of a narrative within which to become strongly involved. Attention is drawn to the fictional conventions, but the frame is not broken ... the sequence of events *could* happen ... within the self-contained diegetic world, even if it might not seem very likely. (King 2002, p. 127)

Tudor and King view *Scream* as inciting a pleasurable, gaming impulse for ('autonomous') fans while functioning referentially as a commercially viable ('heteronomous') realist and popular horror movie (see Tudor 2002, p. 110; Kermode 2003a, p. 5). Tanya Krzywinska (2000 and 2002b) takes the argument a step further, suggesting that *Scream et al.*'s intertextual citations and self-referential dialogue actively help to sustain realism. Recognizing that *Scream*'s characters are watching *Halloween*, or listening to them discuss Jamie Lee Curtis, contributes to the realist illusion that audiences and characters inhabit the same cultural reality. Referring to '[s]elf-referentiality and knowing intertextual references', Krzywinska argues:

> making overt or covert references to other texts, whether they are ... horror films, or popular culture ... engage[s] viewers' cultural or subcultural capital ... the self-referential trend in so-called postmodern slasher films ... has the effect of making the characters as well as viewers into readers of texts. By placing characters and viewers in a similar cultural and interpretational space ... [t]he carefully forged illusion is that the viewer is living in the same cultural space and time. (2002b, p. 190)

Such intertextual references, where previous horror films are discussed as films, can therefore work to open up a space 'in which we can believe that what we are currently watching is "real"' (Krzywinska 2000, p. 267, referring to *Scream* and *Scream 2*). Krzywinska's reference to 'cultural and subcultural capital' also clearly resonates with my own approach here, although I would argue that intertextual subcultural capital does not just activate or 'engage' the subcultural capital that an audience already possesses. As part of a bid for the given text's status within a fan culture, and as a circulation of subcultural capital outside of that fan culture (displaying its references to the 'heteronomous' mass commercial audience), intertextual subcultural capital can actually threaten the distinctiveness of fans' subcultural capital by 'mainstreaming' it (as well as potentially drawing new fans into the subculture, of course).

Intertextual subcultural capital thus very much plays a double-edged role for horror fan cultures; it may deliver new blood, perhaps in the form of new generations of teen horror fans who are incited to watch old 1970s 'scary movies', but it may also undermine the 'inaccessibility' and exclusivity of horror fans' subcultural capital. Mark Jancovich's point with regard to the niche mediation of subcultural capital is highly pertinent here:

> [T]he media [and here, 'postmodern horror films' specifically – MH] exist not as a clearly defined Other [to subcultural knowledges] but rather as a complex range of communication systems that act both to compose and maintain the sense of an 'imagined community', but also threaten to destroy this sense through the profligate dissemination of their exclusive knowledges. (2002c, p. 318)

That is to say, rather than passively carrying cultural or subcultural capital, or only being 'recognized' by the relevant audience, texts can intertextually seek to position themselves by citing forms of (sub)cultural capital – as do both Newman's counterfictions and the 'postmodern' narratives of *Scream et al.* – and can thereby also dynamically challenge the very logics of distinction that they seek to draw on.

In this academic debate, the King-Krzywinska-Tudor axis shares its logic with Philip Brophy's earlier (1986) discussion of 'contemporary' horror as:

> involved in a violent awareness of itself as a saturated genre ... The contemporary Horror film *knows* that you've seen it before; it *knows* that you know what is about to happen; and it knows that you know it knows you know. (Brophy 1986, p. 5)

Despite this citational gaming dimension, Brophy continues to emphasize horror's realist textual effects; regardless of the intertextual knowledge called up, and the fan's subcultural capital, 'what is of prime importance is the textual effect' (ibid.). The opposing Crutchfield-Lake Crane-Wells camp construes any sense of intertextual 'gaming' as a definitive disruption of textual realism, and as an audience reaction – cued by the text – that is morally bankrupt. The question of whether *Scream et al.* can be thought of as immersive narratives or as distanciated games – there seemingly being no discursive space for the notion of an 'immersive game' in this debate, despite the possibilities explored by Brophy – hence becomes an intensely moral question for some critics, rather than just a question of defining the po-mo horror film. It is also worth remembering that the issue of stalker films and textual/audience gaming is hardly a new topic, even if some critics are occasionally wont to display theoretical amnesia. Indeed, the title of Vera Dika's excellent (1990) study of the original 1970s/80s stalker cycle is *Games of Terror*. Dika concludes that:

> The gaming attitude that the films encourage seems particularly appropriate
> to this group [the adolescent audience – MH] ... The predictability of the
> films' elements encourage a play on seeing and not seeing, knowing and not
> knowing. (1990, p. 128)

However, if the stalker cycle encourages gaming via its predictable use of stock
elements – the trick being to recombine them in some novel but subgenerically
recognizable way – then 'neo-stalkers' (Schneider 2000b) simply continue pretty
much in this vein. Bearing this in mind, their intertextual subcultural capital is
perhaps best thought of in two ways: first, as a performative bid to be considered
as sophisticated, ironic 'smart films' (Sconce 2002; Jancovich 2002a) rather than
as dumb, culturally devalued slasher flicks. And secondly, as neo-*stalker* films,
these texts maintain the original stalker cycle's gaming dimension by
supplementing its play with iconography and *mise-en-scène* with further levels
of intertextual and self-reflexive knowingness (something which, of course, some
entries in the original stalker cycle already possessed, e.g. *April Fool's Day* 1986,
dr: Fred Walton).

Refusing to perceive any value in such playfulness or textual gaming, the
Crutchfield-Lake Crane-Wells discursive position defines *Scream* (negatively and
critically) as 'postmodern' by virtue of its slavishly self-referential and
intertextual reiteration of prior stalker films. However, these very arguments
seem to be informed by an internalized and slavishly reiterated Baudrillardian
position, where postmodernism is distinguished by the triumph of simulacra
that do not refer outside themselves, but simply recirculate signifiers. Ironically,
arguments that completely dismiss *Scream* as 'bad' po-mo horror due to its
inability to look 'outwards' and its tendency to look 'inwards' at genre
conventions thus do so on the basis of looking 'inwards' to the codes and
conventions of postmodern theory, citing and repeating such theory's accepted
'truths'.

In this chapter I have contrasted the intertextual subcultural capital of the
Scream films to the wider range of intertextual (sub)cultural and cultural capital
evident in Kim Newman's fictions (Chapter 9). Although *Scream* (1996) and
Anno Dracula (1993) have both been described as 'postmodern', I have suggested
that their intertextualities actually work very differently in relation to bids for
cultural value and forms of cultural distinction. Of course, this begs the question
as to whether other intertextual position-takings are also possible within the
'field of horror'. Intertextuality could, for instance, be based on a *refusal* of
connections to other pop cultural, generic texts. Bids for horror's cultural value –
if we accept that these are relational and field dependent – can be as much
concerned with what is *not* referenced as with what is. It is therefore important
not to restrict our study of 'intertextual relations' only to positive instances of
multiple, proliferating 'cultural interconnectivity' (Orr 2003, p. 170). Unlike
Scream and its ilk, the films of M. Night Shyamalan, say, adopt a series of

intertextual strategies that position these texts as limitedly intertextual and auteurist.

Although *Scream* could be analysed as a Wes Craven film, even the more celebratory end of academic criticism (Schneider 2000b) explores it primarily in relation to Kevin Williamson's authorial agency. *Scream*'s rampant intertextuality has primarily been interpreted academically via postmodern theory rather than *auteur* theory. And where publications target-marketed at horror fans have discussed Wes Craven as an *auteur*, they have emphasized Craven's hesitancy in taking on the project of *Scream* (Robb 1998, p. 177) rather than positioning the film in relation to a directorial 'vision'. Authorial studies of Kim Newman's fictions and their rampant intertextualities have also been thin on the ground, suggesting again that, confronted by a 'monstrous' stitching together of intertextual references, critics have sought to contain these scare quotes via the critical intertext of postmodern theory rather than auteurism.

By contrast, M. Night Shyamalan's films tend to intertextually – and extra-textually via publicity discourses – prioritize a limited range of generic Ur-texts or traditions; *King Kong* (1933, dr: Cooper and Schoedsack) in *The Village* (2004, dr: Shyamalan); *The Birds* (1963, dr: Hitchcock) and *Night of the Living Dead* (1968, dr: Romero) in *Signs* (2002, dr: Shyamalan); vigilante superhero narratives in *Unbreakable* (2000, dr: Shyamalan), and 'subtle' horror in *The Sixth Sense* (2000, dr: Shyamalan). Borrowing intertextually from Hitchcock (Kapsis 1992) as much as from Romero – and restaging Hitchcock's 'cameo' role-playing by appearing in his own films – Shyamalan has been discursively linked to arthouse and commercial *auteurs*. Philip Strick, for example, likens *The Sixth Sense*'s direction to that of Spielberg and Tarkovsky, suggesting that Shyamalan and the film are '[s]tudiously versed in art-house classics as much as in Spielberg' (2002, p. 258). This blending of 'arthouse' and 'popular' cinema suggests that Shyamalan's films attempt the trick of equally interpellating 'autonomous' and 'heteronomous' horror audiences, bidding to occupy a central point in the field between restricted and large-scale cultural production (see Chapter 9). Very much unlike *Scream*, then, Shyamalan's genre films do not bid for a purely populist, heteronomous versioning of subcultural capital, thereby alienating academics who 'morally' refute such a concentration on fan knowledge as well as 'autonomous' fans who wish to preserve the distinctiveness of their subcultural capital. Instead, Shyamalan's films aim for a position that combines reasonably high intertextual subcultural capital (citing previous horror/thriller *auteurs*) with reasonably high intertextual cultural capital (citing film history/film art) and a populist, commercial sensibility – these are self-consciously 'blockbuster' films, at least after the success of *The Sixth Sense*. Deliberately disavowing rampant intertextuality, Shyamalan's films appear to be instances of Jim Collins's (1993) 'new sincerity' in cinema rather than operating via exaggerated semiotic bricolage, thereby reinforcing textual claims to 'originality' rather than exhibiting an 'anxiety of influence' (Bloom 1973). Shyamalan's films could therefore be addressed as mediating between the intertextual position-takings of

Scream (1996) and *Anno Dracula* (1993), typically being discursively framed as 'auteurist' rather than 'postmodern', despite the fact that these are not essentially opposed categorizations.

Part IV of *The Pleasures of Horror* has attempted to set out a number of different, relational intertextual position-takings in the 'field of horror'. By no means an exhaustive study, my Bourdieuian readings have nevertheless challenged monolithic descriptions of 'postmodern' horror. I have addressed the compositions and levels of intertextual capital enacted in texts that could otherwise be simplistically characterized, and lumped together, as displaying 'postmodern' intertextualities. I have argued that the scare quotes of Kim Newman's writing, the *Scream* franchise, and the films of M. Night Shyamalan all work in very different ways – attempting to blend subcultural capital with fuzzy (sub)cultural knowledge and academic 'Theory' (Newman), or seeking to disavow academia and champion popular cultural capital (*Scream*), or even hoping to fuse fuzzy (sub)cultural horror- and film-'art' with a Hollywood culture of commerce, thereby uneasily uniting autonomous and heteronomous poles of the field (Shyamalan). There are different levels of risk in these bids for distinction, and different levels of return: Shyamalan's films could perhaps be described as the most 'successful', given their complex mediation of 'restricted' and 'large-scale' forms of horror, and their emergent academic consecration contra *Scream*'s negative scholarly reception (see Ringstrom 2001; Humphries 2002; Klock 2002, pp. 178–81; La Caze 2002; Žižek 2002, p. xxxiii). Newman's fictions are closer to the autonomous pole of the field of horror, thanks to their reliance on exceptionally high levels of intertextual subcultural capital as well as academic expertise. *Scream*, meanwhile, is far closer to the heteronomous edge of the field, and as such, displays commercial success without academic consecration or uncontested fan-subcultural approval.

I touched on a topic in this chapter that has largely been absent throughout this book, since I addressed academic discourses of *dis*pleasure surrounding *Scream*. To an extent, my lack of focus on displeasure occurs as a result of this book's title and overall project. Nevertheless, to address discourses of pleasure without explicitly analysing how such discourses are refuted or rejected by horror's non-fan *and* fan audiences leaves the business of this study unfinished. I will thus conclude by tackling pleasure's Other.

Leaving discourses of displeasure unexamined would be implicitly to participate in a false and damaging academic logic whereby horror's pleasures are treated as paradoxical and especially deserving of study (Carroll 1990), whereas its displeasures are passed over in silence as if they are unquestionable, natural and wholly understandable. This logic is damaging because even while it produces much scholarly work valorizing horror (Hills 2004e), it begins from a common-sense standpoint that semiotically fixes horror and its pleasures as a 'problem'.

Conclusion

Theorizing the Displeasures of Horror

Over the course of this study, the pleasures of horror have been addressed as a puzzle to be solved in academic work on the genre (Part I), and as a matter of claimed expertise and connoisseurship within fandom (Part II). At the same time, they have been discursively denied or exonominated in relation to horror's 'para-sites' beyond its culturally policed generic boundaries (Part III), while being linked to 'catching-the-reference' in so-called 'postmodern' horror fictions and films dominated by 'scare quotes' from other genre texts (Part IV). Throughout all of this — with the exception of parts of Chapter 10 — audience *dis*pleasure has been left out in the cold.

The framing academic assumption here could be that such displeasure is magically self-evident — why should audiences *not* find the genre's gory representations objectionable? — and thus does not require explanation, justification, or any further consideration in the way that pleasures of horror do. The first major 'problem' of horror's displeasures is thus their relative invisibility in prior academic work. In this closing discussion I will consider the highly limited ways in which horror and displeasure have been theorized. Outside feminist work on horror there has been precious little analysis of the performative non-consumption of 'refusers' or 'allergics' (Barker and Brooks 1998, p. 292 and Barker *et al.* 2001, p. 115; Roberts 1990, p. 82) — that is, audiences who refuse to consume horror.

This absence means that multiple discourses of displeasure require theoretical excavation and recovery, ranging from fan disappointment at a 'derivative' or uninteresting horror flick, through to audiences 'looking away' when a scene becomes too much for them (see Hill 1997, pp. 60–72), and into the cultural realm of those who absolutely will not watch horror films or read horror novels. My heuristic, methodological approach here will once again be performative and constructivist rather than ontological: it is not the 'experienced reality' of displeasure that I am concerned with, but rather discourses, articulations and performances of displeasure. What do discourses of displeasure do, culturally, for audiences who profess to be 'revolted', 'repulsed' or 'disgusted' by horror texts?

Beginning with feminist-inspired readings of horror which assume that the genre should not be pleasurable for female audiences, I then want to briefly consider discourses of dis/pleasure that female horror fans actually draw on to negotiate their gender and subcultural identities. Although fans might be expected to enjoy horror, they certainly do not do so indiscriminately or globally.

HORROR AND FEMINIST/FEMININE DISPLEASURES

Linda Williams begins her essay on horror 'When the Woman Looks' (1996) by referring to the work of Laura Mulvey (1975). Williams's own argument is that female audiences are offered very limited, curtailed pleasures by horror texts, resulting in a generalized female dislike of the genre:

> There are excellent reasons for this refusal of the woman to look [at scenes of generic horror], not the least of which is that she is often asked to bear witness to her own powerlessness in the face of rape, mutilation, and murder. Another excellent reason for the refusal to look is the fact that women are given so little to identify with on the screen. Laura Mulvey's extremely influential article on visual pleasure in narrative cinema has best defined this problem in terms of a dominant male look at the woman that leaves no place for the woman's own pleasure in seeing; she exists only to be looked at. (Williams 1996, p. 15)

In this quotation, women in the audience are directly conflated with onscreen female characters, thought of as victims of violence and abuse, so that 'she [the ideal audience member] is often asked to bear witness to her own [onscreen] powerlessness'. This formulation begs a host of questions, or rather, makes a host of assumptions as to how representation and identification work. Arguments against Mulvey's position are by now extremely well rehearsed (Donald 1989; Penley 1989; Clover 1992; Creed 1993; Thornham 1997 and 1999). What interests me here is not so much the theoretical adequacy of Williams's point, but rather its moral force. Horror's displeasure is put on the agenda as an a priori matter of feminist cultural politics. That *female* audiences may not enjoy horror (an empirical question, in my terms at least, of audience performances of displeasure) is converted prematurely into a totalizing perspective that positions horror as irredeemably misogynistic. Nor can the force of Williams's moral discourse be neutralized by suggesting that it belongs to a certain (now historical) moment in feminist film criticism. In her (1997) study, *Recreational Terror: Women and the Pleasures of Horror Film Viewing*, Isabel Pinedo returns to Laura Mulvey (1975) and Carol Clover's (1992) work to once again allege that horror is generally misogynistic:

A compelling argument for the misogyny of the horror genre is the different character of male and female death. Although victims of both gender are objects of sexual investigation, and despite the evenhandedness of many slasher films in which roughly equal numbers of men and women are killed, male and female death are not the same. As Clover ... argues, male death is swifter, more distanced and more likely to occur offscreen or to be obscured, whereas female death is extended, occurs at close range, and in graphic detail. (1997, p. 75)

Feminist critique of the horror genre has thus displayed a tendency to assume and explain female displeasure. As Brigid Cherry has usefully pointed out:

the majority of academic criticism assume[s] that taking pleasure in horrific or frightening images is a masculine trait, not a feminine one. According to this model, while women may watch horror films, they do so only reluctantly and with displeasure. (1999, p. 188)

By making such an assumption – one that Cherry (1999 and 2002) has challenged on the basis of empirical study – feminist work actually reinforces the very symbolic equation that it is supposedly decrying. Appreciating the horror genre is semiotically fixed in this academic work as an inherently 'masculine' attribute (Freeland 1996, p. 200; Prince 2004b, p. 247). Feminists' moral critique seemingly requires the establishment of a monolithic force and textuality to be opposed. However, by positioning horror as a 'masculine' genre, feminist scholars are participating in a broader process that surrounds the genre's 'natural' (i.e. cultural) identity. Horror, a genre supposedly premised on inspiring affect, is often also discursively positioned by its male fans as a source of 'anti-effeminate' affects such as 'the thrill':

If the characteristic feelings invoked by the sentimental text that marks its reader's body as effeminate are the tightness in the throat and the wetness in the eye that presage crying, then the antieffeminate corollary in this culture would be the pounding heart, the quick breathing, and the mild sweating of the engaged audience. (Warhol 2003, p. 89)

The fan performance of textual agency that I considered in Part II is very much linked to 'anti-effeminate' affects. In Mark Kermode's (1997, p. 60) formulation, fans do not cringe (Warhol 2003, p. 58), instead they invest in knowledge and mastery of horror texts by displaying connoisseurship and expertise. Horror's affects are hence either safely masculinized or denied altogether (Pearce 1997, p. 5; Hoxter 2000). Male horror fans, as with a number of feminist critics (Pinedo 1997; Williams 1996), have attempted to semiotically fix and masculinize the horror genre's affects as absent or as anti-effeminate despite the fact that it can be argued that 'the emergence of horror out of the sentimental has a complicated history' (Elmer 1995, p. 94). Indeed, as Jonathan Elmer has put it:

> Sentimentalism and sensationalism both have their roots in eighteenth-century discourses (literary, political, philosophical), which ground the social tie in the movements of 'sympathy', the dynamics of identificatory affect ... [T]he socially-ameliorative effects of fellow-feeling came to be dramatized almost obsessively by means of 'the death of the other' ... Sentimental literature and sensation-horror share this 'recent loss trope': in their ... treatments of the spectacle of the death of the other, we can see how the sentimental and the sensational are complementary mass-cultural modes, dependent on each other for their own proper functioning. (Elmer 1995, p. 94; see also Hinton 1999, pp. 20 and 27)

Feminist academics and masculinist fans have, I am suggesting, unwittingly colluded in the iteration of horror's pleasures as masculine: fans in order to safely demarcate horror as something to master rather than be affected by, and academics in order to oppose and critique horror as a source of patriarchal, misogynistic imagery. Representing two mutually reinforcing sides of a masculinist-celebratory and feminist-critical reception of horror and dis/pleasure, such fans and academics have pursued their own subculturally situated agendas while concomitantly fuelling monolithic perceptions of the horror genre. Contra fan and academic attempts to masculinize horror, Jonathan Elmer argues that enjoying horror involves being open to horror texts and their sympathetic/identificatory affects:

> the kind of horrified pleasure taken in sudden nosebleeds, liquefying corpses, exploding heads, what have you, is a masochistic pleasure arising ultimately from the reading body's own submission to invasion. It is the nature of such pleasure that one cannot separate it from its threat. On the one hand, the pleasure is that of being mastered by affect, an affect that is itself the index of a sociality based on the principles of sympathy and identification. But this penetration by affect, this opening up of the reading body ... is also a threatening encounter, one with effects that can never be wholly recuperated, for example, by a didactic and memorializing symbolic discourse. (1995, pp. 124–5)

On this account, displeasure is necessarily present within horror's enjoyment: the 'threat' of abject openness is an alleged component of horror's pleasures for both male and female fans/consumers. Yet what Elmer (1995) views as an experiential or logical sameness across gender becomes the occasion for performative constructions of gender difference. Masculinist fandom seeks to discursively ward off such 'openness' in favour of 'mastering' texts, while female non- or 'anti-fans' (Gray 2003) discursively position horror's displeasures as a matter of painful openness to the text (Greenspan 1993, p. 32). Female fans, meanwhile, relate displeasure to specific horror subgenres such as the slasher film, and to versions of realism (preferring gory effects to be comically excessive or lacking in verisimilitude: see Cherry 1999, pp. 193 and 195). Female anti-fans and fans thus appear to share discourses of displeasure as stemming from a 'closeness' to, or immersion in, the text. Both perform their gender identities via a cultural model of being emotionally or viscerally troubled by horror's textual representations, though fans also distinguish between different textual modalities, thus combining performances of their subcultural, fan expertise with their gendered reception of the genre. Contra Mark Kermode's (1997) metaphorical readings of horror, this feminine fan/anti-fan reception of horror is closely linked to 'literalist' reading strategies: images become emotionally troubling because they are treated, imaginatively, as real-seeming rather than as predominantly symbolic or metaphorical.

Masculinized fan reading strategies and feminized fan/anti-fan reading strategies seem amenable to structuralist interpretation: that is, their performative value is culturally relational. Anti-fans can adopt a position that is opposed to 'perverse' fan discourses of pleasure, while fans can likewise position themselves against non-fans' 'failure' to appreciate the genre aesthetically. In a sense, literalist and metaphorical reading strategies work to defend and reproduce (sub)cultural differences between fans and anti-fans as well as gendered differences in responses to popular culture. Female horror fans thus hold on to a modified version of literalist reading – distinguishing between types of horror film special effects and gore – in order to position themselves within culturally constructed fan/non-fan subcultural differences and masculine/feminine gender differences.

Female horror fans also draw on feminist discourses to critique the sexism of specific horror films and film magazines (Cherry 2002, p. 50), meaning that we should not view 'feminist' and female 'fan' discourses as entirely separable. Feminist-informed readings of horror circulate in specific ways within horror fandom, albeit as part of an '"us and them" mentality [that] operates along similar lines to the general population's view of fans as other ..., in this case working along gender lines' (Cherry 2002, p. 56).

Thus far I have begun to consider tensions within horror fandom via gendered discursive approaches to horror and displeasure. In the next section I will address discourses of displeasure that operate alongside gendered and feminist articulations, but are not explicitly gendered themselves: namely, 'individualistic' and 'sub-subcultural' discourses of displeasure.

HORROR AND PHOBIC/PHILIC DISPLEASURES

When using the term 'phobic' displeasure I have two cultural phenomena in mind: first, the fan who relates his/her consumption of horror to a personal experience of some or other phobia, and secondly, the genre 'refuser' who will not go anywhere near a horror text. By contrast, 'philic' displeasure – seemingly an oxymoron – occurs, I will argue, when horror fans express disappointment in specific horror texts. Here the discourse of displeasure drawn upon is based, familiarly enough, around audience claims to knowledgeability and connoisseurship (see Part II). 'Disappointment' in a much-anticipated horror text is a very different type of enacted, discursive displeasure to either versions of phobic displeasure ('genre-refusing' or 'self-testing').

General models of audience 'emotion', 'cognition' and 'affect' (see Part I) have nothing to say about phobias in the reception of horror – this would open the door to allegedly 'subjective' audience interpretations. Subjectivism is virulently opposed by all manner of contemporary academic theories of horror (Noël Carroll's (1990) cognitive philosophy as much as Mark Jancovich's (2000) sociological/cultural studies approach to horror and Steven Jay Schneider's (2000a and 2001) psychoanalytic readings). It threatens to undo the possibility of theoretical generalization and theorists' 'mastery' of the field of horror, challenging aspects of what Pierre Bourdieu has called the 'scholastic fallacy' (Bourdieu 2000, pp. 49–50).

Given this, it should perhaps come as no surprise that work on 'phobic' audience discourses of displeasure has emerged as a result of empirically focused studies (Hill 1997; Barker and Brooks 1998; Barker *et al.* 2001; Gray 2003) rather than through the many 'high theory' frameworks applied to horror. For example, Annette Hill's investigation of how people view violent movies analyses 'social' and 'personal thresholds' (1997, p. 51). Hill describes these as follows:

> Social thresholds indicate participants identify a type of violence they find personally disturbing, but this violence is a common fear shared by a number of other participants; the process of identifying this threshold is collective rather than subjective. Personal thresholds indicate participants identify a type of violence they find personally disturbing, but unlike social thresholds, reasons for this can be traced to a subjective experience unique to that individual. (1997, p. 51)

However, as Hill notes 'many participants' personal thresholds involve the same types of violence identified as social thresholds' (1997, p. 57), such as rape and violence towards women, as well as 'a fear of needles and injections' (1997, p. 57). Personal thresholds also approach the phobic, being concerned with highly specific distastes and dislikes. Participants in Hill's study variously reported that 'seeing blood affects me more than anything else' (1997, p. 58); 'I do not like to see people having their throats cut' (1997, p. 58); and, 'I'm not afraid of dead bodies, but really deep, rumbling voices affect me' (1997, p. 57). These rather idiosyncratic, subjective responses to mediated, fictional violence/horror mean that the respective participants self-monitor and self-censor their consumption of horror, aiming to ensure that they avoid certain types of representational material that especially disturb them. Rather than these discourses of displeasure affirming cultural membership of a community, or performing gender identity *per se*, they appear to work at an *individualistic* level, allowing audiences to reperform and continuously reconstruct an ongoing self-identity that is not wholly reducible to social codes/identities. As one respondent remarks and makes explicit, 'It very much depends on the individual' (1997, p. 57). Discourses of individualism are reinforced through personal thresholds and the phobic material that they carry for audiences.

Of course, 'phobic' displeasures in the second sense that I set out above – 'refusers' of the horror genre – can be more closely linked to performances of feminine cultural identity, as in the case of the following participant in Hill's study:

> I self-censor because I don't want to see women get it as victims. I went to see *The Shining* [1980, dr: Stanley Kubrick] when I was quite young and this film scared me so much I just decided never to go and see another horror movie. The thrill while you're in the cinema isn't worth the risk when you get home, when you can't sleep. And if you live on your own then you certainly don't need that kind of thing, you really don't need to feel that scared when you're at home. (Hill 1997, p. 70)

This discourse of displeasure can usefully be described as 'phobic' given the cultural model of audience activity that is represented here. Unlike masculinist fandom, this female 'refuser' recounts a situation in which she is involuntarily subjected to displeasure: horror films generate the 'risk' of being scared beyond the ritualized boundaries of a film's screening. Seemingly beyond the self-control of this participant, 'being scared' by a film can threaten to move affectively outwards into everyday life and its routines. There is thus a discursively recounted 'penetration by affect' in this instance, an 'opening up of the reading body' that is a threatening encounter, to recall Elmer's (1995) description of horror cited above. This refuser's discursive position is one that performatively iterates feminine cultural identity as related to emotional openness and involuntary affect. It is a bravura performance of 'effeminate affect', in Warhol's (2003) terms.

Phobic genre 'refusers' or 'allergics' also tend to construct their cultural identity reflexively against imagined notions of what it would mean to be a fan of horror. In this performance of cultural distinction, it is less the 'risk' or threat of uncontrollable affect that is an issue, and more the threat of being aligned with dominant, hegemonic connotations surrounding the 'generic community' (Altman 1999, p. 156) of horror fans. As Thomas J. Roberts has suggested:

We do not think of ourselves as having an allergic reaction, of course, but as truth seeing: this or that sort of story is obscenely violent … and those who read it are themselves violent, brutish, stupid. (1990, p. 82)

Such moralizing discourses participate in the cultural pathologization of specific genres, tending to represent horror and those who enjoy it as weird or strange. For instance, in their study of action-adventure 'film-refusers' Martin Barker and Kate Brooks identify how vocabularies of pleasure are firmly refuted by such respondents: 'There is no pleasure at all [to be taken in this kind of film], and none is imaginable, except in *perverse* and *dangerous* forms. This is not our sort of thing at all' (1998, p. 292). By rejecting specific texts as totemic of a genre, such 'refusers' or 'anti-fans' (Gray 2003, p. 70) performatively display culturally 'positive' attributes by discursively positioning themselves against 'negative' and devalued imagined Others. Another good example of this process occurs in the study *Women Viewing Violence* (Schlesinger *et al.* 1992), where the research team appear to accept and validate their respondents' rejection of the horror film *A Nightmare on Elm Street 4: The Dream Master* (1988, dr: Renny Harlin):

A *Nightmare on Elm Street 4* … was not taken seriously by women viewing it in the pilot study, who considered the violence exhibited in the film to be totally unrealistic and far-fetched. It was judged to be a purely escapist film, intended for teenagers, and quite unlikely to be taken seriously by mature women. (1992, pp. 19–20)

The imagined Other mobilized uncritically and non-reflexively here by both research team and pilot study participants is 'the teenager', whose pleasures in such horror are firmly refuted as 'escapist', and as failing to relate to 'mature' concerns and views of the 'real' world. As Thomas J. Roberts reminds us, there is an air of moralistic 'truth seeing' to such rejections. Audiences who enjoy *A Nightmare on Elm Street 4* are, by implication, immature. Pleasures of horror are, in this case, culturally and discursively refuted as inappropriate to the cultural identity of 'mature' femininity. Such anti-fans:

must find cause for their dislike in *something*. This something may vary from having previously watched … [a film/TV show] … and having found it intolerable; to having a dislike for its genre, director or stars; to having seen previews or ads, or seen or heard unfavourable reviews … clearly *anti-fans construct an image of the text* – and, what is more, an image they feel is accurate – sufficiently … that they can react to and against it … anti-fans may not even be viewers in the sense of people who have watched a show [or film]. (Gray 2003, p. 71, my italics)

The discourses of displeasure mobilized by refusers and anti-fans therefore represent a significant challenge to academic and fan performances of readerly

expertise or connoisseurship, for anti-fans' negative interpretations of texts are
not even necessarily based around encountering or viewing the texts that are
rejected or refused. Anti-fans respond to genres and texts through meta-
constructs of para-textuality and 'text stand in[s]':

> Thus while much analysis of texts is steadfastly stuck to close reading, if we
> can show that people engage in distant reading, responding to texts that have
> not been viewed, and more importantly if we can track exactly how the anti-
> fan's text or text stand-in has been pieced together, we will take substantial
> steps forward in understanding textuality. (Gray 2003, p. 71)

In the case of horror's anti-fans, such text stand-ins are arguably inter- and para-
textually constituted in relatively amorphous ways in relation to the negative
stereotype of horror's 'generic community' (Altman 1999) as 'a sign of immature
character development and especially puerile, if not perverse, passions and
sensibilities' (Vorobej 1997, p. 221). What Jonathan Gray's (2003) argument
pushes us to consider, along with the work of Martin Barker *et al.* (2001), is how
genres such as horror do not only or even primarily exist 'in' their texts (Mittell
2004), but also circulate at the level of audiences' moralizing discourses and
performative displays of a range of cultural identities.

This set of concerns is what underpinned my 'third generation' audience
studies approach (Alasuutari 1999) to textuality and genre in Parts III and IV,
where I considered how boundaries around 'the horror genre' and related
discourses of pleasure were contested, as well as analysing horror texts
intertextually as bids for social and cultural positions in the 'field of horror'.
Such textual analysis does not present the 'true' meaning of a given text (and nor
does it trace different audience 'readings' of specific texts); rather, my focus has
been on how *discourses of genre and pleasure* are persistently linked to performative
bids for cultural value or devaluation. This means thinking about popular
cultural texts and genres not just as semiotic material to be decoded, but also as
resources that are available for cultural and subcultural reproduction, within
which audience 'activity' and 'passivity' and 'pleasure' and 'displeasure' are terms
invoked and fought over, rather than existing as an ontology of media use.

In the remainder of this section I want to consider discourses of displeasure
that are mobilized by self-professed horror fans. I have already considered how
female fans express displeasure at certain subgenres (e.g. the slasher film) by way
of opposing masculinist horror fandom, and this feminine-feminist articulation
can be considered as one version of 'philic' displeasure. What other varieties of
fans' 'philic' displeasure can be analytically addressed (Hills 2003a)?

Just as anti-fans oppose media texts, genres, or stars within moralizing
discourses (Schulze *et al.* 1993), fans too draw on moral discourses to devalue
aspects of the texts and genres that they otherwise profess to love. As Jonathan
Gray notes, 'fans can become anti-fans of a sort when an episode or part of a text
is perceived as harming a text as a whole' (2003, p. 73). And as Gray goes on to

point out, '[b]ehind dislike, after all, there are always expectations – of what a text should be like ... of what morality and aesthetics texts should adopt, and what we would like to see others watch or read' (ibid.). A focus on how media audiences' pleasure is articulated through evaluative, moral discourses is also central to S. Elizabeth Bird's (2003) examination of popular aesthetics and to Mark Jancovich's (2000) work on horror fans' tastes and cultural distinctions.

Bird demonstrates how TV drama and soap fans explicitly discuss the 'pleasures of the text' online, but do so self-reflexively, showing an awareness of cultural values and hierarchies. They therefore 'enjoy parodying themselves as besotted fans' while posting 'critical ... analyses' of their favoured text (2003, p. 127; see also Amesley 1989; McKee 2001). Fans thus evaluate their objects of fandom in relation to norms of genre and what might be termed 'textual authenticity' – judging whether episodes are 'true to the genre' (Bird 2003, p. 131). Where characterization or narrative diverge from shared fan-cultural norms of textual authenticity (what makes a 'good' soap, or what makes a 'good' episode of their favourite TV series, or what makes a 'good' horror film) then the offending moments will be criticized and discourses of displeasure articulated (Hills 2003a). Textual authenticity can involve a range of attributes: moral and emotional expression (Bird 2003, p. 136), genre and character, acting/performance styles and writing, design, etc. (McKee 2001). It can also involve anti-commercial evaluations, with texts being judged as 'inauthentic' if they can be placed within discourses of 'commerce' rather than 'art' (which takes us back to Bourdieu-based arguments over the autonomous/heteronomous 'field of horror'; see Part IV).

Mark Jancovich's (2000) work on horror fans engages with just these issues, as he demonstrates how fans, in Jonathan Gray's words, can 'become anti-fans of a sort'. Jancovich's focus falls on how sections of horror fandom have attacked the *Scream* franchise as excessively commercial, feminized and hence 'inauthentic', thereby defending the norms and textual authenticity of 'their' aestheticized, masculinist horror-as-art:

> One film that has particularly provoked ... struggles between horror audiences is *Scream* [1996, dr: Wes Craven], and this is due to its extraordinary commercial success ... The success of the film ... threatens ... [fans'] sense of rarity and distinction and this situation requires these fans to distinguish between the *real* horror fans and the inauthentic interloper. (2000, p. 29; see my discussion of intertextual subcultural capital in Chapter 10)

Jancovich analyses how horror fans opposed to *Scream* devalue it 'through the familiar trope of "mass culture as woman"', dismissively referring to *Scream*'s 'scantily clad, barely legal teen starlets' (2000, p. 29) and implying that the film's audience is made up of the feminized 'consumers of top 40 hits' (2000, p. 30). What such 'philic' discourses of displeasure work to secure, then, is an 'authentic' version of the horror genre that remains relatively inaccessible to 'mainstream' consumers. Fans' subcultural difference is defended through this mobilization of discourses of displeasure and its demarcation of intra-generic distinctions. By opposing the commercialism of *Scream*, these fans closely resemble what Lisa A. Lewis has elsewhere described as the 'contradictory category of the [fan] "hater"' (1992, p. 139). Lewis stresses how fan knowledge and 'textual competency' may be twinned with a critique of consumerism and thus linked to 'masculine identity conflicts' (1992, pp. 139–41). The masculinist fan 'hater' is a fan of a given text or genre, but nevertheless expresses discourses of hate in relation to inauthentic, commercial examples of this text/ genre, hence performing a version of rebellious masculinity (see Hollows 2003 and Read 2003).

A further discourse of fan displeasure can be identified in Steven Jay Schneider's (2003) work on the film *Last House on the Left* (1971, dr: Wes Craven). This type of articulated displeasure strongly challenges the notion that 'popular' horror films necessarily become so because they are 'enjoyed' by audiences. Schneider analyses audience responses to *Last House*:

> two basic types or patterns of response can be distinguished; the amazing thing is that, contrary to what one would expect from such a profitable and long-running film, neither of these response types involve declarations of pleasure. One the one hand, adult viewers, especially those of the middle-class and from suburban locales, were furious after watching *Last House* ... A little harder to make sense of is the fact that most of the young people who lined up to see the film ... didn't 'like it' in the traditional sense all that much either. (Schneider 2003, pp. 87–8)

Schneider suggests that adults professing their dislike for the film were '*parents* ... worried that their children would be the ones eager to see it at the local drive-in' (2003, p. 88). By contrast, teen audiences treated the film as a participatory 'rite of passage' (2003, p. 88) whose cultural value lay not in its pleasurable or enjoyable status *per se* but rather in its ability to define an imagined 'insider' group membership for those who had seen *Last House* and its extreme representations/themes. Arguably, this type of 'participatory' philic displeasure arises around texts that are defined as problem cases in publicity, journalism and other inter- and para-texts. Such attempted predefinitions of textual worth (or lack thereof) lead to audiences reflexively treating such texts as 'controversies' through which in-groups of 'experienced' or 'tough' viewers can be constructed. Similar processes have been identified as occurring around other 'controversial' movies in the work of Thomas Austin (2002, pp. 173–80) and Martin Barker *et al.* (2001, pp. 65 and 95).

If fans' discourses of (dis)pleasure can be linked to the spatiality of 'being there' and participating in a rite of passage, or watching an especially 'gruelling' film, then they can also be articulated through temporalities and histories of the genre. Horror fans and the genre's 'scholar-fans' (Hills 2002, pp. 11–15) tend to reinforce specific versions of textual authenticity by valorizing or devaluing horror films from specific eras (see Jancovich 1996, p. 1; Sanjek 1994, p. 207):

> One of the main problems with most histories of horror is ... that they are 'narrative histories' ... In other words, narratives usually end either in a sense of perfect fulfilment ... or in destruction and failure ... Narrative histories of a genre therefore usually become the story of something – the horror genre – ... [as] an essence which is unfolding before us, and is either heading towards perfect realisation ... or failure or corruption. (Jancovich 2002a, p. 9; see Humphries 2002, pp. 189–95)

Discourses of philic displeasure can thus defend textual authenticity (and for scholar-fans, cultural politics) by attacking the horror films of a given period (Wood 1986, pp. 85–6). Alternatively, within the field of horror, 'heteronomous' fans potentially lacking the subcultural capital to debate the genre's history – or 'autonomous' fans seeking to mark out a generational fan cultural identity – may value contemporary horror while devaluing and rejecting 'old' horror films as lacking in realism (Matravers 2001, p. 91). This articulation of displeasure would perhaps defend *Scream* as 'real' horror – contra Jancovich's (2000) example – while devaluing, say, Val Lewton's 1940s RKO films *and* 1930s and 1950s horror (contra Wood 1986) as all being similarly 'dated'.

Indeed, teaching university undergraduate modules on horror, it is noticeable that student audiences often respond to 'historical' horror of the 1930s, 40s and 50s either with laughter or with that brand of vaguely reverential indifference performatively reserved for 'objects of academic study'. By contrast, when *Scream* and its like are screened then fan engagement typically becomes more evident. Many of these students are self-professed fans of horror, but lack the historical perspectives of scholar-fans such as Mark Jancovich (1996) and Steven Jay Schneider (2000a and 2003). Considering the teaching of horror as a pedagogical 'transmission' of genre histories neglects the point that for these students, their specific fan identities may be premised on a valorization of 'contemporary' horror. This is a form of 'textual authenticity' that values horror 'now' by drawing self-reflexively on discourses of realism, cultural relevance, consumerist 'novelty' and aesthetic innovation. Such expressions of fandom appear to be closely interwoven with the promotional cultures of DVD connoisseurship as well as with the institutionalization of media/film/cultural studies:

> The growth in and diversification of cultures of film connoisseurship that we are witnessing at the present time feeds the expansion of the entertainment and consumer industries in fairly obvious ways, creating demand for ever more state-of-the-art technologies that promise to make attentive, repeat home viewing of films more pleasurable and promoting a consumerist culture of connoisseur-collectors. Here, however, it is important to remember that

along with these industries the institution of film criticism and journalism, ... fan cultures, and film studies courses have also been instrumental in fostering an appreciation of the cinema based on an intellectual and intellectually impassioned engagement with its artifacts. (Pierson 2002, p. 165)

Having noted this, where different versions of textual authenticity ('contemporary' versus a favoured 'era' of horror) occur between student and lecturer, then it is perhaps important to consider whether opposed discourses of dis/pleasure, and related cultural identities, should be appreciated, reflexively analysed, or overwritten by the pedagogical 'aim' of 'expanding' students' knowledge and appreciation of genre histories. This latter pedagogical manoeuvre may, in fact, mask the institutional power of one version of textual authenticity (the lecturer's) rather than opening up for discussion and analysis those different discourses of dis/pleasure that may be in play in film screenings and seminar discussions. As Sara Bragg (2001) has argued, academic work on the meanings of horror has often tended to 'reinforce rather than overcome differences of taste and "cultural capital" between teachers and students' (2001, p. 97). In place of seeking to produce 'the mode of the dutiful student' schooled in horror's meanings and histories (Buckingham 2003, p. 170), Bragg's work on teaching the horror genre at A level suggests that teachers can, alternatively, work to locate students' tastes 'in relation to other possibilities, [encouraging students] ... to participate in the media culture around them' (Bragg 2001, p. 105). Of course, this treats student 'pleasures' as ontological and self-evident, rather than examining them as performative instances of cultural 'ownership', textual agency and cultural reproduction. The further difficulty that Bragg's (2001) work circles around is, I suspect, the problem that students' performances of, and investments in, genre-based textual agency are typically radically different to the textual agency (of exegesis and theory citation) performed by professional academics. The clash of different discourses of pleasure and differently philic displeasures means that horror's scholars and its student fans might sometimes seem alien to one another, both in terms of textual agency and textual authenticity. In short, fans and scholars might seek to do different things with horror's texts, while championing different texts as examples of 'real' horror. Since this clash becomes one of situated cultural power, I would argue that 'responsible' academia should not promote cultural reproduction – positioning student audiences as 'passive' recipients of the lecturer's favoured horror aesthetics – but should rather pursue a reflexive awareness of different discourses of horror's pleasures and displeasures (for both students and lecturers) alongside carrying out 'rational' work on horror's meanings.

As with my earlier conclusions on fandom and academia (see Hills 2002, p. 183), this once again involves calling for increased affective reflexivity in the lecture theatre and beyond. In this instance, it also involves making the performative, claims-based nature of pleasure and displeasure apparent, rather than ontologizing and naturalizing pleasure, which has the potential effect of making it something that supposedly cannot be studied, and instead can only be assumed as a backdrop to the academic study of horror (Leane and Buchanan 2002, p. 253; see the Introduction).

Although we may not be able to get access to the 'thing itself' of horror's pleasures, and hence are dependent on considering discourses of pleasure and displeasure, these discourses – as I have argued throughout this book – can be meaningfully analysed, whether they occur in fans' practices or within particular theoretical frameworks, and whether they are denied in relation to horror's extra-generic para-sites or fixed in relation to its 'postmodern' scare quotes. The pleasures of horror are not ineffable or mysterious. Nor should they be treated as 'naturally' perverse or puzzling. The pleasures – and displeasures – of horror work, finally, to produce and reproduce *cultural* distinctions, differences, moralities and identities. It seems that horror is always 'concerned with a lot more than being scary' (Newman 1995, p. 49).

Bibliography

Aguirre, Manuel (1990), *The Closed Space: Horror Literature and Western Symbolism*, Manchester and New York, Manchester University Press.

Ahmad, Aijaz (1999), 'Reconciling Derrida: "Specters of Marx" and deconstructive politics', in Michael Sprinkler (ed.) *Ghostly Demarcations: A Symposium on Jacques Derrida's Specters of Marx*, London and New York, Verso, pp. 88–109.

Ahmed, Sara (2004), *The Cultural Politics of Emotion*, Edinburgh, Edinburgh University Press.

Alasuutari, Pertti (1999), 'Introduction: three phases of reception studies', in Pertti Alasuutari (ed.), *Rethinking the Media Audience*, London, Sage, pp. 1–21.

Allen, Graham (2000), *Intertextuality*, London and New York, Routledge.

Altman, Rick (1999), *Film/Genre*, London, BFI Publishing.

Amesley, Cassandra (1989), 'How to watch *Star Trek*', *Cultural Studies*, 3: 3, pp. 323–39.

Anderson, Benedict (1991), *Imagined Communities: Reflections on the Origin and Spread of Nationalism*, London, Verso.

Ang, Ien (1985), *Watching Dallas: Soap Opera and the Melodramatic Imagination*, London, Methuen.

Armitt, Lucie (1996), *Theorising the Fantastic*, London, Arnold.

Armon-Jones, Claire (1991), *Varieties of Affect*, Toronto, University of Toronto Press.

Arnzen, Michael (ed.) (1997), *Paradoxa: The Return of the Uncanny*, 3: 3–4.

Auerbach, Nina (1995), *Our Vampires, Ourselves*, Chicago and London, University of Chicago Press.

Austin, J. L. (1976), *How To Do Things With Words*, Oxford and New York, Oxford University Press.

Austin, Thomas (2002), *Hollywood, Hype and Audiences*, Manchester, Manchester University Press.

Bacon-Smith, Camille (2000), *Science Fiction Culture*, Philadelphia, University of Pennsylvania Press.

Badley, Linda (1995), *Film, Horror, and the Body Fantastic*, Westport CT, Greenwood Press.

— (1996), *Writing Horror and the Body: The Fiction of Stephen King, Clive Barker, and Anne Rice*, Westport CT, Greenwood Press.

— (2004), 'The darker side of genius: the (horror) auteur meets Freud's theory', in Steven Jay Schneider (ed.) *Horror Film and Psychoanalysis: Freud's Worst Nightmares*, Cambridge, Cambridge University Press. pp. 222–40.

Baldick, Chris (1987), *In Frankenstein's Shadow: Myth, Monstrosity, and Nineteenth-century Writing*, Oxford, Clarendon Press.

Bann, Stephen (ed.) (1994), *Frankenstein, Creation and Monstrosity*, London, Reaktion Books.

Barcan, Ruth (2003), 'The idleness of academics: reflections on the usefulness of cultural studies', *Continuum*, 17: 4, pp. 363–78.

Barker, Martin (ed.) (1984), *The Video Nasties: Freedom and Censorship in the Media*, London, Pluto Press.

— (1992), *A Haunt of Fears: The Strange History of the British Horror Comics Campaign*, Jackson and London, University Press of Mississippi.

Barker, Martin, Arthurs, Jane and Harindranath, Ramaswami (2001), *The* Crash *Controversy: Censorship Campaigns and Film Reception*, London and New York, Wallflower Press.

Barker, Martin with Austin, Thomas (2000), *From Antz to Titanic: Reinventing Film Analysis*, London, Pluto Press.

Barker, Martin and Brooks, Kate (1998), *Knowing Audiences*: Judge Dredd, *Its Friends, Fans and Foes*, Luton, University of Luton Press.

Barker, Martin and Petley, Julian (eds) (1997), *Ill Effects: The Media/Violence Debate*, London and New York, Routledge.

— (eds) (2001), *Ill Effects: The Media/Violence Debate*, 2nd edn, London and New York, Routledge.

Barlow, Geoffrey and Hill, Alison (1985), *Video Violence and Children*, London, Hodder & Stoughton.

Barrett, Michèle (1999), *Imagination in Theory: Essays on Writing and Culture*, Cambridge, Polity Press.

Barthes, Roland (1972), *Mythologies*, London, Jonathan Cape.

— (1976), *The Pleasure of the Text*, London, Jonathan Cape.

Baudrillard, Jean (1994), *Simulacra and Simulation*, Ann Arbor, University of Michigan Press.

Beard, William (2001), *The Artist as Monster: The Cinema of David Cronenberg*, Toronto and London, University of Toronto Press.

Beck, Ulrich (1992), *Risk Society: Towards a New Modernity*, London, Sage.

Becker, Susanne (1999), *Gothic Forms of Feminine Fictions*, Manchester, Manchester University Press.

Bell-Metereau, Rebecca (2004), 'Searching for blobby fissures: slime, sexuality and the grotesque', in Murray Pomerance (ed.), *Bad: Infamy, Darkness, Evil and Slime on Screen*, New York, State University of New York Press, pp. 287–99.

Bennett, Tony, Emmison, Michael and Frow, John (1999), *Accounting for Tastes: Australian Everyday Cultures*, Cambridge, Cambridge University Press.

Bennett, Tony and Woollacott, Janet (1987), *Bond and Beyond: The Political Career of a Popular Hero*, Basingstoke, Macmillan.

Benshoff, Harry M. (1997), *Monsters in the Closet: Homosexuality and the Horror Film*, Manchester and New York, Manchester University Press.

Berenstein, Rhona J. (1996), *Attack of the Leading Ladies: Gender, Sexuality and Spectatorship in Classic Horror Cinema*, New York, Columbia University Press.

Bianculli, David (1992), *Teleliteracy: Taking Television Seriously*, New York, Continuum.

Bignell, Jonathan (2000), *Postmodern Media Culture*, Edinburgh, Edinburgh University Press.

Billson, Anne (1997), *The Thing*, London, BFI Publishing.

Bingham, Nick (2002), 'In the belly of the monster: Frankenstein, food, factishes and fiction', in Rob Kitchin and James Kneale (eds), *Lost in Space: Geographies of Science Fiction*, London and New York, Continuum, pp. 180–92.

Bird, S. Elizabeth (2003), *The Audience in Everyday Life: Living in a Media World*, New York and London, Routledge.

Biressi, Anita (2001), *Crime, Fear and the Law in True Crime Stories*, London, Palgrave.

Black, Joel (1991), *The Aesthetics of Murder*, Baltimore and London, Johns Hopkins University Press.

— (2002), *The Reality Effect: Film Culture and the Graphic Imperative*, New York and London, Routledge.

Bloom, Clive (ed.) (1993), *Creepers: British Horror and Fantasy in the Twentieth Century*, London, Pluto Press.

Bloom, Harold (1973), *The Anxiety of Influence*, New York and Oxford, Oxford University Press.

Bloustien, Gerry (2002), 'Fans with a lot at stake: serious play and mimetic excess in *Buffy the Vampire Slayer*', *European Journal of Cultural Studies*, 5: 4, pp. 427–49.

— (2004), 'Buffy Night at the Seven Stars: a "subcultural" happening at the "glocal" level', in Andy Bennett and Keith Kahn-Harris (eds), *After Subculture: Critical Studies in Contemporary Youth Culture*, London, Palgrave-Macmillan, pp. 148–61.

Bolin, Göran (2000), 'Film swapping in the public sphere: youth audiences and alternative cultural publicities', *Javnost: The Public*, 7: 2, pp. 57–74.

Booker, M. Keith (2002), *Strange TV: Innovative Television Series from* The Twilight Zone *to* The X-Files, Westport CT and London, Greenwood Press.

Bordwell, David (1989), *Making Meaning: Inference and Rhetoric in the Interpretation of Cinema*, Cambridge MA, Harvard University Press.

— (1996), 'Contemporary film studies and the vicissitudes of grand theory', in David Bordwell and Noël Carroll (eds), *Post-Theory: Reconstructing Film Studies*, Wisconsin, University of Wisconsin Press, pp. 3–36.

Botting, Fred (1996), *Gothic*, London and New York, Routledge.

Bourdieu, Pierre (1986), *Distinction*, London, Routledge.

— (1991), *Language and Symbolic Power*, Cambridge, Polity Press.

— (1992), *The Rules of Art: Genesis and Structure of the Literary Field*, Stanford CA, Stanford University Press.

— (1993), *The Field of Cultural Production*, Cambridge, Polity Press.

— (1998), *Practical Reason*, Cambridge, Polity Press.

— (2000), *Pascalian Meditations*, Cambridge, Polity Press.

Bourdieu, Pierre and Wacquant, Loïc J. D. (1992), *An Invitation to Reflexive Sociology*, Cambridge, Polity Press.

Bragg, Sara (2001), 'Just what the doctors ordered? Media regulation, education and the "problem" of media violence', in Martin Barker and Julian Petley (eds), *Ill Effects: The Media/Violence Debate*, 2nd edn, London and New York, Routledge, pp. 87–110.

Branston, Gill and Stafford, Roy (2003), *The Media Student's Book*, 3rd edn, London and New York, Routledge.

Bronfen, Elisabeth (1998), *The Knotted Subject: Hysteria and Its Discontents*, Princeton, Princeton University Press.

Brooker, Will (2002), *Using the Force: Creativity, Community and* Star Wars *Fans*, New York and London, Continuum.

— (2003), 'Conclusion: overflow and audience', in Will Brooker and Deborah Jermyn (eds), *The Audience Studies Reader*, London and New York, Routledge, pp. 322–34.

Brophy, Philip (1986), 'Horrality: the textuality of contemporary horror films', *Screen*, 27: 1, pp. 2–13.

Brown, Sheila (2003), *Crime and Law in Media Culture*, Buckingham and Philadelphia, Open University Press.

Browne, Nick (ed.) (1998), *Refiguring American Film Genres*, Berkeley, University of California Press.

Buchanan, Ian (2000), *Deleuzism: A Metacommentary*, Edinburgh, Edinburgh University Press.

Buckingham, David (1996), *Moving Images: Understanding Children's Emotional Responses to Television*, Manchester, Manchester University Press.

— (2003), *Media Education: Literacy, Learning and Contemporary Culture*, Cambridge, Polity Press.

Budra, Paul (1998), 'Recurrent monsters: why Freddy, Michael, and Jason keep coming back', in Paul Budra and Betty A. Schellenberg (eds), *Part Two: Reflections on the Sequel*, Toronto and London, University of Toronto Press, pp. 189–99.

Bukatman, Scott (2003), *Matters of Gravity: Special Effects and Supermen in the 20th Century*, Durham NC and London, Duke University Press.

Burn, Andrew and Parker, David (2003), *Analysing Media Texts*, London and New York, Continuum.

Burnett, Robert and Marshall, P. David (2003), *Web Theory: An Introduction*, London and New York, Routledge.

Büssing, Sabine (1987), *Aliens in the Home: The Child in Horror Fiction*, New York and London, Greenwood Press.

Butler, Judith (1993), *Bodies That Matter: On the Discursive Limits of 'Sex'*, New York and London, Routledge.

— (1999a), *Gender Trouble: Feminism and the Subversion of Identity* (10th anniversary edn), New York and London, Routledge.

— (1999b), 'Performativity's social magic', in Richard Shusterman (ed.) *Bourdieu: A Critical Reader*, Oxford, Blackwell, pp. 113–28.

Byrne, Eugene (2000), 'Introduction', in *Unforgivable Stories* (Kim Newman), London, Simon & Schuster UK, pp. 1–9.

Caldwell, John Thornton (1995), *Televisuality: Style, Crisis, and Authority in American Television*, New Brunswick NJ, Rutgers University Press.

— (2003), 'Second-shift media aesthetics', in Anna Everett and John T. Caldwell (eds), *New Media: Theories and Practices of Digitextuality*, New York and London, Routledge, pp. 127–44.

Calinescu, Matei (1993), *Rereading*, New Haven, Yale University Press.

Campbell, Jan (2000), *Arguing with the Phallus: Feminist, Queer and Postcolonial Theory, A Psychoanalytic Contribution*, London and New York, Zed Books.

Cardwell, Sarah (2002), '*American Psycho*: Serial killer film?', *Film Studies: An International Review*, 3, pp. 73–84.

Carroll, Michael Thomas (2000), *Popular Modernity in America: Experience, Technology, Mythohistory*, New York, State University of New York Press.

Carroll, Noël (1990), *The Philosophy of Horror or Paradoxes of the Heart*, New York and London, Routledge.

— (1992a), 'A paradox of the heart: a response to Alex Neill', *Philosophical Studies*, 65: 1–2, pp. 67–74.

— (1992b), 'Disgust or fascination: a response to Susan Feagin', *Philosophical Studies*, 65: 1–2, pp. 85–90.

— (1995), 'Enjoying horror fictions: a reply to Gaut', *The British Journal of Aesthetics*, 35: 1, pp. 67–72.

— (1996), 'Prospects for film theory: a personal assessment', in David Bordwell and Noël Carroll (eds), *Post-Theory: Reconstructing Film Studies*, Wisconsin, University of Wisconsin Press, pp. 37–68.

— (2001), 'Horror and humor' in *Beyond Aesthetics: Philosophical Essays*, Cambridge and New York, Cambridge University Press, pp. 235–54.

— (2004), 'Afterword: psychoanalysis and the horror film', in Steven Jay Schneider (ed.) *Horror Film and Psychoanalysis: Freud's Worst Nightmares*, Cambridge, Cambridge University Press, pp. 257–70.

Carter, Cynthia and Weaver, C. Kay (2003), *Violence and the Media*, Buckingham and Philadelphia, Open University Press.

Casebeer, Edwin F. (1996), 'The art of balance: Stephen King's Canon', in Tony Magistrale and Michael A. Morrison (eds), *A Dark Night's Dreaming: Contemporary American Horror Fiction*, Columbia, University of South Carolina Press, pp. 42–54.

Castricano, Jodey (2001), *Cryptomimesis: The Gothic and Jacques Derrida's Ghost Writing*, Montreal and Kingston, McGill-Queen's University Press.

Cavallaro, Dani (2002), *The Gothic Vision: Three Centuries of Horror, Terror and Fear*, London and New York, Continuum.

Cherry, Brigid (1999), 'Refusing to refuse to look: female viewers of the horror film', in Melvyn Stokes and Richard Maltby (eds), *Identifying Hollywood's Audiences: Cultural Identity and the Movies*, London, BFI Publishing, pp. 187–203.

— (2002), 'Screaming for release: femininity and horror film fandom in Britain', in Steve Chibnall and Julian Petley (eds), *British Horror Cinema*, London and New York, Routledge, pp. 42–57.

Church Gibson, Pamela (2001), '"You've been in my life so long I can't remember anything else": into the labyrinth with Ripley and the Alien', in Matthew Tinkcom and Amy Villarejo (eds), *Keyframes: Popular Cinema and Cultural Studies*, New York and London, Routledge, pp. 35–51.

Cixous, Hélène (1976), 'Fiction and its phantoms: a reading of Freud's *Das Unheimliche*', *New Literary History*, 7: 3, pp. 525–48.

Clark, Lynn Schofield (2003), *From Angels to Aliens: Teenagers, the Media, and the Supernatural*, Oxford and New York, Oxford University Press.

Clemens, Valdine (1999), *The Return of the Repressed: Gothic Horror from* The Castle of Otranto *to* Alien, New York, State University of New York Press.

Clover, Carol J. (1992), *Men, Women and Chainsaws*, London, BFI Publishing.

Coen, Stanley J. (1994), *Between Author and Reader: A Psychoanalytic Approach to Writing and Reading*, New York, Columbia University Press.

Cohen, Jeffrey Jerome (1996), 'Monster culture (seven theses)', in Jeffrey Jerome Cohen (ed.) *Monster Theory: Reading Culture*, Minneapolis and London, University of Minnesota Press, pp. 3–25.

Cohl, H. Aaron (1997), *Are We Scaring Ourselves to Death? How Pessimism, Paranoia and a Misguided Media are Leading Us Toward Disaster*, New York, St Martin's Press.

Collins, Jim (1989), *Uncommon Cultures: Popular Culture and Post-Modernism*, New York and London, Routledge.

— (1993), 'Genericity in the nineties: eclectic irony and the new sincerity', in Jim Collins, Hilary Radner and Ava Preacher Collins (eds), *Film Theory Goes to the Movies*, New York and London, Routledge, pp. 242–63.

— (2002), 'High-pop: an introduction', in Jim Collins (ed.) *High-Pop: Making Culture into Popular Entertainment*, Cambridge MA and Oxford, Blackwell, pp. 1–31.

Conrich, Ian (2000), 'An aesthetic sense: Cronenberg and neo-horror film culture', in Michael Grant (ed.) *The Modern Fantastic: The Films of David Cronenberg*, Trowbridge, Flicks Books, pp. 35–49.

Conrich, Ian and Petley, Julian (eds) (2000), *Journal of Popular British Cinema*, 3, Trowbridge, Flicks Books.

Cook, Roger (2000), 'The mediated manufacture of an "avant garde": a Bourdieusian analysis of the field of contemporary art in London, 1997–9', in Bridget Fowler (ed.) *Reading Bourdieu on Society and Culture*, Oxford, Blackwell, pp. 164–85.

Copjec, Joan (2000), 'Vampires, breast-feeding, and anxiety (extract)', in Ken Gelder (ed.) *The Horror Reader*, London and New York, Routledge, pp. 52–63.

Cornwell, Neil (1990), *The Literary Fantastic: From Gothic to Postmodernism*, London, Harvester Wheatsheaf.

Couldry, Nick (2003), 'Media meta-capital: extending the range of Bourdieu's field theory', *Theory and Society*, 32: 5/6, pp. 653–77.

Craft, Christopher (1984), '"Kiss me with those red lips": gender and inversion in Bram Stoker's *Dracula*', *Representations*, 8, pp. 107–33.

Cranny-Francis, Anne (1990), *Feminist Fiction*, Cambridge, Polity Press.

Crawford, Garry (2004), *Consuming Sport: Fans, Sport and Culture*, London and New York, Routledge.

— (2002), 'Surveying *The Kingdom*: explorations of medicine, memory and modernity in Lars von Trier's *The Kingdom* (1994)', *European Journal of Cultural Studies*, 5: 4, pp. 387–406.

Creeber, Glen (ed.) (2001), *The Television Genre Book*, London, BFI Publishing.

Creed, Barbara (1993), *The Monstrous-Feminine: Film, Feminism, Psychoanalysis*, London and New York, Routledge.

— (2004), 'Freud's worst nightmare: dining with Dr Hannibal Lecter', in Steven Jay Schneider (ed.) *Horror Film and Psychoanalysis: Freud's Worst Nightmares*, Cambridge, Cambridge University Press, pp. 188–202.

Critcher, Chas (2003), *Moral Panics and the Media*, Buckingham and Philadelphia, Open University Press.

Cronin, Anne M. (2000), *Advertising and Consumer Citizenship: Gender, Images and Rights*, London and New York, Routledge.

Crutchfield, Susan (1999), 'Touching scenes and finishing touches: blindness in the slasher film', in Christopher Sharrett (ed.) *Mythologies of Violence in Postmodern Media*, Detroit, Wayne State University Press, pp. 275–99.

Cunningham, Valentine (2002), *Reading After Theory*, Oxford, Blackwell.

Dacre, Anna (1998), 'Predator 3, or, the cultural logic of late capitalism', *The UTS Review*, 4: 2, pp. 1–13.

Dahlgren, Peter (1995), *Television and the Public Sphere: Citizenship, Democracy and the Media*, London, Sage.

Danielewski, Mark (2001), *House of Leaves*, London, Doubleday.

Dant, Tim (1999), *Material Culture in the Social World*, Buckingham and Philadelphia, Open University Press.

Davenport-Hines, Richard (1999), *Gothic: Four Hundred Years of Excess, Horror, Evil and Ruin*, New York, North Point Press.

Day, William Patrick (1985), *In the Circles of Fear and Desire: A Study of Gothic Fantasy*, Chicago and London, University of Chicago Press.

De Certeau, Michel (1988), *The Practice of Everyday Life*, Berkeley and London, University of California Press.

Dean, Jodi (2002), *Publicity's Secret: How Technoculture Capitalizes on Democracy*, Ithaca NY and London, Cornell University Press.

Delasara, Jan (2000), *PopLit, PopCult and* The X-Files, Jefferson NC, McFarland.

Derrida, Jacques (1988), *Limited Inc*, Evanston IL, Northwestern University Press.

— (1992), *Acts of Literature*, New York and London, Routledge.

— (1994), *Specters of Marx: The State of the Debt, the Work of Mourning, and the New International*, New York and London, Routledge.

— (1999), 'Marx & Sons', in Michael Sprinkler (ed.) *Ghostly Demarcations: A Symposium on Jacques Derrida's* Specters of Marx, London and New York, Verso, pp. 213–69.

Dewe Mathews, Tom (1994), *Censored: The Story of Film Censorship in Britain*, London, Chatto & Windus.

Dika, Vera (1990), *Games of Terror:* Halloween, Friday the 13th, *and the Films of the Stalker Cycle*, London and Toronto, Associated University Presses.

— (2003), *Recycled Culture in Contemporary Art and Film: The Uses of Nostalgia*, Cambridge and New York, Cambridge University Press.

Dixon, Wheeler Winston (ed.) (2000), *Film Genre 2000: New Critical Essays*, New York, State University of New York Press.

Donald, James (ed.) (1989), *Fantasy and the Cinema*, London, BFI Publishing.

Donaldson, Mara E. (1997), 'Bordercrossing: fall and fantasy in *Blade Runner* and *Thelma and Louise*', in George Aichele and Tina Pippin (eds), *The Monstrous and the Unspeakable: The Bible as Fantastic Literature*, Sheffield, Sheffield Academic Press, pp. 19–42.

Dresser, Norine (1989), *American Vampires: Fans, Victims, Practitioners*, New York, Vintage Books.

Duclos, Denis (1998), *The Werewolf Complex: America's Fascination with Violence*, Oxford and New York, Berg.

Duncker, Patricia (2002), *The Deadly Space Between*, London, Picador.

Dyer, Richard (2002), 'Three questions about serial killing', in *The Matter of Images: Essays on Representation*, 2nd edn, London and New York, Routledge, pp. 110–17.

Dyson, Jeremy (1997), *Bright Darkness: The Lost Art of the Supernatural Horror Film*, London, Cassell.

Earle, William (1999), 'Bourdieu nouveau', in Richard Shusterman (ed.) *Bourdieu: A Critical Reader*, Oxford, Blackwell, pp. 175–91.

Easthope, Antony (1999), *The Unconscious*, London and New York, Routledge.

Easton Ellis, Bret (1991), *American Psycho*, London, Picador.

Eberly, Rosa A. (2000), *Citizen Critics: Literary Public Spheres*, Urbana and Chicago, University of Illinois Press.

Edmundson, Mark (1997), *Nightmare on Main Street: Angels, Sadomasochism, and the Culture of Gothic*, Cambridge MA, Harvard University Press.

Egan, Kate (2003), 'The amateur historian and the electronic archive: identity, power and the function of lists, facts and memories on "video nasty"-themed websites', *Intensities: The Journal of Cult Media*, 3, 'Horror Special Issue' (Spring), available online at http://www.cult-media.com/issue3/Aegan.htm.

Ekegren, Peter (1999), *The Reading of Theoretical Texts: A Critique of Criticism in the Social Sciences*, London and New York, Routledge.

Elliott, Anthony (2001), *Concepts of the Self*, Cambridge, Polity Press.

Ellis, John (1982), *Visible Fictions*, London, Routledge.

— (2000), *Seeing Things: Television in the Age of Uncertainty*, London and New York, I.B. Tauris.

— (2002), 'A minister is about to resign: on the interpretation of television footage', in Anne Jerslev (ed.), *Realism and 'Reality' in Film and Media*, University of Copenhagen, Museum Tusculanum Press, pp. 193–210.

Ellis, Markman (2000), *The History of Gothic Fiction*, Edinburgh, Edinburgh University Press.

Elmer, Jonathan (1995), *Reading at the Social Limit: Affect, Mass Culture and Edgar Allan Poe*, Stanford CA, Stanford University Press.

Farrell, John (1996), *Freud's Paranoid Quest: Psychoanalysis and Modern Suspicion*, New York and London, New York University Press.

Feagin, Susan L. (1992), 'Monsters, disgust and fascination', *Philosophical Studies*, 65: 1–2, pp. 75–84.

Ferguson, Harvie (1996), *The Lure of Dreams: Sigmund Freud and the Construction of Modernity*, London and New York, Routledge.

Fiedler, Leslie (1987), 'Fantasy as commodity and myth: introduction', in Tim Underwood and Chuck Miller (eds), *Kingdom of Fear: The World of Stephen King*, London, New English Library, pp. 45–50.

Field, John (2003), *Social Capital*, London and New York, Routledge.

Fiske, John (1989), 'Moments of television: neither the text nor the audience', in Ellen Seiter, Hans Borcher, Gabrielle Kreutzner and Eva-Maria Warth (eds), *Remote Control: Television, Audiences and Cultural Power*, London, Routledge, pp. 56–68.

— (1992), 'The cultural economy of fandom', in Lisa A. Lewis (ed.) *The Adoring Audience*, New York and London, Routledge, pp. 30–49.

Fleming, Dan (2000), '*The Blair Witch Project*: film and hypertexts', in Dan Fleming (ed.) *Formations: A 21st Century Media Studies Textbook*, Manchester, Manchester University Press, pp. 248–51.

Flew, Terry (2002), *New Media: An Introduction*, Oxford, Oxford University Press.

Foucault, Michel (1977), *Language, Counter-Memory, Practice*, Ithaca NY, Cornell University Press.

— (1979), 'What is an author?', *Screen*, 20: 1, pp. 13–33.

— (1990), *A History of Sexuality, Volume 1: An Introduction*, New York, Vintage.

— (1991), *Discipline and Punish: The Birth of the Prison*, London, Penguin.

Fowler, Bridget (1997), *Pierre Bourdieu and Cultural Theory*, London, Sage.

Fowles, Jib (1999), *The Case For Television Violence*, London, Sage.

Fraser, Nancy (1992), 'Rethinking the public sphere: a contribution to the critique of actually existing democracy', in Craig Calhoun (ed.) *Critical Social Theory*, Oxford, Blackwell, pp. 109–42.

Freeland, Cynthia (1995), 'Realist horror', in Cynthia A. Freeland and Thomas E. Wartenberg (eds), *Philosophy and Film*, New York and London, Routledge, pp. 126–42.

— (1996), 'Feminist frameworks for horror films', in David Bordwell and Noël Carroll (eds), *Post-Theory: Reconstructing Film Studies*, Madison, University of Wisconsin Press, pp. 195–218.

— (2000), *The Naked and the Undead: Evil and the Appeal of Horror*, Boulder Colorado, Westview Press.

— (2001), 'Explaining the uncanny in *The Double Life of Véronique*', in Daniel Shaw (ed.), *Film and Philosophy: Horror Special Edition*, pp. 34–50.

— (2004), 'Horror and art-dread', in Stephen Prince (ed.), *The Horror Film*, New Jersey and London, Rutgers University Press, pp. 189–205.

Freud, Sigmund (1974[1900]), 'The interpretation of dreams', in *The Standard Edition of the Complete Psychological Works of Sigmund Freud: Volume 4*, London, Hogarth Press, pp. 1–338.

— (1990a[1919]), 'The uncanny', in *The Penguin Freud Library Volume 14: Art and Literature*, Harmondsworth, Penguin, pp. 335–76.

— (1990b[1920]), 'Beyond the pleasure principle', in *The Penguin Freud Library Volume 11: On Metapsychology*, Harmondsworth, Penguin, pp. 269–338.

Fuss, Diana (1993), 'Monsters of perversion: Jeffrey Dahmer and *The Silence of the Lambs*', in Marjorie Garber, Jann Matlock and Rebecca L. Walkowitz (eds), *Media Spectacles*, New York and London, Routledge, pp. 181–205.

Gabbard, Glen O. (2001), 'Introduction', in Glen O. Gabbard (ed.) *Psychoanalysis and Film*, London, Karnac Books, pp. 1–16.

Gabler, Neal (1998), *Life – The Movie: How Entertainment Conquered Reality*, New York, Alfred A. Knopf.

Gallagher, Stephen (1988), *Oktober*, London, New English Library.

— (2000), 'We want it dark!', *Dreamwatch*, 66, p. 82.

— (2004), 'State of the art', *Dreamwatch*, 115, p. 82.

Gallardo C., Ximena and Smith, C. Jason (2004), *Alien Woman: Ripley as Cinematic Icon*, New York and London, Continuum.

Game, Ann (1991), *Undoing the Social: Towards a Deconstructive Sociology*, Toronto, University of Toronto Press.

Game, Ann and Metcalfe, Andrew (1996), *Passionate Sociology*, London, Sage.

Gamer, Michael (2000), *Romanticism and the Gothic: Genre, Reception and Canon Formation*, Cambridge, Cambridge University Press.

García Canclini, Nestor (2001), *Consumers and Citizens: Globalization and Multicultural Conflicts*, Minneapolis and London, University of Minnesota Press.

Garnham, Nicholas (2000), *Emancipation, the Media, and Modernity: Arguments about the Media and Social Theory*, Oxford, Oxford University Press.

Gauntlett, David (1995), *Moving Experiences: Understanding Television's Influences and Effects*, Luton, John Libbey.

— (2001), 'The worrying influence of "media effects" studies', in Martin Barker and Julian Petley (eds), *Ill Effects: The Media/Violence Debate*, 2nd edn, London and New York, Routledge, pp. 47–62.

Gaut, Berys (1993), 'The paradox of horror', *The British Journal of Aesthetics*, 33: 4, pp. 333–45.

— (1995), 'The enjoyment theory of horror: a reply to Carroll', *The British Journal of Aesthetics*, 35: 3, pp. 284–9.

Gelder, Ken (1994), *Reading the Vampire*, London and New York, Routledge.

— (1996), 'The vampire writes back: Anne Rice and the (re)turn of the author in the field of cultural production', in Deborah Cartmell, I.Q. Hunter, Heidi Kaye and Imelda Whelehan (eds), *Pulping Fictions*, London, Pluto Press, pp. 29–41.

— (ed.) (2000), *The Horror Reader*, London and New York, Routledge.

Gibson, Andrew (1996), *Towards a Postmodern Theory of Narrative*, Edinburgh, Edinburgh University Press.

Giles, Dennis (1984), 'Conditions of pleasure in horror cinema', in Barry Keith Grant (ed.) *Planks of Reason: Essays on the Horror Film*, Lanham MD, Scarecrow Press, pp. 38–52.

Gomel, Elana (2003), *Bloodscripts: Writing the Violent Subject*, Columbus, Ohio State University Press.

Grainge, Paul (2003), 'Colouring the past: *Pleasantville* and the textuality of media memory', in Paul Grainge (ed.) *Memory and Popular Film*, Manchester, Manchester University Press, pp. 202–19.

Grant, Michael (1999), 'The modern fantastic', in Andy Black (ed.) *Necronomicon: The Journal of Horror and Erotic Cinema*, Book Three, pp. 51–72.

Gray, Jonathan (2003), 'New audiences, new textualities: anti-fans and non-fans', *International Journal of Cultural Studies*, 6: 1, pp. 64–81.

Green, André (2002), *Time in Psychoanalysis: Some Contradictory Aspects*, London, Free Association Books.

— (2003), *Diachrony in Psychoanalysis*, London, Free Association Books.

Greenberg, Harvey Roy (2004), 'Heimlich maneuvres: on a certain tendency of horror and speculative cinema', in Steven Jay Schneider (ed.) *Horror Film and Psychoanalysis: Freud's Worst Nightmares*, Cambridge, Cambridge University Press, pp. 122–41.

Greenspan, Patricia S. (1993), *Emotions and Reasons: An Inquiry into Emotional Justifications*, New York and London, Routledge.

Greig, Mary (2004), 'Habermas and the holy grail of reason: *The Philosophical Discourse of Modernity* between theatre and theory', *Social Semiotics*, 14: 2, pp. 215–32.

Grenfell, Michael and James, David with Hodkinson, Philip, Reay, Diane and Robbins, Derek (1998), *Bourdieu and Education: Acts of Practical Theory*, London, Falmer Press.

Grixti, Joseph (1989), *Terrors of Uncertainty: The Cultural Contexts of Horror Fiction*, London and New York, Routledge.

Grodal, Torben (1999), *Moving Pictures: A New Theory of Film Genres, Feelings, and Cognitions*, Oxford, Oxford University Press.

Guillory, John (2000), 'Bourdieu's refusal', in Nicholas Brown and Imre Szeman (eds), *Pierre Bourdieu: Fieldwork in Culture*, Lanham MD, Rowman & Littlefield, pp. 19–43.

Haas, Lynda and Haas, Robert (1996), 'Living with(out) boundaries: the novels of Anne Rice', in Tony Magistrale and Michael A. Morrison (eds), *A Dark Night's Dreaming: Contemporary American Horror Fiction*, Columbia, University of South Carolina Press, pp. 55–67.

Habermas, Jürgen (1989), *The Structural Transformation of the Public Sphere*, Cambridge, Polity Press.

Haggerty, George E. (1989), *Gothic Fiction/Gothic Form*, University Park and London, Pennsylvania State University Press.

Halberstam, Judith (1995), *Skin Shows: Gothic Horror and the Technology of Monsters*, Durham NC and London, Duke University Press.

Hallam, Julia with Marshment, Margaret (2000), *Realism and Popular Cinema*, Manchester, Manchester University Press.

Halttunen, Karen (1998), *Murder Most Foul: The Killer and the American Gothic Imagination*, Cambridge MA, Harvard University Press.

Hansen, Miriam (1990), 'Early cinema: whose public sphere?', in Thomas Elsaesser (ed.) *Early Cinema: Space, Frame, Narrative*, London, BFI Publishing, pp. 228–46.

— (1991), *Babel and Babylon: Spectatorship in American Silent Film*, Cambridge MA, Harvard University Press.

— (1993), 'Foreword', in Oskar Negt and Alexander Kluge *Public Sphere and Experience: Towards an Analysis of the Bourgeois and Proletarian Public Sphere*, Minneapolis and London, University of Minnesota Press, pp. ix–xli.

Hanson, Clare (1990), 'Stephen King: powers of horror', in Brian Docherty (ed.) *American Horror Fiction: From Brockden Brown to Stephen King*, London, Macmillan, pp. 135–54.

Hantke, Steffen (2002), 'Shudder as we think: reflections on horror and/or criticism', *Paradoxa*, 17, pp. 1–9.

Harbord, Janet (2002), *Film Cultures*, London, Sage.

Harker, Richard, Mahar, Cheleen and Wilkes, Chris (eds) (1990), *An Introduction to the Work of Pierre Bourdieu*, London, Macmillan.

Harries, Dan (2000), *Film Parody*, London, BFI Publishing.

— (2002), 'Film parody and the resuscitation of genre' in Steve Neale (ed.), *Genre and Contemporary Hollywood*, London, BFI Publishing, pp. 281–93.

Harrington, C. Lee and Bielby, Denise D. (1995), *Soap Fans: Pursuing Pleasure and Making Meaning in Everyday Life*, Philadelphia PA, Temple University Press.

Harris, David (1992), *From Class Struggle to the Politics of Pleasure: The Effects of Gramscianism on Cultural Studies*, London and New York, Routledge.

Hartley, John (1999), *Uses of Television*, London and New York, Routledge.

Hawkins, Joan (2000), *Cutting Edge: Art-Horror and the Horrific Avant-garde*, Minneapolis, University of Minnesota Press.

Heffernan, Kevin (2004), *Ghouls, Gimmicks, and Gold: Horror Films and the American Movie Business, 1953–1968*, Durham NC and London, Duke University Press.

Heller, Terry (1987), *The Delights of Terror: An Aesthetics of the Tale of Terror*, Urbana and Chicago, University of Illinois Press.

Hendershot, Cyndy (1998), *The Animal Within*, Ann Arbor, University of Michigan Press.

Hermes, Joke (1998), 'Cultural citizenship and popular fiction', in Kees Brants, Joke Hermes and Liesbet van Zoonen (eds), *The Media in Question: Popular Cultures and Public Interests*, London, Sage, pp. 157–67.

Herron, Don (1987), 'King: the good, the bad and the academic', in Tim Underwood and Chuck Miller (eds), *Kingdom of Fear: The World of Stephen King*, London, New English Library, pp. 131–64.

Higley, Sarah L. and Weinstock, Jeffrey Andrew (eds), (2004), *Nothing That Is: Millennial Cinema and the Blair Witch Controversies*, Detroit MI, Wayne State University Press.

Hill, Annette (1997), *Shocking Entertainment: Viewer Response to Violent Movies*, Luton, University of Luton Press.

Hills, Matt (2002), *Fan Cultures*, London and New York, Routledge.

— (2003a), 'Putting away childish things: Jar Jar Binks and the "Virtual Star" as an object of fan loathing', in Thomas Austin and Martin Barker (eds), *Contemporary Hollywood Stardom*, London, Arnold, pp. 74–89.

— (2003b), 'An event-based definition of art-horror', in Steven Jay Schneider and Daniel Shaw (eds), *Dark Thoughts: Philosophic Reflections on Cinematic Horror*, Lanham, MD, Scarecrow Press, pp. 138–57.

— (2003c), 'Counterfictions in the work of Kim Newman: rewriting Gothic SF as "alternate story stories"', *Science Fiction Studies*, 30: Part 3, pp. 436–55.

— (2003d), 'Whose "postmodern" horror?', *Kinoeye*, 3: Issue 5, available online at http://www.kinoeye.org/03/05/hills05.php.

— (2004a), '*Dawson's Creek*: "quality teen TV" and "mainstream cult"?', in Glyn Davis and Kay Dickinson (eds), *Teen TV: Genre, Consumption and Identity*, London, BFI Publishing, pp. 54–67.

— (2004b), 'Defining cult TV: texts, inter-texts and fan audiences', in Robert C. Allen and Annette Hill (eds), *The Television Studies Reader*, London and New York, Routledge, pp. 509–23.

— (2004c), '*The Twilight Zone*', in Glen Creeber (ed.), *Fifty Key Television Programmes*, London, Arnold, pp. 217–21.

— (2004d), 'Strategies, tactics and the question of *Un Lieu Propre*: what/where is "media theory"', *Social Semiotics*, 14: 2, pp. 133–49.

— (2004e), 'Doing things with theory: from Freud's worst nightmare to (disciplinary) dreams of horror's cultural value', in Steven Jay Schneider (ed.), *Horror Film and Psychoanalysis: Freud's Worst Nightmares*, Cambridge, Cambridge University Press, pp. 205–21.

Hills, Matt and Williams, Rebecca (forthcoming) '*Angel*'s monstrous mothers and vampires with souls: investigating the abject in "television horror"', in Stacey Abbott (ed.), *Reading Angel*, London and New York, I.B. Tauris.

Hinton, Laura (1999), *The Perverse Gaze of Sympathy: Sadomasochistic Sentiments from Clarissa to Rescue 911*, New York, State University of New York Press.

Hipsky, Marty (2000), 'Romancing Bourdieu: a case study in gender politics in the literary field', in Nicholas Brown and Imre Szeman (eds), *Pierre Bourdieu: Fieldwork in Culture*, Lanham, MD, Rowman & Littlefield, pp. 186–206.

Hockley, Luke (2001), *Cinematic Projections: The Analytical Psychology of C.G. Jung and Film Theory*, Luton, University of Luton Press.

Hodges, Devon and Doane, Janice L. (1991), 'Undoing feminism in Anne Rice's vampire chronicles', in James Naremore and Patrick Brantlinger (eds), *Modernity and Mass Culture*, Bloomington, Indiana University Press, pp. 158–75.

Hodkinson, Paul (2002), *Goth: Identity, Style and Subculture*, Oxford and New York, Berg.

Hoesterey, Ingeborg (2001), *Pastiche: Cultural Memory in Art, Film and Literature*, Bloomington and Indianapolis, Indiana University Press.

Hogan, David J. (1988), *Dark Romance: Sex and Death in the Horror Film*, Wellingborough, Equation.

Hogle, Jerrold E. (2002), *The Undergrounds of the Phantom of the Opera: Sublimation and the Gothic in Leroux's Novel and Its Progeny*, London, Palgrave.

Höijer, Birgitta (1999), 'To be an audience', in Pertti Alasuutari (ed.) *Rethinking the Media Audience*, London, Sage, pp. 179–94.

Hollows, Joanne (2003), 'The masculinity of cult', in Mark Jancovich, Antonio Lázaro Reboll, Julian Stringer and Andy Willis (eds), *Defining Cult Movies: The Cultural Politics of Oppositional Taste*, Manchester, Manchester University Press, pp. 35–53.

Hollway, Wendy and Jefferson, Tony (2000), *Doing Qualitative Research Differently*, London, Sage.

Hoppenstand, Gary (1996), 'The pleasures of evil: hedonism and the contemporary horror film', in Paul Loukides and Linda K. Fuller (eds), *Beyond the Stars: Studies in American Popular Film*, Bowling Green OH, Bowling Green State University Popular Press, pp. 249–63.

Hoxter, Julian (1996), 'The evil dead – die and chase: from slapstick to splatshtick', in Andy Black (ed.) *Necronomicon: The Journal of Horror and Erotic Cinema*, Book One, pp. 71–83.

— (2000), 'Taking possession: cult learning in *The Exorcist*', in Xavier Mendik and Graeme Harper (eds), *Unruly Pleasures*, Guildford, FAB Press, pp. 171–85.

Hume, Kathryn (1984), *Fantasy and Mimesis: Responses to Reality in Western Literature*, New York and London, Methuen.

Humphries, Reynold (2002), *The American Horror Film: An Introduction*, Edinburgh, Edinburgh University Press.

Hunt, Nathan (2003), 'The importance of trivia: ownership, exclusion and authority in science fiction fandom', in Mark Jancovich, Antonio Lázaro Reboll, Julian Stringer and Andy Willis (eds), *Defining Cult Movies: The Cultural Politics of Oppositional Taste*, Manchester, Manchester University Press, pp. 185–201.

Hutchings, Peter (1993), *Hammer and Beyond: The British Horror Film*, Manchester, Manchester University Press.

— (1996), 'Tearing your soul apart: horror's new monsters', in Victor Sage and Allan Lloyd Smith (eds), *Modern Gothic: A Reader*, Manchester, Manchester University Press, pp. 89–103.

— (2001), *Terence Fisher*, Manchester and New York, Manchester University Press.

— (2003), 'The Argento effect', in Mark Jancovich, Antonio Lázaro Reboll, Julian Stringer and Andy Willis (eds), *Defining Cult Movies: The Cultural Politics of Oppositional Taste*, Manchester, Manchester University Press, pp. 127–41.

Iaccino, James F. (1994), *Psychological Reflections on Cinematic Terror: Jungian Archetypes in Horror Films*, Westport CT, Praeger.

Illouz, Eva (1997), *Consuming the Romantic Utopia: Love and the Cultural Contradictions of Capitalism*, Berkeley and London, University of California Press.

Indiana, Gary (1999), *Three Month Fever: The Andrew Cunanan Story*, London, Quartet Books.

Ingebretsen, Edward J. (2001), *At Stake: Monsters and the Rhetoric of Fear in Public Culture*, Chicago IL and London, University of Chicago Press.

Inglis, David and Hughson, John (2003), *Confronting Culture: Sociological Vistas*, Cambridge, Polity Press.

Isin, Engin F. and Wood, Patricia K. (1999), *Citizenship and Identity*, London, Sage.

Jackson, Rosemary (1981), *Fantasy: The Literature of Subversion*, London and New York, Methuen.

Jacobs, Jason (2003), *Body Trauma TV: The New Hospital Dramas*, London, BFI Publishing.

Jameson, Fredric (1983), 'Pleasure: a political issue' in Formations Editorial Collective (eds), *Formations of Pleasure*, London, Routledge & Kegan Paul, pp. 1–14.

— (1985), 'Postmodernism and consumer society', in Hal Foster (ed.), *Postmodern Culture*, London, Pluto Press, pp. 111–25.

— (1991), *Postmodernism, or, The Cultural Logic of Late Capitalism*, London, Verso.

— (1999), 'Marx's purloined letter', in Michael Sprinkler (ed.), *Ghostly Demarcations: A Symposium on Jacques Derrida's* Specters of Marx, London and New York, Verso, pp. 26–67.

— (2003), 'The dialectics of disaster', in Stanley Hauerwas and Frank Lentricchia (eds), *Dissent from the Homeland: Essays After September 11th*, Durham NC and London, Duke University Press, pp. 55–62.

Jancovich, Mark (1992), *Horror*, London, Batsford.

— (1996), *Rational Fears: American Horror in the 1950s*, Manchester, Manchester University Press.

— (2000), '"A real shocker": authenticity, genre and the struggle for distinction', *Continuum*, 14: 1, pp. 23–35.

— (2002a), 'Introduction', in Mark Jancovich (ed.), *Horror, The Film Reader*, London and New York, Routledge, pp. 1–19.

— (2002b), 'Genre and the audience: genre classifications and cultural distinctions in the mediation of *The Silence of the Lambs*', in Mark Jancovich (ed.), *Horror, The Film Reader*, London and New York, Routledge, pp. 151–61.

— (2002c), 'Cult fictions: cult movies, subcultural capital and the production of cultural distinctions', *Cultural Studies*, 16: 2, pp. 306–22.

Jancovich, Mark and Lyons, James (2003), 'Introduction', in Mark Jancovich and James Lyons (eds), *Quality Popular Television*, London, BFI Publishing, pp. 1–8.

Jansen, Sue Curry (1990), *Censorship: The Knot That Binds Power and Knowledge*, Oxford, Oxford University Press.

Jenkins, Henry (1992), *Textual Poachers*, New York and London, Routledge.

— (2002), 'Interactive audiences?', in Dan Harries (ed.) *The New Media Book*, London, BFI Publishing, pp. 157–70.

— (2003), 'Quentin Tarantino's *Star Wars*? Digital cinema, media convergence, and participatory culture', in David Thorburn and Henry Jenkins (eds), *Rethinking Media Change: The Aesthetics of Transition*, Cambridge MA and London, MIT Press, pp. 281–312.

Jenkins, Philip (1994), *Using Murder: The Social Construction of Serial Homicide*, New York, Aldine de Gruyter.

Jenkins, Richard (2002), *Pierre Bourdieu* rev. edn, London and New York, Routledge.

Jenks, Chris (2003), *Transgression*, London and New York, Routledge.

Jensen, Joli (1992), 'Fandom as pathology: the consequences of characterization', in Lisa A. Lewis (ed.) *The Adoring Audience*, New York and London, Routledge, pp. 9–29.

Johnson, Catherine (2001a), '*The X-Files*' in Glen Creeber (ed.) *The Television Genre Book*, London, BFI Publishing, p. 30.

— (2001b), '*Buffy the Vampire Slayer*', in Glen Creeber (ed.) *The Television Genre Book*, London, BFI Publishing, p. 42.

Jones, Darryl (2002), *Horror: A Thematic History in Fiction and Film*, London, Arnold.

Jones, E. Michael (2000), *Monsters From The Id: The Rise of Horror in Fiction and Film*, Dallas TX, Spence Publishing.

Jones, Stephen (1994), *The Illustrated Frankenstein Movie Guide*, London, Titan Books.

Jones, Stephen and Newman, Kim (eds) (1988), *Horror: 100 Best Books*, London, Xanadu Publications.

Joshi, S.T. (2001a), *The Modern Weird Tale*, Jefferson NC, McFarland.

— (2001b), *Ramsey Campbell and Modern Horror Fiction*, Liverpool, Liverpool University Press.

Kaminsky, Stuart M. with Mahan, Jeffrey H. (1985), *American Television Genres*, Chicago IL, Nelson-Hall.

Kapsis, Robert E. (1992), *Hitchcock: The Making of a Reputation*, Chicago IL and London, University of Chicago Press.

Kaveney, Roz (1990), 'Kim Newman: Interview', *Interzone*, 36, June, pp. 17–19.

Kavka, Misha (2002), 'The Gothic on screen', in Jerrold E. Hogle (ed.) *The Cambridge Companion to Gothic Fiction*, Cambridge, Cambridge University Press, pp. 209–28.

Kearney, Richard (2003), *Strangers, Gods and Monsters: Interpreting Otherness*, London and New York, Routledge.

Kellner, Douglas (2003), *Media Spectacle*, London and New York, Routledge.

Kelso, Sylvia (2002), 'Writing about *On Writing*', *Paradoxa*, 17, pp. 200–9.

Kendall, Gavin and Wickham, Gary (2001), *Understanding Culture: Cultural Studies, Order, Ordering*, London, Sage.

Kennedy, Barbara M. (2000), *Deleuze and Cinema: The Aesthetics of Sensation*, Edinburgh, Edinburgh University Press.

Kerekes, David and Slater, David (2000), *See No Evil: Banned Films and Video Controversy*, Manchester, Critical Vision.

Kermode, Mark (1997), 'I was a teenage horror fan: or, "How I learned to stop worrying and love Linda Blair"', in Martin Barker and Julian Petley (eds), *Ill Effects: The Media/Violence Debate*, London and New York, Routledge, pp. 57–66.

— (2002), 'The British censors and horror cinema', in Steve Chibnall and Julian Petley (eds), *British Horror Cinema*, London and New York, Routledge, pp. 10–22.

— (2003a), 'All fright on the night', *The Observer Review* 19 October, p. 5.

— (2003b) 'What a carve up!', *Sight and Sound*, December, pp. 13–16.

Kilgour, Maggie (1995), *The Rise of the Gothic Novel*, London and New York, Routledge.

— (1998), 'Dr Frankenstein Meets Dr Freud', in Robert K. Martin and Eric Savoy (eds), *American Gothic: New Interventions in a National Narrative*, Iowa City, University of Iowa Press, pp. 40–53.

Kimber, Shaun (2002), 'Including the excluded: genre fans' views on film violence and the regulative censorship of film violence in Britain', paper presented at 'Exploiting Fear: The Art and Appeal of Horror on Film' International Film Conference, University of Hull, 11–13 October.

King, Geoff (2002), *Film Comedy*, London and New York, Wallflower Press.

King, Stephen (1975), *'Salem's Lot*, New York, Doubleday.

— (1982), *Danse Macabre: The Anatomy of Horror*, London, Futura.

— (1983), *Pet Sematary*, New York, Doubleday.

— (2001), *On Writing: A Memoir of the Craft*, New York, Pocket Books.

Klinger, Barbara (1991), 'Digressions at the cinema: commodification and reception in mass culture', in James Naremore and Patrick Brantlinger (eds), *Modernity and Mass Culture*, Bloomington, Indiana University Press, pp. 117–34.

Klock, Geoff (2002), *How to Read Superhero Comics and Why*, New York and London, Continuum.

Knox, Sara L. (1998), *Murder: A Tale of Modern American Life*, Durham NC and London, Duke University Press.

Kofman, Sarah (1991), *Freud and Fiction*, Cambridge, Polity Press.

Konigsberg, Ira (1998), 'How many Draculas does it take to change a lightbulb?', in Andrew Horton and Stuart Y. Dougal (eds), *Play It Again, Sam: Retakes on Remakes*, Berkeley, University of California Press, pp. 250–75.

Krips, Henry (1999), *Fetish: An Erotics of Culture*, London, Free Association Books.

Kristeva, Julia (1982), *Powers of Horror: An Essay on Abjection*, New York, Columbia University Press.

Krzywinska, Tanya (2000), 'Demon daddies: gender, ecstasy and terror in the possession film', in Alain Silver and James Ursini (eds), *Horror Film Reader*, New York, Limelight Editions, pp. 247–67.

— (2002a), 'Hands-on horror', in Geoff King and Tanya Krzywinska (eds), *ScreenPlay: Cinema/videogames/interfaces*, London and New York, Wallflower Press, pp. 206–23.

— (2002b), 'Hubble-bubble, herbs and grimoires: magic, Manichaeanism, and witchcraft in *Buffy*', in Rhonda V. Wilcox and David Lavery (eds), *Fighting the Forces: What's at Stake in Buffy the Vampire Slayer*, Lanham MD, Rowman & Littlefield, pp. 178–94.

Kuhn, Annette (1988), *Cinema, Censorship, and Sexuality, 1909–1925*, London, Routledge.

— (1999), '"That day *did* last me all my life": cinema memory and enduring fandom', in Melvyn Stokes and Richard Maltby (eds), *Identifying Hollywood's Audiences: Cultural Identity and the Movies*, London, BFI Publishing, pp. 135–46.

— (2002), *An Everyday Magic: Cinema and Cultural Memory*, London and New York, I.B. Tauris.

La Caze, Marguerite (2002), 'The mourning of loss in *The Sixth Sense*', *PostScript*, 21: 3, pp. 111–121.

LaFollette, Hugh (1996), *Personal Relationships: Love, Identity and Morality*, Oxford, Blackwell.

Lake Crane, Jonathan (1994), *Terror and Everyday Life: Singular Moments in the History of the Horror Film*, London, Sage.

— (2000), 'A body apart: Cronenberg and genre', in Michael Grant (ed.) *The Modern Fantastic: The Films of David Cronenberg*, Trowbridge, Flicks Books, pp. 50–68.

— (2004), '"It was a dark and stormy night . . . ": horror films and the problem of irony', in Steven Jay Schneider (ed.) *Horror Film and Psychoanalysis: Freud's Worst Nightmares*, Cambridge, Cambridge University Press, pp. 142–56.

Lamont, Michèle and Lareau, Annette (1988), 'Cultural capital: allusions, gaps and glissandos in recent theoretical developments', *Sociological Theory*, 6: 1, pp. 153–68.

Lareau, Annette and Weininger, Elliott B. (2003), 'Cultural capital in educational research: a critical assessment', *Theory and Society*, 32: 5/6, pp. 567–606.

Lash, Scott (1990), *Sociology of Postmodernism*, London and New York, Routledge.

— (1993), 'Pierre Bourdieu: cultural economy and social change', in Craig Calhoun, Edward LiPuma and Moishe Postone (eds), *Bourdieu: Critical Perspectives*, Cambridge, Polity Press, pp. 193–211.

Latham, Rob (2001), 'VR Noir: Kim Newman's *The Night Mayor*', *ParaDoxa: Studies in World Literary Genres*, 16, pp. 95–122.

— (2002), *Consuming Youth: Vampires, Cyborgs, and the Culture of Consumption*, Chicago IL and London, University of Chicago Press.

Lawrence, Patricia A. and Palmgreen, Philip C. (1996) 'A uses and gratifications analysis of horror film preference', in James B. Weaver III and Ron Tamborini (eds), *Horror Films: Current Research on Audience Preferences and Reactions*, Saddle River NJ, Lawrence Erlbaum, pp. 161–78.

Leane, Elle and Buchanan, Ian (2002), 'What's left of theory?', *Continuum*, 16: 3, pp. 253–8.

Lee, Judith (1997), 'Sacred horror: faith and fantasy in the revelation to John', in George Aichele and Tina Pippin (eds), *The Monstrous and the Unspeakable: The Bible as Fantastic Literature*, Sheffield, Sheffield Academic Press, pp. 220–39.

Leffler, Yvonne (2000), *Horror as Pleasure: The Aesthetics of Horror Fiction*, Stockholm, Almqvist & Wiksell International.

Leledakis, Kanakis (1995), *Society and Psyche: Social Theory and the Unconscious Dimension of the Social*, Oxford, Berg.

Lem, Stanislaw (1985), *Microworlds: Writings on Science Fiction and Fantasy*, London, Mandarin.

Lembo, Ron (2000), *Thinking Through Television*, Cambridge, Cambridge University Press.

Levine, George and Knoepflmacher, U.C. (eds) (1982), *The Endurance of Frankenstein*, Berkeley, University of California Press.

Levinson, Jerrold (1990), 'The place of real emotion in response to fictions', *Journal of Aesthetics and Art Criticism*, 48, pp. 79–80.

— (1991), 'Review of Carroll's *Philosophy of Horror*', *Journal of Aesthetics and Art Criticism*, 49, pp. 253–8.

Lévy, Pierre (1999), *Collective Intelligence: Mankind's Emerging World in Cyberspace*, Boulder CO, Perseus Books.

Lewis, Lisa A. (1992), '"Something more than love": fan stories on film', in Lisa A. Lewis (ed.) *The Adoring Audience: Fan Culture and Popular Media*, London and New York, Routledge, pp. 135–59.

Lewis, Tom (1999), 'The politics of "hauntology" in Derrida's *Specters of Marx*', in Michael Sprinkler (ed.) *Ghostly Demarcations: A Symposium on Jacques Derrida's* Specters of Marx, London and New York, Verso, pp. 134–67.

Leyland, Matthew (2003), 'Review of *Identity*', *Sight and Sound*, August, p. 50.

Lin, Nan (2001), *Social Capital: A Theory of Social Structure and Action*, Cambridge, Cambridge University Press.

Lister, Martin, Dovey, Jon, Giddings, Seth, Grant, Iain and Kelly, Kieran (2003), *New Media: A Critical Introduction*, London and New York, Routledge.

Lopes, Paul (2000), 'Pierre Bourdieu's fields of cultural production: a case study of modern jazz', in Nicholas Brown and Imre Szeman (eds), *Pierre Bourdieu: Fieldwork in Culture*, Lanham MD, Rowman & Littlefield, pp. 165–85.

López, José (2003), *Society and Its Metaphors: Language, Social Theory and Social Structure*, New York and London, Continuum.

Lucanio, Patrick (1987), *Them or Us: Archetypal Interpretations of Fifties Alien Invasion Films*, Bloomington and Indianapolis, Indiana University Press.

Luckhurst, Roger (2002), 'The contemporary London Gothic and the limits of the spectral turn', *Textual Practice* 16: 3, pp. 527–46.

Lupton, Deborah (1999), *Risk*, London and New York, Routledge.

Lyons, William (1980), *Emotion*, New York, Cambridge University Press.

Lyotard, Jean-François (1993), *Libidinal Economy*, London, Athlone Press.
Magistrale, Tony (2003), *Hollywood's Stephen King*, New York and London, Palgrave-Macmillan.
Malcolm, Janet (1991), *The Journalist and the Murderer*, London, Bloomsbury.
Maley, Willy (1999), 'Spectres of Engels', in Peter Buse and Andrew Stott (eds), *Ghosts: Deconstruction, Psychoanalysis, History*, London, Macmillan, pp. 23–49.
Marcus, Jana (1997), *In the Shadow of the Vampire: Reflections from the World of Anne Rice*, New York, Thunder's Mouth Press.
Marcuse, Herbert (1987), *Eros and Civilisation: A Philosophical Inquiry into Freud*, London, Ark.
Marx, Karl and Engels, Friedrich (1998[1848]), 'The Communist Manifesto' in Leo Panitch and Colin Leys (eds), *The Communist Manifesto Now: Socialist Register 1998*, Rendlesham, Merlin Press, pp. 240–68.
Massumi, Brian (2002), *Parables for the Virtual: Movement, Affect, Sensation*, Durham NC and London, Duke University Press.
Matravers, Derek (2001), *Art and Emotion*, Oxford, Oxford University Press.
Mäyrä, Ilkka (1999), *Demonic Texts and Textual Demons: The Demonic Tradition, the Self, and Popular Fiction*, Tampere, Tampere University Press.
McAfee, Noëlle (2000), *Habermas, Kristeva, and Citizenship*, Ithaca NY and London, Cornell University Press.
McCracken-Flesher, Caroline (1994), 'Cultural projections: the "strange case" of Dr Jekyll, Mr Hyde, and cinematic response', in Janice Carlisle and Daniel R. Schwarz (eds), *Narrative and Culture*, Athens, University of Georgia Press, pp. 179–99.
McDayter, Ghislaine (1999), 'Conjuring Byron: Byromania, literary commodification and the birth of celebrity', in Frances Wilson (ed.) *Byromania: Portraits of the Artist in Nineteenth- and Twentieth-century Culture*, London, Macmillan, pp. 43–62.
McGinn, Colin (1997), *Ethics, Evil and Fiction*, Oxford, Oxford University Press.
McGuigan, Jim (1999), *Modernity and Postmodern Culture*, Buckingham, Open University Press.
McHale, Brian (1992), *Constructing Postmodernism*, London and New York, Routledge.
McKee, Alan (2001), 'Which is the best *Doctor Who* story? A case study in value judgements outside the Academy', *Intensities: The Journal of Cult Media*, 1, available online at http://www.cult-media.com/issue1/Amckee.htm.
— (2002), 'Fandom', in Toby Miller (ed.), *Television Studies*, London, BFI Publishing, pp. 66–70.
— (2003a), 'Review of *Fan Cultures*', *The International Journal of Cultural Studies*, 6: 1, pp. 126–8.
— (2003b), *Textual Analysis*, London, Sage.
Mendik, Xavier (1998), 'From the monstrous mother to the third sex: female abjection in the films of Dario Argento', in Andy Black (ed.), *Necronomicon: The Journal of Horror and Erotic Cinema*, Book Two, pp. 110–33.
— (2001), 'Looking down Irma's throat: monstrous viewing in *Demons*', in Andy Black (ed.) *Necronomicon: The Journal of Horror and Erotic Cinema*, Book Four, pp. 161–77.
Mercer, Colin (1983), 'A poverty of desire: pleasure and popular politics', in Formations Editorial Collective (eds), *Formations of Pleasure*, London, Routledge & Kegan Paul, pp. 84–100.
Messenger Davies, Máire (2001), *'Dear BBC': children, television storytelling and the public sphere*, Cambridge, Cambridge University Press.
Meyers, Chris and Waller, Sara (2001), 'Disenstoried horror: art horror without narrative', in Daniel Shaw (ed.) *Film and Philosophy Horror Special Edition*, pp. 117–26.
Meyers, Helene (2001), *Femicidal Fears: Narratives of the Female Gothic Experience*, New York, State University of New York Press.

Millard Daugherty, Anne (2001), 'Just a girl: Buffy as icon', in Roz Kaveney (ed.) *Reading the Vampire Slayer*, London, I.B. Tauris, pp. 148–65.

Miller, D.A. (1988), *The Novel and the Police*, Berkeley and London, University of California Press.

Miller, Jeffrey S. (2000), *The Horror Spoofs of Abbott and Costello*, Jefferson NC and London, McFarland.

Miller, Toby (1993), *The Well-tempered Self: Citizenship, Culture, and the Postmodern Subject*, Baltimore MD and London, Johns Hopkins University Press.

— (ed.) (2002), *Television Studies*, London, BFI Publishing.

Miller, William Ian (1997), *The Anatomy of Disgust*, Cambridge MA, Harvard University Press.

Minsky, Rosalind (1998), *Psychoanalysis and Culture: Contemporary States of Mind*, Cambridge, Polity Press.

Mittell, Jason (2004), *Genre and Television: From Cop Shows to Cartoons in American Culture*, New York and London, Routledge.

Modleski, Tania (1986), 'The terror of pleasure: the contemporary horror film and postmodern theory', in Tania Modleski (ed.) *Studies in Entertainment: Critical Approaches to Mass Culture*, Bloomington and Indianapolis, Indiana University Press, pp. 155–66.

Moi, Toril (1999), *What Is A Woman?*, Oxford, Oxford University Press.

Monleón, José B. (1990), *A Specter is Haunting Europe: A Sociohistorical Approach to the Fantastic*, Princeton NJ, Princeton University Press.

Moretti, Franco (1988), *Signs Taken for Wonders*, rev. edn, London and New York, Verso.

Morgan, Jack (2002), *The Biology of Horror: Gothic Literature and Film*, Carbondale and Edwardsville, Southern Illinois University Press.

Morley, David (1999), '"To boldly go . . . ": the "third generation" of reception studies', in Pertti Alasuutari (ed.) *Rethinking the Media Audience*, London, Sage, pp. 195–205.

Morrison, Michael (1996), 'After the danse: horror at the end of the century', in Tony Magistrale and Michael A. Morrison (eds), *A Dark Night's Dreaming: Contemporary American Horror Fiction*, Columbia, University of South Carolina Press, pp. 9–26.

Muir, John Kenneth (1998), *Wes Craven: The Art of Horror*, Jefferson NC, McFarland.

— (2001), *Terror Television: American Series, 1970–1999* Jefferson NC, McFarland.

Mulvey, Laura (1975), 'Visual pleasure and narrative cinema', *Screen*, 16: 3, pp. 6–18.

Murray, Timothy (1993), *Like A Film: Ideological Fantasy on Screen, Camera and Canvas*, London and New York, Routledge.

Ndalianis, Angela (1999), '"Evil will walk once more": *Phantasmagoria* – the stalker film as interactive movie?', in Greg M. Smith (ed.), *On a Silver Platter: CD-ROMs and the Promises of a New Technology*, New York, New York University Press, pp. 87–112.

Neale, Stephen (1980), *Genre*, London, BFI Publishing.

— (1996), '*Halloween*: suspense, aggression and the look', in Barry Keith Grant (ed.), *Planks of Reason: Essays on the Horror Film*, Lanham MD, Scarecrow Press, pp. 331–45.

— (2000), *Genre and Hollywood*, London and New York, Routledge.

— (ed.) (2002), *Genre and Contemporary Hollywood*, London, BFI Publishing.

Needham, Gary (2003), 'Playing with genre: defining the Italian *giallo*', in Steven Jay Schneider (ed.), *Fear Without Frontiers: Horror Cinema Across the Globe*, Guildford, Fab Press, pp. 135–44.

Negt, Oskar and Kluge, Alexander (1993), *Public Sphere and Experience: Towards an Analysis of the Bourgeois and Proletarian Public Sphere*, Minneapolis and London, University of Minnesota Press.

Neill, Alex (1992), 'On a paradox of the heart', *Philosophical Studies*, 65: 1–2, pp. 53–65.

Newitz, Annalee (1999), 'Serial killers, true crime, and economic performance anxiety', in Christopher Sharrett (ed.) *Mythologies of Violence in Postmodern Media*, Detroit MI, Wayne State University Press, pp. 65–83.

Newman, Kim (1988), *Nightmare Movies: A Critical Guide to Contemporary Horror Films*, New York, Harmony Books.

— (1993), *Anno Dracula*, London, Simon & Schuster UK.

— (1995), 'Kim Newman', *Beyond*, 1, April/May, pp. 48–9.

— (ed.) (1996), *The BFI Companion to Horror*, London, BFI Publishing/Cassell.

— (1999a), *Millennium Movies: End of the World Cinema*, London, Titan Books.

— (1999b), *Cat People*, London, BFI Publishing.

— (1999c), *Andy Warhol's Dracula*, Leeds, PS Publishing.

— (1999d), *Life's Lottery*, London, Simon & Schuster UK.

— (2000a), 'Further developments in the strange case of Dr Jekyll and Mr Hyde', in *Unforgivable Stories*, London, Simon & Schuster UK, pp. 13–52.

— (2000b), *Dracula Cha Cha Cha*, London, Simon & Schuster UK.

— (2000c), *Where the Bodies Are Buried*, Birmingham, Alchemy Press.

— (2000d), 'Quetzalcón', in *Unforgivable Stories*, London, Simon & Schuster UK, pp. 209–23.

— (2000e), 'Completist heaven', in *Unforgivable Stories*, London, Simon & Schuster UK, pp. 185–97.

— (2001a), 'Bloodlines', in Ginette Vincendeau (ed.) *Film/Literature/Heritage: A Sight and Sound Reader*, London, BFI Publishing, pp. 97–101.

— (2001b), *Time and Relative*, Tolworth, Telos Publishing.

— (ed.) (2002a), *Science Fiction/Horror: A Sight and Sound Reader*, London, BFI Publishing.

— (2002b), 'A drug on the market', in Stephen Jones and David Sutton (eds), *Dark Terrors 6*, London, Gollancz, pp. 338–72.

Newman, Robert D. (1993), *Transgressions of Reading: Narrative Engagement as Exile and Return*, Durham NC and London, Duke University Press.

Nixon, Nicola (1998), 'Making monsters, or serializing killers', in Robert K. Martin and Eric Savoy (eds), *American Gothic: New Interventions in a National Narrative*, Iowa City, University of Iowa Press, pp. 217–36.

Oakes, David A. (2000), *Science and Destabilization in the Modern American Gothic: Lovecraft, Matheson and King*, Westport CT and London, Greenwood Press.

Oates, Joyce Carol (1997), 'Reflections on the grotesque', in Christoph Grunenberg (ed.) *Gothic: Transmutations of Horror in Late Twentieth Century Art*, Cambridge MA, MIT Press, pp. 38–34 (NB: page numbers run backwards).

Oliver, Mary Beth and Sanders, Meghan (2004), 'The appeal of horror and suspense', in Stephen Prince (ed.), *The Horror Film*, New Brunswick NJ and London, Rutgers University Press, pp. 242–59.

Ono, Kent A. (2000), 'To be a vampire on *Buffy the Vampire Slayer*: race and ("Other") socially marginalizing positions on horror TV', in Elyce Rae Helford (ed.), *Fantasy Girls: Gender in the New Universe of Science Fiction and Fantasy Television*, Lanham MD, Rowman & Littlefield, pp. 163–86.

Orr, Mary (2003), *Intertextuality: Debates and Contexts*, Cambridge, Polity Press.

Osborne, Peter (1998), 'Remember the future? The Communist Manifesto as historical and cultural form', in Leo Panitch and Colin Leys (eds), *The Communist Manifesto Now: Socialist Register 1998*, Rendlesham, Merlin Press, pp. 190–204.

— (2000), *Philosophy in Cultural Theory*, London and New York, Routledge.

Page, Adrian (2001), '*Twin Peaks*', in Glen Creeber (ed.), *The Television Genre Book*, London, BFI Publishing, p. 44.

Parker, John (2000), *Structuration*, Buckingham, Open University Press.

Parkin-Gounelas, Ruth (1999), 'Anachrony and anatopia: spectres of Marx, Derrida and Gothic fiction', in Peter Buse and Andrew Stott (eds), *Ghosts: Deconstruction, Psychoanalysis, History*, London, Macmillan, pp. 127–43.

Parks, Lisa (2003), 'Brave new *Buffy*: rethinking "TV violence"', in Mark Jancovich and James Lyons (eds), *Quality Popular Television*, London, BFI Publishing, pp. 118–33.

Paul, William (1994), *Laughing Screaming: Modern Hollywood Horror and Comedy*, New York, Columbia University Press.

— (2004), 'What does Dr Judd want? Transformation, transference, and divided selves in *Cat People*', in Steven Jay Schneider (ed.), *Horror Film and Psychoanalysis: Freud's Worst Nightmares*, Cambridge, Cambridge University Press, pp. 159–76.

Pearce, Lynne (1997), *Feminism and the Politics of Reading*, London, Arnold.

Peim, Nick (2000), '"If only you could see what I've seen with your eyes": *Blade Runner* and *La Symphonie Pastorale*', in Deborah Cartmell, I.Q. Hunter, Heidi Kaye and Imelda Whelehan (eds), *Classics in Film and Fiction*, London, Pluto Press, pp. 14–33.

Penley, Constance (1989), *The Future of an Illusion: Film, Feminism and Psychoanalysis*, New York and London, Routledge.

Petley, Julian (2000), '"Snuffed out": nightmares in a trading standards officer's brain', in Xavier Mendik and Graeme Harper (eds), *Unruly Pleasures: The Cult Film and Its Critics*, Guildford, FAB Press, pp. 205–19.

Picart, Caroline Joan S. (2003), *Remaking the Frankenstein Myth on Film: Between Laughter and Horror*, New York, State University of New York Press.

Pierson, Michele (2002), *Special Effects: Still in Search of Wonder*, New York, Columbia University Press.

Pinedo, Isabel Cristina (1997), *Recreational Terror: Women and the Pleasures of Horror Film Viewing*, New York, State University of New York Press.

Pippin, Tina and Aichele, George (1997), 'Introduction: imagining God', in George Aichele and Tina Pippin (eds), *The Monstrous and the Unspeakable: The Bible as Fantastic Literature*, Sheffield, Sheffield Academic Press, pp. 11–18.

Pitkin, Hanna Fenichel (1998), *The Attack of the Blob: Hannah Arendt's Concept of the Social*, Chicago IL and London, University of Chicago Press.

Pizzato, Mark (1999), 'Jeffrey Dahmer and media cannibalism: the lure and failure of sacrifice', in Christopher Sharrett (ed.), *Mythologies of Violence in Postmodern Media*, Detroit MI, Wayne State University Press, pp. 85–118.

Polan, Dana (1997), 'Eros and syphilization: the contemporary horror film', in Peter Gibian (ed.), *Mass Culture and Everyday Life*, New York and London, Routledge, pp. 119–27.

Pollard, Tom (2000), 'Postmodern cinema and the death of the hero', *Cineaction: Horror*, 53, pp. 40–8.

Prawer, S. S. (1980), *Caligari's Children: The Film as Tale of Terror*, Oxford, Oxford University Press.

Prince, Stephen (2004a), 'Dread, taboo and *The Thing*: toward a social theory of the horror film', in Stephen Prince (ed.), *The Horror Film*, New Brunswick NJ and London, Rutgers University Press, pp. 118–30.

— (2004b), 'Violence and psychophysiology in horror cinema', in Steven Jay Schneider (ed.) *Horror Film and Psychoanalysis: Freud's Worst Nightmares*, Cambridge, Cambridge University Press, pp. 241–56.

Prior, Nick (2000), 'A different field of vision: gentlemen and players in Edinburgh, 1826–1851', in Bridget Fowler (ed.) *Reading Bourdieu on Society and Culture*, Oxford, Blackwell, pp. 142–63.

Punter, David (1996), 'Problems of recollection and construction: Stephen King', in Victor Sage and Allan Lloyd Smith (eds), *Modern Gothic: A Reader*, Manchester, Manchester University Press, pp. 121–40.

Rand, Nicholas and Torok, Maria (1994), 'The sandman looks at "the uncanny": the return of the repressed or of the secret; Hoffman's question to Freud', in Sonu Shamdasani and Michael Munchow (eds), *Speculations after Freud: Psychoanalysis, Philosophy and Culture*, London, Routledge, pp. 185–203.

Rank, Otto (1989), *The Double: A Psychoanalytic Study*, London, Karnac Books.

Read, Jacinda (2003), 'The cult of masculinity: from fan-boys to academic bad-boys', in Mark Jancovich, Antonio Lázaro Reboll, Julian Stringer and Andy Willis (eds), *Defining Cult Movies: The Cultural Politics of Oppositional Taste*, Manchester, Manchester University Press, pp. 54–70.

Reeves, Jimmie, Rodgers, Mark C. and Epstein, Michael (1996), 'Rewriting popularity: the cult files', in David Lavery, Angela Hague and Marla Cartwright (eds), *Deny All Knowledge: Reading* The X-Files, London, Faber & Faber, pp. 22–35.

Reich, Jacqueline (2001), 'The mother of all horror: witches, gender and the films of Dario Argento', in Keala Jewell (ed.) *Monsters in the Italian Literary Imagination*, Detroit MI, Wayne State University Press, pp. 89–105.

Reynolds, Kimberley, Brennan, Geraldine and McCarron, Kevin (2001), *Frightening Fictions: R.L. Stine, Robert Westall, David Almond and others*, London and New York, Continuum.

Rhodes, Gary D. (2002), 'Mockumentaries and the production of realist horror', *PostScript*, 21: 3, pp. 46–60.

Richards, Barry (1994), *Disciplines of Delight: The Psychoanalysis of Popular Culture*, London, Free Association Books.

Rickels, Laurence A. (1999), *The Vampire Lectures*, Minneapolis and London, University of Minnesota Press.

— (2002), *Nazi Psychoanalysis Volume III: Psy Fi*, Minneapolis and London, University of Minnesota Press.

Ringstrom, Philip A. (2001), '*The Sixth Sense*' in Glen O. Gabbard (ed.) *Psychoanalysis and Film*, London, Karnac Books, pp. 235–9.

Ritzer, George (1998), *The McDonaldisation Thesis*, London, Sage.

— (2001), *Explorations in Social Theory: From Metatheorizing to Rationalization*, London, Sage.

Robb, Brian J. (1998), *Screams and Nightmares: The Films of Wes Craven*, London, Titan Books.

Robbins, Derek (1991), *The Work of Pierre Bourdieu*, Buckingham, Open University Press.

— (2000), *Bourdieu and Culture*, London, Sage.

Roberts, Mark S. (2003), 'Addicts without drugs: the media addiction', in Anna Alexander and Mark S. Roberts (eds), *High Culture: Reflections on Addiction and Modernity*, New York, State University of New York Press, pp. 339–53.

Roberts, Thomas J. (1990), *An Aesthetics of Junk Fiction*, Athens and London, University of Georgia Press.

Rockett, Will H. (1988), *Devouring Whirlwind: Terror and Transcendence in the Cinema of Cruelty*, New York, Greenwood Press.

Roscoe, Jane and Hight, Craig (2001), *Faking It: Mock-documentary and the Subversion of Factuality*, Manchester, Manchester University Press.

Rose, Anita (2002), 'Of creatures and creators: *Buffy* does *Frankenstein*', in Rhonda V. Wilcox and David Lavery (eds), *Fighting the Forces: What's at Stake in* Buffy the Vampire Slayer, Lanham MD, Rowman & Littlefield, pp. 133–42.

Royle, Nicholas (2003), *The Uncanny*, New York, Routledge.

Russell, David (1998), 'Monster roundup: reintegrating the horror genre', in Nick Browne (ed.) *Refiguring American Film Genres*, Berkeley, University of California Press, pp. 233–54.

Sabbadini, Andrea (ed.) (2003), *The Couch and the Silver Screen: Psychoanalytic Reflections on European Cinema*, Hove and New York, Brunner-Routledge.

Sage, Victor (1988), *Horror Fiction in the Protestant Tradition*, New York, St Martin's Press.

Salisbury, Mark and Hedgcock, Alan (1994), *Behind the Mask: The Secrets of Hollywood's Monster Makers*, London, Titan Books.

Salomon, Roger B. (2002), *Mazes of the Serpent: An Anatomy of Horror Narrative*, Ithaca NY and London, Cornell University Press.

Sandvoss, Cornel (2003), *A Game of Two Halves: Football, Television and Globalization*, London and New York, Routledge.

Sanjek, David (1994), 'Twilight of the monsters: the English horror film 1968–1975', in Wheeler Winston Dixon (ed.) *Re-viewing British Cinema, 1900–1992*, New York, State University of New York Press, pp. 195–209.

— (2000), 'Fans' notes: the horror film fanzine', in Ken Gelder (ed.) *The Horror Reader*, London and New York, Routledge, pp. 314–23.

Sarrantonio, Al (1988), 'Stephen King: *'Salem's Lot*', in Stephen Jones and Kim Newman (eds), *Horror: 100 Best Books*, London, Xanadu Publications, pp. 161–2.

Saunders, Michael William (1998), *Imps of the Perverse: Gay Monsters in Film*, Westport CT, Praeger.

Schlesinger, Philip, Dobash, R. Emerson, Dobash, Russell P., Weaver, C. Kay (1992), *Women Viewing Violence*, London, BFI Publishing.

Schneider, Alfred R. with Pullen, Kaye (2001), *The Gatekeeper: My 30 Years as a TV Censor*, New York, Syracuse University Press.

Schneider, Steven Jay (2000a), 'Monsters as (uncanny) metaphors: Freud, Lakoff, and the representation of monstrosity in cinematic horror', in Alain Silver and James Ursini (eds), *Horror Film Reader*, New York, Limelight Editions, pp. 167–91.

— (2000b), 'Kevin Williamson and the rise of the neo-stalker', *PostScript*, 19: 2, pp. 73–87.

— (2001), 'Manifestations of the literary double in modern horror cinema', in Daniel Shaw (ed.), *Film and Philosophy: Horror Special Edition*, pp. 51–62.

— (2003), 'The legacy of *Last House on the Left*', in Gary D. Rhodes (ed.), *Horror at the Drive-In*, Jefferson NC and London, McFarland, pp. 79–93.

— (2004a), 'Toward an aesthetics of cinematic horror', in Stephen Prince (ed.), *The Horror Film*, New Brunswick NJ and London, Rutgers University Press, pp. 131–49.

— (ed.) (2004b), *Horror Film and Psychoanalysis: Freud's Worst Nightmares*, Cambridge, Cambridge University Press.

Schubart, Rikke (1995), 'From desire to deconstruction: horror films and audience reactions', in David Kidd-Hewitt and Richard Osborne (eds), *Crime and the Media: The Post-modern Spectacle*, London, Pluto Press, pp. 219–42.

Schuller, Tom, Baron, Stephen and Field, John (2000), 'Social capital: a review and critique', in Stephen Baron, John Field and Tom Schuller (eds), *Social Capital: Critical Perspectives*, Oxford, Oxford University Press, pp. 1–38.

Schulze, Laurie, Barton White, Anne and Brown, Jane D. (1993), '"A sacred monster in her prime": audience construction of Madonna as Low-Other', in Cathy Schwichtenberg (ed.), *The Madonna Connection*, Boulder CO, Westview Press, pp. 15–37.

Sconce, Jeffrey (1993), 'Spectacles of death: identification, reflexivity, and contemporary horror', in Jim Collins, Hilary Radner and Ava Preacher Collins (eds), *Film Theory Goes to the Movies*, New York and London, Routledge, pp. 103–19.

— (2000), *Haunted Media: Electronic Presence from Telegraphy to Television*, Durham NC and London, Duke University Press.

— (2002), 'Irony, nihilism and the new American "smart" film', *Screen*, 43: 4, pp. 349–69.

Seltzer, Mark (1998), *Serial Killers: Death and Life in America's Wound Culture*, New York and London, Routledge.

Shaw, Daniel (2001), 'Power, horror and ambivalence', in Daniel Shaw (ed.), *Film and Philosophy: Horror Special Edition*, pp. 1–12.

— (2003), 'A reply to "real horror"', in Steven Jay Schneider and Daniel Shaw (eds), *Dark Thoughts: Philosophic Reflections on Cinematic Horror*, Lanham MD, Scarecrow Press, pp. 260–3.

Showalter, Elaine (2000), 'Dr Jekyll's closet (extract)', in Ken Gelder (ed.) *The Horror Reader*, London and New York, Routledge, pp. 190–7.

Silverstone, Roger (1994), *Television and Everyday Life*, London and New York, Routledge.

Simons, Ronald C. (1996), *Boo! Culture, Experience, and the Startle Reflex*, Oxford, Oxford University Press.

Simpson, Philip L. (2000), *Psycho Paths: Tracking the Serial Killer through Contemporary American Film and Fiction*, Carbondale, Southern Illinois University Press.

Skal, David J. (1993), *The Monster Show: A Cultural History of Horror*, New York and London, W.W. Norton.

— (2002), *Death Makes a Holiday: A Cultural History of Halloween*, New York and London, Bloomsbury.

Smith, Andrew (2000), *Gothic Radicalism: Literature, Philosophy and Psychoanalysis in the Nineteenth Century*, London, Macmillan.

Smith, Murray (1999), 'Gangsters, cannibals, aesthetes, or apparently perverse allegiances', in Carl Plantinga and Greg M. Smith (eds), *Passionate Views: Film, Cognition, and Emotion*, Baltimore MD and London, Johns Hopkins University Press, pp. 217–38.

Solomon, Robert C. (1992), 'The philosophy of horror, or, why did Godzilla cross the road?', in *Entertaining Ideas – Popular Philosophical Essays: 1970–1990*, New York, Prometheus Books, pp. 119–30.

— (2003), 'Real horror', in Steven Jay Schneider and Daniel Shaw (eds), *Dark Thoughts: Philosophic Reflections on Cinematic Horror*, Lanham MD, Scarecrow Press, pp. 230–59.

Stacey, Jackie (1997), *Teratologies*, London and New York, Routledge.

Stahl, Roger (2000), 'Blair witchery: simulacra, propaganda, and documentary', *Mythosphere*, 2, Issue 3, pp. 307–19.

Staiger, Janet (1993), 'Taboos and totems: cultural meanings of *The Silence of the Lambs*', in Jim Collins, Hilary Radner and Ava Preacher Collins (eds), *Film Theory Goes to the Movies*, New York and London, Routledge, pp. 142–54.

— (2000), *Perverse Spectators: The Practices of Film Reception*, New York and London, New York University Press.

Steinert, Heinz (2003), *Culture Industry*, Cambridge, Polity Press.

Stern, Lesley (1997), 'I think Sebastian, therefore I ... somersault: film and the uncanny', *Paradoxa: The Return of the Uncanny*, 3: 3–4, pp. 348–66.

Stevenson, Nick (ed.) (2001), *Culture and Citizenship*, London, Sage.

Stevenson, Robert Louis (1979[1886]), *Dr Jekyll and Mr Hyde and Other Stories*, Harmondsworth, Penguin.

Stockwell, Peter (2000), *The Poetics of Science Fiction*, Harlow, Pearson Education.

Stoker, Bram (1994[1897]), *Dracula*, Harmondsworth, Penguin.

Strick, Philip (2002), '*The Sixth Sense*', in Kim Newman (ed.), *Science Fiction/Horror*, London, BFI Publishing, pp. 257–8.

Talbot, Mary M. (1995), *Fictions at Work: Language and Social Practice in Fiction*, London and New York, Pearson Education.

Tan, Ed S. (1996), *Emotion and the Structure of Narrative Film: Film as an Emotion Machine*, Saddle River NJ, Lawrence Erlbaum.

Tasker, Yvonne (2002), *The Silence of the Lambs*, London, BFI Publishing.

Taylor, John (1998), *Body Horror: Photojournalism, Catastrophe and War*, Manchester, Manchester University Press.

Telotte, J. P. (1991), 'Beyond all reason: the nature of the cult' in J.P. Telotte (ed.), *The Cult Film Experience*, Austin, University of Texas Press, pp. 5–17.

Terada, Rei (2001), *Feeling in Theory: Emotion after the 'Death of the Subject'*, Cambridge, MA, Harvard University Press.

Thomas, Lyn (2002), *Fans, Feminisms and 'Quality' Media*, London and New York, Routledge.

Thomas, Paul (1998), 'Seeing is believing: Marx's manifesto, Derrida's apparition', in Leo Panitch and Colin Leys (eds), *The Communist Manifesto Now: Socialist Register 1998*, Rendlesham, Merlin Press: pp. 205–17.

Thornham, Sue (1997), *Passionate Detachments: An Introduction to Feminist Film Theory*, London, Arnold.

— (ed.) (1999), *Feminist Film Theory: A Reader*, Edinburgh, Edinburgh University Press.

Thornton, Sarah (1995), *Club Cultures*, Cambridge, Polity Press.

Threadgold, Terry (1997), *Feminist Poetics: Poesis, Performance, Histories*, London and New York, Routledge.

Tithecott, Richard (1997), *Of Men and Monsters: Jeffrey Dahmer and the Construction of the Serial Killer*, Madison, University of Wisconsin Press.

Todorov, Tzvetan (1975), *The Fantastic: A Structural Approach to a Literary Genre*, Ithaca NY, Cornell University Press.

Tolson, Andrew (1996), *Mediations: Text and Discourse in Media Studies*, London, Arnold.

Tomc, Sandra (1997), 'Dieting and damnation: Anne Rice's *Interview with the Vampire*', in Joan Gordon and Veronica Hollinger (eds), *Blood Read: The Vampire as Metaphor in Contemporary Culture*, Philadelphia, University of Pennsylvania Press, pp. 95–113.

Tonkin, Boyd (2001), 'Entropy as demon: Buffy in Southern California', in Roz Kaveney (ed.), *Reading the Vampire Slayer*, London, I.B. Tauris, pp. 37–52.

Tropp, Martin (1990), *Images of Fear: How Horror Stories Helped Shape Modern Culture (1818–1918)*, Jefferson NC, McFarland.

Tudor, Andrew (1974), *Image and Influence: Studies in the Sociology of Film*, London, Allen & Unwin.

— (1989), *Monsters and Mad Scientists: A Cultural History of the Horror Movie*, Oxford, Blackwell.

— (1995), 'Unruly bodies, unquiet minds', *Body and Society*, 1: 1, pp. 25–41.

— (1997), 'Why horror? The peculiar pleasures of a popular genre', *Cultural Studies*, 11: 3, pp. 443–63.

— (2002), 'From paranoia to postmodernism? The horror movie in late modern society', in Steve Neale (ed.), *Genre and Contemporary Hollywood*, London, BFI Publishing, pp. 105–16.

Turner, Graeme (2001), 'The uses and limitations of genre', in Glen Creeber (ed.), *The Television Genre Book*, London, BFI Publishing, pp. 4–5.

Turney, Jon (1998), *Frankenstein's Footsteps*, London, Yale University Press.

Turvey, Malcolm (2004), 'Philosophical problems concerning the concept of pleasure in psychoanalytical theories of (the horror) film', in Steven Jay Schneider (ed.), *Horror Film and Psychoanalysis: Freud's Worst Nightmares*, Cambridge, Cambridge University Press, pp. 68–83.

Twitchell, James B. (1985), *Dreadful Pleasures: An Anatomy of Modern Horror*, New York and Oxford, Oxford University Press.

Urbano, Cosimo (2004), '"What's the matter with Melanie?": Reflections on the merits of psychoanalytic approaches to modern horror cinema', in Steven Jay Schneider (ed.), *Horror Film and Psychoanalysis: Freud's Worst Nightmares*, Cambridge, Cambridge University Press, pp. 17–34.

Veeder, William and Hirsch, Gordon (eds) (1988), *Dr Jekyll and Mr Hyde After One Hundred Years*, Chicago IL, University of Chicago Press.

Volk, Stephen (2003), 'Faking it: *Ghostwatch* 10 years on', *Fortean Times*, 166, pp. 36–41.

Vorobej, Mark (1997), 'Monsters and the paradox of horror', *Dialogue: Canadian Philosophical Review*, XXXVI: 2 (Spring), pp. 219–46.

Waller, Gregory A. (1986), *The Living and the Undead: From Stoker's Dracula to Romero's Dawn of the Dead*, Urbana and Chicago, University of Illinois Press.

— (1987), 'Made-for-television horror Films', in Gregory A. Waller (ed.) *American Horrors: Essays on the Modern American Horror Film*, Urbana and Chicago, University of Illinois Press, pp. 145–61.

Walton, Kendall L. (1990), *Mimesis as Make-Believe: On the Foundations of the Representational Arts*, Cambridge MA, Harvard University Press.

Ward, Geoff (2002), *The Writing of America: Literature and Cultural Identity from the Puritans to the Present*, Cambridge, Polity Press.

Ward, Graham (2003), *True Religion*, Oxford, Blackwell.

Warhol, Robyn R. (2003), *Having a Good Cry: Effeminate Feelings and Pop-culture Forms*, Columbus, Ohio State University Press.

Wayne, Mike (2003), *Marxism and Media Studies: Key Concepts and Contemporary Trends*, London, Pluto Press.

Weaver III, James B. and Tamborini, Ron (eds) (1996), *Horror Films: Current Research on Audience Preferences and Reactions*, Saddle River NJ, Lawrence Erlbaum.

Webb, Jen, Schirato, Tony and Danaher, Geoff (2002), *Understanding Bourdieu*, London, Sage.

Weber, Samuel (2000), *The Legend of Freud* Expanded edn, Stanford CA, Stanford University Press.

Weigl, Charles E. (2002), 'Introducing horror', in Henry Jenkins, Tara McPherson, and Jane Shattuc (eds), *Hop on Pop: The Politics and Pleasures of Popular Culture*, Durham NC and London, Duke University Press, pp. 700–19.

Wells, Paul (2000), *The Horror Genre: From Beelzebub to Blair Witch*, London, Wallflower Press.

Wheatley, Helen (2002), 'Mystery and imagination: anatomy of a Gothic anthology series', in Janet Thumim (ed.) *Small Screens, Big Ideas: Television in the 1950s*, London and New York, I.B. Tauris, pp. 165–80.

Wiater, Stanley (1992), '"Reach out and touch some thing": blurbs and Stephen King', in Don Herron (ed.), *Reign of Fear: The Fiction and the Films of Stephen King*, Novato CA and Lancaster, Underwood-Miller, pp. 109–22.

Wigley, Mark (1993), *The Architecture of Deconstruction: Derrida's Haunt*, Cambridge MA, MIT Press.

Wilkinson, Gary (2000), 'Stepping through the silver screen: the fiction of Kim Newman', *Vector: The Critical Journal of the BSFA*, 210, pp. 15–17.

Williams, Anne (1995), *Art of Darkness: A Poetics of Gothic*, Chicago IL and London, University of Chicago Press.

Williams, Linda (1996), 'When the woman looks' in Barry Keith Grant (ed.), *The Dread of Difference: Gender and the Horror Film*, Austin, University of Texas Press, pp. 15–34.

— (1999), 'Film bodies: gender, genre and excess', in Sue Thornham (ed.) *Feminist Film Theory: A Reader*, Edinburgh, Edinburgh University Press, pp. 267–81.

— (2000), 'Discipline and fun: *Psycho* and postmodern cinema', in Christine Gledhill and Linda Williams (eds), *Reinventing Film Studies*, London, Arnold, pp. 351–78.

Williams, Linda Ruth (1999), 'The inside-out of masculinity: David Cronenberg's visceral pleasures', in Michele Aaron (ed.), *The Body's Perilous Pleasures: Dangerous Desires and Contemporary Culture*, Edinburgh, Edinburgh University Press, pp. 30–48.

Williams, Raymond (1965), *The Long Revolution*, London, Pelican.

— (1975), *Television, Technology and Cultural Form*, New York, Schocken.

— (1979), *Politics and Letters: Interviews with* New Left Review, London, Verso.

Williams, Simon (2001), *Emotion and Social Theory: Corporeal Reflections on the (Ir)Rational*, London, Sage.

Williams, Tony (1996), *Hearths of Darkness: The Family in the American Horror Film*, London, Associated University Presses.

— (2003), *The Cinema of George A. Romero: Knight of the Living Dead*, London and New York, Wallflower Press.

Williamson, Milly (2001), 'Vampires and goths: fandom, gender and cult dress', in William J.F. Keenan (ed.), *Dressed to Impress: Looking the Part*, Oxford and New York, Berg, pp. 141–57.

Wilson, F. Paul (1999), 'Introduction', in Kim Newman, *Andy Warhol's Dracula*, PS Publishing, Leeds, pp. 5–7.

Winter, Douglas E. (2000), 'The pathos of genre', in Ellen Datlow and Terri Windling (eds), *The Year's Best Fantasy and Horror*, New York, St Martin's Press, pp. 176–83.

Wolfreys, Julian (2002), *Victorian Hauntings: Spectrality, Gothic, the Uncanny and Literature*, London, Palgrave.

Wood, Robin (1978), 'The return of the repressed', *Film Comment*, 14, pp. 25–32.

— (1986), *Hollywood from Vietnam to Reagan*, New York, Columbia University Press.

— (1996), 'Burying the undead: the use and obsolescence of Count Dracula', in Barry Keith Grant (ed.), *The Dread of Difference: Gender and the Horror Film*, Austin, University of Texas Press, pp. 364–78.

— (2004), 'What lies beneath', in Steven Jay Schneider (ed.), *Horror Film and Psychoanalysis: Freud's Worst Nightmares*, Cambridge, Cambridge University Press, pp. xiii–xviii.

Woodiwiss, Anthony (2001), *The Visual in Social Theory*, London and New York, Athlone Press.

Young, Elizabeth (2001), 'Bods and monsters: the return of the Bride of Frankenstein', in Jon Lewis (ed.), *The End of Cinema As We Know It: American Film in the Nineties*, London, Pluto Press, pp. 225–36.

Young, Robert J.C. (1999), 'Freud's secret: *The Interpretation of Dreams* was a Gothic novel', in Laura Marcus (ed.) *Sigmund Freud's* The Interpretation of Dreams: *New Interdisciplinary Essays*, Manchester and New York, Manchester University Press, pp. 206–31.

Zelizer, Barbie and Allan, Stuart (eds) (2002), *Journalism After September 11th*, London and New York, Routledge.

Zizek, Slavoj (1997), *The Plague of Fantasies*, London, Verso.

— (2000), 'In his bold gaze my ruin is writ large (extract)', in Ken Gelder (ed.) *The Horror Reader*, London and New York, Routledge, pp. 71–7.

— (2002), *For They Know Not What They Do: Enjoyment as a Political Factor*, London, Verso.

Index

Author's note: I'd like to thank Amy Luther for compiling this index.